WATERSHED

THE 2022 AUSTRALIAN
FEDERAL ELECTION

WATERSHED

THE 2022 AUSTRALIAN
FEDERAL ELECTION

EDITED BY ANIKA GAUJA,
MARIAN SAWER
AND JILL SHEPPARD

Australian
National
University

ANU PRESS

In memory of Marian Simms, who inspired and sustained the partnership between the Academy of the Social Sciences in Australia and the federal election series.

Australian
National
University

ANU PRESS

Published by ANU Press
The Australian National University
Canberra ACT 2600, Australia
Email: anupress@anu.edu.au

Available to download for free at press.anu.edu.au

ISBN (print): 9781760465810
ISBN (online): 9781760465827

WorldCat (print): 1391124095
WorldCat (online): 1391124210

DOI: 10.22459/W.2023

Cover design and layout by ANU Press. Cover photograph: Supporters of Dr Monique Ryan keep an eye on the screens as they watch the count at a reception for the 2022 federal election (Auburn Hotel, seat of Kooyong, Melbourne, Saturday 21 May 2022), AAP Image/Luis Ascui.

This book is published under the aegis of the Social Sciences editorial committee of ANU Press.

Contents

Part 3: Results

List of illustrations

Figures

Plates

Tables

Abbreviations

2PP	two-party-preferred
ABC	Australian Broadcasting Corporation
ACL	Australian Christian Lobby
ACT	Australian Capital Territory
ACTU	Australian Council of Trade Unions
AEC	Australian Electoral Commission
ALP	Australian Labor Party
ICAC	Independent Commission Against Corruption
JSCEM	Joint Standing Committee on Electoral Matters
LNP	Liberal National Party of Queensland
MP	Member of Parliament
NDIS	National Disability Insurance Scheme
NSW	New South Wales
NT	Northern Territory
PHON	Pauline Hanson's One Nation
Qld	Queensland
RBA	Reserve Bank of Australia
SA	South Australia
Tas.	Tasmania
UAP	United Australia Party
UK	United Kingdom
UN	United Nations
US	United States
Vic.	Victoria
WA	Western Australia

Acknowledgements

The Australian federal election books are always a demanding enterprise and the editors have many people to thank.

First and foremost, the Academy of the Social Sciences in Australia remains unwavering in its continuing support for this series. We acknowledge, in particular, the help of its chief executive officer, Chris Hatherly, and events manager, Anna Dennis, with the organisation of the election workshop held at the Museum of Australian Democracy in June 2022.

In addition to the Academy, funding support came from the Museum of Australian Democracy, the School of Politics and International Relations at The Australian National University, and the Global Institute for Women's Leadership at The Australian National University (GIWL at ANU). The workshop was held over two days, with authors and discussants engaging in sustained conversation about the draft chapters and the key themes that emerged. Discussants included Damon Muller (Parliamentary Library), Natalie Barr (GIWL), Andrew Hughes (ANU), Mark Kenny (ANU) and Chris Wallace (University of Canberra).

Following the workshop, the generous support of our funders enabled us to hold a public seminar in the former House of Representatives chamber. This highly topical seminar was entitled 'Women in the 2022 Federal Election: Will politics be done differently?' and attracted an enthusiastic audience. The seminar was chaired by Andrea Carson (La Trobe University) and the speakers were Antony Green (ABC), Michelle Ryan (GIWL at ANU), Kim Rubenstein (50/50 Foundation and Senate candidate) and Tharini Rouwette (Centre of Multicultural Political Engagement, Literacy and Leadership).

We thank the anonymous reviewer of our book manuscript for helpful suggestions, as well as Frank Bongiorno, chair of the Social Sciences editorial committee of ANU Press, and other committee members. We are grateful to the ANU Publication Subsidy Fund, the University of Sydney and the Social Sciences editorial committee for publishing support, to the staff of ANU Press and once again to Jan Borrie for her meticulous copyediting.

Finally, we thank all those who have given permission for reproduction of the photos, cartoons and other images that help tell the story of the visual politics of the 2022 campaign—the memes that now win elections.

Contributors

A.J. Brown is a professor of public policy and law in the Centre for Governance and Public Policy at Griffith University, Brisbane, and a board member of Transparency International globally and in Australia. His Australian Research Council–funded research includes two national integrity system assessments of Australia and three of the world's largest research projects on public interest whistleblowing. Shortlisted in 2012 for the Prime Minister's Literary Award (Non-Fiction), he is also a fellow of the Australian Academy of Law.

Andrea Carson is a professor of political communication in the Department of Politics, Media and Philosophy at La Trobe University, Melbourne. She studies the role of the media in democracy. Her research interests include investigative journalism, political communication, politics and gender, and measures to counter misinformation and disinformation.

Emily Foley is a PhD candidate and lecturer in politics at La Trobe University, Melbourne. Her research focuses on the relationship between the Australian Labor Party and temporary migration. Her broader research interests include examining the role of unions in contemporary Australian politics and Australia's immigration policies.

Anika Gauja is a professor of politics in the Department of Government and International Relations at the University of Sydney. She researches political parties, Australian politics and electoral law and has co-edited two previous volumes of the federal election book series: *Morrison's Miracle* (ANU Press, 2020) and *Double Disillusion* (ANU Press, 2018).

Murray Goot is an emeritus professor of politics at Macquarie University, Sydney, and a fellow of the Academy of the Social Sciences in Australia. His main publications cover polls, the media and electoral behaviour. His next book (with Tim Rowse), on Indigenous recognition and the referendum on the Voice, will be published in 2024.

Antony Green is the chief election analyst at the Australian Broadcasting Corporation. He is also an adjunct professor in the Department of Government and International Relations at the University of Sydney.

Carolyn M. Hendriks is a professor at the Crawford School of Public Policy at The Australian National University. She undertakes social research on democratic aspects of contemporary governance, including public participation, community organising, deliberation, inclusion, listening and representation. Carolyn is the author of three books: *Mending Democracy* (with Selen A. Ercan and John Boswell, Oxford University Press, 2020), *The Politics of Public Deliberation* (Palgrave, 2011) and *Environmental Decision-Making: Exploring Complexity and Context* (with Ronnie Harding and Mehreen Faruqi, The Federation Press, 2009).

Josh Holloway is a lecturer in the College of Business, Government and Law at Flinders University, Adelaide. His research covers political parties, election management and democratic resilience to crisis. His most recent publications can be found in *Government & Opposition*, *Contemporary Politics* and *Defence Studies*.

Simon Jackman is an honorary professor at the University of Sydney and a fellow of the Academy of the Social Sciences in Australia. He studies public opinion, elections and electoral systems, using rigorous data analysis to better understand democratic processes and their frailties. His current research projects include machine-learning methods for classifying and modelling large corpora of political text and ensuring the validity and reliability of social and political measurement in the digital age.

Stewart Jackson is a senior lecturer in the Department of Government and International Relations at the University of Sydney. He is the author of *The Australian Greens: From Activism to Australia's Third Party* (Melbourne University Publishing, 2016) as well as textbooks and journal articles covering Australian, Green and environmental politics. He is working on a new multi-university, Australian Research Council–funded project examining youth engagement in climate change protests.

Carol Johnson is an emerita professor in the Department of Politics and International Relations at the University of Adelaide and a fellow of the Academy of the Social Sciences in Australia. She has published extensively on Australian politics, with a particular interest in issues of ideology, gender, sexuality and the politics of emotion. Her most recent book is *Social Democracy and the Crisis of Equality: Australian Social Democracy in a Changing World* (Springer, 2019).

Glenn Kefford is the author of *Political Parties and Campaigning in Australia: Data, Digital and Field* (Palgrave, 2021) and has a forthcoming monograph on data-driven campaigning across advanced democracies with Oxford University Press, co-authored with Katharine Dommett and Simon Kruschinski.

Lucien Leon is an independent researcher who writes on political satire and contemporary new media. His publications include 'Cartoons, Memes and Videos', in Anika Gauja, Marian Sawer and Marian Simms (eds), *Morrison's Miracle: The 2019 Australian Federal Election* (ANU Press, 2020); and 'The Evolution of Political Cartooning in the New Media Age: Cases from Australia, the USA and the UK', in Jessica Milner Davis (ed.), *Satire and Politics: The Interplay of Heritage and Practice* (Palgrave Macmillan, 2017). He was a judge for the Museum of Australian Democracy's annual Behind the Lines political cartoon exhibitions in 2021 and 2022.

Michael Maley had a 30-year career at the Australian Electoral Commission, retiring in 2012 as a special adviser on electoral reform and international services. He has also worked as a consultant to the United Nations, the International Foundation for Electoral Systems, the International Institute for Democracy and Electoral Assistance, and the Commonwealth Secretariat. He is a member of the editorial board of the *Election Law Journal*, was awarded the Australian Public Service Medal in 2001 and received the International Foundation for Electoral Systems' Joe C. Baxter Award in 2015.

Rob Manwaring is an associate professor at Flinders University, Adelaide. Rob researches political parties, comparative politics and the centre-left. He is the author of *The Politics of Social Democracy* (Routledge, 2021).

Ferran Martinez i Coma is a senior lecturer and the director of engagement in the School of Government and International Relations at Griffith University, Brisbane. His current research specialises in elections, electoral integrity, comparative politics, political parties and electoral behaviour. He has published articles in *Electoral Studies*, the *European Journal of Political Research*, *Party Politics* and *Parliamentary Affairs*, among other leading journals, and has written 17 policy reports for international organisations such as the Organization of American States and International IDEA.

Stephen Mills is an honorary senior lecturer with the School of Social and Political Sciences at the University of Sydney. He has written widely on election campaign management, party professionalisation and public opinion polling. He is a former journalist with Fairfax newspapers and was an adviser (and speechwriter) to Prime Minister Bob Hawke.

Ben Raue is an adjunct associate lecturer in the Department of Government and International Relations at the University of Sydney and an electoral and data analyst who writes about elections for *The Tally Room* and *The Guardian*. He has been writing about elections in Australia and around the world since 2008.

Richard Reid is a researcher in politics and political history at The Australian National University. He researches contemporary rural and regional politics in Australia and Australian and British conservative politics in the 1950s and 1960s.

Serrin Rutledge-Prior is a research fellow with the Crawford School of Public Policy at The Australian National University. Her research centres on animal and environmental politics and political participation and inclusion.

Marian Sawer is an emeritus professor in the School of Politics and International Relations at The Australian National University and a fellow of the Academy of the Social Sciences in Australia. She has led the Democratic Audit of Australia and has a longstanding interest in political finance and electoral regulation. Her most recent book is the *Handbook of Feminist Governance*, co-edited with Lee Ann Banaszak, Jacqui True and Johanna Kantola (Edward Elgar, 2023).

Richard Scully is an associate professor in modern history at the University of New England. His main field of research is the global history and function of political cartoons. He is the author of *Eminent Victorian Cartoonists* (three volumes, London, 2018).

Jill Sheppard is a senior lecturer in politics at The Australian National University. She is an investigator with the Australian Election Study and researches public opinion, political participation and political parties in Australia.

Rodney Smith is a professor of Australian politics in the Department of Government and International Relations at the University of Sydney. His research has focused on national and regional elections in Australia.

He has published articles in the *European Journal of Political Research*, *Party Politics*, *Governance* and *The Australian Journal of Political Science*, among other journals, and has written reports on recent trends in voting methods for the Electoral Regulation Research Network and the NSW Electoral Commission.

Marija Taflaga is a senior lecturer at The Australian National University and the director of the Australian Politics Studies Centre. Her research focuses on the career paths of political elites and how they interact with political institutions such as political parties and parliaments in Australia and other Westminster countries.

Ariadne Vromen is the Sir John Bunting Chair of Public Administration at the Crawford School of Public Policy, The Australian National University, and a fellow of the Academy of the Social Sciences in Australia. She has long-term research interests in citizen engagement and her latest book, with Darren Halpin and Michael Vaughan, is *Crowdsourced Politics: The Rise of Online Petitions and Micro-Donations* (Palgrave Macmillan, 2022).

Blair Williams is a lecturer in Australian politics at Monash University, Melbourne, and was previously a research fellow at the Global Institute for Women's Leadership at The Australian National University. Her research focuses on gendered media coverage of women in politics—most recently published in *Feminist Media Studies*, *Politics & Gender* and *Parliamentary Affairs*. She is working on an analysis of the gendered media coverage of leaders' responses to the Covid-19 pandemic and the gendered double standards of the Murdoch media's coverage of political women.

1

Watershed: The 2022 Australian federal election

Anika Gauja, Marian Sawer and Jill Sheppard

On election night, as Labor gradually inched towards government, the most remarkable news was the success of the 'Teal wave' of women Independents winning previously safe Liberal seats. They had campaigned on a platform of climate change, integrity and women's issues and presented themselves as a community-based alternative to the way the major parties operated. This, together with the success of the Australian Greens in winning lower house seats in Brisbane, sent a strong message that voters, and particularly women voters, wanted politics done differently.

Many saw the election result as a tipping point, signalling that Australia's longstanding and very stable two-party system was finally on its way out. Its dominance had been gradually eroding and, this time, more than 30 per cent of voters looked elsewhere to cast their primary vote. As it transpired, Labor won government with a majority of 77 seats in the House of Representatives, but with a lower primary vote than it had achieved in 2019. It optimistically attributed this to 'strategic' voting and supporters temporarily shifting their primary votes to non-Labor candidates deemed capable of beating Liberal incumbents. Labor polled exceptionally strongly in Western Australia, winning four seats from the Liberal Party.

While the Coalition parties (Liberal and National) made much of their primary vote being slightly higher than Labor's, the Liberal Party also had a historically low primary vote. In other democracies, the Covid-19 pandemic shored up some faith in the 'wartime' governments dealing with it, at least initially. By 2022, the same incumbency benefit was not enjoyed by the federal government in Australia. Nor did the lowest unemployment rate in almost 50 years save the government from defeat (or the treasurer from losing his own seat in Kooyong). The prime minister had become the most unpopular Liberal leader for more than 30 years and was targeted relentlessly during the campaign. The 'miracle' that came to characterise Scott Morrison's 2019 electoral victory in the face of opinion polling that predicted a Labor win (see Gauja et al. 2020) did not occur twice.

The longer-term trend in Western democracies—reinforced by the Australian election result—was that the major (or traditional) parties could no longer rely on lifelong voters. The success of the Teal Independents in Australia reflected widespread reaction against what was perceived as the major parties operating in the interests of the political class and donors, ignoring substantive policy issues—such as climate change—that mattered to Australians. Political scandals over sexual misconduct contributed to this disenchantment and to the increased salience of gender issues.

If the 2022 election could be seen as a watershed moment, or a 'tipping point', for voters in Australia, the extraordinary events that transpired between the 2019 and 2022 elections certainly increased the salience of certain policy issues and voters' critical stance towards the government. The Morrison Government, like its counterparts across the globe, faced the daunting task of dealing with a global pandemic. It is important to note that the 2022 Australian election campaign coincided with a period in which the country had the highest daily infection rates in the world (Booker and Sambul 2022).

Climate change also loomed large in the wake of record-breaking bushfires and floods since the 2019 election. The summer of 2019–20 became known as 'Black Summer' because of the bushfires that, between September 2019 and March 2020, burned an unprecedented 18.6 million hectares of bushland. 'Once in a century' floods in March 2021 severely affected communities in greater Sydney, the Hunter region and Mid North Coast of New South Wales, and around Queensland's Gold Coast. These events were repeated a year later, with severe flooding affecting Brisbane, the NSW Northern Rivers and Sydney. The Insurance Council of Australia (2022) reported almost 200,000 claims from the 2022 floods, or more than $3.3 billion in insured losses.

Despite the severity of these events, the theme of climate change was not prominent in the campaigns of the major parties, although the prime minister's apparent lack of empathy with flood and fire victims became part of the negative campaign directed against him. The Coalition Government was particularly vulnerable on climate change and its attempts to reframe the issue were singularly unsuccessful. One discursive tactic tried well before the campaign proper was that climate change would 'ultimately be solved by "can-do" capitalism, not "don't-do" government'. This attempt at free-market framing was no more successful than the ubiquitous 'freedom' ads of the United Australia Party (UAP) funded by billionaire Clive Palmer.

Voters were looking for alternatives to the two-party system and they were also engaging in politics in new ways, both online and offline, in the community organising of the 'Voices For' movements. The election campaign moved further into the digital space and citizen actors creating and sharing memes were as visible as more traditional party actors. Within this landscape the visual elements of campaigning were more important than ever. Digital disruption and disinformation—so prominent in 2019— were also a feature, but so were more concerted efforts to deal with them.

In this Introduction, we will highlight key themes of the 2022 federal election campaign. We will also analyse some of the regulatory issues highlighted by the campaign, including how to deal with electoral disinformation and fake news. We then introduce the place of this book in the federal election series and each of the chapters. It is telling that this volume—the eighteenth in the series—is the first that has needed a separate chapter on corruption and integrity issues.

Election themes

The 2022 federal election—called by Prime Minister Scott Morrison on 10 April 2022 and ending with the return of the election writs on 28 June 2022—played out in ways that very few observers could have expected.

Not only did the election bring a change in government; it also saw the lowest primary votes for both major parties and the election of the greatest number of Independents to the lower house since the formation of the Australian party system. The success of the Teal Independents and the Greens and the appetite voters showed for 'doing politics differently' suggested that the dominant model of electoral competition might no longer be the two-party system. At the very least, the continued usefulness of the 'two-party-preferred' vote as a way of conceptualising and predicting Australians' voting behaviour has been cast into serious doubt.

Table 1.1 2022 federal election timetable

Date	Event
10 April	Prime minister calls the election
11 April	Writs issued for the House and half-Senate elections
18 April	Close of rolls
21 April	Close of nominations
9 May	Early voting begins
21 May	Election day
23 May	Anthony Albanese sworn in as Australia's thirty-first prime minister
28 June	Return of writs

Source: Australian Electoral Commission.

A key outcome of the election was a widening split between the salience for voters and the salience for the major parties of long-term issues such as climate change and transparency in government. 'Localised' politics, community campaigning and candidate quality were more prominent than in recent elections, in combination with the changing nature of campaigning in an evolving digital media landscape.

Another issue that unexpectedly took off was the Coalition's broken promise to introduce a federal integrity commission. Integrity issues were highlighted by the Teal Independents and the Greens and, along with gender issues, became part of the negative depiction of Morrison that dominated social media. The Coalition unsuccessfully attempted to deflect attention from integrity issues by suggesting they were of no interest to ordinary voters and that the focus should instead be on cost-of-living issues and economic management—their usual electoral strengths.

Along with climate change and integrity issues must be mentioned the salience of gender issues—more prominent than in any election since 1972. The Morrison Government had seemed incapable of dealing with issues of sexual misconduct in the parliamentary precinct and this served as a touchstone for women's disenchantment with the government on a range of issues. Veteran political journalist Paul Kelly was taken by surprise and won a Gold Ernie award for his 2021 prediction that 'the women's movement won't decide the next election'.

With so many high-profile ministers (and purported future party leaders) falling victim to Independents' campaigns on these issues, the Liberal Party faces the daunting task of rebuilding and—along with the Nationals—re-establishing its relevance with Australian voters, particularly women, socially progressive economic liberals and younger Australians.

The 2022 federal election also marked a profound shift in how the country runs its elections. A record proportion of voters cast their ballot before election day through either early or postal voting. While this trend was no doubt accelerated in 2022 due to Covid-19, it builds on an underlying preference for convenience and arguably on disengagement from politics—with voters casting an early ballot to switch off from the long campaign. With fewer than half of all voters casting their vote on election day, it appears that we have moved from an election *day* to an election *period*. This is a trend that is highly unlikely to be reversed, with potentially significant implications for the nature of elections as democratic rituals. It also has implications for the level playing field because non-incumbent candidates can struggle to staff polling booths for extended periods.

The traditional media was criticised during the campaign for a seeming preoccupation with the performance of leaders and the possibility of missteps, with the hashtag '#ThisisNotJournalism' trending on Twitter. In the very first week, Labor leader Anthony Albanese was unable to recall either the unemployment or the cash rates during a press conference. The Morrison Government and conservative media seized on the misstep to discredit Albanese's economic expertise and cast doubt on his leadership abilities. However, it also became illustrative of a style of politics that characterised the election: a focus on 'gotcha' moments and detail from which bigger policy issues and debates were notably absent.

Having learned from the mistake of campaigning in 2019 on complex reforms (such as overhauling tax policy in areas like imputation credit refunds), the Labor Party focused on a slimmed agenda of manufacturing, wage growth, gender pay parity and housing. The Coalition responded by repeatedly emphasising its record of economic management, leading to what it described as 'jobs and growth'. The result of this dynamic was to leave major policy issues that were salient in the minds of voters—such as climate change—out of the contest between the major parties and in the hands of the Greens and the Teals.

Despite the major parties' best efforts to keep the campaign focused on preset announcements and policy agendas, significant events occurred during the official campaign period that challenged both leaders to respond in ways that were not scripted. This included the announcement of Solomon Islands' security pact with China early in the campaign, which made regional security a significant issue but not in a way favourable to the government.

On 3 May, the Reserve Bank of Australia lifted the official cash rate by 0.25 per cent—the first of eight increases that would occur during 2022. This was the first time since the 2007 federal election (when Liberal prime minister John Howard was ousted by Labor's Kevin Rudd) that such an increase had occurred during a campaign, and it cemented economic management, the cost of living and housing affordability as key campaign issues (see Table 1.2).

Compared with other recent federal election campaigns, the 2022 election saw a heightened focus on individual candidates and constituencies. While all elections feature scandals involving candidates, the attention given not just to individual seats, but also to the competencies of individual candidates, was highly unusual. In part this can be explained by the momentum behind the localised campaigns of the Teal and 'Voices For' Independents, but it could have also been a broader consequence of the renewed importance of place and community that was felt so acutely during the Covid lockdowns.

The national media was captivated by the controversial candidate Katherine Deves, who was selected by Morrison to contest the northern Sydney seat of Warringah against Independent Zali Steggall. Deves's vocal stance against the rights of trans Australians was interpreted as a 'dog whistle' to the Liberals' conservative voter base (see Chapter 5). However, in other electorates, the suitability of candidates was being questioned based on geographic representation and appropriate reflection of ethnic diversity.

Labor's Andrew Charlton and Kristina Keneally—both contesting seats in western Sydney—were caught up in these debates. Charlton—despite his political credentials as a former adviser to Prime Minister Kevin Rudd—was criticised for not living in the electorate. Former NSW premier and senator Kristina Keneally, in her attempt to win a House of Representatives seat, was criticised in a similar way—but the party also faced strong opposition to the fact that it had not fielded a candidate who reflected the diversity of the electorate's population. Independent and Vietnam-born candidate Dai Le ultimately won the seat of Fowler from the Australian Labor Party (ALP).

Table 1.2 Key campaign events, 2022

Date	Event
16 February	Prime Minister Scott Morrison launches an attack on Labor as 'soft' on China and suggests the Labor deputy leader is a 'Manchurian candidate'.
7 March	The AEC launches a disinformation register to tackle fake news about the electoral process.
16 March	The AEC warns Advance Australia that its 'truth truck' showing Chinese president Xi Jinping voting Labor could be in contravention of the *Electoral Act*.
11 April	Opposition leader Anthony Albanese is unable to state the cash or unemployment rates when a journalist asks a 'gotcha' question.
13 April	Labor refuses to commit to an increase in JobSeeker payments.
	Greens leader Adam Bandt tells a journalist to 'Google it, mate' when asked a gotcha question about the wage price index.
16 April	Albanese commits to introducing an anti-corruption watchdog by the end of 2022.
	The United Australia Party holds its campaign launch on Queensland's Sunshine Coast.
20 April	Morrison supports Katherine Deves, his 'captain's pick' to contest the seat of Warringah, despite her comments about transgender people. The first leaders' debate is held in Brisbane, with Albanese declared the winner.
21 April	Albanese tests positive for Covid-19 and must self-isolate for seven days.
22 April	Former Liberal foreign minister Julie Bishop and former defence chief Chris Barrie criticise the Morrison Government for not doing enough to stop Solomon Islands' security pact with China.
29 April	Albanese comes out of isolation.
	The AEC warns Pauline Hanson's One Nation over a video making claims about voter fraud.
1 May	Labor holds its election campaign launch in Perth.
3 May	The Reserve Bank lifts the official cash (interest) rate, ending the record low maintained during the Covid pandemic.
5 May	A debate at the National Press Club in Canberra between Minister for Defence Peter Dutton and shadow minister Brendan O'Connor.
8 May	Second leaders' debate, in Sydney.
11 May	Albanese supports an increase of 5.1 per cent to the minimum wage tied to the inflation rate; Morrison claims this would increase interest rates.
	Third leaders' debate, in Sydney.
13 May	A debate at the National Press Club in Canberra between Minister for Foreign Affairs Marise Payne and shadow minister Penny Wong.

Date	Event
15 May	The Liberal Party holds its election campaign launch in Brisbane. Morrison promises to allow people to purchase their first home using funds from their superannuation.
16 May	The Australian Greens launch their campaign in Brisbane.
18 May	Albanese addresses the National Press Club. Morrison becomes the first prime minister since 1969 not to do so in the final week of the campaign.
21 May (Election day)	Australian Border Force reveals that a boat with asylum-seekers from Sri Lanka onboard has been intercepted. Voters receive a text message from the Liberal Party about the boat turnback, urging them to vote Liberal to maintain border security. Albanese begins his victory speech by committing in full to the Uluru Statement from the Heart.

Sources: The authors and Wikipedia.

Regulatory issues

Both formal and informal changes in the regulatory framework took place for the 2022 election. At the formal level there were several amendments to the *Electoral Act* in 2021, including changes to eligibility for party registration. The number of members required for registration was raised from 500 to 1,500, which contributed to a drop in the number of parties contesting the election compared with 2019. However, there was an increased number of candidates, in part due to minor parties such as the UAP, Pauline Hanson's One Nation (PHON) and the Liberal Democratic Party running in more House of Representatives seats. An attempt to eliminate the Liberal Democratic Party through a new requirement preventing registration of parties with similar names eventually failed due to a legal technicality. A reduction in the period for pre-poll voting from three weeks to two had little effect on the increase in pre-poll voting, most of which occurred in the final week before election day.

Also at the formal level, the Coalition Government attempted in 2021 to introduce voter ID requirements for voting in federal elections—something long on the agenda of conservative governments in Australia. It had been recommended by the Joint Standing Committee on Electoral Matters but was strongly opposed by Labor, the Australian Greens and Independent senator Rex Patrick. The government dropped the proposal after Senator Jacqui Lambie made it clear she would oppose it in the Senate, meaning it could not pass. Senator Lambie had conducted a poll on her website and two-thirds of the 33,000 respondents had opposed it (Giannini 2021). A particular concern was disenfranchisement of Indigenous voters in remote communities.

One change to the regulatory framework that was achieved with the support of Labor responded to the rise of the 'Voices For' movement and funding support from the Climate 200 crowdfunding initiative. In its final form, the change required 'significant third parties' that spent more than $250,000 on 'electoral expenditure' in that year (or in any one of the three previous financial years) to register and have detailed disclosure requirements like those of political parties. The change was strongly opposed by charities on several grounds. They argued that advocating for policy change was an important part of their work, that the definition of 'electoral expenditure' was much too broad and would capture issue-based advocacy only tangentially related to an election and that the new disclosure requirements would deter charitable donors. Labor's support for the change was apparently part of a deal over the voter ID bill, but Labor committed to revisiting the matter once in government (Karp 2021).

One area where no change occurred was in the very narrow proscription of misleading advertising in the *Electoral Act*, which had been found by the High Court (in *Evans v Crichton-Browne*, 1981) to only cover the process of casting a vote. The limits of the existing provision were vividly illustrated before the campaign proper had even begun. Already in March, the right-wing advocacy group Advance Australia (see Chapter 15, this volume) was organising 'truth trucks' depicting Chinese president Xi Jinping voting Labor. The initial version seen in Canberra (Plate 1.1) resulted in a warning from the Australian Electoral Commission (AEC), but only because it depicted President Xi marking his ballot with a tick rather than a number, which could mislead voters as to how to cast a valid vote. Advance Australia met this objection in subsequent versions of the 'truth truck' by substituting '1' for the tick, but also added a hammer and a sickle to ensure voters got the message. The message—that Labor was the cat's paw of the Chinese Communist Party—did not contravene the misleading advertising provision of the *Electoral Act*. The narrow scope of the existing provision has led both Labor and the Australian Greens to support truth in political advertising legislation such as that enacted in South Australia in 1985 and more recently in the Australian Capital Territory.

Plate 1.1 The 'Truth Truck', March 2022
Source: Ian Bushnell.

Changes at the more informal level took place to meet the broader challenge of rapidly disseminated digital disinformation, particularly concerning the electoral process. The AEC took a much more assertive approach than in 2019 to tackling such disinformation, which was important given its increased volume. In the runup to the election, the AEC developed an agreement with online platforms Meta (Facebook, Instagram), Twitter, Microsoft and TikTok that complemented the industry code on disinformation and misinformation in operation for the first time in the 2022 election. Meta was an important partner and, for example, provided one-off grants for the election to each of its third-party fact-checking agencies, the Australian Associated Press (AAP), Agence France-Presse (AFP) and RMIT FactLab. It claims to have rejected about 17,000 ads during the campaign for not complying with its policies (Meta 2022: 3).

In March 2022, the AEC launched a disinformation register, listing items of disinformation, the date detected and the action taken by the commission in conjunction with digital platforms or through videos of its own on social media. The increased quantum of disinformation included claims echoing the Trump campaign in the United States that the election would be stolen through the use of rigged Dominion voting machines, even though voting machines are not used in Australian elections. There was a prompt response to this conspiracy theory, with AAP Factcheck compiling a report and the AEC producing a video and forwarding the Factcheck to journalists. The AEC also used its Twitter account (on a Sunday!) to engage in an exchange of tweets on the subject with former senator Rod Culleton, now leader of the Great Australian Party.

In recognition of the speed at which disinformation spreads on social media, the AEC's digital engagement director, Evan Ekin-Smyth, had been given unprecedented freedom to be an active voice on Twitter responding to disinformation, as in the Culleton case. Social media logic is incompatible with bureaucratic hierarchy, but freedom can be used for a good bureaucratic purpose such as managing the AEC's reputation and positioning it as the foremost expert on electoral matters (Ekin-Smyth 2022). Together with his team of six, Ekin-Smyth was tweeting up to two dozen times an hour as well as running the AEC's accounts on Facebook, Instagram, LinkedIn and YouTube. He also partnered with TikTok on an election guide and held an 'Ask me anything' session on Reddit. While the snappy AEC tweets occasionally drew pushback from critics, Ekin-Smyth was able to stand his ground on the importance of engaging with people in their own terms rather than talking like a public servant.

Where candidates were involved, dealing with disinformation was sometimes sensitive because of the need to preserve political neutrality. For example, legal and executive advice was sought before crafting a response to a video by PHON on 29 April suggesting the 2010 federal election had been decided by illegal votes. Meanwhile, social media companies were contacted and either took the video down or labelled it as misleading. *The Washington Post* was so impressed, it ran a story on the AEC's digital engagement headlined: 'The Twitter account defending Australian democracy' (Miller and Vinall 2022).

The structure of the book

Australian political scientists have been producing studies of federal election campaigns since 1958. This is the eighteenth in the series that has been supported since the 1996 election by the Academy of the Social Sciences in Australia. After each election there is a workshop identifying the key themes of the campaign, patterns of voting behaviour, the campaign strategies of political and third parties, the performance of opinion polls, administrative issues, political discourses, and visual politics. The workshop brings together academics and practitioners and pairs established scholars with early career researchers to ensure a diverse range of perspectives on the event.

In 2022 we needed, for the first time in an Australian election book, to include a chapter on corruption and integrity issues. Another salient feature of the election was the gap between the campaign as reported in the traditional media and the dynamic campaigns taking place on social media. We found that the election was a watershed in several ways, with a record number of voters rejecting the electoral patterns of the past and the forms taken by professional party politics.

To address what led to the 2022 election being a watershed moment in Australian electoral history, the volume is divided into three parts:

1. The campaign and its context, covering administrative arrangements for an election held during the Covid-19 pandemic, populism, the major parties' campaign techniques, gender, the visual politics of the campaign, social media and traditional media reporting, and corruption and integrity issues.
2. The actors involved in the campaign, including the political parties, the Teal Independents, the Voices For community groups and third parties such as Climate 200.
3. The results in the House and the Senate, also covering analyses of voter behaviour, early voting and the polls.

Following this Introduction, Michael Maley begins the first part of the book with a chapter outlining the effect of the pandemic on the operation of Australian democracy and how the AEC was able to deliver a Covid-safe election. In particular, he highlights the work of the federal parliament's Joint Standing Committee on Electoral Matters in achieving a nonpartisan approach. Another factor he finds important is the reservoir of public trust in election administrators. Despite the great increase in early voting and the innovation of telephone voting for Covid-affected electors, no election outcomes were challenged in the Court of Disputed Returns.

In the third chapter, 'The integrity election', A.J. Brown examines how government accountability became a highly salient issue in 2022, which was dramatised by the success of the Teal Independents. While accountability covered a broad range of factors, including lobbying and political finance, its symbol became the need for a federal integrity commission. This chapter shows how revelations of 'industrial-scale' pork-barrelling and Australia's sliding position on the global Corruption Perceptions Index provided the background for legislative initiatives by federal Independents and the Australian Greens. Labor also became committed to reform in early 2018 while Prime Minister Scott Morrison unsuccessfully attempted to deflect issues of integrity on to questions of economic management.

In Chapter 4, Carol Johnson examines the variants of populism in the 2022 election. She finds it differed from the populism of the 2019 election, with Labor no longer mobilising left-wing populist discourse against the 'top end of town'. Rather, Labor contested 'us versus them' rhetoric by arguing that it would bring both business and the unions to the table rather than dividing them. The Coalition presented a post-pandemic form of market populism, seeking to exploit resentment about continuing restrictions by promoting 'can-do capitalism' as an alternative to 'don't-do government'. The chapter also looks at populist elements in the strategies of other parties, including Clive Palmer's UAP and PHON, both of which targeted elites or the 'political class' for selling out Australia's interests.

Next, Blair Williams and Marian Sawer examine how the 2022 federal election was a watershed in terms of women's disaffection with the Morrison Government and its handling of 'their' issues. Women's safety became a salient electoral issue, along with climate change and an integrity commission, and women Independents helped loosen the grip of the two-party system. This chapter examines how despite continuing revelations of women's mistreatment in politics there was an increased number of women standing for the federal parliament and increased diversity in the forty-seventh parliament. The chapter also analyses the gendered nature of campaign discourses, whether centring on hardhats or the care economy, and assesses the nature of party offerings for women.

In Chapter 6, Glenn Kefford and Stephen Mills review the campaign strategies adopted by the Labor and Liberal parties. Labor had methodically rectified the organisational failures identified by its 2019 review, particularly the lack of a formal campaign committee. In 2022, the predominant frame used by both parties for campaign communications was leadership, exemplifying the personalisation of politics now seen internationally. Both sides boosted the credentials of their own leader while exploiting the weaknesses of the other. The chapter also uses data available for the first time from the Meta Ad Library to analyse resource allocation to target seats, finding the Coalition outspent Labor in this form of digital campaigning.

Analysis of the media coverage of federal elections has been a strength of the election series and in Chapter 7 Andrea Carson and Simon Jackman examine the relationship between traditional media and the digital domain. They analyse election coverage on the front pages of Australia's major daily newspapers and in Facebook posts by a wide range of media organisations and then assess the engagement of Facebook readers with the varying topics covered in these election-relevant posts. Housing affordability— a traditional hip-pocket-nerve issue—was the largest single issue on front pages, accounted for one-third of media organisations' election-relevant Facebook posts and generated most user interaction. However, adjusting for subscriber counts and the volume of posts, the highest user engagement was with personalities such as posts about individual leaders, Independent candidates and Katherine Deves's candidacy.

In Chapter 8, Lucien Leon and Richard Scully examine the cartoons, memes and videos circulating during the 2022 campaign, a selection based on readership and viewing figures. TikTok had become the major social media platform for both political actors and citizen actors during the campaign, but the Coalition fundamentally misunderstood the dynamics of this platform, achieving little engagement. Labor's digital strategy was more successful than the Coalition's, unlike in 2019. Cartoons in the mainstream media were somewhat more favourable to the Coalition but, in general, visual politics, including the bin sticker campaign in Sydney, reflected and reinforced disenchantment with the government.

The second section of the book examines the key actors involved in the campaign. In Chapter 9, Rob Manwaring and Emily Foley examine the distinctive factors underpinning Labor's 2022 electoral performance, focusing on the key transitions the party made from the disappointing 2019 result under Bill Shorten. They outline Anthony Albanese's four-stage strategy for electoral victory, built on a process of review, vision-making, policy clearing/setting and the 'short' campaign. The authors map the shift to a 'thin labourist' agenda, as well as a greater willingness to cooperate with business—an approach echoing other successful centre-left parties that have captured a distinctive post-Covid environment with something of a 'back to basics' agenda.

In Chapter 10, Marija Taflaga provides an analysis of the organisational, personality and policy factors impacting on the Liberal Party's defeat at the 2022 federal election and reflects on the party's future viability. She examines changes to the organisation of the party and its candidate selection procedures, which impacted on its campaign and electoral performance, as well as perceptions of its performance in government and its policy positioning. Looking forward, the chapter reflects on how the 2022 result has significantly altered the Coalition party room: the dominance of the Liberal National Party of Queensland (LNP), the loss of heartland seats in the party's wealthiest and oldest strongholds and the resulting shift in the balance of power, as well as the party's future relationship with the Nationals.

Continuing the analysis of the Coalition, in Chapter 11, Anika Gauja examines the campaign and electoral performance of the National Party of Australia. She analyses the party's decision to contest seats and the candidates they selected, focusing on contests where the party faced challenges from popular Independents and the community-based 'Voices For' groups. The chapter argues that the Nationals' campaign was characterised by a small-target, locally focused strategy built on a war-chest of pre-election infrastructure and spending promises. It was conducted, however, in the context of a broader fragmentation within the party and its supporter base over climate change policy.

In Chapter 12, Stewart Jackson and Josh Holloway look at the performance of the Greens—a result that surprised many media commentators but one that the authors argue was a result of years of local campaigning and advocacy on progressive policy issues. The party placed greater emphasis on grassroots organising, waging 'ground' campaigns in several key seats of unprecedented scale and duration for a minor party. The Queensland Greens coupled this with 'mutual aid' programs, embedding themselves in communities to provide, for instance, aid packages and cleanup following floods. On policy, the Greens advocated a distinctly green-centred social democracy. Campaign appeals spoke of climate action holistically, but also gave prominence to classic left-redistributionist policies such as expanding the welfare system, building public housing, increasing taxes on big business and including dental health in Medicare.

Chapter 13 examines the success of Independent candidates in 2022 in the context of voters' long-term disenchantment with the major parties, arguing we should acknowledge the unsung Independents who have spent decades chipping away at the major parties' electoral bases. Jill Sheppard outlines how the professionalisation of non-party candidacy (largely underwritten by third-party and community groups) led to a 'Teal wave' in which Independent candidates gained national media attention and toppled a generation of the Liberal Party's future leaders. The chapter argues that the longstanding presence of Independent candidates (and small parties like the Democrats and the Greens) over several decades helped to pave the way for the 2022 result that saw seven new Independents elected, forming a House of Representatives crossbench of 16 members. The chapter details the strategies of Independent and other candidates outside the major organised groups in 2022, their ideological bases, their successes and failures, and their role in creating a post–two-party system.

Carolyn M. Hendriks and Richard Reid analyse in Chapter 14 one of the most distinctive features of the 2022 election: the rise of the 'Voices For' groups as well as local Community Independent candidate groups. The authors argue that the movement for Community Independents is a loose network of place-based groups, each carving out a local pathway for improving political representation. The place-based variation across community groups is an important nuance that has been overlooked in the national media, both by those celebrating the 'Teal wave' and by those critiquing the 'party-like' behaviour of the movement. The analysis reveals considerable diversity within the movement; some local groups selected or endorsed a Community Independent candidate in the 2022 election, while others chose not to follow this path and instead facilitated broader community engagement with all local candidates.

In Chapter 15, Ariadne Vromen and Serrin Rutledge-Prior focus on the activities of four different campaigning organisations that were active as third parties during the 2022 election campaign: GetUp!, Climate 200, the Australian Christian Lobby and Advance (formerly Advance Australia). The authors argue that while some tactics were shared across the groups, particularly their use of digital campaigning via social media and Facebook advertising, they differed in their emphasis on a range of campaign issues, tactics and overall influence on the election campaign discourse. There is also an interdependency between the campaign work of these third parties and their capacity to raise large amounts of money, as well as the organic reach of their brand of ideas.

Ben Raue outlines the results in the House of Representatives in Chapter 16, focusing on changes between the 2019 and 2022 elections, who stood for election in 2022, differences between the States, and the steep rise in 'non-classic' electoral races (that is, those seats where an Independent or minor-party candidate was one of the top two vote winners). The chapter observes that Labor performed poorly in several geographic areas, including Tasmania and outer Melbourne, while winning far more seats than expected in Western Australia. The Greens' electoral efforts in Queensland paid off, but they had little success elsewhere, while the Liberals lost key seats to Teal Independents in Sydney, Melbourne and Perth.

In Chapter 17, Antony Green notes that the Coalition received its lowest-ever share of the Senate vote and that both major parties received fewer votes than the combined minor-party and Independent candidates. Also notable is the Greens' result in 2022: not quite matching the lofty heights of 2010 but reflecting long-term growth in its electoral popularity and the emerging group of lifelong Greens voters who provide reliable support to the party. PHON performed strongly across New South Wales, Queensland and South Australia, while Palmer's UAP reached 4 per cent of the final vote in Victoria. Surprising everyone, the Legalise Cannabis party won 5 per cent of the vote in Queensland and 6 per cent in the Northern Territory. While the resulting crossbench will prove a challenge for the government in the Senate, the ongoing normalisation of Independent and minor-party voting in the upper house will challenge both major parties over the longer term.

In Chapter 18, Murray Goot finds that polling in the 2022 election was distinctive for several reasons: first, the almost total collapse of media-sponsored opinion polls; second, and largely as a consequence, the very small number of single-seat polls that were conducted and released—mostly in marginal seats but also in seats, otherwise safe or very safe, under challenge from Teal Independents; and third, and most importantly, the publication of a poll that sought to predict the outcome not just in some seats but in every seat—a poll whose novel method could have changed election-watching in Australia for ever had it lived up to its promise. This chapter shows that Australia's first published multilevel regression post-stratification (MRP) poll generally overestimated the Coalition's vote share—something a national swing towards the Coalition late in the campaign would have compounded. But it also shows that in Liberal seats where the Teals mounted a challenge, and in Labor seats in Western Australia, the last stretch of the campaign may have worked against the Coalition.

Finally, in Chapter 19, Ferran Martinez i Coma and Rodney Smith observe that for the first time in Australian elections a minority—just under half—of Australian voters cast their ballots at a polling place on polling day. Record numbers and proportions of citizens voted before polling day, with almost all either voting in person at early voting centres (5,541,757 voters, or 36 per cent) or voting by post (2,210,408 voters, or 14 per cent). While some of this was driven by Covid-19–related contingencies, the trend has led to serious questions about how we conduct elections and campaigns in Australia. The chapter finds that most early voters cast their ballots in the five days before polling day, and pre-poll voting was more common in safe seats than in marginal contests, suggesting the major parties may not have to do much to adjust their campaigns in response to the rise of early voting. On the other hand, the 2022 successes of well-organised and well-resourced minor parties and Independents in House of Representatives seats in which there were average to high levels of postal and/or pre-poll voting indicate that early voting will not protect major-party candidates from defeat, even in previously safe seats.

Conclusion

Just weeks into its first term, the Albanese Government had embarked at high speed on its election commitments, including preparation for a referendum on a Voice to Parliament, legislation to introduce a federal integrity commission, and a Jobs and Skills Summit. Both Albanese and Foreign Minister Penny Wong embarked on international diplomatic visits to the Pacific region, security summits in Japan and Spain, and Paris to 'reset' Australia's relationship with France, which deteriorated after the cancellation of a multibillion-dollar defence submarine contract in 2018. The government itself was more diverse than ever before, with a record number of women—including an Indigenous woman, Linda Burney, holding the Indigenous Australians portfolio.

In the months after the election, doubt has continued over the enduring legacy of the Morrison Government. In August 2022, it was revealed that Morrison had been secretly sworn into multiple ministerial portfolios, including health, finance, home affairs and industry. Morrison defended these actions as necessary in a time of unprecedented crisis and uncertainty caused by the Covid-19 pandemic, but his actions were widely criticised as contrary to fundamental principles of collective ministerial responsibility and open and transparent government.

While the implementation of Albanese's policy agenda has begun with considerable speed, the economic context has created—and will continue to create—significant challenges for the new government. Saddled with its election commitment to proceed with the 'Stage 3' tax cuts for the wealthy, the government faces an incredibly difficult mix of rising inflation, rising interest rates and falling wages. This will significantly constrain the government's fiscal policy options and presents a scenario for industrial unrest that could become difficult for Labor to resolve given its voter base and election commitments.

References

Booker, Chloe and Najma Sambul. 2002. 'We're living with COVID but more of us are dying than ever'. *Sydney Morning Herald*, 7 May. Available from: www.smh. com.au/national/we-re-living-with-covid-but-more-of-us-are-dying-than-ever-20220429-p5ah7y.html.

Ekin-Smyth, Evan. 2022. Interviewed by Marian Sawer, 23 July.

Gauja, Anika, Marian Sawer and Marian Simms (eds). 2020. *Morrison's Miracle: The 2019 Australian Federal Election*. Canberra: ANU Press. doi.org/10.22459/ MM.2020.

Giannini, Dominic. 2021. 'Jacqui Lambie pulls support for voter ID laws prompting government to quietly kill bill'. *7News.com.au*, 18 August. Available from: 7news.com.au/politics/voter-identity-laws-heading-towards-defeat-c-4771484.

Insurance Council of Australia. 2022. 'Updated data shows 2022 flood was Australia's costliest'. Media release, 3 May. Sydney: Insurance Council of Australia. Available from: insurancecouncil.com.au/resource/updated-data-shows-2022-flood-was-australias-costliest/.

Karp, Paul. 2021. 'Morrison government urges MPs to dob in climate and "Voices for" groups under new donor rules'. *The Guardian*, [Australia], 13 December. Available from: www.theguardian.com/australia-news/2021/dec/13/morrison-government-urges-mps-to-dob-in-climate-and-voices-for-groups-under-new-donor-rules.

Meta. 2022. 'Meta's submission to the inquiry into the 2022 federal election'. Submission 421 to the Joint Standing Committee on Electoral Matters Inquiry into the 2022 Federal Election, October. Canberra: Parliament of Australia. Available from: www.aph.gov.au/Parliamentary_Business/Committees/Joint/ Electoral_Matters/2022federalelection/Submissions.

Miller, Michael E. and Frances Vinall. 2022. 'The Twitter account defending Australian democracy'. *The Washington Post*, 14 May. Available from: www. washingtonpost.com/world/2022/05/14/australia-electoral-commission/.

Part 1: Campaign and context

2

Administrative issues in a time of Covid

Michael Maley

The 2022 federal election took place in a singular environment of threat: the Covid-19 pandemic. To find a comparable phenomenon that so dominated the political, social, economic and administrative contexts of a federal poll, one would have to go back to World War II. The pivotal election of 1943 saw the collapse of the original United Australia Party, which had been the dominant conservative force since 1931. The effect of Covid-19 on the key institutions of Australian democracy was sudden and striking. In response to the initial impact of the virus, Mills (2020: 7) notes, 'the Federal Parliament was reduced to an unrepresentative "rump" and then adjourned for twenty weeks'.

Clearly a problem capable of producing such dramatic consequences also had potentially major implications for the normal conduct of an election. It is worth highlighting at the outset the sheer scale of electoral processes: they are the largest and most complex logistical operations a country undertakes in peacetime—and thus uniquely susceptible to disruption at a range of points—since they involve the delivery of a service to the entire adult citizenry of the country in a highly compressed time frame. Furthermore, one of the burdens electoral administrators must bear is that the better they do their work, the easier it looks from the outside.

They also have only one chance to get things right and depend on a huge election day workforce, some of whom will be doing their job for the first time. This became especially problematical in 2022, when about 20,000 polling and counting staff (of a target figure of approximately 105,000) dropped out, largely due to Covid-19, in the fortnight before polling day, necessitating massive and ultimately successful efforts by the Australian Electoral Commission (AEC) to cover the shortfall. In addition, some 8,000 staff had to be engaged and trained to provide, on a unique scale, a facility for telephone voting by those required to isolate because of Covid infection.

The aims of this chapter are therefore to explore in more detail the problems the Covid-19 pandemic caused or could have caused at the 2022 election; to highlight why the AEC was well placed to implement a relatively Covid-safe election; to describe the main policy options for dealing with Covid-19 and the mechanisms and processes by which the AEC explored them; to note the changes that were made to the legal framework for elections; and to describe the implementation and impact of the key measures that had been agreed on.

Problems

The Covid-19 pandemic, declared by the World Health Organization on 30 January 2020 to be a global public health emergency, had four characteristics that gave rise to challenges for the administration of elections.

First, Covid-19 had been clearly identified as a dangerous disease, with a significant fatality rate, particularly among the elderly and those with certain pre-existing medical conditions. Its danger was especially concerning at the outset of the pandemic when neither vaccines nor proven treatments other than interventions to alleviate symptoms were available. Given these circumstances, it rapidly became clear that the pandemic would place significant strains on public health systems worldwide.

Second, it was a highly communicable disease. While initial cases appeared to flow from transmission from animals to humans, it soon became apparent that human-to-human transmission was also possible, the disease could be passed on by infected but asymptomatic individuals and respiratory secretions were a key transmission vector but airborne transmission also played a major role. In the absence of vaccines and treatments, it was therefore necessary in the first instance to rely on limiting physical transmission using disinfectants, protective clothing and equipment, and regimes for 'social distancing' or even isolation. By the time of the 2022 election, the global dominance of the highly communicable 'Omicron' variant of Covid-19 had made the achievement of herd immunity against the disease seem ever more elusive. The ease with which Covid-19 could be transmitted also provided an early warning that, unlike a natural disaster, its impact was unlikely to be confined to a small geographical area.

Third, it was at the outset, and remained at the time of the 2022 election, a novel and evolving disease, making its future character and course difficult to model and predict, either virologically or epidemiologically.

Fourth, for all the reasons listed above, Covid-19 rapidly gave rise to societal disruption on a grand scale. Measures such as lockdowns, compulsory isolation and 'working from home' arrangements were put in place that greatly disrupted patterns of daily life, with major flow-on economic effects, including a large increase in the federal budget deficit.

Given these characteristics, the problems looming for the conduct of elections were obvious. Elections represent the antithesis of social distancing, as they bring people together in large numbers; an international study of electoral processes in general, undertaken early in the pandemic, noted that '[m]ore than 40 points in the electoral process involve the assembly of people or transfer of objects and therefore pose risks of virus transmission if no preventive measures are taken' (Buril et al. 2020: 4).

By November 2020, the AEC (2020: 4–5) had identified that emergencies, including that arising from Covid-19, 'could force significant compromises, delays, or even render an election partially or fully undeliverable'. It identified six key areas of particular concern: staffing, materials and logistics, turnout, premises, service suppliers and the exacerbation of existing challenges (such as the provision of access to electoral services to regional or overseas voters, or to voters living with disability or experiencing homelessness; early voting; the reliability of postal services; and the provision of voting facilities in Indigenous communities). A further source of complexity that rapidly became apparent was the existence of disparate rules and health orders across the States and Territories, which had the potential to be especially challenging given the need for the AEC to ensure nationwide consistency in the provision of services to voters.

Beyond those specific concerns, there is a more general challenge to the conduct of successful elections in the Covid-19 era: uncertainty. The concept of the electoral cycle clearly points to the desirability of identifying major planning constraints and pinning down key parameters well before the election period, so that planning can proceed effectively, staff can be recruited and trained and the public can be made aware of how the process will unfold. For that reason, electoral administrators very much prefer to avoid last-minute changes to the legal or procedural framework for elections.

Reasons the AEC was well placed

The AEC was, for a range of reasons, especially well placed at the 2022 election to meet the challenges posed by Covid-19.

First, the timing of the election was fortuitous, falling as it did at a point in the pandemic when there had been a substantial rollout of vaccinations across the country, with more than 95 per cent of the population aged 16 or over fully vaccinated nationwide by polling day, and with a substantial percentage also having received a first booster. Had the election been due in 2020 or held close to the earliest possible date for simultaneous House of Representatives and Senate elections (in 2021), the health risks—both real and perceived—associated with the electoral process would have been much greater. There would also have been far greater challenges associated with the conduct of the election had lockdowns been in place, forcing AEC staff to work from home and quite possibly compromising the ability of key suppliers to deliver necessary materials on time.

Second, the federal election was not the first the AEC had been required to conduct in the Covid-19 era; there had been a by-election in the NSW division of Eden-Monaro in June 2020 and in the division of Groom in Queensland in November 2020. That ensured, among other things, that preparatory steps required for the implementation at polling and counting of Covid-specific public health measures had been not only initiated within the organisation, but also field-tested, almost two years before the 2022 election. There had also, since the declaration of the pandemic, been State, Territory or local government elections in every Australian jurisdiction, giving the AEC considerable opportunities to benefit from the experience of its counterparts.

Third, steps to take the pressure off queueing on election day and to reduce the need for personal interactions between voters more generally did not require major last-minute architectural changes, but merely the expansion of enrolment and voting modalities that were already well developed. Most federal elections in the twentieth century were marked by many enrolment transactions generated by the announcement of an election date, which required the voter to complete an electoral enrolment form and have it witnessed by someone else. That potentially involved a good deal of face-to-face contact. Now, the Commonwealth roll is predominantly based on information received by the AEC from other government agencies; voters missed by this process have the option of enrolling online; and voters' identities are generally confirmed by cross-referencing to passport and driver's licence databases, rather than by the attestation of a witness. Early voting has also become well established. In 2022, for the first time in Australian federal electoral history, more than 50 per cent of those who voted did so before polling day. In fact, the AEC (2008: 41) had identified to the federal parliament's Joint Standing Committee on Electoral Matters (JSCEM) some 14 years earlier that Australia no longer had just a polling day for federal elections, but rather a polling period. The number of votes being cast before polling day has increased at every federal election since 1993, and the process of applying for a postal vote has become more sophisticated but also simpler, with online applications taking only a few minutes to complete. The telephone voting system built on one originally developed for vision-impaired voters that was later extended to Antarctic voters as well.

Fourth, and more generally, the administration of federal elections in Australia has become increasingly automated. In recent years, the most striking example of that has been the reconfiguration of Senate counting, which is now based on scanning and optical character recognition technology—still, however, supplemented by a parallel manual checking and data entry process. The process of delivering postal vote packs to postal voters has also substantially been automated, eliminating much labour-intensive activity. The development of enhanced online training packages for polling staff also proved its worth when large numbers of replacement staff had to be found in the weeks before polling day. (It is worth emphasising, however, that a dependence on centralised automated systems also carries risks. All of them require, to a greater or lesser extent, management and maintenance, which in normal circumstances would be done by a small team of specialists. An outbreak of Covid-19 within such a team could have had an impact across the entire country rather than being limited, for example, to the electoral divisions served by a single AEC field office. Significant contingency planning is needed to mitigate such risks.)

Fifth, the AEC's administrative approach to elections has become much more integrated. At the time of its establishment in 1984, the AEC had a nationwide network of divisional offices—one for each federal constituency—which functioned with a considerable degree of autonomy, in effect conducting discrete elections. The network is now much smaller, with offices regionalised and able to access nationwide systems that help to ensure a consistency of approach across the country. In that sense, field staff are now less like feudal lords and more like cogs in a machine. While the feudal model worked well in its time and proved to be relatively robust, it is almost inconceivable that many small offices, each essentially fending for itself, could have met the unique challenges posed by Covid-19.

Sixth, two parliamentary committees, the JSCEM and its predecessor, the Joint Select Committee on Electoral Reform, have since 1983 provided a well-defined mechanism through which the federal parliament can address electoral policy issues in a systematic way. The JSCEM has proven to be adept at distinguishing between electoral changes that are controversial (such as the proposed introduction of requirements for voters to produce documentary proof of identity when voting) and those in relation to which there is scope for consensus to be forged. When, in 2020, there was clearly an urgent need for the consideration of new policy approaches to the pandemic, the committee was ready and able to conduct an effective inquiry that produced by June 2021 a set of unanimous recommendations (JSCEM 2021: ix–x), thereby reducing the risk that measures taken by the AEC could become matters of partisan dispute, as happened in the United States in the runup to the 2020 presidential election.

Finally, Australia benefits greatly from the reservoir of public trust in its election administrators that has been built up over the years. In most countries, as one goes from election to election, incremental changes to processes are much commoner than radical ones. That helps to develop public familiarity with how elections are run, reinforcing trust. When significant changes to procedures are made necessary by external shocks such as the Covid-19 pandemic, such familiarity cannot be relied on to the same extent, and then, public trust that the AEC will be doing its best to provide a service in a politically neutral way becomes a more important element of the perceived legitimacy of the election process. As noted in Chapter 1, the AEC in the runup to the 2022 election made major efforts to respond rapidly to disinformation being spread about the electoral process. Rumours relating to Covid-19—that the unvaccinated would be unable to vote or to serve as scrutineers—were promptly contradicted.

Exploration of policy options

The Covid-19 pandemic gave rise to a situation—unique in living memory—in which virtually all electoral administrators worldwide were focusing on the same problems at the same time. The existence of the internet, furthermore, made it possible for their practical experiences and conclusions about lessons learned to be shared almost in real time.[1] Three broad categories of response to the pandemic emerged.

First, in some cases, it was possible for elections simply to be postponed. That was done for certain Australian local government elections but was not constitutionally feasible at the federal level.

Second, changes were possible to the architecture (broadly defined) of an election process—for example, measures as diverse as conducting polling outdoors rather than inside buildings, shifting to universal postal voting or extending polling beyond a single day. The common element in each case was a need to reduce the risk of disease transmission during the polling.

Third, standard public health measures of the type implemented in most public places at the height of the pandemic could also be implemented in the electoral context. Such measures typically included the use of face masks and shields, the provision of single-use pencils for the marking of votes and the widespread use of disinfectant.

Anticipating that a great deal of work would be required to research and explore these diverse policy options and to implement those ultimately adopted, and noting that an increase in early voting could be anticipated, the AEC in 2020 undertook an 'Early Voting Trends Volumetrics Project' in an attempt to clarify likely demand as much as possible to ensure that capacity would exist to meet it. Building on that work and other lessons learned in the earlier stages of the pandemic, the AEC in August 2021 established a Covid Variants Response Unit (CVRU) within its Strategic Election Priorities Branch. Its role was summarised as follows:

> [T]he CRVU [sic] provides the agency with a central source of up-to-date information across all Australian jurisdictions, acts as a central point of coordination with key external stakeholders such

---

1   For a global overview of electoral policy measures adopted in response to Covid-19, see International IDEA (2022). For a detailed exploration prepared early in the pandemic of policy options that could be considered in the Australian context, see Maley (2020).

as the Chief Health Officers and the Australian Health Protection
Principal Committee (AHPPC) and has supported operational
areas with scenarios to allow them to test their responsiveness to
complexities of delivery that may occur … [due] to COVID. Some
of [the] other … key outputs of this unit are:

- a **COVID-19 Management Handbook**
- updates to the **COVID-19 Working Safely Framework** with
  People and Property Branch
- **research on international responses** to delivering elections
  during pandemic conditions
- COVID election **best practice information sharing** with States
  and Territories
- **COVID dashboard** leveraging Commonwealth and State data
- the establishment of **COVID Executive Officer roles** in each
  State and Territory office. (AEC 2022a: 19; emphasis in original)

More generally, the AEC put mechanisms in place for high-level liaison
and cooperation with a wide range of other government organisations,
including the Department of Health and that department's State and
Territory counterparts.

Legal initiatives

The regulatory framework for the conduct of federal elections has long
been highly prescriptive (Maley and Orr 2019), so it was inevitable that
legislation of some sort would be required to authorise changed processes.
As it happened, the changes recommended by the JSCEM in 2021 in
response to the pandemic were not as broad as had been suggested in
some submissions to the committee's inquiry, including that of the AEC.
To give but one example, the AEC (2020: 6) had raised the possibility that
'[t]o provide greater flexibility in the event of an emergency situation, the
Electoral Act could be modified, for example, to … conduct an election
solely by postal vote (in some or all geographic areas)'.

The JSCEM was not prepared to go that far: its ultimate recommendation
in relation to postal voting (JSCEM 2021: ix) envisaged that the electoral
commissioner could be authorised to 'extend the reasons electors can
vote by post or pre-poll' and 'streamline application and/or declaration

requirements for postal and pre-poll voting', but such changes would not have enabled the requirement that electors apply individually for a postal vote to be set aside so that all voters could be sent postal ballot papers directly.

Ultimately, the *Commonwealth Electoral Act 1918* was twice amended to facilitate elections conducted against the background of Covid-19: by the *Electoral Legislation Amendment (Contingency Measures) Act 2021* (primarily to expand the electoral commissioner's powers to make certain limited determinations and contingency arrangements) and the *Electoral Legislation Amendment (COVID Enfranchisement) Act 2022* (to enable telephone voting to be extended to people in isolation due to Covid-19).

Implementation and impact

For the 2022 election, the expansion of telephone voting proved to be the main architectural innovation. While as noted above this built on a foundation already in place, the extent to which the existing system had to be expanded represented a quantum leap from the past. At the 2019 election, 2,044 blind or vision-impaired electors voted by telephone (AEC 2022d: 7). In the runup to the 2022 election, the AEC undertook detailed modelling in conjunction with the Department of Health, the Australian Bureau of Statistics and others, and found it necessary to plan for the worst-case possibility that up to 360,000 people would utilise the system. Challengingly, the detailed legal framework for the operation was promulgated only on 31 March 2022, less than two months before the election, in the form of the Commonwealth Electoral (COVID Enfranchisement) Regulations 2022. Through a partnership with Services Australia and seven other government agencies, call centre facilities were assembled and some 8,000 existing public servants were engaged and trained. At the close of business on election day, 74,255 Covid-affected individuals had voted by telephone, along with 2,794 blind or vision-impaired electors and 65 electors in the Antarctic (AEC 2022b). The scale of the service provided is even more remarkable when it is considered that the system is not like automated opinion polling where choices can be indicated simply by pressing a button on a keypad, but requires—unavoidably—an interaction between the voter and AEC employees.

Plate 2.1 AEC staff with facemasks and sanitiser
Source: AEC.

There was also a large increase in the number of people voting before polling day. Of those who turned out, 36.4 per cent voted at pre-poll voting centres and 14.3 per cent voted by post. As noted above, this represented a substantial scaling up of voting modalities already in place, rather than an architectural change per se.

There was no mobile polling conducted in general hospitals or prisons and mobile polling in residential aged care homes proceeded only to a very limited extent. Consultations with the Department of Health had highlighted the infection risks to the elderly that entry to such premises would involve, and it became necessary for the AEC to discuss possible access and risk mitigations with each aged care facility individually. The AEC accordingly established support cells in all States and Territories that engaged with residential aged care facilities to ensure support was in place for electors to cast their votes. This included provision of support materials, posters and information for families, postal vote applications, expedited delivery of postal vote certificates if needed and onsite support (with controls in place) in some instances. There was also high-level engagement with several peak bodies ahead of the election to best support the sector.

Ultimately, the number of results reported from Special Hospital Teams fell from 489 at the 2019 election to only 60 in 2022, and the number of formal House of Representatives votes taken by such teams fell from 83,240 to 3,632 (AEC 2019a, 2022e). The bulk of residents were left dependent on postal voting, as had been the case before 1984; the number of postal votes cast by such electors was not separately published. While postal voting has long been a legally recognised voting modality, the development was nonetheless a regrettable one, not least because mobile polling had been introduced against the background of distrust between the major parties of the way in which postal voting had worked in aged care homes in the past. In that context, it is worth noting that with postal voting, unlike mobile polling, the AEC cannot provide a guarantee that voters, especially in an institutional setting, will be able to cast a secret ballot; nor are scrutineers able to monitor the voting process.

Voting at diplomatic missions was also cut back severely, being offered at only 19 posts (AEC 2022c), compared with 85 in 2019 (AEC 2019b). Again, those arrangements reflected risk assessments that had to be undertaken country by country. This process was made significantly more complicated by the fact that every host country could in the Covid-19 era be expected to have its own evolving legal framework for handling the pandemic, which could potentially include measures such as lockdowns that would disrupt access to embassy polling facilities.

Most overseas voters therefore had to rely on postal voting. All their postal ballot papers were sent by the AEC from Australia, and they still ultimately had to depend on the postal service or courier services in their country of residence to receive their ballots; in the event, more than 80 per cent of overseas postal votes were sent by courier. The quality of postal and courier services of course varies from country to country. Timor-Leste, for example, has no functioning postal service and courier services face significant challenges in delivering consignments to remote areas; the number of votes received from there fell from 372 in 2019 to only 43 in 2022. Globally, mechanisms were put in place for overseas votes (pre-poll and postal) to be returned to the AEC by diplomatic bag; the number so dispatched fell from 61,838 in 2019 to 39,363 in 2022.

The AEC also implemented a broad suite of basic public health measures of the type that had become standard in elections in Australia since the start of the pandemic. All steps were taken based on advice from the relevant public health authorities.

In general, the election proved to be highly successful from a Covid-19 point of view; there is no evidence that it became a 'super spreader' event. Turnout fell slightly compared with 2019, but that could partly be explained by reductions in mobile polling and overseas voting. Some voters' concerns about Covid-19 risks could have been great enough to deter them from voting, but that does not appear to have been a mass phenomenon. Others could have assumed that fear of catching Covid-19 would be accepted as a valid and sufficient reason to not vote; the AEC, in a major departure from previous practice, had in fact made a public announcement to that effect in the runup to the 2020 Eden-Monaro by-election.

Changes to the voting process proved to be relatively uncontroversial and certainly did not give rise to any major disputation. Notably, no election outcomes were challenged in the Court of Disputed Returns. Except at the extreme margins, the legitimacy of the election was accepted much as had always been the case in the past.

That is not to say, however, that the AEC's task was easy. In particular, the need to replace a significant proportion of polling and counting staff in the weeks before polling day was without precedent in living memory. That such a challenge was met successfully exemplifies, perhaps more than anything else, the benefit to Australia from having professional, permanent, independent and neutral election management bodies at all levels of government.

In the short term, the measures to make the election relatively Covid safe gave rise to a very significant increase in the overall cost of the process, of the order of $50 million. Factors driving this included the recruitment of thousands of additional polling staff to reduce voters' time spent in the polling place; the need to obtain appropriate personal protective equipment, some of which came from a national stockpile; the appointment of a dedicated hygiene officer for every polling place; the procurement of equipment such as plastic liners placed in cardboard voting screens to enable them to be disinfected; and the hire of much larger premises for the conduct of counting to enable social distancing to be better maintained.

A more subtle longer-term cost driver is the fact that the rise of pre-poll and postal voting cannot easily be offset by reductions in the numbers of polling places established and polling staff employed for election day. By law, a polling place cannot be abolished once the writs for an election have been issued, and at that point, pre-poll and postal voting will not even have started, making it uncertain how many people will be voting on polling day. This uncertainty is compounded by the relative generosity of the prescribed grounds for voting pre-poll or by post set out in Schedule 2 to the *Commonwealth Electoral Act 1918*. In the Covid-19 era, virtually any elector could have sought so to vote by virtue of being 'unable to attend a polling booth on polling day because of a reasonable fear for, or a reasonable apprehension about, his or her personal well-being or safety'.

Finally, even the short-term administrative consequences of the measures taken to ameliorate the impact of Covid-19 in 2022 remain unclear, not least because the extent to which the virus will still be a problem at the time of the next election remains uncertain. Overall, the need to cope with Covid-19 has added significant complexity to the AEC's tasks, as well as to its day-to-day management. It is reasonable to speculate, however, that in the longer term the pandemic's turbocharging of early voting will have the most enduring effect.

References

Australian Electoral Commission (AEC). 2008. 'Submission 169'. Inquiry by the Joint Standing Committee on Electoral Matters (JSCEM) into the 2007 Federal Election. Canberra: Parliament of Australia. Available from: www.aph.gov.au/ Parliamentary_Business/Committees/House_of_Representatives_Committees? url=em/elect07/subs/sub169.pdf.

Australian Electoral Commission (AEC). 2019a. 'House of Representatives: Two candidate preferred by candidate by polling place'. *Results*. Canberra: AEC. Available from: results.aec.gov.au/24310/Website/Downloads/HouseTcpBy CandidateByPollingPlaceDownload-24310.csv.

Australian Electoral Commission (AEC). 2019b. 'Overseas voting: Overseas votes by post'. *2019 Federal Election Downloads and Statistics*. [Online.] Canberra: AEC. Available from: www.aec.gov.au/Elections/federal_elections/2019/files/ downloads/2019-os-votes-by-post.xlsx.

Australian Electoral Commission (AEC). 2020. 'Submission 17: Australian Electoral Commission submission to the Joint Standing Committee on Electoral Matters'. *Inquiry on the Future Conduct of Elections Operating during Times of Emergency Situations*. Canberra: Parliament of the Commonwealth of Australia. Available from: www.aph.gov.au/DocumentStore.ashx?id=468399f7-c762-4914-a041-9b 596b4d6626&subId=695854.

Australian Electoral Commission (AEC). 2022a. *Delivering the 2022 Federal Election: Addressing the Challenges of an Increasingly Complex Operating Environment.* March. Canberra: AEC. Available from: aec.gov.au/About_AEC/files/election-2022-addressing-the-challenges-of-australias-most-complex-election.pdf.

Australian Electoral Commission (AEC). 2022b. *Downloads and Statistics: 2022 Federal Election.* [Online.] Canberra: AEC. Available from: www.aec.gov.au/Elections/Federal_Elections/2022/downloads.htm.

Australian Electoral Commission (AEC). 2022c. *Downloads and Statistics: 2022 Federal Election—Overseas Voting: Overseas Votes by Post.* [Online.] Canberra: AEC. Available from: www.aec.gov.au/Elections/Federal_Elections/2022/files/downloads/2022-os-votes-by-post.csv.

Australian Electoral Commission (AEC). 2022d. *Federal Election Reporting Guide.* Canberra: AEC. Available from: www.aec.gov.au/media/files/aec-federal-election-reporting-guide-digital.pdf.

Australian Electoral Commission (AEC). 2022e. *House of Representatives Downloads: Two Candidate Preferred by Candidate by Polling Place.* [Online.] Canberra: AEC. Available from: results.aec.gov.au/27966/Website/Downloads/HouseTcpByCandidateByPollingPlaceDownload-27966.csv.

Buril, Fernanda, Staffan Darnolf and Muluken Aseresa. 2020. *Safeguarding Health and Elections.* IFES COVID-19 Briefing Series. Arlington, VA: International Foundation for Electoral Systems. Available from: www.ifes.org/sites/default/files/ifes_covid19_briefing_series_safeguarding_health_and_elections_may_2020.pdf.

International Institute for Democracy and Electoral Assistance (International IDEA). 2022. *Global Overview of COVID-19: Impact on Elections.* Stockholm: International IDEA. Available from: www.idea.int/news-media/multimedia-reports/global-overview-covid-19-impact-elections.

Joint Standing Committee on Electoral Matters (JSCEM). 2021. *Report of the Inquiry on the Future Conduct of Elections Operating during Times of Emergency Situations.* June. Canberra: Parliament of the Commonwealth of Australia. Available from: parlinfo.aph.gov.au/parlInfo/download/committees/reportjnt/024638/toc_pdf/Reportoftheinquiryonthefutureconductofelectionsoperatingduringtimesofemergencysituations.pdf.

Maley, Michael. 2020. *Electoral management under Covid-19.* Electoral Regulation Research Network/Democratic Audit of Australia Joint Working Paper Series, No. 71, May. Melbourne: Electoral Regulation Research Network, University of Melbourne. Available from: law.unimelb.edu.au/__data/assets/pdf_file/0003/3393066/WP71_Maley.pdf.

Maley, Michael and Graeme Orr. 2019. *Developing a legislative framework for a complex and dynamic electoral environment: Discussion paper*. Electoral Regulation Research Network/Democratic Audit of Australia Joint Working Paper, No. 64, November. Melbourne: Electoral Regulation Research Network, University of Melbourne. Available from: law.unimelb.edu.au/__data/assets/pdf_file/0006/3237864/WP_64_Maley_Orr.pdf.

Mills, Stephen. 2020. 'Parliament in a time of virus: Representative democracy as a "non-essential service".' *Australasian Parliamentary Review* 34(2): 7–26.

3

The integrity election: Public trust and the promise of change

A.J. Brown

With two weeks to go, progressive thinktank The Australia Institute declared the 2022 federal poll would be 'the integrity election' (2022). Against a prevailing elite wisdom that elections are won or lost on 'hip-pocket' issues and appeals to voter self-interest, the 2022 election was unprecedented in turning significantly on an iconic issue of government accountability: support for a national integrity or anti-corruption commission.

As a symbol of wide demands for public integrity reform, this issue became a major point of perceived difference between the parties. It was a clear factor in the victory of the Albanese Government, with Labor the first of the two major parties to formally support a national integrity commission, in 2018; and also in the historic expansion of representation of the Greens, which was the first party to propose such a reform, in 2010. It featured especially dramatically in the success of the 'Teal' wave of (women) Independents whose conservative-seat campaigns for overdue climate action, integrity and gender equality drove the longest nails into the Morrison Government's coffin.

Far from arriving out of the blue, however, the integrity issue was long in the brewing. All the ingredients of the 2022 result were taking shape in the previous federal election—dubbed 'Morrison's miracle'—and were already epitomised by the increasing personalisation of politics and falling trust in political institutions (Gauja et al. 2020: 1). This chapter charts how the specific question of a national integrity commission came to be central and iconic in the 2022 campaign and result, and its implications for the challenges of sustaining base levels of public trust in and restoring constructive stability to federal politics. First, it reviews the background to the issue, then how it played out in the 2022 campaign and results, followed by the implications for the forty-seventh parliament and beyond.

The path to 2022

Every election is important as a marker of trajectories of public trust, but the 2022 election proved to be the culmination of longstanding concerns about the quality of Australia's federal 'integrity system' and the efforts of civil society and diverse individual parliamentarians to make reform a central issue. While federal institutions had generally escaped the scale of corruption scandals that prompted serious integrity reforms at the State level since the 1980s, by the 2019 election, evidence that federal politics and administration were not keeping pace with the ever-present threats of official corruption had forced a major change in position for all political parties—from one of relative complacency that existing institutions were good enough for the job to concrete commitments to reform.

The centrepiece commitment was the most obvious difference between the Commonwealth's architecture and those of Australia's States: the lack of a 'broad-based' specialist agency to detect, investigate and prevent corruption at the federal level. First recommended in 2005 as part of a wider suite of reforms (Brown and Sampford 2005), the issue became real after the Howard Coalition Government was prompted by Victorian political events to promise an 'independent national anti-corruption body' (Ruddock and Ellison 2004) but proceeded only to establish the Australian Commission for Law Enforcement Integrity. This provided anti-corruption oversight for just two federal agencies—the Australian Federal Police and Australian Crime Commission—on the questionable logic that these, in turn, were enough to deal with corruption across the rest of federal politics and administration (Brown 2005, 2008).

Consequently, the Australian Greens introduced bills for a broader 'national integrity commission' into every parliament from 2010. But it was not until early 2018 that a major party, Labor, committed publicly to the reform (Remeikis and Murphy 2018). A catalyst for the shifting of opinion was increasing evidence that federal governments were not only failing to regulate against bribery and money-laundering in Australia, but also propagating it internationally through current and former government-owned companies like the Australian Wheat Board and Note Printing Australia (TI 2013: 13–16). By 2022, as discussed below, more general domestic corruption concerns also took hold.

Central to the debate was Australia's sliding position on the global Corruption Perceptions Index (CPI) published annually by Transparency International—one of a range of international nongovernmental organisations (NGOs) that had become influential in standard-setting for good governance (Sawer and Gauja 2016: 11; Figure 3.1). From the outset, this slide was cited by the architect of Labor's policy shift, shadow attorney-general Mark Dreyfus (2018), as confirming the imperative for reform. Later in 2018, when the original Teal Independents brought on a parliamentary debate on the issue, Coalition attorney-general Christian Porter used the CPI to defend the status quo, observing that Australia had remained 'consistently in the top 20 countries on Earth for low corruption'—only for former Liberal staffer Rebekha Sharkie, now a Centre Alliance Independent (Mayo), to point out that Australia had fallen from the top 10; 'the trajectory is not good' (Hansard 2018a: 8802, 8810). By March 2022, when Opposition leader Anthony Albanese again cited the CPI result in support of Labor's reform pledge, Australia had slid further (Albanese 2022).

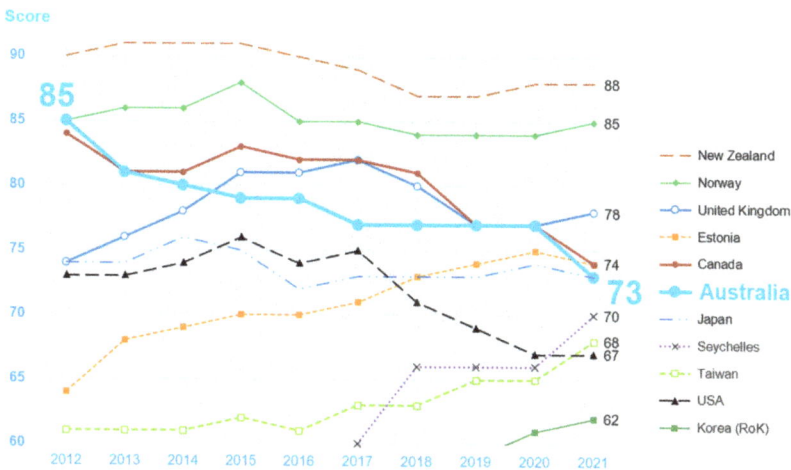

Figure 3.1 Corruption Perceptions Index, 2012–2021
Source: Transparency International Australia (www.transparency.org/en/cpi/2021).

In fact, the Coalition had slowly started working on its own integrity commission reform before Labor's announcement, after a Senate Select Committee in November 2017 reached a consensus validating the idea as at least worth considering. But the government's slow movement was widely—and probably accurately—interpreted as indicating a weak and increasingly reactive commitment to the idea, which was to plague it for the next four years.

In November 2018, after the demise of Malcolm Turnbull as prime minister saw the Coalition reduced to minority government, the crossbenchers—Independents and Greens—were the ones who seized the initiative, defining the political dynamic that ultimately unfolded in the 2022 campaign. Seconded by Sharkie, Community Independent Cathy McGowan (Indi) introduced a package of highly developed integrity commission bills, which if put to the vote would have passed whether the government liked it or not. This forced the Morrison Government to finalise and announce its own proposed model in December 2018. Criticised from the outset as clunky and ineffective, the Coalition plan was not fleshed out in a draft Commonwealth Integrity Commission Bill for another two years (Brown 2020), and from then to election day continued to attract a barrage of criticism.

At the 2019 election, the issue of integrity reform was therefore not simply warming up; it was already well on the way to the boil. Mainstream media coverage and academic commentary mostly failed to detect it, but all the political ingredients of the 2022 result were brewing. The Teal Independents movement took its major next step, with the community-based Voices of Indi replacing the retiring McGowan with a new candidate, Dr Helen Haines. Not only did Haines become the first Independent to succeed another in a federal electorate, but also new Independent Zali Steggall (Warringah) unseated former prime minister Tony Abbott (Curtin and Sheppard 2020). Steggall, too, was committed to a strong national integrity commission, as well as other reforms such as truth in political advertising. With Sharkie re-elected in Mayo, as well as former whistleblower Andrew Wilkie in Denison (now Clark), the pro-integrity crossbench Independents were on the march.

The first factor behind the 2022 outcome was thus the long burn of the integrity reform issue as driven by civil society, culminating in the policy shift by which Labor took and retained its 'first-mover advantage'. In this, Transparency International Australia, The Australia Institute, the

Melbourne-based Accountability Round Table and, more recently, the Centre for Public Integrity all played crucial roles. But the second factor—the potential for yet more Independents and/or Greens to join Labor in capitalising on the issue—was an especially clear and present danger for the re-elected Morrison Government, unless it dealt with the issue in the forty-sixth parliament. After all, Independents and Greens not only had staked out the territory federally, but also had a proven track record of using the balance of power to drive equivalent reforms in most Australian States and Territories.

And capitalise they did: without delay, soon after the 2019 election, the Greens reintroduced their own Integrity Commission Bill to the Senate, closely matching McGowan's bill, where it passed with the active support of Labor and the tacit support of Pauline Hanson's One Nation. As the government's own plans continued to languish—attributable only in part to the Covid-19 pandemic—Haines and Steggall updated and reintroduced their own Australian Federal Integrity Commission Bill in October 2020. By late February 2021, when the first national conference of Community Independents was held online as a foundation for what was to become the Teal wave, integrity reform had joined climate action as its unifying mantra (see Chapter 20, this volume).

With Labor adding no new detail to its plans as the 2022 campaign loomed, the question quickly became what, if anything, would the Coalition do to capitalise on, or at least neutralise, the integrity issue?

The long campaign: Bad leadership, bad policy, bad politics

In the end, the Morrison Government did nothing to successfully neutralise the issue by the time polling opened and closed in May 2022. The reasons for this political failure reinforce the significance of the election watershed.

The third factor behind the outcome was the Morrison Government's failure to bring its own reform proposal to fruition in the forty-sixth parliament. Even if criticised and voted down by a volatile Senate, this would have enabled the Coalition to go the election with a claim to have genuinely tried and a readiness to pursue reform in the future. The failure to achieve even this result was due to poor leadership, political mismanagement and misfortune, bordering on tragedy.

The poor leadership began with the architect and custodian of the Coalition's proposals, Attorney-General Christian Porter, who proved unmoveable on improving his original, defective model, whether through personal intransigence, Cabinet constraints or both. This was notwithstanding two major rounds of public consultation and many internal ones, even within his own party, making stakeholders as exhausted as they were distrustful. Porter also brought a propensity to twist facts for rhetorical points that undermined confidence and progress. Examples included not only his attempt to paint Australia as still doing well on the CPI, as mentioned earlier, but also his claims that his proposed body would have the powers of a royal commission, which were later parroted by numerous Coalition colleagues. In fact, given that his proposal denied the power to hold public hearings in any corruption matters involving 80 per cent of the public sector, including politicians, the claim was highly inaccurate and must have been knowingly so (RMIT ABC Fact Check 2022).

The entire issue also then went off the rails when Porter was forced to stand down as attorney-general in March 2021 after launching defamation action against the Australian Broadcasting Corporation (ABC) over its reporting of a historical rape allegation from Porter's youth. The controversy joined other allegations against federal parliamentarians and their staffers of sexual and gendered misconduct, more recently and in parliamentary workplaces (see Chapter 5, this volume). Porter ultimately resigned in September 2021, after declining to reveal the confidential donors who contributed to his legal fees in the case, and announced in December that he would not contest the 2022 election. His seat of Pearce was lost by the Coalition to Labor. While work was done under the replacement attorney-general, Senator Michaelia Cash, to improve some parts of Porter's bill and prepare it for introduction, leadership on the issue essentially collapsed. Moreover, the entire misconduct saga fed concerns that the government was not serious about integrity and ethics matters, providing yet further campaign ammunition to the Labor opposition, Greens and Independents.

Of course, ultimate responsibility for the Coalition's mishandling of the issue lay with Prime Minister Scott Morrison, whose explanation for failing to present the government's bill—improved or unimproved—became increasingly unconvincing. In the end, the primary explanation became that the Opposition refused to support the government's proposal, which most onlookers found bizarre. The reality was that Morrison was losing both the confidence and the control of his party room, on this issue and others, as demonstrated when Tasmanian Liberal Bridget Archer (Bass) crossed the floor to support debate on Independent Helen Haines's bill (Martin 2021b). The next day, Morrison shut down any chance of the government's bill being brought on, unable to manage the risk that it might not even survive a vote in the lower house.

Importantly, though, the roots of Coalition mismanagement ran even deeper. While a solid core of Liberal and National members was ready to support a reasonable outcome, or at least wanted the government's proposal put to a vote, the prime minister had always responded somewhat bizarrely to the issue. Back in November 2018, when McGowan introduced her private member's bill and both houses supported a resolution that a commission was needed, Morrison had given this response in Question Time:

> Mr SHORTEN (Leader of the Opposition): Why did the government vote today to support a national integrity commission if it still hasn't decided whether it wants one?
>
> Mr MORRISON (Prime Minister): The government is considering its position through a normal cabinet process. When it comes to the issues, this is what responsible governments do … But it says something about this Leader of the Opposition that, of the issues that he wants to bring into this chamber, when it comes to families and small businesses that are struggling to deal with getting access to finance or families that are dealing with electricity prices, the issues that he wants to raise don't relate to these … While the Leader of the Opposition is off on *some sort of fringe issue*, what we're focused on is the strength of our economy because that's what delivers the services … The Leader of the Opposition likes to come in and talk about *anything under the sun* other than what makes an economy stronger. (Hansard 2018b; emphasis added)

In fact, there was a logic behind Morrison's attempt to deflect issues of integrity on to questions of economic management. As will be discussed in the conclusion, the failure of that attempt points to the wider, longer-term implications of the 2022 outcome for federal political debates about public trust. At the time, Morrison's declaration that the issue was marginal simply made it more difficult for Coalition members to convince themselves, let alone their electorates, that the government was serious. Morrison's personal reputation for integrity and accountability would receive a further, perhaps final, trashing when it was revealed post-election that he secretly had himself sworn into five central government ministries without anyone knowing (Beck 2022).

The fourth and final factor behind the salience of the integrity commission issue, by the time of the election, were successive revelations throughout 2020 and 2021 of the government's abuse of public funds for political 'pork-barrelling'—especially as part of the Coalition's 2019 re-election campaign. Previously, questions of integrity system reform had seemed dry and technical, with real corruption, even if serious, seemingly isolated and remote from voters' everyday experiences. The main domestic, systemic abuses were limited to distrust about the access bought by political donations and perceived abuse of entitlements by politicians, such as charging private or party travel to the public purse (Gauja et al. 2020: 4).

This changed after the Australian National Audit Office reported in early 2020 that party-political imperatives had contaminated a $100 million community sports grants scheme administered by then sports minister Bridget McKenzie (Speers 2020). The 'Sports Rorts' scandal became the first in a series, with similar controversies unfolding over federal funding grants for commuter carparks and regional development, to name a few. The various rorts scandals further compounded the leadership and credibility problems of the government, especially after Porter confirmed that his proposed Commonwealth integrity commission would not investigate such abuses (because they were 'grey area' political corruption rather than clear criminal offences). It worsened after Prime Minister Morrison took a public stance in support of former NSW premier Gladys Berejiklian, whose resignation was prompted by a NSW Independent Commission Against Corruption (ICAC) probe into undisclosed conflicts of interest associated with similar grants programs—found by the NSW auditor-general to constitute pork-barrelling on an even more industrial scale.

As well as adding difficulties to the Coalition's management of the issue, the rorts scandals proved important in exposing to voters that the federal government was indeed subject to corruption risks, threatening fairness and honesty at the community level—even if this was political or institutional corruption, rather than personal or individual self-enrichment (Sawer 2021). Public attitudes against pork-barrelling also seemed to visibly harden as the debate went on. Contrary to the traditional claims repeated by Berejiklian, Morrison and others that winning elector support through flexible ministerial spending was simply a normal part of government, the electorate seemed increasingly persuaded that large-scale financial favouritism towards politically loyal and/or marginal communities, in a direct bid to sway votes, was wrong. Detailed analysis suggested that, in fact, the pork-barrelling failed to have its intended effect (McAllister 2021). But the issue gave unprecedented life to the need for stronger integrity and anti-corruption oversight.

The 2022 results

By the time of the federal election, these factors were compounding to make integrity reform—symbolised by the issue of a broad-based integrity commission—a hugely influential issue in the minds of voters and the behaviour of parties and candidates. Unsurprisingly, polling by The Australia Institute and others had long suggested overwhelming support for such a reform as a stand-alone question, but it was unknown what role the issue would play in the complex mix of the election contest. The ABC's Vote Compass research confirmed that it was far from the only issue driving voting behaviour; climate action, economic issues and cost of living all still rated higher. Nevertheless, government integrity, accountability and corruption ranked at an unprecedented level, higher even than quality of health care amid a global pandemic that was still far from over (Brennan 2022).

For Labor, the issue naturally played well, vindicating its 2018 policy shift together with its decision to retain the integrity commission among an otherwise simplified suite of election policies. In fact, Labor had still done little preparatory work on its proposal and, if anything, had narrowed its scope from an 'integrity commission' to a 'national anticorruption commission', prompting mixed reviews from expert observers (Griffiths et al. 2022). But the general idea continued to resonate, becoming an attractive element of Labor's basic but reliable campaign theme of 'a better future':

> The health of our democracy, the integrity of our institutions, the transparency and fairness of our laws, the harmony and cohesion of our population. These aren't just noble ideals. They are a powerful defence against the threat of modern authoritarianism. Because behind authoritarianism's reliance on disinformation, crude nationalism and false nostalgia and its insidious appeal to the disillusioned and disenfranchised is the implicit and explicit argument that democracy, diversity and progress have failed us.
>
> It's why measures to strengthen faith in our institutions and our democracy—including our commitment to a National Anti-Corruption Commission—are so important in building national cohesion … Nation-building is about more than economic strength.

> Democratic strength is also critical to our long-term stability and security … Responding to this trend requires building the legitimacy and trust in our democratic institutions.
>
> Unfortunately, the Morrison Government has waged a prolonged assault on accountability, dragging Australia down to its lowest level on record in Transparency International's Corruption Perceptions Index. The doctrine of ministerial responsibility has been comprehensively trashed. And the Prime Minister [Scott Morrison] has reneged on his promise of a national anti-corruption commission. I will deliver one. (Albanese 2022)

By contrast, the Coalition went into the campaign with an uncertain message from Prime Minister Morrison about whether it would attempt to introduce its own bill, even if successfully re-elected. On top of its other self-created problems, the ultimate killer was the fact that, for the Coalition, the failure to establish any commission now represented a broken election promise. This fed into basic doubts about whether Morrison and his government could any longer be trusted to come through on other issues— ranging from responses to natural disasters and pandemic preparedness to the belated, apparently still half-hearted commitment to achieve 'net zero' greenhouse gas emissions by 2050.

That the issue had cut through to voters was exemplified when Morrison visited a Newcastle pub on the pre-campaign trail, only to be accosted angrily by a random elderly voter—first, about a personal cost-of-living issue and, second, on 'another promise' the government had made but not delivered on: '[Y]ou were going to have an integrity commission' (Butler 2022). Other pubgoers chimed in their support: 'Good on you, mate.' For his part, Morrison appeared blindsided about how the 'fringe issue' had become so mainstream.

Even more blindsided, however, were the many Coalition parliamentarians who had been ready, willing and able to embrace integrity reform as a positive campaign message of their own, but who were now left high and dry by the government's failure to bring forward its bill or provide any other credible response. Committed to reform but sensing electoral danger, a number began sounding the alarm publicly about the government's unworkable position more than six months out, in October 2021 (Martin 2021a).

Plate 3.1 An elderly voter accosts Scott Morrison on his failure to create an integrity commission, Edgeworth Tavern, Newcastle, 6 April 2022
Source: Peter Lorimer, *Newcastle Herald*/ACM.

Left with no answers for a concerned electorate, all those Coalition members ended up losing their seats, predominantly to the expanding wave of Community Independents. The full scope and impact of the Teal wave are detailed elsewhere, including their common theme of integrity reform, alongside the re-election of Haines, Sharkie and Wilkie and the dramatic expansion of the pro-integrity Greens (see Chapter 12, this volume). But there was supreme irony, if not tragedy, that the Liberal members thus sacrificed by Morrison were those who most strongly supported integrity reform. Lawyer and former university vice-chancellor Celia Hammond, who had taken over Liberal deputy leader Julie Bishop's heartland seat of Curtin, in Western Australia, lost her seat to Independent Kate Chaney. Respected former diplomat Dave Sharma had regained the Liberal NSW heartland seat of Wentworth from Independent Kerryn Phelps, but now lost it, to a new Independent, Allegra Spender. Jason Falinski had won Mackellar in 2016 and 2019—previously held by Liberal elders Bronwyn Bishop and Jim Carlton—but now lost it to Independent Sophie Scamps. Dr Katie Allen lost her Melbourne seat of Higgins—previously held by Liberal prime minister Harold Holt and treasurer Peter Costello—to Labor's Michelle Ananda-Rajah.

From a Liberal Party perspective, the wreckage was appalling. Ironically, the election survivor among internal critics of the government's approach, despite being in the nation's most marginal seat, was Tasmanian Bridget Archer. Described as 'the lion of the forty-sixth parliament' by Helen Haines, Archer was the only Coalition member who had the advantage of having independently demonstrated her personal commitment to the issue, in a very public way, by crossing the floor in November 2021 (Martin 2021b).

Conclusions: Implications for the future

Will the dramatic results of 'the integrity election' contribute to a turnaround in public trust in federal politics or government generally—the avowed objective of all those, elected or defeated, advocating serious integrity reform? While that is impossible to predict, the prominence of the integrity issue has at least three implications for life in and beyond the forty-seventh parliament, which will shape the ultimate answer.

First, the new Albanese Government's push to rapidly implement its promised national anti-corruption commission reform was always headed for tension with the reality that this was just the most iconic of a wider range of integrity issues. Indeed, within weeks, the pre-election promise that the new government's bill would be 'extremely similar' to the previous crossbench integrity bills (Knott 2022) was threatening to unravel, met with concern from the expanded crossbench that its scope would be limited only to 'serious and systemic corruption' and its design would not include a range of key issues relating to corruption prevention, national coordination, civic engagement and especially whistleblower protection (Karp 2022a, 2022b, 2022c).

More broadly, it was at least initially unclear whether the government planned to advance a yet further range of reforms associated with Australia's falling place in international rankings (Brown 2022)—widely identified as imperative to meeting public trust challenges (TI Australia 2020, 2022; Browne 2022). These included the scope of reform of parliamentary standards as highlighted in the previous parliament, lobbying reform, truth in political advertising and, especially, 'the regulation of political finance, consequent perceived purchase of political access and influence … the role of private money in federal elections, [and] use of public money, such as parliamentary allowances, for electioneering'—all previously identified as making Australia increasingly out of step with comparable democracies and even the States (Gauja et al. 2020: 3, 4). The new government began with individual backers of electoral finance reform, such as new finance minister and former ACT chief minister Katy Gallagher, but no concrete commitment or plan (Jervis-Bardy 2022).

Consequently, there remained substantial scope for further public disappointment and disaffection unless the new government transitioned from pursuing 'integrity' through a single national anticorruption commission reform to advancing a more holistic transparency and accountability agenda. That transition, which is slow and ongoing, holds the first key to addressing known drivers of falling trust.

The second, more complex challenge was whether reactions to the new reforms would see greater multipartisanship return to the parliament on integrity and trust reform—or whether continued politicisation of the idea of a federal corruption agency 'with teeth' would undermine durability and political support.

Early signs were positive. As part of his avoidance tactics, outgoing prime minister Scott Morrison had attacked existing anti-corruption agencies like the NSW ICAC and any Labor proposal as 'kangaroo courts' that undermined the rule of law (McGowan and Agencies 2022). Rejected by many, the attack had superficial traction because no State anti-corruption legislation had yet established a clear best-practice model for managing the use of crucial powers by these agencies, such as public hearings—increasing both the burden and the opportunity for the Commonwealth in needing to do so (TI Australia 2020).

However, new Liberal leader Peter Dutton began his post-election role by declaring himself a supporter of a strong independent commission, consciously uncoupling himself from 'Morrison's integrity commission car crash', as it was described by *Guardian* journalist Katharine Murphy (2022). Ultimately, the Coalition finally backed the proposal put forward by Labor—and it was the Independents and Greens whose proposals for an even stronger model ended up slightly unsatisfied.

Finally, a potentially more enduring implication of the 2022 outcome was a positive shift in the way in which 'public trust' itself was defined as an electoral tactic. As seen earlier in the chapter, Morrison mystified many in November 2018 by dismissing integrity as 'some sort of fringe issue'.

However, his underlying tactic was a proven one. This was to meet questions about integrity, in which trust hinged on the honesty and propriety of leaders and parliaments, with an answer about confidence in a government to deliver economic and financial benefits in the immediate self-interests of voters—trust in the performance of a government being more important than trust in its integrity.

Morrison carried on with this style of non-response on numerous occasions. Its poor execution confirmed that the prime minister simply did not understand public integrity as an issue—for example, in December 2021, when he responded to further evidence of Coalition pork-barrelling with the unashamed claim that the favoured Coalition-held seats must simply 'have a very good local member', skilled in delivering their constituents the money they needed (Shepherd 2021; Moore 2021). Nevertheless, the deflection was a time-honoured tactic, especially of populist leaders. Morrison had perhaps received tips from former prime minister John Howard, who in the 2004 federal election campaign deflected serious challenges to his government's honesty into a question of 'who you can trust' to deliver economic performance. Indeed, as Liberal tactician Mark Textor told journalists afterwards, this deflection involved a deliberate 'redefinition of honesty' away from probity standards towards dependability on matters of self-interest—'a kind of consistency honesty' rather than 'the-letter-of-the-law honesty' (see Uhr 2005: 11–12).

But by 2022, it seems, this kind of redefinitional tactic had reached its expiry date, at least in Australian federal politics or as executed by Morrison. The focus on integrity reform as a real and pressing issue, buoyed especially by the pork-barrelling that Morrison himself had masterminded and overseen, saw the need for trust in the honesty, fairness and accountability of government win out over simple promises to meet individuals' hip-pocket needs. For once, in a prominent way, trust in honesty and probity mattered to a critical proportion of voters and was not obscured by appeals to reliable economic performance and self-interest. Whether this represented an enduring shift in the political discourse of trust remains to be seen. But perhaps—just perhaps—the unprecedented and decisive prominence of the integrity reform issue in 2022 showed there is hope for politics yet.

References

Albanese, Anthony. 2022. 'An address by Opposition leader Anthony Albanese'. Lowy Institute, Sydney, 4 March. Available from: www.lowyinstitute.org/publications/address-opposition-leader-anthony-albanese.

Beck, Luke. 2022. 'Parliament must act to ensure Australia never has "secret ministers" again'. *The Conversation*, 17 August. Available from: theconversation.com/parliament-must-act-to-ensure-australia-never-has-secret-ministers-again-188884.

Brennan, Bridget. 2022. 'Vote Compass shows Australians are worried about corruption in politics'. *ABC News Online*, 14 April. Available from: www.abc.net.au/news/2022-04-14/vote-compass-australians-worried-corruption-politics-election/100990918.

Brown, A.J. 2005. 'Federal anti-corruption policy takes a new turn … but which way? Issues and options for a Commonwealth integrity agency'. *Public Law Review* 16(2): 93–98.

Brown, A.J. 2008. 'Towards a federal integrity commission: The challenge of institutional capacity-building in Australia'. In *Promoting Integrity: Evaluating and Improving Public Institutions*, edited by Brian Head, A.J. Brown and Carmel Connors, 169–96. Aldershot, UK: Ashgate.

Brown, A.J. 2020. 'Explainer: What is the proposed Commonwealth integrity commission and how would it work?'. *The Conversation*, 2 November. Available from: theconversation.com/explainer-what-is-the-proposed-commonwealth-integrity-commission-and-how-would-it-work-140734.

Brown, A.J. 2022. 'Australia and Norway were once tied in global anti-corruption rankings. Now, we're heading in opposite directions'. *The Conversation*, 25 January. Available from: theconversation.com/australia-and-norway-were-once-tied-in-global-anti-corruption-rankings-now-were-heading-in-opposite-directions-174966.

Brown, A.J. and Charles Sampford. 2005. *Chaos or Coherence? Strengths, Challenges and Opportunities for Australia's Integrity Systems*. National Integrity Systems Assessment Final Report. Melbourne: Transparency International Australia & Griffith University.

Brown, A.J., Samuel Ankamah, Ken Coghill, Adam Graycar, Kym Kelly, John McMillan, Tim Prenzler and Janet Ransley. 2020. *Australia's National Integrity System: The Blueprint for Action.* Report of the ARC Linkage Project: Strengthening Australia's National Integrity System—Priorities for Reform. Melbourne: Transparency International Australia & Griffith University. Available from: transparency.org.au/australias-national-integrity-system/.

Browne, Bill. 2022. *Democracy Agenda for the 47th Parliament of Australia: Options for Reform.* Report, 31 March. Canberra: The Australia Institute. Available from: australiainstitute.org.au/report/democracy-agenda-for-the-47th-parliament-of-australia/.

Butler, Josh. 2022. 'Furious pensioner confronts Scott Morrison as Newcastle pub photo-opp backfires'. *The Guardian*, [Australia], 7 April. Available from: www.theguardian.com/australia-news/2022/apr/07/furious-pensioner-confronts-scott-morrison-as-newcastle-pub-photo-opp-backfires.

Curtin, Jennifer and Jill Sheppard. 2020. 'The Independents'. In *Morrison's Miracle: The 2019 Australian Federal Election*, edited by Anika Gauja, Marian Sawer and Marian Simms, 357–71. Canberra: ANU Press. doi.org/10.22459/MM.2020.18.

Dreyfus, Mark. 2018. 'Corruption Perceptions Index shows need for national integrity commission'. Media release, 22 February. Melbourne. Available from: www.markdreyfus.com/media/media-releases/corruption-perceptions-index-shows-need-for-national-integrity-commission-mark-dreyfus-qc-mp/.

Gauja, Anika, Marian Sawer and Marian Simms. 2020. 'Morrison's miracle: Analysing the 2019 Australian federal election'. In *Morrison's Miracle: The 2019 Australian Federal Election*, edited by Anika Gauja, Marian Sawer and Marian Simms, 1–17. Canberra: ANU Press. doi.org/10.22459/MM.2020.01.

Griffiths, Kate, Adam Graycar, A.J. Brown, Gabrielle Appleby and Yee-Fui Ng. 2022. 'How do the major parties rate on an independent anti-corruption commission? We asked 5 experts'. *The Conversation*, 28 April. Available from: theconversation.com/how-do-the-major-parties-rate-on-an-independent-anti-corruption-commission-we-asked-5-experts-181077.

Hansard (Commonwealth Parliamentary Debates). 2018a. 'Matter of Public Importance: National Integrity Commission'. *House of Representatives Debates*, Wednesday, 12 September 2018. Canberra: Parliament of Australia.

Hansard (Commonwealth Parliamentary Debates). 2018b. 'Questions Without Notice'. *House of Representatives Debates*, Monday, 26 November 2018. Canberra: Parliament of Australia.

Jervis-Bardy, Dan. 2022. 'Katy Gallagher backs review into election spending caps'. *The Canberra Times*, 29 May. Available from: www.canberratimes.com.au/story/7757611/you-can-change-the-campaign-gallagher-backs-review-into-election-spending-caps/.

Karp, Paul. 2022a. 'Labor urged to bolster federal Icac plan with more protection for whistleblowers'. *The Guardian*, [Australia], 6 July. Available from: www.theguardian.com/australia-news/2022/jul/06/labor-urged-to-bolster-federal-icac-plan-with-more-protection-for-whistleblowers.

Karp, Paul. 2022b. 'Greens to seek changes to Labor's integrity commission legislation to protect whistleblowers'. *The Guardian*, [Australia], 10 July. Available from: www.theguardian.com/australia-news/2022/jul/10/greens-to-seek-changes-to-labors-integrity-commission-legislation-to-protect-whistleblowers.

Karp, Paul. 2022c. 'Federal Icac should be overseen by non-government MPs to ensure funding, crossbench says'. *The Guardian*, [Australia], 4 August. Available from: www.theguardian.com/australia-news/2022/aug/04/federal-icac-should-be-overseen-by-non-government-mps-to-ensure-funding-crossbench-says.

Knott, Matthew. 2022. 'Labor integrity commission to investigate allegations from a "long time ago"'. *Sydney Morning Herald*, 13 May. Available from: www.smh.com.au/politics/federal/labor-integrity-commission-to-investigate-allegations-from-a-long-time-ago-20220512-p5akvr.html.

Martin, Sarah. 2021a. '"It needs more work": Liberal MPs call for tougher federal integrity commission'. *The Guardian*, [Australia], 15 October. Available from: www.theguardian.com/australia-news/2021/oct/15/it-needs-more-work-liberal-mps-call-for-tougher-federal-integrity-commission.

Martin, Sarah. 2021b. 'Liberal MP crosses the floor to support independent bill for federal integrity commission'. *The Guardian*, [Australia], 25 November. Available from: www.theguardian.com/australia-news/2021/nov/25/liberal-mp-attacks-morrison-government-for-failing-to-act-on-integrity-commission-pledge.

McAllister, Ian. 2021. 'Does pork-barrelling actually work? New research suggests it's not a big vote winner'. *The Conversation*, 31 January. Available from: theconversation.com/does-pork-barrelling-actually-work-new-research-suggests-its-not-a-big-vote-winner-173329.

McGowan, Michael and Agencies. 2022. 'Dominic Perrottet says Scott Morrison "absolutely" went too far by calling ICAC a kangaroo court'. *The Guardian*, [Australia], 3 May. Available from: www.theguardian.com/australia-news/2022/may/03/dominic-perrottet-says-scott-morrison-absolutely-went-too-far-by-calling-icac-a-kangaroo-court.

Moore, Tony. 2021. 'LNP-held Queensland seat gets 47 times more funding than its Labor neighbour'. *Brisbane Times*, 15 December. Available from: www.brisbane times.com.au/politics/federal/lnp-held-queensland-seat-gets-47-times-more-funding-than-its-labor-neighbour-20211213-p59h87.html.

Murphy, Katharine. 2022. 'Peter Dutton is consciously uncoupling himself and the Liberals from Morrison's integrity commission car crash'. *The Guardian*, [Australia], 4 June. Available from: www.theguardian.com/australia-news/2022/jun/04/peter-dutton-is-consciously-uncoupling-himself-and-the-liberals-from-morrisons-integrity-commission-car-crash.

Remeikis, Amy and Katharine Murphy. 2018. 'Labor promises federal integrity commission if it wins next election'. *The Guardian*, [Australia], 30 January. Available from: www.theguardian.com/australia-news/2018/jan/30/labor-promises-federal-integrity-commission-if-it-wins-the-next-election.

RMIT ABC Fact Check. 2022. 'Scott Morrison says the government's proposed integrity commission would have the powers of a royal commission. Is that correct?'. *ABC News Online*, 20 May. Available from: www.abc.net.au/news/2022-05-20/fact-check-scott-morrison-federal-integrity-commission-icac/101081616.

Ruddock, Philip and Chris Ellison. 2004. 'Commonwealth to set up independent national anti-corruption body'. Joint media release, 16 June, Offices of the Commonwealth Attorney-General and Minister for Justice, Canberra.

Sawer, Marian. 2021. 'Understanding corruption: There's no need to get personal'. *Pearls & Irritations: John Menadue's Public Policy Journal*, 10 November. Available from: johnmenadue.com/marian-sawer-institutional-corruption-and-australian-democracy/.

Sawer, Marian and Anika Gauja. 2016. 'Party rules: Promises and pitfalls'. In *Party Rules: Dilemmas of Political Party Regulation in Australia*, edited by Anika Gauja and Marian Sawer, 1–36. Canberra: ANU Press. doi.org/10.22459/PR.10.2016.01.

Shepherd, Tory. 2021. 'Sorting facts from spin in the Coalition's response to grants pork-barrelling claims'. *The Guardian*, [Australia], 16 December. Available from: www.theguardian.com/australia-news/2021/dec/16/sorting-facts-from-spin-in-the-coalitions-response-to-grants-pork-barrelling-claims.

Speers, David. 2020. 'Bridget McKenzie's sport grant cash splash is a particularly brazen example of pork-barrelling'. *ABC News*, 16 January. Available from: www.abc.net.au/news/2020-01-16/bridget-mckenzie-saga-pork-barrelling-brazen-example/11874224.

The Australia Institute. 2022a. *The Integrity Election*. Webinar, 11 May. Available from: australiainstitute.org.au/event/the-integrity-election/.

Transparency International (TI). 2013. *Exporting Corruption: Assessing Enforcement of the OECD Convention on Combating Foreign Bribery.* Berlin: Transparency International. Available from: www.transparency.org/en/publications/exporting-corruption-progress-report-2013-assessing-enforcement-of-the-oecd.

Transparency International Australia (TI Australia). 2020. *Australia's National Integrity System: The Blueprint for Action.* National Integrity System Assessment, Australia, November 2020. Melbourne: Transparency International Australia and Griffith University. Available from: transparency.org.au/australias-national-integrity-system/.

Transparency International Australia (TI Australia). 2022. *A Fairer, More Transparent and More Trustworthy System of Government: An Integrity Pack for Members of Australia's 47th Parliament.* Melbourne: Transparency International Australia. Available from: transparency.org.au/integrity-pack/.

Uhr, John. 2005. *Terms of Trust: Arguments over Ethics in Australian Government.* Sydney: UNSW Press.

4

Variants of populism

Carol Johnson

This chapter argues that analysing populist elements throws a useful light on aspects of the 2022 federal election campaign that might otherwise be neglected. These include not only Liberal Party strategy and Labor's response to it but also the strategies of minor parties and even the Teal Independents. However, the 2022 election revealed a more complex populist landscape than in the 2019 election. The previous campaign saw a clear contest between different forms of major-party populism in which both the Liberals and Labor argued they were representing the people, 'us', against an enemy constructed as 'them'. Labor depicted itself as representing ordinary people (particularly the working and middle classes) against a wealthy 'top end of town'. By contrast, Scott Morrison depicted himself as an ordinary suburban bloke whose party was representing the people against a Labor big government that would rip off and spend taxpayers' hard-earned money while ruining the economy. Both forms of populism had underlying ideological agendas. Labor was shifting away from a neoliberal-influenced form of social democracy to one that focused more on issues of class inequality. The Liberals were displaying a form of free-market populism influenced by a neoliberal opposition to big-government intrusions into the economy and citizens' lives. Meanwhile, Pauline Hanson's One Nation (PHON) and Clive Palmer's United Australia Party (UAP) pursued more extreme right-wing populist agendas.

Definitions of populism remain highly contested (Hunger and Paxton 2022); however, 'us' versus 'them' arguments are a regular trope in populism. For example, populism commonly mobilises the people against claimed powerful, corrupt elites and the groups they protect. In 2022, Labor's 'small-target' strategy and emphasis on cooperating with business resulted in it no longer mobilising left-wing populism against the 'top end of town'. Rather, Labor contested right-wing populist 'us' versus 'them' rhetoric by arguing that it would bring the Australian people together for the common good. The Liberals' campaign saw more similarities with their 2019 one. They tried to mobilise a post-pandemic form of market populism that emphasised the role of 'can-do capitalism' as opposed to big-government (and strong Covid-19) restrictions that they tried to associate with Labor. The Liberals also drew on national security and anti-gender campaign forms of populism. However, their plans were undermined not only by Labor's small-target strategy but also by multiple factors to be discussed in this chapter.

Significantly, the Liberals were also challenged by a new form of populism: the largely centre-right populism of the so-called Teal Independents. The Teals promised to represent the people (in the form of local communities) against an elite, out-of-touch and corrupt federal government. Meanwhile, the populist parties of the right were more critical of the Liberals than previously. The UAP and PHON targeted (claimed) tyrannical actions by both Liberal and Labor governments during the Covid-19 pandemic, while Hanson also targeted 'woke' liberalism. The Greens had populist elements in their arguments that the major parties had corruptly sold the people out to big business polluters/emitters—a form of left-wing populism that also intersected with some of the largely centre-right populism of the Teals.

Elections are decided by multiple factors. Variants of populism can only explain limited elements of the election campaign and the parties' ideological agendas. However, it will be argued here that they did play a role. This chapter will focus on analysing the Liberal and Labor parties as the major parties of government but will also make some brief comments about the minor parties and the Teals. The Liberals' populism will be analysed in greater depth to identify some aspects that contributed to the Coalition's defeat.

The Liberals

Morrison's intended 2022 election strategy was clear by the end of 2021, as State and international borders were opened, restrictions were eased and Covid-19 was let rip. Morrison argued that the Coalition would be winding back the big-government measures and restrictions that had been necessary earlier during the pandemic. Instead, it would rely on 'can-do capitalism' to build the economy and improve standards of living. In his words:

'Can do capitalism', not 'don't do Governments'. I think that's a good motto for us to follow … right across the spectrum of economic policy in this country. We've got a bit used to Governments telling us what to do over the last couple of years, I think we have to break that habit. (Morrison 2021)

It was a form of post-pandemic free-market populism (see further Sawer and Laycock 2009) designed not only to attack Labor's claimed big-government agenda on the left, but also to counter Palmer's critique of big-government attacks on freedom from the right. It built on the Coalition's successful 2019 strategy.

Morrison's (2022b) election launch speech argued that Australians were 'tired of politics … and they've certainly had enough of Governments telling them how to live their lives'. He claimed that the Coalition's policies of lower taxes and less regulation for businesses would put 'you', the people, 'back in the driver's seat' (Morrison 2022c). By contrast, 'Labor wants to tell you what to do … with your own money' and, he claimed: 'We've had enough of governments telling people … where they can go and what they can do' (Morrison 2022c). Post-pandemic market populism reinforced a longstanding neoliberal emphasis on individual 'choice' (albeit before the pandemic had ended).

The Liberals also attempted to mobilise other forms of populism, including nationalist ones. They suggested that Labor would not adequately protect the Australian people from an increasingly aggressive China. Labor was depicted as not just weak but also—drawing on a common nationalist populist trope—a potentially traitorous political elite. Peter Dutton claimed that China had been trying to influence Labor's candidate selection (Hurst 2022), while Morrison called deputy Labor leader Richard Marles 'the Manchurian candidate' (ABC 2022a).

Morrison's Pentecostalism had already (Morrison 2018, 2019) made him familiar with populist campaigns against 'gender ideology' and its challenges to traditional (fixed) gender identities. These campaigns started in Europe, where they were used by far-right populist movements and elected leaders such as Hungary's Viktor Orbán (Kuhar and Paternotte 2017). They subsequently influenced religious conservatives in the United States, with populist Republicans especially targeting transgender issues (Sosin 2022). Morrison used his support for hand-picked anti-transgender candidate Katherine Deves (see Chapter 5, this volume) not only to try to appeal to socially conservative religious voters but also to suggest that he would protect women from a claimed influx of transgender athletes into women's sport. While not endorsing all of Deves's extreme language, Morrison did contribute to a populist scare campaign himself, including by wrongly claiming that transgender adolescents could access life-transforming surgery (Morrison 2022a).[1] Transgender Australians were depicted as a new threatening 'Other' supported by a woke elite, in a context in which questioning gender or same-sex equality was no longer as electorally acceptable in Australia as it had been in the past.[2]

Howard-era populism encouraged an ethnic identity politics of 'us' versus 'them' that had increasingly focused on a threatening Muslim Other protected by politically correct elites (George and Huynh 2009; Johnson 2004). By contrast, Morrison (2022b) affirmed that 'we understand how important faith and culture is to … local communities … Australia is the most successful multicultural, multifaith, immigration nation on earth'. He was hoping that Deves's candidature would mobilise diverse religious conservative voters, including Muslim ones, especially in the electorates of western Sydney.

Morrison also attempted to re-energise his populist personal image. Leaders' personal images have now become increasingly important in politics as a focus on candidates' personal stories combines with the use of visual communication (Arbour 2014; Barnhurst and Quinn 2012) in a context in which many voters are disengaged from conventional politics. Moffitt (2016: 51) has emphasised the important role of 'the leader as a performer of populism'. It is very different from a historical context in which male leaders' images tended to be far more authoritative, statesmanlike and overwhelmingly monochrome (for example, a conservative suit with only a tie possibly adding a spot of colour). In 2019, Morrison had reinforced his populist argument that he would protect ordinary Australians against

---

1   Albanese (Albanese et al. 2022) argued that these issues were already covered by the *Sex Discrimination Act* and were the responsibility of sporting codes, although he did also add the ambiguous statement that 'girls should be able to play sport against girls and boys should be able to play sport against boys' without stating how boys and girls would be defined. Albanese had also answered a question from Joe Hildebrand (2022) about whether men could have babies with the response 'no'.

2   Though, of course, abortion and same-sex rights are still very much being targeted in the United States.

a Labor big government by rejecting his 'tall poppy' Sydney's eastern suburbs origins and instead fostering his image as an ordinary 'top bloke from the Sutherland Shire' (Blaine 2021: 7). Morrison was 'ScoMo', the likeable daggy dad from the suburbs who loved his footy and a beer (see further Johnson 2021a). The ScoMo image undercut Labor's left-populist arguments that the Liberals supported the 'top end of town'—a campaign that might have worked better against Malcom Turnbull, the wealthy former banker, than an apparent suburban dad.

Morrison favoured photo opportunities during the campaign in manufacturing facilities (preferably in a high-vis vest) as he tried to appeal to the bloke vote (see further Crabb 2022; Chapter 5, this volume). However, Morrison also displayed a confusing kaleidoscope of images in other workplaces as he desperately tried to refashion his populist ordinary Australian image. Morrison washed a woman's hair, sewed and swept a basketball court. There were also his more homely images: building a kid's cubby house, cooking curries and playing the ukulele.

Presumably, at least some of these images were intended to gel with Morrison's market populism, appealing to the manufacturing worker, tradie and small business vote. However, Morrison's focus on can-do capitalism and the government inaction that resulted also played into Labor's counterimage of Morrison, to be discussed later in this chapter, which depicted him as not taking government action when needed and shirking responsibility.

As well, Morrison's original populist image revolved around a form of protective masculinity in which he promised to be a strong male leader who would protect ordinary Australians from harm, whether that be from Labor big government or China. However, I have argued elsewhere that Morrison had repeated protective masculinity failures, including on climate change–related bushfires, the pandemic and protecting women from harm (see further Johnson 2021a: 20–23; 2021b; 2022b).

As it became clear that he had a major image problem, Morrison tried to recalibrate. He promised to be more empathetic, arguing that he had been a 'strong leader, and yes, I can be a bit of a bulldozer, and that's certainly what we've needed to get through these difficult times'. However, he pledged to move into another 'gear' as Australia went forward 'into a period of real great opportunity' (Morrison 2022c). Unfortunately for Morrison, he was to be denied that opportunity, partly because his populist leadership credentials had been seriously undermined.

Populism and the Teal Independents

As already indicated, the Liberals found themselves facing not just a challenge from Labor but also a populist challenge from the largely centre-right Teal Independents. The Teals' policies in a range of areas from gender equality to climate change were influenced more by social liberalism than neoliberalism, allowing a more active role for an ethical state (Sawer 2003) in furthering equal opportunity and ensuring social wellbeing, while still supporting a healthy private sector economy. Hence their appeal to some former Liberal voters who felt that the Liberal Party had lost its way as it became more conservative and neoliberal. Prominent Teal Allegra Spender, who defeated Liberal Dave Sharma in Wentworth, specifically acknowledged the influence of small-'l' social liberalism on her values (ABC 2022b).

While the Teals are categorised as largely centre-right here, with some Teals such as Spender and Kate Chaney coming from well-known Liberal family backgrounds, it should be noted that other Teals are somewhat more difficult to pigeonhole. For example, Monique Ryan, who defeated Liberal treasurer Josh Frydenberg in Kooyong, described herself as a small-'l' liberal but had been a Labor Party member from 2007 to 2010. She claimed her politics had changed since then (Minear 2022). The Teals also benefited from strategic Labor and Greens votes.

The Teals' appeals for greater integrity also had distinct populist elements. The Teals would reject those forms of populism that were anti-government and hostile to the role of independent experts. However, this chapter argues that while they used a variety of organisational approaches (see Chapters 14 and 15, this volume), the Teals represented a form of community-based populism that seeks to improve democratic input and trust in democratic institutions (see further Dzur and Hendriks 2018; Moffitt 2020: 94–114). The Teals argued that, unlike the political parties, they would be genuinely representing the people of their electorates against a government and party-political system that were verging on corruption due to the influence of vested interests.

For example, Monique Ryan argued:

> The establishment of an anti-corruption body is only a partial solution to restoring integrity: Australia's system of political donations and campaign finance also needs root and branch reform.

> Australia's lax federal donation laws have had a corrupting influence on politics and must be reformed in order to ensure a well functioning democracy that acts on expert advice and the wishes of the people rather than vested interests. (Ryan n.d.)

Similarly, Allegra Spender (n.d.) supported legislating for 'transparent, accountable government' to 'stop vested interests undermining our democracy'. Zoe Daniel (2022a), who defeated Liberal Tim Wilson in Goldstein, asserted that she was 'running on a platform that places integrity, and stamping out corruption and rorts, at the very centre of my candidacy'.

The Teals argued that their communities had not had their voices heard by the party system on issues ranging from climate change to gender equality. For example, Daniel (2022b) placed great emphasis on their movement representing their community in all its diversity against a party system that had fostered disunity and division, and she pledged to keep her community safe. Daniel stressed that 'this is your community campaign, your community movement, you are carrying me forward' (Daniel 2022b).

In short, the Teals were mobilising a community-based, largely centre-right reformulation of the populist trope of 'we the people' versus the corrupt and divisive establishment elites. While the Coalition and News Corp tried to dismiss Teal candidates as being from a privileged elite themselves (see Chapter 5, this volume), such attempts were to prove unsuccessful in key seats.

Palmer's United Australia Party

At the same time as the Liberals were being challenged by a largely centre-right populist movement, they were also being challenged by more far-right populist forces, particularly Clive Palmer's spectacularly well-funded UAP. The UAP campaigned on a libertarian right agenda, promising it would protect the Australian people against claimed tyrannical major-party politicians, foreign control and economic disaster. Palmer (2022e) pledged that the UAP would 'save Australia' while ensuring 'freedom forever'.

The UAP argued that neither of the major parties could be trusted after the pandemic restrictions that included lockdowns and vaccine mandates. Craig Kelly, the party's leader, argued that both major parties would lock down Australians again after the election. Consequently, the UAP would bring in a bill of rights that would ban lockdowns, ensure Australians could access the medical treatment of their choice and ensure freedom of speech (Kelly 2022b). The UAP (2022a; Kelly 2022b; Palmer 2022a, 2022e) claimed that the Australian Government was already compiling a database from mass biometric surveillance and facial recognition, ominously named 'the capability', which would be used by major-party governments to oppress opponents.

Palmer also claimed that Australia was facing a major economic 'catastrophe' due to the massive debt run up by the elite 'political class' of the major parties both before and after the pandemic. He asserted that 'weak politicians' had failed to protect Australian resources from being pillaged by Asian countries when they could have generated revenue via a 15 per cent export licence fee on iron ore, which could have been used to pay off the government debt and improve health, education and aged care services (Palmer 2022b; Kelly 2022b). In addition, the UAP claimed that the high interest rates resulting from government debt would see vast numbers of Australians losing their homes, so it pledged to cap home interest rates at 3 per cent for five years (UAP 2022b). Otherwise, Palmer (2022e) claimed there would be a dystopian future in which 60–80 per cent of mortgages would fail and Australians would become 'economic slaves in their own country'. By contrast, Kelly (2022b) claimed that the UAP would improve standards of living, increase incomes and end the cost-of-living crisis.

Palmer appealed to nationalistic forms of populism in which the UAP promised to defend against various foreign threats from which local political elites had failed to protect ordinary Australians. The UAP denounced the investment of Australian superannuation overseas: 'Just like when John Curtin in World War 2 brought the troops back to save Australia, the United Australia Party will bring back a Trillion Dollars of Australian Super back [sic] to Australia to save Australia' (Kelly 2022a). Meanwhile, Palmer (2022c) alleged that Chinese state-owned companies were 'seeking control over hundreds of square kilometres of Western Australian land' (Palmer 2022d). A final election-day advertisement (UAP 2022d) proclaimed: 'Stop Liberals and Labor transferring all our health assets and hospitals to the Chinese controlled WHO [World Health Organization] at the World Health Assembly in Geneva this May.' The UAP was evoking an established nationalist populist trope, suggesting elite politicians were traitorous.

While the UAP won only a single Senate seat and MP Craig Kelly, a former Liberal, lost his seat in the lower house, the party arguably had an impact that went beyond its own candidates' success or preference distribution.

In the 2019 election, Palmer's massive election spend had targeted Labor leader Bill Shorten. In 2022, the UAP (2022c) produced regular full-page newspaper advertisements prominently displaying personal criticisms of Scott Morrison by Barnaby Joyce and Liberal senator Concetta Fierravanti-Wells, with Joyce accusing Morrison of being a 'hypocrite and a liar' and Fierravanti-Wells calling him 'an autocrat and a bully who has no moral compass'.

The Liberals were therefore in the unfortunate position of facing both a well-funded centre-right populist campaign from the Teals and a well-funded far-right campaign from the UAP. They also faced a far-right populist campaign from One Nation.

Pauline Hanson's One Nation (PHON)

PHON also sought to attract votes from anti-vaxxers and lockdown opponents, with the unvaccinated Hanson testing positive for Covid-19 shortly before election day. However, PHON also drew on more traditional identarian radical right politics, as it had throughout Hanson's career (Betz and Johnson 2004), albeit updated to incorporate contemporary US right-wing discourse around 'wokeness' and critical race theory. Hanson (2022a) argued that Australian schoolchildren were being 'taught critical race theory so they feel guilt and shame for being white'. She opposed an Indigenous voice to parliament on the grounds it would undermine racial equality by giving Aboriginal Australians more than one vote (Hanson 2022a). PHON aimed to particularly target so-called woke Liberal parliamentarians, claiming: 'For too long conservative Australian values have been undermined by woke, lefty-Liberals … This is why I am targeting the woke Liberals in five of the 151 lower house seats' (Hanson 2022b).

Those targeted included Bridget Archer in Bass, Tim Wilson in Goldstein, Trent Zimmerman in North Sydney and James Stevens in Sturt, as well as Independent Helen Haines in Indi. Hanson claimed:

> [L]eft-leaning Liberals aren't giving conservative Australian voters much reason to hope their party will act differently to Labor on issues such as immigration, the housing crisis, religious freedom, critical race theory, gender reassignment, trans women competing in women's sports and climate change. (Hanson 2022b)

Hanson also aimed to gain support from Nationals voters unhappy at the supposed left turn of the Liberals.

However, Haines and Archer retained their seats, while Zimmerman and Wilson lost to Teal Independents. In fact, Hanson came close to losing her own Senate seat, defeating a conservative rather than a woke Liberal senator (Amanda Stoker) in the process.

The Greens

While the Liberals faced centre-right populist challenges from the Teals and far-right challenges from the UAP and PHON, both they and Labor faced a left-wing populist challenge (see further Moffitt 2020: 50–70, 94–113) from the Greens.

There were clear elements of 'us' versus 'them' populism in the Greens' pledge to 'tax the billionaires & big corporations, and provide the things we all need for a better life' (The Greens 2022a). The Greens' policies included a treaty with Indigenous Australians, having 100 per cent renewable energy replace coal and gas, including dental and improved mental health funding in Medicare funding, providing free education and scrapping student debt, providing affordable housing and well-paid and secure jobs and ending 'all forms of discrimination' (The Greens 2022a).

The Greens (2022b) pledged to provide 'politics for people, not corporations and billionaires', claiming:

> People have lost confidence in politicians. There's [sic] too many dirty donations, dodgy deals, a revolving door between politicians and big corporations, and no Independent Commission Against Corruption.
>
> Big corporations and billionaires have too much power over politicians. Liberal & Labor take millions in donations from big corporations and billionaires, they will never put people first.
>
> Strengthening our democracy benefits everyone. We will stamp out corruption and cap the influence of big corporations and billionaires to ensure politics works for everyone, not just the rich and powerful. (The Greens 2022b)

In short, the Greens' program included a pitch of the left's populist 'us', the people, versus 'them', the wealthy corrupt elites, with wealthy carbon polluters particularly, but not exclusively, in their sights. Interestingly, the Greens attracted not only voters normally on the left but also some former Liberal voters who might otherwise have voted Teal Independent in seats where Teals were standing. As a result, the Greens succeeded in winning Brisbane and Ryan in Queensland from the Liberal National Party and Griffith in Queensland from Labor.

Labor moves away from left populism

Anthony Albanese signalled that he would be moving away from Labor's populist targeting of the 'top end of town' soon after Labor's 2019 election defeat. He argued: 'The language used was terrible … [U]nions and employers have a common interest. Successful businesses are a precondition for employing more workers' (quoted in Benson et al. 2019). The new shadow treasurer, Jim Chalmers, expressed similar reservations (ABC 2019). In the campaign, Albanese made a conscious effort to avoid the 'us' versus 'them' style of arguments that are a hallmark of populism. Instead, he drew on a long-term Labor ideological tradition (Johnson 1989) of stressing the harmony of interests between various groups in Australian society. These included capital and labour who, it was argued, had a common interest in a healthy economy that would generate good-quality jobs.

Consequently, Albanese (2022c) pledged to move away from the 'conflict fatigue' that he argued the Australian people felt 'to bring people together'. That included bringing business and labour together to tackle the cost-of-living crisis:

> Because bringing business and unions together at the enterprise bargaining table, with productivity gains as a focal point, is how we increase both profits and wages without adding inflationary pressure. This is the fundamental economic challenge right now, and we must view government, business, unions and employees as partners in tackling it. (Albanese 2022c)

Albanese was drawing on the legacy of Bob Hawke, albeit without acknowledging that Hawke's success in wooing business was partly due to substituting a 'social wage' of government benefits for wage increases, which eventually resulted in not just wage restraint but also real wage cuts (Johnson 1989: 98–102). Nonetheless, Albanese (2022c) pledged his government's basic principle would be 'no-one held back, no-one left behind'. In other words, Labor would support aspiration, including that of businesspeople, but also welfare for the most disadvantaged and better pay for low-paid workers, including the many women working in the care economy.

Similarly, Albanese (2022c) pledged to 'end the climate wars', stressing that both the Australian Council of Trade Unions (ACTU) and various business groups supported Labor's approach. A Labor government would also foster reconciliation between Indigenous and non-Indigenous Australians by grasping 'the opportunity for healing and truth and reconciliation offered by the Uluru Statement from the Heart' (Albanese 2022c). Overall, Labor urged Australians to '[v]ote for hope and optimism over fear and division. Vote Labor, so together, we can build a … better future for all Australians' (Albanese 2022b). In contrast to Morrison, Albanese (2022c) argued that government had a crucial and positive role to play in creating that future. It was an argument that also appealed to those who believed government had played a positive role in protecting and supporting Australians during the pandemic.

Albanese projected a personal image that was compatible with Labor's approach. His life story of growing up in social housing with a disabled single mother was used as evidence of his ability to empathise with the disadvantaged and to recognise the role government could play in improving their lives, while the fact that he had bettered himself by going to university and becoming leader of the Australian Labor Party (ALP) provided evidence of his support for aspiration (Albanese 2022a). 'Albo' would be a kind, caring and compassionate leader. It was a more caring and compassionate image that Bob Hawke and Kevin Rudd (Johnson 2021a: 12, 15) had also fostered to defeat conservative governments, as had more recent overseas leaders such as Joe Biden and Jacinda Ardern (Johnson 2022a). Consequently, while Albanese did sometimes wear a high-vis vest like Morrison, he tended to favour photo opportunities with workers in the health or caring professions (Crabb 2022). Williams (2022) has characterised the leadership image contest as being between conservative 'daggy dads' and caring 'state daddies', with Albanese's image designed to appeal more to the female than the male gaze.

By contrast, Labor depicted Morrison as uncaring, unempathetic and out of touch, thereby undermining his image as a strong leader who would look after Australians. He was also depicted as incompetent and shirking responsibility (Albanese 2022c). Morrison's multiple attempts to change his image were made fun of, with Queensland Labor's (2022) website stating: 'Scott Morrison will pretend to do everyone else's job but he won't do his own.' Or, as Chalmers (2022) put it, if Morrison were re-elected, one would see a second decade of 'calamities and cosplay when we need calm and competence'.

Labor's attacks on Morrison were aided by his own missteps—for example, holidaying and stating he did not hold a hose during the bushfires, delays on sourcing Covid-19 vaccines and rapid antigen tests and his repeated failures to empathise with women. As already mentioned, these also caused problems for Morrison's own image of protective masculinity. Furthermore, Labor was ready to exploit the issue, already alluded to, that Morrison's market populism contributed to government inaction (see further Johnson 2022b), thereby reinforcing Labor's criticisms of him. Paul Erickson (2022), national secretary of the ALP, identified one of the factors leading to the Liberal's defeat as 'a pathological refusal to take responsibility for anything which comes from their small government mindset'.

The Liberals attempted to respond to Albanese's kinder, softer image by depicting him as a weak leader, who would produce a weak economy (LPA 2022). In short, as with accusations about China, they tried to question Albanese's masculinity. However, Albanese shored up his own masculine image, not only emphasising Labor's economic and national security credibility but also countering Morrison's bulldozer metaphor by arguing that while a bulldozer 'wrecks things … I'm a builder' (Butler 2022). Meanwhile, the populist image of ScoMo, the likeable ordinary bloke who loved a beer and the footy, that had been so successful in 2019 was no longer working. Indeed, depicting oneself as an ordinary bloke had lost part of its raison d'être now that Labor was no longer targeting the Liberals' close relationship with the 'top end of town'. Morrison was attempting a populist campaign but without a successful populist leadership image and against an opponent who had shifted the goalposts.

Conclusion

The Liberal's attempts to mobilise market populism against Labor were unsuccessful this time around. Labor moved to neutralise such campaigns via a small-target strategy, while countering 'us' versus 'them' arguments with an emphasis on bringing Australians together. At the same time, the Coalition faced centre-right, far-right and left-populist campaigns against it by minor parties and Independents. Meanwhile, Morrison's image, far from reinforcing the Liberal's populist appeal as it had in 2019, was turned into a negative. It was a perfect storm for the Coalition.

Labor's move away from left populism could have reassured some less left-wing voters concerned about how Labor would manage its relationship with business and the private sector economy. Nonetheless, in moving away from its own 2019 version of left populism, Labor risked vacating fertile ground to the Greens (and possibly in future to the Teals), particularly in some progressive inner-city seats. Furthermore, it is noticeable that the issue of climate change is playing a key role in both centre-right and left populism. Labor's electorally cautious climate change policies could make it harder to counter Teals' and Greens' campaigns mobilising the people against political elites accused of selling out to big business carbon emitters. Populism, in its various forms, seems likely to continue to play a role in Australian elections.

References

Albanese, Anthony. 2022a. *Anthony's Story*. [Online.] Available from: anthony albanese.com.au/anthonys-story.

Albanese, Anthony. 2022b. 'Vote for a better future'. Speech [Transcript]. Australian Labor Party Federal Election Campaign Launch, Perth, 1 May. Available from: anthonyalbanese.com.au/media-centre/vote-for-a-better-future-2022-campaign-launch.

Albanese, Anthony. 2022c. 'Address to the National Press Club'. Speech [Transcript]. Canberra, 18 May. Available from: anthonyalbanese.com.au/media-centre/address-to-the-national-press-club-18-may.

Albanese, Anthony, Jim Chalmers and Tony Burke. 2022. 'Doorstop interview Toll NQX national office'. [Transcript.] Berrinba, Qld, 20 April. Available from: jimchalmers.org/latest-news/transcripts/berrinba-doorstop-20-04-22/.

Arbour, Brian. 2014. *Candidate-Centered Campaigns: Political Messages, Winning Personalities, and Personal Appeals*. New York, NY: Palgrave Macmillan. doi.org/10.1093/poq/nfw035.

Australian Broadcasting Corporation (ABC). 2019. 'Jim Chalmers joins Insiders'. *Insiders*, [ABC TV], 23 June. Available from: www.abc.net.au/news/2017-03-26/jim-chalmers-joins-insiders./8387580.

Australian Broadcasting Corporation (ABC). 2022a. 'What is "a Manchurian candidate"? Five quick questions, answered'. *ABC News*, 18 February. Available from: www.abc.net.au/news/2022-02-18/what-is-a-manchurian-candidate-scott-morrison/100842190.

Australian Broadcasting Corporation (ABC). 2022b. 'Allegra Spender on the energy crisis and federal ICAC'. *RN Breakfast*, [ABC Radio], 9 June. Available from: www.abc.net.au/radionational/programs/breakfast/allegra-spender-on-the-energy-crisis-and-federal-icac/13921698.

Barnhurst, Kevin G. and Kelly Quinn. 2012. 'Political visions: Visual studies in political communication'. In *The Sage Handbook of Political Communication*, edited by Holly A. Semetko and Margaret Scammell, 276–91. Thousand Oaks, CA: Sage. doi.org/10.4135/9781446201015.n23.

Benson, Simon, Greg Brown and Michael McKenna. 2019. 'Albanese vows to end Labor's class-war rhetoric'. *The Australian*, 23 May. Available from: www.theaustralian.com.au/nation/politics/albanese-vows-to-end-labors-classwar-rhetoric/news-story/5dccd3b687017f55145bdf4750be803c.

Betz, Hans-Georg and Carol Johnson. 2004. 'Against the current—Stemming the tide: The nostalgic ideology of the contemporary radical populist right'. *Journal of Political Ideologies* 9(3): 311–27. doi.org/10.1080/1356931042000263546.

Blaine, Lech. 2021. 'Top blokes: The larrikin myth, class and power'. *Quarterly Essay* 83.

Butler, Josh. 2022. 'Builders and bulldozers: Anthony Albanese rubbishes Scott Morrison's late attempts at change'. *The Guardian*, [Australia], 13 May. Available from: www.theguardian.com/australia-news/2022/may/13/builders-and-bulldozers-anthony-albanese-rubbishes-scott-morrisons-late-attempts-at-change.

Chalmers, Jim. 2022. 'A cause worth the winning'. Speech [Transcript]. Melbourne, 3 March. Available from: jimchalmers.org/latest-news/speeches/a-cause-worth-the-winning/.

Crabb, Annabel. 2022. 'The lost women'. *ABC News*, 23 May. Available from: www.abc.net.au/news/2022-05-23/election-2022-morrison-women-vote/101089978.

Daniel, Zoe. 2022a. *Integrity Policy*. [Online.] Available from: www.zoedaniel.com.au/policies/integrity/.

Daniel, Zoe. 2022b. 'Zoe's campaign launch speech: Video & transcript'. [Transcript.] Melbourne, 10 April. Available from: www.zoedaniel.com.au/2022/04/11/zoes-campaign-launch-speech-video-transcript-10th-april-2022/.

Dzur, Albert W. and Carolyn M. Hendriks. 2018. 'Thick populism: Democracy-enhancing popular participation'. *Policy Studies* 39(3): 334–51. doi.org/10.1080/01442872.2018.1478408.

Erickson, Paul. 2022. 'Campaign director's address to the National Press Club of Australia'. Speech. Canberra, 15 June. Available from: www.npc.org.au/speaker/2022/1028-paul-erickson.

George, Jim and Kim Huynh. eds. 2009. *The Culture Wars: Australian and American Politics in the 21st Century*. Melbourne: Palgrave Macmillan.

Hanson, Pauline. 2022a. 'Say no to a third tier of government'. [Online.] Available from: www.onenation.org.au/aboriginal-voice-to-parliament.

Hanson, Pauline. 2022b. 'Pauline Hanson targets woke lefty Liberals'. [Online.] 4 May. Available from: www.onenation.org.au/pauline-hanson-targets-woke-lefty-liberals.

Hildebrand, Joe. 2022. 'Federal election 2022: Anthony Albanese to change Labor's class war rhetoric'. Herald Sun, [Melbourne], 22 March. Available from: www.heraldsun.com.au/news/national/federal-election/federal-election-2022-anthony-albanese-to-change-labors-class-war-rhetoric/news-story/f276923ff8dc247f89c38472ccc4ab6e.

Hunger, Sophia and Fred Paxton. 2022. 'What's in a buzzword? A systematic review of the state of populism research in political science'. *Political Science Research and Methods* 10(3): 617–33. doi.org/10.1017/psrm.2021.44.

Hurst, Daniel. 2022. 'Anthony Albanese hits back at "nonsense" suggestion China wants Labor to win federal election'. *The Guardian*, [Australia], 11 February. Available from: www.theguardian.com/australia-news/2022/feb/11/anthony-albanese-hits-back-at-nonsense-suggestion-china-wants-labor-to-win-federal-poll.

Johnson, Carol. 1989. *The Labor Legacy: Curtin, Chifley, Whitlam, Hawke*. Sydney: Allen & Unwin.

Johnson, Carol. 2004. 'Anti-elitist discourse in Australia: International influences and comparisons'. In *Us and Them: Anti-Elitist Discourse in Australia*, edited by Marian Sawer and Barry Hindess, 117–36. Perth: API Network.

Johnson, Carol. 2021a. 'The gendered identities of Australian political leaders: From Hawkie to ScoMo'. In *Gender Politics: Navigating Political Leadership in Australia*, edited by Zareh Ghazarian and Katrina Lee-Koo, 11–23. Sydney: NewSouth Publishing.

Johnson, Carol. 2021b. 'Scott Morrison doesn't just have a "woman problem", he has a masculinity problem as well'. *Inside Story*, [Melbourne], 24 March. Available from: insidestory.org.au/in-harms-way/.

Johnson, Carol. 2022a. 'Feeling protected: Protective masculinity and femininity from Donald Trump and Joe Biden to Jacinda Ardern'. *Emotions and Society* 4(1): 7–26. doi.org/10.1332/263169021X16310949038420.

Johnson, Carol. 2022b. 'Why Morrison's "can-do" capitalism and conservative masculinity may not be cutting through anymore'. *The Conversation*, 17 May. Available from: theconversation.com/why-morrisons-can-do-capitalism-and-conservative-masculinity-may-not-be-cutting-through-anymore-183118.

Kelly, Craig. 2022a. 'Letter to fellow Australians'. [Advertisement.] *The Australian*, 11 May: 7.

Kelly, Craig. 2022b. 'United Australia policy launch 2022'. *YouTube*, 17 May. Available from: www.youtube.com/watch?v=wIBGmhi2vM4.

Kuhar, Roman and David Paternotte. eds. 2017. *Anti-Gender Campaigns in Europe: Mobilizing against Equality*. New York, NY: Rowman & Littlefield International.

Liberal Party of Australia (LPA). 2022. 'It won't be easy under Albanese: Weak economy, weak leadership'. Election leaflet. Canberra: LPA.

Minear, Tom. 2022. '"Independent" candidate Dr Monique Ryan accused of "hypocrisy" over social media posts'. *Herald Sun*, [Melbourne], 4 March. Available from: www.heraldsun.com.au/news/victoria/independent-candidate-dr-monique-ryan-accused-of-hypocrisy-over-social-media-posts/news-story/6e1a6e0a990299ac99c94da0c53d924c.

Moffitt, Benjamin. 2016. *The Global Rise of Populism: Performance, Political Style, and Representation*. Stanford, CA: Stanford University Press. doi.org/10.11126/stanford/9780804796132.001.0001.

Moffitt, Benjamin. 2020. *Populism*. Cambridge, UK: Polity.

Morrison, Scott. 2018. 'We do not need "gender whisperers" in our schools. Let kids be kids'. *Twitter*, 5 September. Available from: twitter.com/scottmorrisonmp/status/1037100764294836224?lang=en.

Morrison, Scott. 2019. 'Interview with Ben Fordham'. [Transcript.] *2GB Radio*, 29 August. Available from: pmtranscripts.pmc.gov.au/release/transcript-42388.

Morrison, Scott. 2021. 'Address, Victorian Chamber of Commerce and Industry'. Speech [Transcript]. Melbourne, 10 November. Available from: pmtranscripts.pmc.gov.au/release/transcript-43653.

Morrison, Scott. 2022a. 'Press conference: Epping, NSW'. [Transcript.] Sydney, 10 May. Available from: webarchive.nla.gov.au/awa/20220519151952/https://www.liberal.org.au/latest-news/2022/05/10/prime-minister-transcript-press-conference-epping-nsw.

Morrison, Scott. 2022b. 'Liberal election campaign launch'. Speech [Transcript]. Brisbane, 15 May. Available from: webarchive.nla.gov.au/awa/20220516145253/https://nswliberal.org.au/Shared-Content/News/2022/Prime-Minister-Speech-Liberal-Election-Campaign-Launch.

Morrison, Scott. 2022c. 'Interview with Allison Langdon'. [Transcript.] *Today*, [Nine Network], 16 May. Available from: webarchive.nla.gov.au/awa/20220519143739/https://www.liberal.org.au/latest-news/2022/05/16/prime-minister-transcript-interview-allison-langdon-today.

Palmer, Clive. 2022a. 'Don't let the government do this to us'. *YouTube*, 1 February. Available from: www.youtube.com/watch?v=m6-7Uc2Yv3A.

Palmer, Clive. 2022b. 'Clive Palmer's National Press Club speech'. Canberra, 7 April. Available from: www.unitedaustraliaparty.org.au/video/clive-palmers-national-press-club-speech/.

Palmer, Clive. 2022c. 'China makes land grab in Western Australia'. Media release, 22 April. Gold Coast, Qld: United Australia Party. Available from: www.unitedaustraliaparty.org.au/china-makes-land-grab-in-western-australia-clive-palmer/.

Palmer, Clive. 2022d. 'China to control the health of Australians'. Media release, 17 May. Gold Coast, Qld: United Australia Party. Available from: www.unitedaustraliaparty.org.au/china-to-control-the-health-of-australians-palmer/.

Palmer, Clive. 2022e. 'United Australia policy launch 2022'. *YouTube*, 18 May. Available from: www.youtube.com/watch?v=wIBGmhi2vM4.

Queensland Labor. 2022. 'Scott Morrison will pretend to do everyone else's job, but he won't do his own'. *Twitter*, 28 March. Available from: twitter.com/QLDLabor/status/1508284690398326792.

Ryan, Monique. n.d. 'Frequently asked questions'. [Online.] Available from: www.moniqueryan.com.au/frequently_asked_questions.

Sawer, Marian. 2003. *The Ethical State? Social Liberalism in Australia*. Melbourne: Melbourne University Press.

Sawer, Marian and David Laycock. 2009. 'Down with elites and up with inequality: Market populism in Australia and Canada'. *Commonwealth & Comparative Politics* 47(2): 133–50. doi.org/10.1080/14662040902842836.

Sosin, Kate. 2022. 'Why is the GOP escalating attacks on trans rights? Experts say the goal is to make sure evangelicals vote'. PBS *News Hour*, 20 May. Available from: www.pbs.org/newshour/politics/why-is-the-gop-escalating-attacks-on-trans-rights-experts-say-the-goal-is-to-make-sure-evangelicals-vote.

Spender, Allegra. n.d. 'Policies'. [Online.] Available from: www.allegraspender.com.au/policies.

The Greens. 2022a. *Greens Policy Platform*. Canberra: The Australian Greens. Available from: greens.org.au/platform.

The Greens. 2022b. *Greens Policy Platform—Democracy: Politics for People, Not Corporations and Billionaires*. Canberra: The Australian Greens. Available from: greens.org.au/platform/democracy.

United Australia Party (UAP). 2022a. '"The capability": Australia's mass biometric surveillance plan'. Advertisement, 11 February. Gold Coast, Qld: United Australia Party. Available from: www.unitedaustraliaparty.org.au/video/the-capability-australias-mass-biometric-surveillance-plan/.

United Australia Party (UAP). 2022b. 'Home loan interest rates under threat'. Media release, 4 May. Gold Coast, Qld: United Australia Party. Available from: www.unitedaustraliaparty.org.au/home-loan-interest-rates-under-threat/.

United Australia Party (UAP). 2022c. 'What does the Deputy Prime Minister and Liberal Senator think of Scomo?'. [Advertisement.] *The Australian*, 9 May: 7.

United Australia Party (UAP). 2022d. 'Stop Liberals and Labor transferring all our health assets and hospitals to the Chinese controlled WHO at the World Health Assembly in Geneva this May'. [Advertisement.] *The Weekend Australian*, 21 May: 3.

Williams, Blair. 2022. 'When the state daddy takes on the daggy dad'. *The Canberra Times*, 3 May: 10–11.

5

High-vis and hard hats versus the care economy

Blair Williams and Marian Sawer

Gender was a very important part of the story of the 2022 federal election, particularly the perception of many women that 'their' issues were being ignored or dismissed by the Morrison Government. In seats such as Goldstein, Kooyong, North Sydney and Wentworth, where women voters outnumbered men on a ratio of about 53–47, women's concerns about climate change, integrity issues and women's safety became pivotal issues. There was a disconnect between women's discontent and the predominant image of the prime minister during the campaign wearing a high-vis vest and hard hat to relay a message about his target voters.

The back story of gender in the 2022 campaign began in March 2021 when Brittany Higgins made her explosive allegations about being raped in Parliament House and the way it had been hushed up two years before. Women took their anger to the streets, with some 10,000 demonstrating outside Parliament House in Canberra and some 100,000 more around Australia. Polls conducted at the time showed a steep increase in women's disaffection with the Morrison Government and this 'modern' gender gap (with women to the left of men) continued until the election. While some commentators asked where women's anger had gone as they disappeared from the streets, it became clear that, among other things, it had fuelled the campaigns of the Teal Independents. The 2022 election showed that women had turned sexual misconduct in the parliamentary workplace into a highly salient political issue.

This chapter will track the increased diversity of active participants in the 2022 election and in its outcomes. It will also examine the gendered nature of the electoral discourses employed by the political parties, Independents and other political actors, including visual discourses and memes. Finally, it will apply a gender lens to policy offerings and assess the extent to which the distributive injustice of the care economy received serious attention during the campaign.

Candidates

Despite continuing revelations and media stories about women's mistreatment in politics, there was a significant increase in the number of women standing for federal parliament—rising from 32 to 38 per cent of candidates for the House of Representatives. The most striking increase was in the number of women standing as Independent candidates—rising to 43 per cent from 23 per cent in 2019. Women became closely identified with the rejection of politics as usual that characterised the 2022 election and made up nine of the 10 Independents elected to the House of Representatives.

The successes of Helen Haines and Zali Steggall in 2019 had inspired the emergence of new 'Voices For' movements protesting major-party politics (see Chapter 14, this volume), arguing that the major parties had taken their safe seats for granted and failed to address the issues of most concern to communities. Women dominated this so-called Teal wave of Independent candidates: professional women standing in previously safe conservative seats on platforms prioritising climate change, a federal integrity commission and women's safety or gender justice. Also elected was the community-based Independent Dai Le, a Vietnam-born refugee and deputy mayor of Fairfield in western Sydney, who won the previously safe Labor seat of Fowler after local reaction against Australian Labor Party (ALP) preselection of outsider Kristina Keneally.

The gender breakdown of candidate nominations of the major parties and the Australian Greens was less surprising. The Greens led with women making up 51 per cent of its House of Representatives candidates (as well as three nonbinary candidates), followed by the ALP with 44 per cent and the Coalition with 29 per cent (no real change from 2019). The ALP has had a policy since 2015 of achieving a 50 per cent quota by 2025, with 45 per cent by 2022. The policy pays dividends, as could be seen in the 2022 results, with women winning the largest swings to Labor in each State.

While the Coalition has traditionally objected to quotas, on the basis that they override the merit principle, voters have become increasingly in favour (The Australia Institute 2021).

Labor more than achieved its 2022 goal, with women becoming a majority (52.4 per cent) of its federal parliamentary party for the first time thanks to Labor women senators outnumbering men 18 to eight. The parliamentary Labor Party was also becoming more diverse, with newly elected Indigenous and South Asian members and senators.

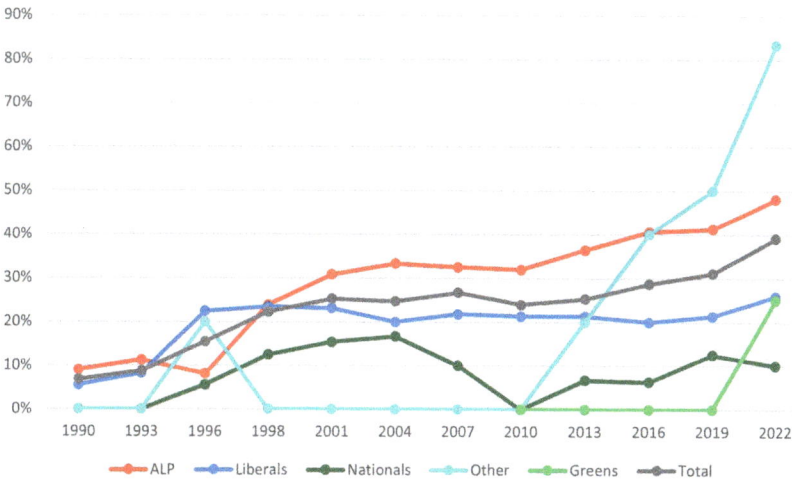

Figure 5.1 Women as a percentage of MPs in the House of Representatives by party, 1990–2022

Note: The Greens did not have a single MP in the House of Representatives until briefly from 2002 to 2004 and then from 2010 onwards.

Source: Compiled by Blair Williams, based on Parliamentary Library figures.

Table 5.1 Gender breakdown of the Senate after the 2022 election

Party	Female	Male	Female (%)
Labor	17	9	65.4
Coalition	14	18	43.8
Greens	8	4	66.7
Pauline Hanson's One Nation	1	1	50
Jacqui Lambie Network	2	0	100
David Pocock	0	1	0
United Australia Party	0	1	0
Total	**42**	**34**	**55.3**

Source: Compiled by Blair Williams, based on Parliamentary Library figures.

Three Labor branches (New South Wales, Queensland and Western Australia) have quotas for Indigenous candidates in held or winnable seats. Recent research has found that Labor has been much more likely than the Liberal Party/Country Liberal Party to preselect Indigenous candidates for winnable seats and much more likely to preselect Indigenous women (Evans and McDonnell 2022). In the Senate, Labor now had two Indigenous women senators (Malarndirri McCarthy and Jana Stewart) as well as Indigenous senator Pat Dodson. In the House of Representatives, Marion Scrymgour, a former deputy chief minister of the Northern Territory, was elected for the seat of Lingiari and Gordon Reid won the seat of Robertson. Linda Burney was re-elected for Barton and became minister for Indigenous Australians in the new Labor Government.

The Coalition also now had two Indigenous senators, Jacinta Nampijinpa Price (Northern Territory) and Kerrynne Liddle (South Australia), as did the Greens: Lidia Thorpe (Victoria) and Dorinda Cox (Western Australia).[1] Overall Indigenous representation in the federal parliament rose from six before the election to 11 afterwards, with nine of those women (Richards 2021). At 4.8 per cent, Indigenous parliamentary representation now exceeded the percentage of the Australian population identifying as Aboriginal or Torres Strait Islander at the 2021 census (3.2 per cent).

There was an increase in another form of diversity with, for example, four more women from non-European backgrounds elected for Labor in the House of Representatives. In the Senate, Afghanistan-born Fatima Payman was elected as a Labor senator for Western Australia. At 27, she was one of the youngest elected representatives and the first to wear the hijab. Of the two other Muslim women in the Australian Parliament, Labor's Anne Aly now entered the ministry while Greens senator Mehreen Faruqi was returned. On the Coalition side, Gladys Liu lost the seat of Chisholm and the Coalition also lost Ken Wyatt, their only Indigenous MP (and Cabinet minister).

While diversity in the Australian Parliament was generally increasing, there was a slight diminution in LGBTIQ+ representatives (see Table 5.2). Three gay Liberal MPs lost their seats—in Goldstein, North Sydney and Brisbane (for historical information on LGBTIQ+ representation, see Richards 2022). However, in Brisbane, Trevor Evans was replaced with the Australian Greens' Stephen Bates, who not only was gay but also ran election ads on the gay dating site Grindr. The Queensland Labor Party remains the only Labor

---

1   In February 2023, Thorpe resigned from the Greens and moved to the crossbench to sit as an Independent.

Party branch with a quota (5 per cent) for LGBTIQ+ candidates in held or winnable seats. Though the success of the Teal Independents helped increase women's representation in parliament, most were straight white women.

Table 5.2 Diversity in the federal parliament, 2022

	ALP	Coalition	Greens	Other	Total
Indigenous	6	2	2	1	11 (4.8%)
Non-European	9	3	1	2	15 (6.6%)
LGBTIQ+	4	2	2	0	8 (3.5%)
Aged under 30	1	0	2	0	3 (1.3%)

Notes: The Independents are notably non-diverse, apart from Dai Le in Fowler. The one parliamentarian in the 'Other' column identifying as Indigenous is Senator Jacqui Lambie.

Albanese's Cabinet is the most diverse in Australia to date. It includes a record number of women, in 10 of 23 positions or 43.5 per cent— a significant increase on Morrison's Cabinets (see Table 5.3). The ministry also includes numerous firsts, such as Penny Wong becoming the first Asian Australian and openly LGBTIQ+ minister for foreign affairs, Linda Burney becoming the first Indigenous woman Cabinet minister and minister for Indigenous Australians and Dr Anne Aly becoming Australia's first Muslim woman minister. The previous ministry had little cultural and linguistic diversity, with an all-white Cabinet apart from Ken Wyatt, the minister for Indigenous Australians (and Michael Sukkar in the outer ministry). The increased number of women in Cabinet has flowed naturally from the increased pool of women in the parliamentary Labor Party. Women occupy some key portfolios, including Wong in foreign affairs (now almost a gender-stereotyped portfolio) and Katy Gallagher in finance. Gallagher is also the minister for women—a useful conjunction given the government's commitment to reintroduce gender budgeting.

Table 5.3 Gender breakdown of Cabinet, 2010–22

Cabinet	Female	Male	Female (%)
Gillard, August 2010	4	16	20.0
Rudd, 2013	6	14	30.0
Abbott, 2013	1	18	5.2
Turnbull, 2016	6	17	26.1
Morrison, 2019	7	16	30.4
Albanese, 2022	10	13	43.5

Source: Compiled by Blair Williams, based on Parliamentary Library figures.

On diversity, the UK House of Commons provides a useful point of comparison. While it has a slightly smaller proportion of women than the Australian House of Representatives (35 per cent against 38 per cent), it has a larger percentage of LGBTIQ+ MPs: 9 per cent—second only to New Zealand. The House of Commons also has a greater number of MPs from ethnic-minority backgrounds (10 per cent), including six Cabinet members as of November 2021 (Uberoi and Tunnicliffe 2021) and prime minister as of October 2022.

Campaign discourses

The campaign was characterised by highly gendered visual discourses, with the prime minister's photo opportunities conveying a predominantly masculine message, while the Opposition leader chose a more feminine message, reinforcing the priority he was giving to the care economy (Williams 2022).

Another part of the story was the Covid-19 pandemic, which brought home the centrality of the care economy, with all its unpaid and poorly paid work. While the pandemic had a disproportionate impact on women, including the need to undertake home schooling on top of other care work, this did not receive adequate policy focus from the Morrison Government. Analysis by the *Australian Financial Review* one month into the campaign found that while Morrison visited 16 manufacturing and engineering worksites, Albanese favoured hospitals and aged care facilities to provide visual telegraphing of the care economy message (McCubbing and Mizen 2022). This visual discourse underpinned Morrison's highly masculinised campaign strategy, which focused not only on 'tradies' but also on economic management and higher taxes and weaker national security under Labor.

These were the kind of issues usually given greater priority by men than by women. For example, in the 2019 election, the biggest issue for men was management of the economy (men, 32 per cent; women, 17 per cent), while for women the biggest issue was health (30 per cent; men, 14 per cent) (Cameron and McAllister 2019: 17). The April 2022 ANU Poll found similar gender gaps on the issue of the care economy (Biddle 2022). The biggest issue for women was 'fixing the aged care system' (68.8 per cent; men, 51.3), with a similar gender gap on increasing wages in the aged care system, while more men than women put priority on 'strengthening the nation's economy' (58.2 per cent to 51.2 per cent).

Not only the Coalition's economic management theme but also the tax discourse was notably gender-blind, as had been the case since the tax cuts package was first announced in 2018. The government had at that time refused to allow the Office for Women to do a gender-impact analysis of the proposal. There was widespread criticism from outside government of the impact of the Stage 3 tax cuts on gender equality (as well as equality more generally), with men receiving two-thirds of the benefits and women disproportionately affected by loss of revenue to support the care economy (PBO 2021; Grudnoff 2022). When the gender impact of the package was pointed out, then treasurer Scott Morrison dismissed this as ridiculous, commenting: 'You don't get pink forms and blue forms to fill out your tax return. That's not how it works' (Morrison 2018).

The insouciant dismissal of the gender impacts of budgets showed how much the Australian Government had forgotten since it was a pioneer of gender budgeting in the 1980s—the invention that travelled around the world and is now practised in about half of Organisation for Economic Co-operation and Development (OECD) countries. When *Women's Agenda* applied a gender lens to the big-spending budget of 2020 and its lack of attention to the care economy, the author received a call from the Prime Minister's Office to complain that 'no-one credible was making such a complaint and that nothing in the budget is gendered' (Dawson 2020). A hashtag, '#CredibleWomen', sprang into action, attracting economists, business leaders, politicians and journalists.

Despite Labor's emphasis on the care economy in the 2022 federal election campaign, and its commitment to gender-responsive budgeting, it remained wedded to the Stage 3 tax cuts for fear that the Coalition would mount a massive tax-scare campaign as it had done successfully in 2019. Labor's support for tax cuts was in stark contrast to its 1987 women's policy, which highlighted the costs to women of John Howard's proposed tax cuts and their consequences for the funding of community services (Simms 1988: 157–58).

Labor's nervousness about tax left it to the Greens to campaign for a 'wealth tax' on billionaires to pay for an ambitious platform of policies such as universal childcare. They proposed an annual 6 per cent wealth tax for this purpose as well as abolishing the Stage 3 tax cuts, which, they argued, would predominantly benefit older men and disadvantage women of all ages. The Greens used numerous memes throughout the election campaign to advertise their tax plan, as well as other key policies. Instead of following the approach of the major parties in creating their own memes, the Greens collaborated with already existing and popular meme pages and online creators, frequently reposting memes from unaffiliated pages such as Australian Green Memes for Actually Progressive Teens and The Simpsons against the Liberals.

The most successful—created by Australian Green Memes for Actually Progressive Teens—was the meme format: 'If you recognise [X] then you will not be affected by the Greens plans to tax billionaires and corporations' (see Chapter 8, this volume). The official Australian Greens Instagram page reposted this meme with the caption 'If you've ever wanted to get dental & mental health into Medicare, increase JobSeeker to $88 a day and wipe student debt, you will benefit from the Greens plan to tax billionaires & big corporations', which received more than 24,000 likes and hundreds of comments. This effectively communicated the wealth tax plan while reaching out to younger voters in an informal and accessible way, allowing them to follow the format and contribute their own humorous examples demonstrating how a wealth tax would not affect lower and middle-income people.

The Greens ran a largely positive campaign focusing on change. Apart from an occasional meme targeting the government, their social media discourse generally evoked optimism. Greens leader Adam Bandt took to TikTok to respond to the Nine Network leadership debate between Morrison and Albanese, expressing his frustration at the incoherent yelling on display and noting that while the major parties were 'talking over each other', the Greens were 'talking about the big issues that matter to you'. In comparable democracies like Canada, the leaders of all parliamentary parties participate in leaders' debates, so the Greens leader would have had the opportunity to talk about the big issues. Yet, although the Greens' platform included many commitments to ending 'racism, sexism, ableism and homophobia', their social media discourse was far less explicit, championing policies that would positively affect many Australians but particularly those most marginalised.

Greens discourse has always highlighted their social movement origins and difference from traditional party politics—signalled by not using the word 'party' in their name. They have long led the way with social media campaigning, making up for their general absence from traditional print media and television advertising. As mentioned earlier, Stephen Bates, the candidate for Brisbane, took his campaign ads to the gay dating app Grindr with sexually suggestive slogans such as 'The best parliaments are hung'.

The seat of Brisbane is home to many LGBTIQ+ voters and the second-highest percentage of voters aged 18–29 in the country. Bates remarked that 'these ads are just another way to connect with the community and have fun while doing it', but they also included a 'serious underlying message of the potential of a hung parliament with the Greens holding the balance of power' (Rogers 2022). By demonstrating a queer and playful approach to politics, these ads also helped distinguish Bates from the incumbent Liberal National Party of Queensland (LNP) MP Trevor Evans—the first openly LGBTIQ+ federal politician from Queensland. Evans had received criticism from the LBGTIQ+ community for not joining the five Liberal MPs who crossed the floor to support the repeal of provisions in the Religious Discrimination Bill allowing religious schools to discriminate against students on the grounds of sexuality or gender identity.

Meanwhile, the Teal Independents were very effectively promoting a narrative suggesting that the two-party system was not serving the best interests of women, the environment or democracy. It fed into the populist distrust of political parties and the 'political class' discussed in Chapter 4 of this volume by suggesting that although they were professional women, they were not professional politicians. Such discourse was common on their campaign websites. For example, Dr Monique Ryan, who won former Liberal treasurer Josh Frydenberg's 'blue-ribbon' seat of Kooyong, presented herself as 'certainly not a career politician' but a 'real alternative: a fresh independent voice truly dedicated to our community'. Likewise, Dr Sophie Scamps, who won Liberal MP Jason Falinski's seat of Mackellar, promoted herself as 'stepping up to take our community's concerns to Canberra, free from party politics and political factions'.

In response, the Teals were attacked by Coalition members and in News Corp mastheads as either puppets lacking agency of their own or cashed-up elites with luxury concerns far from the issues affecting blue-collar voters. Former Liberal treasurer Alexander Downer wrote in the *Australian Financial Review* that the Teals presented an impediment to the careers of (male) politicians like Frydenberg and Dave Sharma, who could become 'truly great men', while the Independents would be forgotten within a decade (Downer 2022). They were regularly framed as 'fake Independents' controlled by 'puppet-master' Simon Holmes à Court, founder of the fundraising organisation Climate 200 (Devine 2022). Their platforms of gender equality, climate action and anti-corruption were portrayed as 'luxury beliefs' (Lehmann 2022; Andrews 2022).

While the Coalition largely ignored gender issues during the campaign, there was one issue for which the prime minister expressed enthusiasm: banning trans women from playing women's sport. Just a week before he called the election, Morrison hand-picked Katherine Deves, a lawyer and co-founder of the Save Women's Sport organisation, to be the Liberal candidate for Warringah. On the second day of the election campaign, Morrison stood behind his controversial 'captain's pick' and declared that he shared her views:

> Katherine is, you know, an outstanding individual. And she's standing up for things that she believes in, and I share her views on those topics. This is just about, you know, common sense and what's right. And I think Katherine's right on the money there. (Baj 2022)

The day after this statement, thousands of Deves's previously deleted anti-transgender tweets resurfaced, including comments claiming that 'half of all males with trans identities are sex offenders', describing transgender children as 'surgically mutilated and sterilised' and likening transgender activists to Nazis and anti-transgender activists to opponents of the Holocaust. Morrison reaffirmed his support and there were reports of Deves's campaign being run from the Prime Minister's Office. Numerous Liberal MPs criticised both Deves and Morrison, including moderates Dave Sharma, Trent Zimmerman and Warren Entsch. Likewise, NSW treasurer Matt Kean demanded that Morrison disendorse Deves as 'there is no place for that vile bigotry in a mainstream political party or quite frankly anywhere' (Belot 2022). In response, Morrison labelled these demands a symptom of 'cancel culture', arguing that 'others might want to cancel her, others might want to cancel other Australians for standing up for things they believe in' and that Australians were 'fed up with having to walk on eggshells' (Withers 2022).

The Coalition has often been accused of using LGBTIQ+ Australians as political footballs, as evidenced by their attacks on the Safe Schools anti-bullying program, their anti-transgender discourse during the marriage equality plebiscite and, more recently, their attempt to pass the Religious Discrimination Bill. Morrison's support of Deves appeared to be another attempt to reignite the culture wars—this time, framing transgender rights as a wedge issue. Many within his own party accused Morrison of gambling with the future of the Liberal Party to win socially conservative and religious outer-suburban seats at the risk of socially progressive blue-ribbon inner-city votes. Morrison's gamble backfired as the Liberals both failed to win any outer-suburban seats and lost inner-city ones. In Warringah, there was a 5 per cent swing against Deves and towards the incumbent, Independent Zali Steggall. Morrison's attempt at a culture war election nonetheless could have had a significant impact on transgender Australians as there was a 53 per cent increase in calls to QLife, the national LGBTIQ+ helpline, on days with significant media coverage of Deves (O'Halloran 2022). Measures that improve the mental health of transgender Australians are also those that Deves and Morrison staunchly opposed: increased social inclusion, acceptance and gender-affirming interventions (Cheung and Zwickl 2021).

Issues and their perception

A year of revelations by women staffers and politicians of bullying, harassment and assault on the Coalition side of politics and the prime minister's 'tin ear' in dealing with these issues contributed to perceptions of the government's 'women problem'. Unlike Opposition leader Anthony Albanese, Morrison refused to come out to address the March4Justice gathered outside Parliament House in March 2021 and the minister for women, Senator Marise Payne, was also absent. Morrison's statement that the demonstration was a triumph of democracy because 'not far from here such marches, even now, are being met with bullets' reverberated around the country. Revelations continued relentlessly. Only a week after the March4Justice, government staffers were found to be sharing a video of a male staffer masturbating on a female MP's desk. Surveys in Westminster democracies have found a consistent pattern of about 30 per cent of women working in parliament experiencing some form of sexual harassment and becoming more ready to speak out about it since the arrival of the #MeToo movement (Sawer 2021). The fact that such issues have become major political issues in Australia owes much to the women who now have senior roles in the press gallery. Journalists Laura Tingle, Katharine Murphy, Samantha Maiden and Annabel Crabb are celebrated along with advocates and women politicians in the 'Fight Like a Girl' tea towel on sale in the Museum of Australian Democracy shop. The Morrison Government's response failed to convince, and surveys showed a steep rise in women's disenchantment (Roy Morgan 2022). The Murdoch press was dismissive, with editor-at-large of *The Australian* newspaper Paul Kelly writing: 'Albanese knows he cannot rely on the 2021 zeitgeist—the emotional demand by women to reset the norms of respect and justice—to deliver victory' (Kelly 2021).

Plate 5.1 March4Justice, Canberra, 15 March 2021
Source: Courtesy of Angelika Heurich.

However, the disenchantment did last until the election. Laura Tingle, in her role as president of the National Press Club, chaired a powerful joint address in February 2022 by Brittany Higgins and advocate Grace Tame that helped keep the issue on the political agenda. In April 2022, the ANU Poll revealed that while most Australians thought that equality for women had not gone far enough, two-thirds had little confidence in the Liberal Party with regards to the issue. There was even less confidence in the Nationals and least of all in the minor parties further to the right. In contrast, half had confidence in Labor on issues of gender equality, although this was still not overwhelming. In general, women had less confidence than men in parties' commitment to gender equality, with confidence in the Greens an exception (Biddle and Gray 2022). These pre-election poll findings were reinforced by The Australia Institute's exit poll, which found that two-thirds of voters thought that the state of aged care and the treatment of women in politics were weaknesses for the Coalition (The Australia Institute 2022).

Quite apart from the direct question of gender equality policy, an important part of the story was the Covid-19 pandemic and the lack of adequate policy attention from the Morrison Government, leaving the way open for Labor to build its campaign on the care economy. The Opposition leader's budget reply speech in March 2022 set the scene for a such a campaign, with major commitments to childcare and aged care—for example, the funding of pay increases for aged care workers and better ratios of staff to residents. The fact that such a campaign was hitting home was confirmed by an Essential poll (20 April 2022) that found voters rated Labor much more highly than the Coalition in terms of managing the care economy, specifically in relation to Medicare, aged care, childcare and disability and the National Disability Insurance Scheme (NDIS).

As Labor said in its election policy on the gender pay gap: '[O]ne of the main causes of the gender pay gap is low pay and poor conditions in care sectors like aged care, early childhood education and care and disability care—where the vast majority of workers are women' (Albanese et al. 2022).

Labor's 2022 *Women's Budget Statement*, released the morning after the budget reply and emphasising the care economy, served instead of a women's policy launch during the campaign, in line with the general small-target strategy.

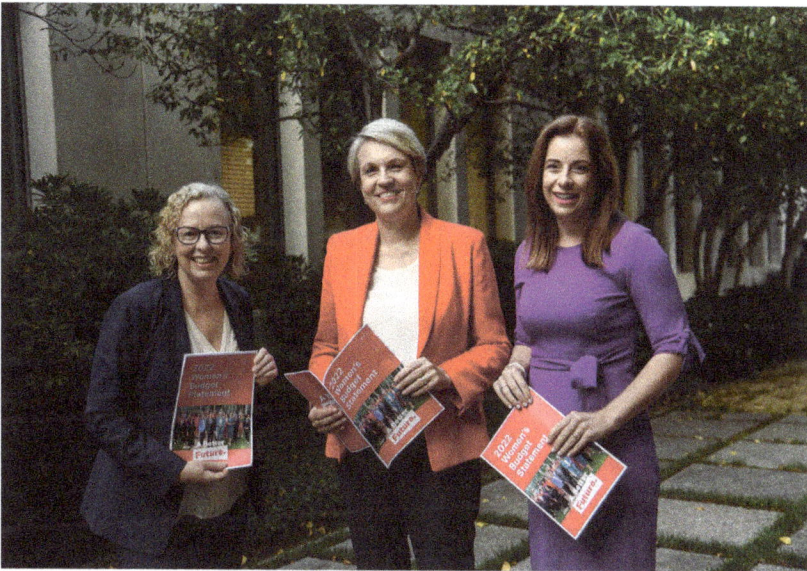

Plate 5.2 From left: Sharon Claydon MP (chair, Caucus Status of Women Committee), Tanya Plibersek MP (shadow minister for women) and Anika Wells MP with Labor's *Women's Budget Statement*, 31 March 2022
Source: Supplied by the office of Tanya Plibersek MP.

To address the gender pay gap, Labor offered to make pay equity an objective of the *Fair Work Act*, to introduce a statutory equal remuneration principle and to set up expert panels in the Fair Work Commission to hear equal remuneration and care-sector cases, supported by a restored research unit. The commission's Pay Equity Unit had been abolished by the Coalition Government in 2015. This was a familiar story: in the 1990s, the Equal Pay Unit in the workplace relations portfolio had fallen victim to the Howard Government, which also defunded most of the working women's centres.

Labor's major commitments to the care economy in child, aged and disability care were backed up by commitment to a national strategy to achieve gender equality. In 2018, the treaty body responsible for the UN Convention on the Elimination of All Forms of Discrimination against Women expressed concern about Australia's lack of such a strategy (CEDAW 2018: 4) but no progress had been made. To underpin a national strategy, the solid machinery-of-government commitments made in 2016 and 2019 were repeated. They included strengthening the Office for Women's capacity to oversee the gender-impact assessment of Cabinet submissions and the introduction of gender-responsive budgeting. As seen by the travesty referred to earlier of Morrison's comments about pink and blue tax forms, the reintroduction of gender-responsive budgeting at the federal level is long overdue.

In general, Labor's offerings, including on violence against women and implementation of recommendations of the *Respect@Work* report, such as the 'positive duty' for employers to provide safe workplaces, were well received by women's advocacy organisations, although funding commitments for services were rated as less than what was needed (Fair Agenda 2022; WEL 2022). Labor did not take a commitment to expand paid parental leave (currently funded at less than half the OECD average) to the election, although this changed after it became a repeated theme at the Jobs and Skills Summit in September 2022.

From a different direction, the Cherish Life organisation campaigned against sitting Labor MP Susan Templeman in the highly marginal seat of Macquarie, with leaflets claiming: 'Labor wants you to fund abortions' (Murray 2022). Although the word 'abortion' had disappeared from the 2021 National Platform, Labor was committed to improving access to sexual and reproductive health services and expanding service provision in the public sector.

In terms of LGBTIQ+ policy, it was notable that while at the 2016 and 2019 elections Labor had been committed to establishing a dedicated LGBTI or LGBTIQ commissioner in the Human Rights Commission, there was no mention of it in the 2022 Labor policy for 'An Equal and Inclusive Nation'. This, and the removal of a commitment to a dedicated ministerial advisory council, was part of the general slimming down of the Labor platform and, perhaps, the desire to show Labor was not captive to a 'woke' agenda. Labor did, however, commit to including questions about gender identity and sexual orientation in the next census (questions removed from the 2021 census at the wish of the then assistant treasurer) and to a human rights ambassador with a mandate to advance internationally the rights of people living with disability, ethnic and religious minorities and LGBTIQ+ individuals (Equality Australia 2022).

Coalition policy

The Coalition did not launch its women's policy and the minister for women, Senator Payne, was 'unavailable' for any debate on women's issues in the election. However, 'Our Plan for Women's Safety, Economic Security and Health' appeared on the Coalition's election policy website and outlined existing policies and budget commitments. The Coalition had made some significant investments in areas such as women's safety and women's economic security (encouraging more women into science, technology, engineering and mathematics, or STEM, fields), had achieved its target of 50 per cent female representation on government boards and continued with the appointment of ambassadors for women to promote gender equality internationally and regionally. Oddly, its women's policy statement did not include an item regarded by insiders as the best thing done by the Coalition Government on the gender equality front: the new time-use survey undertaken in 2020–21—the first since 2006. The Coalition was rated poorly by the women's advocacy organisations that produced scorecards on parties' policies. It was widely noted that while lip-service had been paid to women in the care economy bearing the brunt of the Covid-19 pandemic, the economic stimulus investment was in manufacturing and construction rather than in social infrastructure.

Despite the appointment of Senator Jane Hume as a dedicated minister for women's economic security in 2021, some policy developments seemed to lead in the opposite direction. One example was the decision in 2020 to allow early release of up to $20,000 from superannuation accounts to help those under financial stress due to the pandemic. This had a disparate impact on women, who were already very disadvantaged in post-retirement income support. More women than men completely emptied their super accounts and, as a result, the gender gap in superannuation balances widened over the period 2019–21 (Preston 2022). The Coalition Government did introduce free childcare for three months during the pandemic, but unfortunately, childcare was then the first sector of the economy to lose the JobKeeper wage subsidy. Some improvements were made to the Child Care Subsidy System, but not enough to deliver affordable quality care for most families. Although there was a welcome increase in funding for the Workplace Gender Equality Agency, there was no commitment to closing the gender pay gap by doing something about its main cause: low pay in care sectors.

While changes had been introduced to make paid parental leave more flexible, the removal of 'use it or lose it' dad and partner pay was highly controversial. Senator Hume justified it in terms of the government's commitment to freedom of choice rather than social engineering. In contrast, the Work + Family Policy Roundtable said that it unpicked good policy architecture designed to 'nudge' men to take leave. Both major parties were criticised for their failure to support payment of superannuation on paid parental leave— 'a major oversight that weakens women's economic security and retirement income' (W+FPR 2022).

Greens policy

The Greens presented an overarching 'Equality and Justice for All' platform, reminiscent of Labor's 'An Equal and Inclusive Nation' election policy. Under the forthright title 'End Sexism', the Greens promised to 'shut down the old boys' club, close the gender pay gap, and make sure workplaces are fair, respectful and safe'. Like Labor, the Greens were committed to implementing all recommendations from the *Respect@Work* and *Set the Standard* reports but also had commitments to free universal childcare, strengthening paid parental leave entitlements and ensuring above-average pay rises in women-dominated industries. The Australian Gender Equality Council's 'women's scorecard' for the election praised the Greens' 'comprehensive policy statement', giving them five stars (out of five) for free universal childcare and 4.5 stars on women's economic security, safety and respect for women, and women's representation and leadership (AGEC 2022).

Conclusion

While the political parties did not overtly compete with women's policy launches or a debate on women's policy, gender issues made a major contribution to disenchantment with the Morrison Government. The prime minister's lack of credibility in addressing issues of safety in the parliamentary workplace fed into perceptions of a lack of credibility across a broad range of issues. As we have noted, the treatment of sexual misconduct as a serious political issue owed much to the senior women in the press gallery.

In terms of policy, Labor presented a redistributive gender equality policy through the priority it gave to the care economy. This wholistic approach distinguished its gender equality policy from the Coalition's more neoliberal approach relying on market mechanisms and some discrete initiatives to boost women's workforce participation, particularly in non-traditional STEM areas (Johnson 2022). The unprecedented prominence of the care economy in Labor's campaign was bolstered both by the Greens and by the campaigns of the Teal Independents. In contrast, the Coalition's campaign and its visual discourse were clearly targeting blue-collar male voters.

Commentators sometimes failed to see the highly gendered nature of Labor's campaign, asking where the women's policy was. Nonetheless, there was a widespread perception that, as Senator Penny Wong expressed it on election night, 'a government for women' had been elected. Whether this perception will survive austerity policies and the albatross of the Stage 3 tax cuts remains to be seen.

References

Albanese, Anthony, Tony Burke and Tanya Plibersek. 2022. 'Labor to deliver fair pay and conditions for working women'. Media release, 1 May. Available from: anthonyalbanese.com.au/media-centre/labor-to-deliver-fair-pay-conditions-for-working-women-burke-plibersek.

Andrews, Lillian. 2022. 'Anti–working class vote of the elite fuels teal victory'. The Australian, 24 May. Available from: www.theaustralian.com.au/commentary/antiworking-class-vote-of-the-elite-fuels-teal-victory/news-story/eefcb32a380fae308e06c37270569ef8.

The Australia Institute. 2021. *Polling: Gender Issues and Quotas*. Research Report, 28 March. Canberra: The Australia Institute. Available from: australiainstitute. org.au/report/polling-gender-issues-and-quotas/.

The Australia Institute. 2022. *Exit Poll: Coalition Strengths and Weaknesses in the Election*. Report, 30 May. Canberra: The Australia Institute. Available from: australiainstitute.org.au/report/exit-poll-2022/.

Australian Gender Equality Council (AGEC). 2022. *2022 Federal Election*. Canberra: AGEC. Available from: www.agec.org.au/federalelection/.

Baj, Lavendar. 2022. 'Surprise, surprise, the candidate Scott Morrison hand-picked for Warringah is a TERF'. *Junkee*, 13 April. Available from: junkee.com/scott-morrison-transphobia-katherine-deves/327618.

Belot, Henry. 2022. 'Scott Morrison sticks by Katherine Deves after NSW Treasurer calls for Liberal candidate in Warringah to be dumped'. *ABC News*, 16 April, [Updated 17 April]. Available from: www.abc.net.au/news/2022-04-16/nsw-treasurer-calls-for-liberal-candidate-warringah-to-be-dumped/100995112.

Biddle, Nicholas. 2022. 'ANU Poll 50: Volunteering, aged care, policy priorities and experiences with COVID-19'. *ADA Dataverse, V1*. April. doi.org/10.26193/AXQPSE.

Biddle, Nicholas and Matthew Gray. 2022. *Australians' views on gender equity and the political parties*. Discussion Paper, 17 May. Canberra: Centre for Social Research and Methods, The Australian National University. Available from: apo.org.au/node/317864.

Cameron, Sarah and Ian McAllister. 2019. *The 2019 Australian Federal Election: Results from the Australian Election Study*. Canberra: School of Politics and International Relations, The Australian National University. Available from: australianelectionstudy.org. doi.org/10.1080/10361146.2020.1776679.

Cheung, Ada and Sav Zwickl. 2021. 'Why have nearly half of transgender Australians attempted suicide?'. *Pursuit*, 23 March. Melbourne: University of Melbourne. Available from: pursuit.unimelb.edu.au/articles/why-have-nearly-half-of-transgender-australians-attempted-suicide.

Committee on the Elimination of Discrimination against Women (CEDAW). 2018. *Concluding Observations on the 8th Periodic Report of Australia: Committee on the Elimination of Discrimination against Women*. July. Geneva: CEDAW. Available from: digitallibrary.un.org/record/1641944?ln=en.

Dawson, Emma. 2020. 'There are thousands of very credible women across Australia fighting for equal rights'. *The Guardian*, 8 October. Available from: www.theguardian.com/commentisfree/2020/oct/08/there-are-thousands-of-very-credible-women-across-australia-fighting-for-equal-rights.

Devine, Miranda. 2022. 'Labor, Teals wipe out generation of Lib leaders'. *Daily Telegraph*, [Sydney], 21 May. Available from: www.dailytelegraph.com.au/news/opinion/miranda-devine-labor-teal-independents-wipe-out-generation-of-leaders/news-story/ca6b55dc1167e3e5e4f2aff6abaa6206.

Downer, Alexander. 2022. 'Election 2022: Four questions to make the election about Australia's future'. *Australian Financial Review*, 10 April. Available from: www.afr.com/politics/federal/four-questions-to-make-the-election-about-australia-s-future-20220407-p5abt9.

Equality Australia. 2022. *#EqualityVotes 2022: Summary of Federal Election Party Survey Responses*. 20 May. Sydney: Equality Australia. Available from: equalityaustralia.org.au/wp-content/uploads/2022/05/EqualityVotes-2022-Summary-of-Federal-Election-party-survey-responses.pdf.

Evans, Michelle and Duncan McDonnell. 2022. 'More partisans than parachutes, more successful than not: Indigenous candidates of the major Australian parties'. *Australian Journal of Political Science* 57(4): 346–67. doi.org/10.1080/10361146.2022.2065968.

Fair Agenda. 2022. *Election 2022: Together for Women's Safety—Scoring the Major Parties' Track Records*. [Online.] Melbourne: Fair Agenda. Available from: votefor safety.com.au/.

Grudnoff, Matt. 2022. *Rich Man's World: Gender Distribution of the Stage 3 Tax Cuts*. Research Report, 17 February. Canberra: The Australia Institute. Available from: australiainstitute.org.au/report/rich-mans-world-gender-distribution-of-the-stage-3-tax-cuts/.

Johnson, Carol. 2022. 'What COVID-19 revealed about gender equality policy framing'. *Australian Journal of Political Science* 57(1): 93–112. doi.org/10.1080/10361146.2021.2023094.

Kelly, Paul. 2021. 'Women's movement won't decide next election'. *The Australian*, 2 April.

Lehmann, Claire. 2022. 'Teal power a luxury the poor can ill-afford'. *The Australian*, 6 May. Available from: www.theaustralian.com.au/commentary/climate-action-teal-power-a-luxury-the-poor-can-illafford/news-story/cfd852adbd9ca46a0a55a206f9db463b.

McCubbing, Gus and Ronald Mizen. 2022. 'PM sets a cracking high-visibility pace'. *Australian Financial Review*, 7 May.

Morrison, Scott. 2018. 'Transcript, press conference'. Canberra, 6 June.

Murray, Duncan. 2022. 'Labor targeted by anti-abortion campaign'. *News.com.au*, 9 May. Available from: www.news.com.au/national/federal-election/labor-targeted-by-antiabortion-campaign/news-story/b04e73152f71528bdf5915627 e72db37.

O'Halloran, Kate. 2022. 'Trans women's participation in sport has been framed as an election issue. This is what some trans athletes think'. *ABC News*, 27 April. Available from: www.abc.net.au/news/2022-04-27/trans-inclusion-womens-sport-participation-politics-election/101015082.

Parliamentary Budget Office (PBO). 2021. *Distributional Analysis of the Stage 3 Tax Cuts*. Request for Budget Analysis. Canberra: PBO. Available from: www.aph.gov.au/-/media/05_About_Parliament/54_Parliamentary_Depts/548_Parliamentary_Budget_Office/Costings/Publicly_released_costings/2021/Distributional_analysis_of_the_stage_3_tax_cuts.docx?la=en&hash=6B35B00FD26AB5C486 2E4E25FCB4457A2962B897.

Preston, Alison. 2022. 'Raiding super early has already left women worse off. Let's not repeat the mistake for home deposits'. *The Conversation*, 19 May. Available from: theconversation.com/raiding-super-early-has-already-left-women-worse-off-lets-not-repeat-the-mistake-for-home-deposits-183351.

Richards, Lisa. 2021. *Indigenous Australian parliamentarians in federal and State/Territory parliaments: A quick guide*. Research Paper Series 2020–21, 15 June. Canberra: Parliamentary Library.

Richards, Lisa. 2022. *LGBTIQ+ parliamentarians in Australian parliaments: A quick guide*. Research Paper Series 2021–22, 20 January. Canberra: Parliamentary Library.

Rogers, Destiny. 2022. 'Greens Brisbane candidate says "Best parliaments are hung"'. *QNews*, [Brisbane], 29 April. Available from: qnews.com.au/greens-brisbane-candidate-says-best-parliaments-are-hung/.

Roy Morgan. 2022. 'Australian federal voting intention: Two-party preferred (2019–2022)'. In 'ALP 54.5% leads the L-NP 45.5% on a two-party preferred basis as early voting begins this week'. Press release, 10 May, Federal Poll Finding No. 8967. Sydney: Roy Morgan Research. Available from: www.roymorgan.com/findings/8967-roy-morgan-poll-on-federal-voting-intention-may-2022-2022 05091128.

Sawer, Marian. 2021. 'Dealing with toxic parliaments: Lessons from elsewhere'. *Australasian Parliamentary Review* 36(1): 7–22. Available from: www.aspg.org. au/wp-content/uploads/2021/07/Dealing-with-Toxic-Parliaments.pdf.

Simms, Marian. 1988. 'Women'. In *Australia Votes: The 1987 Federal Election*, edited by Ian McAllister and John Warhurst, 146–61. Melbourne: Longman Cheshire.

Uberoi, Elisa and Richard Tunnicliffe. 2021. *Ethnic Diversity in Politics and Public Life*. Research Briefing, 26 November. London: House of Commons Library. Available from: commonslibrary.parliament.uk/research-briefings/sn01156/.

Williams, Blair. 2022. 'Morrison's carefully cultivated caricature as daggy dad PM is coming undone'. *The Canberra Times*, 3 May, [Updated 6 May]. Available from: www.canberratimes.com.au/story/7714805/morrisons-carefully-cultivated-caricature-as-daggy-dad-pm-is-coming-undone/.

Withers, Rachel. 2022. 'The "culture war" election'. *The Politics*, 20 April. Available from: www.themonthly.com.au/the-politics/rachel-withers/2022/04/20/culture-war-election.

Women's Electoral Lobby (WEL). 2022. *2022 WEL Federal Election Scorecard*. Sydney: WEL. Available from: www.wel.org.au/2022_wel_federal_election_scorecard.

Work + Family Policy Roundtable (W+FPR). 2022. *The Work + Family Policy Roundtable Federal Election 2022 Scorecard: How the Major Parties' Policies Rate against the Research Evidence*. Sydney: W+FPR. Available from: www.workand familypolicyroundtable.org/wp-content/uploads/2022/05/WFPR-Election-Benchmarks-2022-Scorecard_s.pdf.

6

Strategy and leadership in the Labor and Liberal campaigns

Glenn Kefford and Stephen Mills

In their critique of Labor's failed 2019 election campaign, Labor Party elders Craig Emerson and Jay Weatherill observed that 'any successful major undertaking requires a sound strategy' (2019: 21). Using advertising data, media reports and background interviews with participants in both parties' campaign organisations, this chapter reviews the strategies adopted by the Labor and Liberal parties in the 2022 federal election campaign. Understanding these rival strategies and how the two parties sought to implement them helps explain the election outcome. The strategies themselves—essentially, detailed plans setting out how each party proposed to win the election—remain tightly held within the party head offices. But they can be inferred from the actions the parties took to implement them— in particular, how they organised their campaigns, how they allocated their resources and how they communicated with voters through advertising. We will consider each of these in turn.

By focusing on the major parties, we do not suggest that minor parties and Independents did not develop and implement their own strategies; rather, only the major-party strategies were aimed at winning government—that is, winning (in the case of the Liberals, in coalition) a majority of seats in the House of Representatives. In the same sense, only the leaders of the two major parties—Prime Minister Scott Morrison and Opposition leader Anthony Albanese—were in realistic contention to emerge from the campaign as prime minister. Both major-party strategies were accordingly centred on the party leaders. Leaders, we observe, were the principal actors in party campaign activities and leadership was the predominant frame of party campaign communications; each side sought to boost the credentials of its own leader and, even more vigorously, to exploit the perceived weaknesses of the other. The 2022 federal election campaign thus illustrates the broader trend towards the 'personalisation' of politics that has been observed in democratic politics internationally.

Campaign organisation

The campaign strategy remains the distinctive concern of the parties' head offices, which, with the elected parliamentarians and grassroots supporters, constitute the party's 'three faces' (Katz and Mair 1993). The head office is responsible for designing the strategy, resourcing it and efficiently coordinating the various actors within and outside the party to implement it. The Labor and Liberal head offices have adopted broadly similar organisational responses to this imperative, selecting campaign professionals as their organisational heads (Mills 2014). In the 2022 federal election campaign, the Liberals' federal director Andrew Hirst and Labor's national secretary Paul Erickson served as campaign managers of the respective campaigns. Hirst, the architect of the 2019 'Morrison miracle', was managing his second federal election campaign. Erickson—assistant national secretary in 2019—was appointed to the top job after the post-election departure of his predecessor, Noah Carroll.

In each party, the campaign organisation featured an 'assemblage' (Nielsen 2011) of campaign personnel: a combination of federal and State party officials, parliamentary advisers drawn from their leaders' offices and external marketing specialists engaged for short-term campaign roles as 'creatives'. These organisational arrangements have proven broadly stable over time, albeit with Labor typically experiencing a higher turnover of personnel than the Liberals. Alongside Erickson in Labor's Sydney campaign headquarters were party officials including assistant national secretary Jen Light, a digital team led by Kate Ryan and Ross Caldwell, advertising director David Nelson, a launch team led by Kate Dykes and research leads Bryce Roney and Lachlan Poulter, and parliamentary staffers—including Albanese's chief of staff, Tim Gartrell. Gartrell, manager of Albanese's first election campaign as the Member for Grayndler in 1996, had helmed Labor's successful 'Kevin 07' campaign in 2007 as national secretary. His involvement in the

2022 campaign—as a former national secretary now serving in the most senior advisory role to the parliamentary leader—was unprecedented in Australian campaigns. External agencies included researchers YouGov, Essential Media and New Zealand–based Talbot-Mills and advertising creatives Dee Madigan (Campaign Edge) and Darren Moss (Moss Group).

Alongside Hirst in the Liberals' Brisbane campaign headquarters were deputy director Simon Berger and Morrison's chief of staff John Kunkel. Senior consultant Isaac Levido and inhouse pollster Mike Turner both joined the campaign from CT Group, the United Kingdom–based advisory agency still managed by former Liberal national director Lynton Crosby. Neither Crosby nor business partner Mark Textor had official roles, but Textor did dial in on strategy calls and offered advice to members of the senior leadership team. Separate 'departments' managed tactics and research, digital media, policy and campaign support, including direct voter contact and direct mail (Kefford 2021). Television advertising was again managed by Adelaide-based KWP!, and returning to work on digital for the third time were New Zealand–based Topham Guerin founders and principals, Ben Guerin and Sean Topham (Patrick 2022). The Nationals' campaign director Jonathan Hawkes and his team also worked in what was effectively a joint Coalition campaign headquarters.

A striking feature of Labor's campaign strategy was the conscious and methodical way it rectified the organisational errors that beset its 2019 campaign. These errors were identified in the party's post-election review conducted by former federal minister Craig Emerson and former South Australian premier Jay Weatherill. They attributed the defeat to a weak strategy combined with poor adaptability and an unpopular leader. A prominent finding was that Labor 'did not settle on a persuasive strategy for winning the election':

> We could not find any documented strategy that had been discussed, contested and agreed across the whole campaign organisation, the leadership and the wider Labor Party ... We found no body that was empowered to discuss and settle a strategy or any process to monitor its implementation ... No formal campaign committee was established, creating no forum for formulating an effective strategy or for receiving reports evaluating progress against the strategy. (Emerson and Weatherill 2019: 21)

Figure 6.1 The organisational structure of the Labor Party's campaign

* National secretary, leader's chief of staff, other party officials and parliamentary advisers.

** Parliamentary leadership (4) plus economic shadow ministers; representatives of National Executive; State secretaries (NSW, Victoria, Queensland and Western Australia); Caucus factional convenors; and representatives of affiliated unions.

FPLP = Federal Parliamentary Labor Party

Sources: Interview data; media reports.

In response to these criticisms, Labor's National Executive established the National Campaign Committee (NCC) in August 2020 and vested it with authority over the campaign strategy. A campaign budget review committee was established at the same time. The NCC's broad membership included the four parliamentary leaders plus the shadow treasurer and finance minister, representatives of the National Executive, representatives of affiliated unions, the State secretaries of New South Wales, Victoria, Queensland and Western Australia, and Caucus factional convenors. The NCC was convened for the first time in January 2021 and continued meeting at six-weekly intervals—although, thanks to pandemic lockdowns, never in person.

The convenor of the NCC was national secretary Paul Erickson. Before any strategy was presented to the NCC, Erickson worked with Gartrell in an informal senior strategy group to generate themes and ideas informed by the party's qualitative and quantitative social researchers. They presented their proposals in the first instance to the parliamentary leaders, and iteratively modified them to incorporate their feedback. The refined strategy was then documented by Erickson, presented to the NCC, debated, further refined if necessary and approved; thence, it was communicated to shadow Cabinet and Caucus and, on the party side, to party secretaries (campaign directors) in each State and Territory and through them to organisers in target seats and to the branch network. By July 2021, with the possibility of a September election, Erickson delivered the first version of Labor's strategy to the NCC; with the possibility of a March election, it was revised in December, further refined in February 2022 and again in March, as a May election date emerged as the certainty. This process encapsulated in every respect the advice set out by Emerson and Weatherill that 'best practice' strategic development required 'an iterative process involving all the key players, informed by research, [which] should then arrive at a settled approach. The strategy should then be reduced to writing and monitored, with progress against it measured' (Emerson and Weatherill 2019: 21).

Strategy and leadership

Labor's campaign strategy sought to make the election a referendum on Scott Morrison. As Erickson explained after the election, 'the first core objective of our campaign [was] to cultivate, elevate and stoke a mood for change', complemented by a second objective to 'ensure that, for anyone still sitting on the fence, the spectre that haunted them into the polling booth was three more years of Scott Morrison' (Erickson 2022). A third goal, clearly, was to build public trust in Anthony Albanese as a credible alternative. The Liberals' strategy was designed, as the incumbent, to re-establish in voters' minds the government's achievements, particularly its economic and health management of the pandemic and putting Australia in a strong position, and to identify Labor, and specifically Albanese, as a risk to that position.

For both parties, the contrast between the character and experience of the rival leaders provided the centre of their strategy. This approach was based on research that presented both parties with a similar dilemma: neither leader was much liked by voters; both were flawed. Morrison was respected as a leader, particularly as a decision-maker during the pandemic, but not liked as a person. This was familiar territory for the Liberals, who had successfully managed a similarly not-much-liked but grudgingly respected John Howard; but Morrison's difficulties were more severe: 'missing in action' during bushfires and floods; insensitive to women in the workplace, notably in Parliament House and his own party; and as 'Scotty from Marketing'—a figure who was in a permanent campaign mode with no agenda for the future, a 'flat character' without authentic definition (Kelly 2021: 47–49). As the pandemic endured into late 2021, incumbency shifted from a boon to a drawback, with Morrison's government blamed for drift and incompetency during a slow vaccine rollout and the further disruption of the Omicron variant wave. The prime minister had become a 'punching bag' not only for Labor but also for Liberals (Coorey 2022).

By contrast, Albanese was liked, in the sense of being a good bloke to have a beer with and a likeable knockabout from Marrickville; but he simply was not perceived as a leader. Until a makeover in late 2021, he had presented as a slightly overweight Canberra insider with bad suits and slurred speech, sidelined during the pandemic by premiers, ministers and health officials and forced into passive acceptance of government decisions. Right until the campaign, many disengaged voters had heard and knew little about him. Both major parties, then, had fertile soil for negative advertising but would struggle to promote a positive message. It was a low-expectations campaign: the Liberals' best argument was basically 'better the devil you know', while Albanese's gaffes early in the first week of the campaign nearly derailed his entire effort; Labor's momentum was only restored when he disappeared from view when forced to isolate after contracting Covid-19.

In this sense, Australia's 2022 federal election exemplified a trend observed in many democratic contests in recent years. While there is significant debate about whether changes to institutional structures and democratic practices have affected the capacity of leaders to shape the institutions around them (Poguntke and Webb 2005), there is little doubt that leadership, however projected, is a key strategic frame used by political parties in their campaigns. The literature on the role of leaders and the projection of 'leadership' in election campaigns is well established (Mackintosh 1968; Crossman 1963: 51). In subsequent decades, this literature has spawned significant international debate about the effects of changing institutional structures and democratic practices, including debates about 'presidentialisation' (Poguntke and Webb 2005; Dowding 2012).

Especially relevant to our analysis is personalisation. According to McAllister (2007: 571), the personalisation of politics refers to the idea that democratic systems are experiencing fundamental changes 'without any concomitant change in their formal institutional structures'. While there is debate about how these changes manifest, Walter and Strangio (2007: 12) have suggested that 'as greater expectations are invested in leaders, more extensive responsibilities are delegated to them by the parties and the public and they consequently act as superheroes'. For Poguntke (2000: 7), personalisation describes 'the growing influence of candidate effects on voting choice'. We argue here that while personalisation is often seen as arising from system-level factors such as the predominant role of the media and the substitution of parliamentary and Cabinet governance by executive power, it can also be seen as a function of actor-level factors—in particular, as an aspect of political management. In this sense, personalisation can form part of a campaign design or strategy, adopted by campaign managers to frame an electoral contest through the projection of leadership.

A significant question, therefore, is how was the 'leadership frame' employed by political parties in the 2022 Australian federal election? What did they do to implement their strategic objectives? We have already considered the organisational arrangements they put in place to manage their campaigns. What further steps did they take and what campaign activities did they undertake to achieve their goals?

Resource allocation

Campaigns are exercises in allocating finite resources. Campaign managers like Erickson and Hirst must choose where to allocate money (TV advertising, digital media or direct mail), volunteer phone-banking (this electorate or that) and the leader's itinerary (Tasmania again, western Sydney or the Northern Territory). In the 2022 election, such choices were exacerbated by the ever-evolving media landscape: the proliferation of digital media channels and platforms, the increasing cost and diminishing reach of free-to-air television and the enduring penetration of direct mail.[1] Campaign managers use public opinion polling, analytical processes and informed judgement to determine which seats and regions are most winnable or most vulnerable to loss and therefore most deserving of extra resources. The target-seat list clarifies for the campaign just how it intends to win: a documented 'path to victory' that specifies those seats the party must defend and/or flip to assemble a majority in the House of Representatives.

In Labor's campaign, the shadow of 2019 loomed large. Emerson and Weatherill (2019: 23) reported that Labor had targeted 'too many' seats and identified 'multiple' paths to victory, spreading its resources too thinly and depriving the campaign of proper focus. In 2022, Labor addressed this concern with a more precise target list. Given favourable polls, Labor believed it could defend all 69 Labor-held seats; only Gilmore and Lyons were on the radar as seriously at risk. The more challenging task was to identify Coalition-held seats to attack. Labor made a critical decision to target only four seats in Queensland—not the 10 or so of 2019—instead

---

1   Several of our interviewees commented that, despite the coverage that digital media receives in popular commentary, direct mail operations remain a core component of the major parties' voter outreach.

aiming to win more seats in States where it was already dominant (Victoria and New South Wales), to win back previously held seats (in Tasmania) and, critically, to build on its strong incumbency under extremely popular premiers in Western Australia and South Australia. This approach identified an estimated 15 to 17 target seats (see Table 6.1) that would yield a seat tally in the low to mid eighties and a small but solid (less than 10) majority in the House. The Coalition needed to win only one additional seat to retain its majority. Leaving the Nationals to defend their 10 seats, the Liberals' initial strategy required the successful defence of 66 seats, plus flipping a Labor-held marginal such as Gilmore, Lyons or Lingiari. This was a defensive strategy, offering a very narrow but plausible path to victory along the lines of 2019. Unlike 2019, however, the published opinion polls were correct in showing the Coalition well behind Labor.

Table 6.1 Labor's path to victory?

Labor's path to victory required:			
Target		**Actual**	
1. Retain all currently held Labor seats			
Including target seats to defend: Gilmore (NSW), Lyons (Tas.)	69	Minus Labor seats lost: Fowler (NSW), Griffith (Qld)	67
2. Gain 15–17 Coalition seats			
Qld: Longman, Leichhardt, Brisbane, Flynn	4		0
Tas.: Bass, Braddon	2		0
NSW: Reid, Robertson, Bennelong	3		3
Vic.: Chisholm, Higgins, (Casey?)	2–3		2
SA: Boothby	1		1
WA: Swan, Pearce, Hasluck, (Tangney?)	3–4		4
Total	**84–86**		**77**

Source: Authors' estimates based on interview data and media reports.

The resource allocations that arose from these different strategies can be discerned in the data showing party spending on digital media (Figures 6.2 and 6.3). These data—made publicly available for the first time via the Meta Ad library—showed in real time on individual candidates' 'pages' how much each party was spending. For Labor, three of the four seats with the greatest spending (Brisbane, Boothby and Bennelong) were seats the party targeted to flip; another (Fowler) reflected the party's desperate efforts to save this safe seat from an Independent challenger. The essentially defensive strategy of the Liberals is revealed by the fact that all but three of their top-30 candidate spends were in House of Representatives seats they already held (the exceptions being Braddon, McEwen and Cowan). Further, 10 of the top-30 page spends were in the top 30 for both Labor and the Liberal Party/LNP. If we use this as a proxy for where the contest was hardest fought, we end up with Brisbane, Boothby, Bennelong, Pearce, Swan, Hasluck, Tangney, Cowan, McEwen and Flynn. The results in these seats were devastating for the Liberal Party and the LNP. Labor won all four of the West Australian seats; it won Bennelong and Boothby, retained McEwen and Cowan and lost to the Greens in Brisbane in a very close contest; of these 10 contests, the government only won Flynn. Indeed, of the 10 seats that changed hands from the government to Labor, the only two not in the top-30 spend by both parties were Chisholm and Higgins; both were in the top 30 for the Liberal/LNP but missed out (just) in the figures for Labor. It is also worth noting that positions 31 and 32 for candidate page spending for Labor were Bass and Reid and for the Liberals/LNP, Ryan and Curtin.

The Liberals and LNP spent more than double that of Labor according to the Meta Library's top-30 candidate spending pages. If we use this as a proxy for digital spending overall, this seems to counter campaign commentary that Labor was outspending the government in vast sums online. Of course, it may be true that if we include all pages—including leader and federal and State party pages—this gap is narrowed or Labor did spend more. But the government did deploy significant resources to its digital campaign in its defensive strategy.

Finally, the data reveal extraordinarily heavy spending in the Queensland Senate contest. In an underappreciated part of the narrative about the federal election, then Senator Amanda Stoker's candidate page showed the most spending of any page from the Liberal Party, LNP or Labor nationally between 19 April and election day. Relegated to third spot on the LNP's Senate ticket, Stoker's expenditure was approximately $129,000 during this period. The candidate pages for Labor senators Murray Watt and Anthony Chisholm also revealed significant spending, of approximately $30,000 each, during this period. This suggests parties placed extra significance on the Queensland Senate contest.

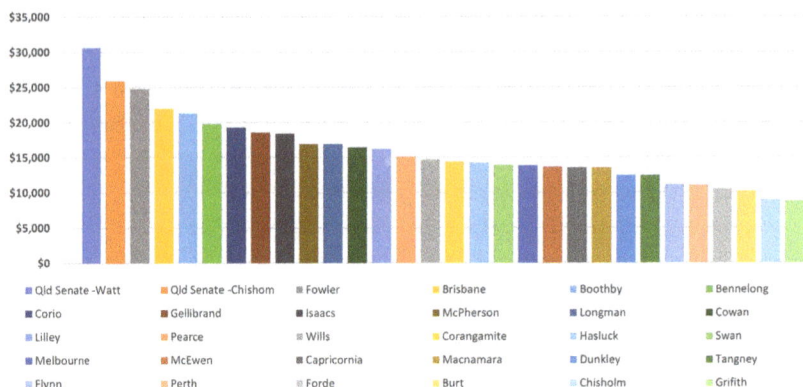

Figure 6.2 Top-30 Labor candidates' page spending on Facebook, 19 April – 22 May 2022

Sources: Meta Ad library; UQ Election Data Dashboard.

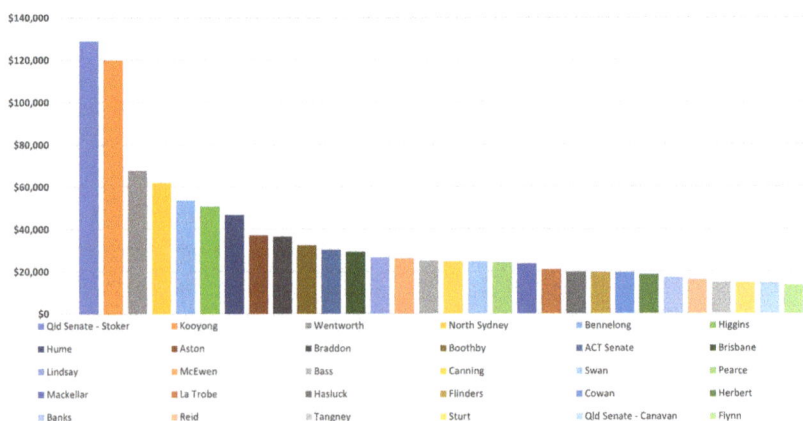

Figure 6.3 Top-30 Liberal and LNP candidates' page spending on Facebook, 19 April – 22 May 2022

Sources: Meta Ad library; UQ Election Data Dashboard.

These data deal only with advertising on Facebook. TikTok, which emerged as a significant new theatre of the election contest in 2022, is harder to assess. While strategies must be well researched, clearly developed and widely understood within the campaign, the proliferation of social media channels tests these boundaries and pushes campaign managers to empower parts of their assemblage to create content and messaging that is 'edgy'—beyond the reach of the formal campaign. The point is underlined by TikTok's reliance on 'organic' (user-created) content that may or may not follow the lead of the party's sponsored (paid) content on other channels (see Chapter 8, this volume). It is important to recognise that TikTok does not allow political advertising on its platform but does allow commentary. Questions remain about how coordinated the content evident on TikTok is with the broader campaign organisations.

A further demonstration of parties devoting resources to their target seats is provided in the leaders' itineraries. Leaders and senior frontbenchers are more likely to concentrate campaign visits on target seats than on unwinnable seats. Albanese campaigned predominantly in government-held marginal seats; his week of Covid-enforced isolation allowed Labor to showcase some of its other frontbench talent. Labor also broke with convention to launch Albanese's campaign in Perth and reinforced its pitch to West Australian voters through the appointment of a dedicated ad agency (Moss Group) to produce broadcast material for that State.

Morrison's itinerary was more compromised. He visited marginal Coalition seats in outer-suburban Queensland, western Sydney and Tasmania, but political and organisational problems presented significant constraints. In New South Wales, factional manoeuvring delayed preselection in several key seats (Grattan 2022). In Victoria, the hard lockdowns during the pandemic were perceived to have encouraged that State's division to campaign against the premier, Dan Andrews (Kolovos 2022). The West Australian division—decimated at the State election in 2021—was underresourced and some commentators perceived factional manoeuvrings there as hampering the campaign (Bennet 2022). All this made the Liberals' defensive task of sandbagging their marginal seats against a Labor tide much harder. Aggressive anti-China rhetoric by the Coalition alienated Chinese-Australian voters, undermining the Liberal vote in Chisholm, Reid, Bennelong, Tangney and North Sydney. Further, as the campaign progressed, the growing Teal assault on formerly safe Liberal seats in Sydney and Melbourne changed the arithmetic. 'Wedged' on climate change issues due to competition from Teals and Greens in inner-city seats in Sydney, Melbourne, Brisbane and Perth, the prime minister found himself unable to campaign alongside Liberal incumbents; Nationals leader Barnaby Joyce and senior Queenslander Peter Dutton were likewise unwelcome. Josh Frydenberg, who presented a more moderate face, was besieged in his own seat and unable to contribute to the national campaign. Liberals—seemingly accepting the inevitability of inner-city losses—now needed to win Labor-held seats like outer-metropolitan Hunter (NSW) and McEwen (Victoria).

In any event, the Liberals failed to win any Labor seats and, despite holding all their Queensland and Tasmanian seats against Labor challengers, were overwhelmed by the loss of 10 marginals in other States to Labor (plus, unexpectedly, two to the Greens in greater Brisbane), along with six safe seats to Teals. The Liberal Party and LNP lost 13 'inner-metropolitan' seats, as classified by the AEC (2022), and five 'outer-metropolitan', but none in provincial or rural areas. Labor swept Western Australia and made further inroads in Victoria and New South Wales. But thanks to unexpected losses in Fowler and Griffith, and with no gains in Queensland or Tasmania, Labor's majority failed to reach its target of the low eighties, ending with 77 seats.

Advertising messages: The leadership frame

Commercial television advertising remained the largest single campaign expense in 2022 for both major parties. The Teals declared after the election that 'TV advertising is dead' (Coper 2022); however, while it was logical, and cheaper, for Independent candidates to use digital media to target affluent inner-city professionals, for the major parties, broadcast advertising into metropolitan markets remained a cost-effective way of reaching the large numbers of voters in outer-suburban seats with generally low engagement in politics. Even so, advertisements are becoming ever shorter: 15-second ads—cheaper to put to air—were broadcast by both parties. Longer, TV-style ads were posted to YouTube and other platforms to attract smaller, elite audiences in the media and policy communities.

Plate 6.1 Still from 'Why I love Australia' advertisement
Source: Liberal Party of Australia.

Initially, the Liberal Party chose to focus on a presidential-style contest that contrasted Morrison, with his record of addressing key economic and social issues, against Albanese, who had never served in a senior ministry. The Liberals opened their advertising campaign with a documentary-style ad showing the prime minister working alone late at night in the office—a national flag and portrait of the Queen prominently displayed. His voiceover opens with an admission—'You always have setbacks, you always have imperfect information'—designed to neutralise criticism of his errors, before he asserts that 'things are tough', listing drought, floods, fires, the pandemic and war. 'We're dealing with a world that has never been more unstable since the time of the Second World War,' he says. This last statement is accompanied by a close-up photo of his wedding ring. The scene shifts to a Cabinet meeting as he claims credit for saving lives and jobs during the pandemic. The ad concludes with an anecdote, delivered by Morrison in interview style, in praise of high school students he met in Brisbane who wanted to start their own businesses: 'How good's that? That's why I love Australia.' The lengthy ad (it runs for 1 minute 40 seconds) was posted on YouTube immediately before Morrison announced the election date. It was intended as a scene-setter, in line with the strategic purpose of reminding voters of the government's achievements and to reveal—through a catch in his voice—the prime minister's private emotions. It was a classic incumbency-style advertisement, with the prime minister displaying the symbols of the nation, owning the responsibilities, failings and achievements of his record in office, and ultimately embodying love of country itself.

Yet while well constructed, the ad was inconsistent with the campaign the prime minister conducted. Morrison did not stay in his office in Canberra; rather, his campaign itinerary was all about generating performative images of him alongside the people—in factories and workplaces and on sporting fields, reinforcing for the evening TV news his theme of a low-unemployment economic recovery. These challenges manifested during the campaign in a lack of consistency in messaging, with difficulties in successfully framing what the campaign was about or about what it should be fought.

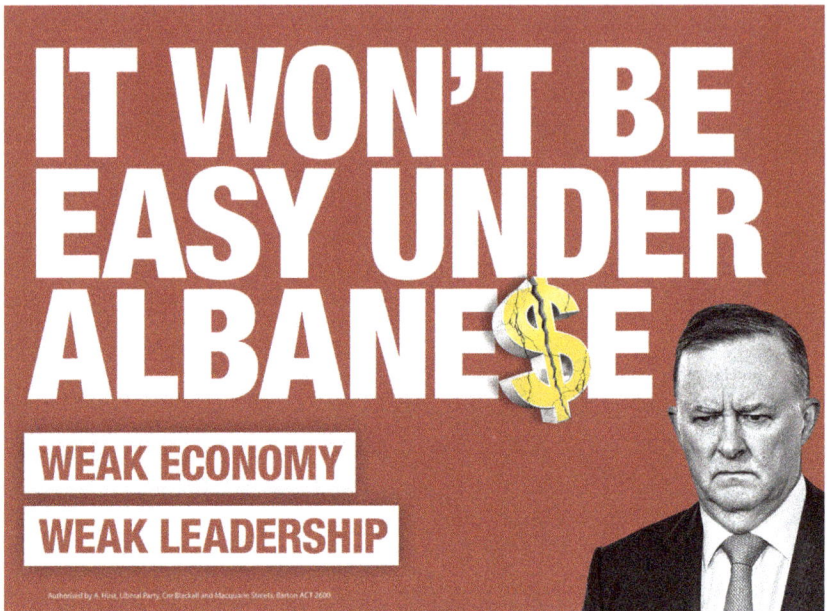

Plate 6.2 Still from 'It won't be easy under Albanese' YouTube advertisement

Source: Liberal Party of Australia.

More effective, and more assiduously pursued, were the Liberals' negative attacks on Albanese. The Liberals' task was to ensure that Albanese was never seen as a credible alternative prime minister; he was presented as inexperienced and untested in economic portfolios, a weathervane erratically changing directions on key policies in opposition and a dangerous risk to the economy if elected. Albanese's gaffes in the first week strongly empowered this narrative and were documented with relish in a series of Liberal ads posted to YouTube. The most effective vehicle for these charges—hard-hitting and annoyingly memorable—was an ad showing coins dropping into, and falling out of, a rusty broken bucket, with the mocking song: 'There's a hole in your budget, dear Labor, dear Labor.' The ad played to Labor's perceived weakness on economic management and—despite the government's pandemic-inspired fiscal generosity—budget deficits and the threatened flow-on hit to family budgets of increased taxes. And the tagline swung the critique back on to the individual: 'It won't be easy under Albanese' echoed the Liberals' 2019 smear of then Labor leader Bill Shorten as 'the Bill you can't afford'. By the final 10 days of the campaign, the 15-second ad constituted virtually the entire Liberal campaign effort.

Labor started its campaign in positive form, with a message centred on Albanese's argument for a 'better future'. In the ad, Albanese declares:

> Australians deserve a prime minister who shows up, who takes responsibility and who works with people. I'll work with business to invest in manufacturing—making more things here will create more secure jobs here. I'll help families get ahead, by making childcare cheaper, by reducing power bills and investing in fee-free TAFE. And I'll make it easier to see the doctor. It's my plan for a better future.

Apparently about policies, the ad in fact used those policies as vehicles to introduce and define an Opposition leader who was still unknown to many disengaged voters. The advertisement filled this information gap with propositions about Albanese having a set of practical plans to make life better for typical Australians. At the same time, the ad presented Albanese—his name and title prominently displayed—in a professional and contemporary office setting; with his neutral suit and new glasses, here was someone ready to lead the nation. Likewise, the opening sentence of the ad deftly contrasted Albanese's and Morrison's preparedness to work collaboratively and responsibly. This was an advertisement that reduced the electoral contest to one of pure personality. Labor insiders confirm that this was deeply researched, approved by the national campaign committee and supported by expensive national media purchases for the first week of the campaign; its impact was neutralised, however, as this coincided with Albanese's press conference gaffe on the unemployment rate.

Plate 6.3 Still from Labor's 'A better future' advertisement
Source: ALP.

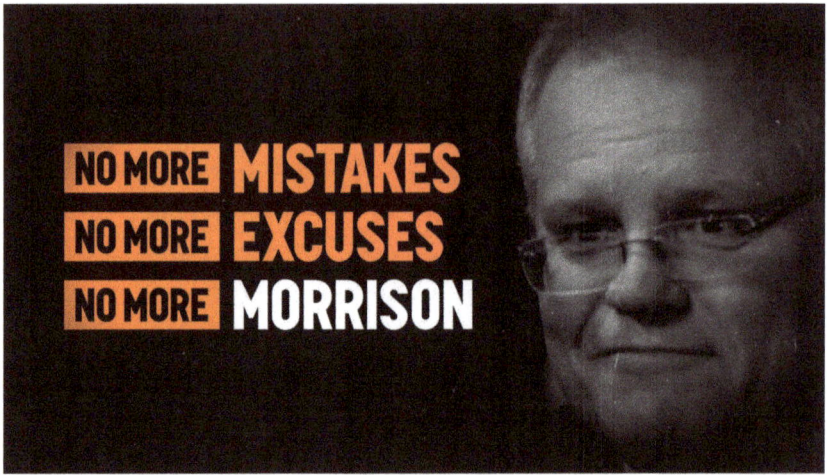

Plate 6.4 Still from Labor's 'No more Morrison' advertisement
Source: ALP.

Labor's negative advertising was informed by focus group research that, according to Erickson, showed voters were 'regularly referring to Morrison and the Liberals as "mishandling things", "making too many mistakes" and "stuffing things up"' (Erickson 2022). Labor's most expensive advertisement exploited and reinforced such sentiments by using images and words of Morrison himself. Versions featured Morrison on holiday in Hawai`i during the bushfire crisis and declaring 'I don't hold a hose'; trying to shake the hand of an exhausted volunteer firefighter and being rebuffed; or declaring the vaccine rollout was 'not a race, not a competition'. The voiceover is stark: 'No-one gets it right all the time. But Scott Morrison makes too many mistakes and too many excuses' and then, in Morrison's own words, 'That's not my job … That's not my job … That's not my job to do that'.

The ad ends with a black and white image of a slightly dazed-looking Morrison with the tagline: 'No More Mistakes. No More Excuses. No More Morrison.' Another version ends with the voiceover: 'Next time something goes wrong, do you trust him to make it right?' Then, as if on cue, Morrison says: 'That's not my job.'

By the end of the campaign, Labor believed it had successfully prosecuted the case against Morrison. The 'not my job' ad had stung the Liberals into a 'dirty tricks' response, claiming Morrison's words had been taken out of context. More tellingly, in a press conference at the end of the penultimate week of the campaign, Morrison confessed that he was 'a bit of a bulldozer' who would 'have to change' the way he operated (Murphy 2022). The confession handed Albanese an easy response ('A bulldozer wrecks things. A bulldozer knocks things over. I'm a builder'), and was later seemingly confirmed when Morrison, pretending to play soccer for the cameras, accidentally knocked over a child. Still, some voters sat on the fence, clearly unhappy with Morrison but not yet convinced about Albanese. To galvanise them into voting for change, Labor modified its 'Better future' ad to highlight the cost of *not* changing the government. In the final days of the campaign, Albanese reminded voters in the ad of what they would miss out on if Morrison was re-elected:

> The world has changed, and I don't want Australia to miss out on the opportunities that presents. I'll invest in renewables so we don't miss out on lower power prices and well-paid advanced industry jobs. I'll make more things here so we don't miss the chance to rebuild our manufacturing. Strengthening Medicare means Australians won't miss out on better health care. A Labor government means Australia won't miss out on a better future.

In a final twist in the campaign, the Liberal Party decided to mass send text messages to voters in marginal seats on election day about the interception of asylum-seeker boats in Australian waters. The text message read: 'BREAKING: Australian Border Force has intercepted an illegal boat trying to reach Australia. Keep our borders secure by voting Liberal today. https://vote.liberal.org.au' (Worthington and Bogle 2022).

Conclusion

The campaign of 2022 was a contest of rival strategies about leadership. Leaders' individual personalities—their character, values and experience—have rarely been more prominent than in 2022. Both leaders were flawed and these flaws became central to the strategies of both parties as they sought to neutralise their own weaknesses while vigorously attacking those of their opponent. The Liberal Party projected an inconsistent story about Prime Minister Morrison, from serious, hardworking incumbent to participant in community activities to a 'bulldozer'. Labor meanwhile poured a relentless and effective torrent of criticism on to Morrison for his errors and excuses, while successfully presenting the hitherto little-known Albanese as suitably qualified to step up to the prime ministership.

The strategies of the major parties provided a contrast—offensive versus defensive—and the context of an election fought during a global pandemic may have been unusual, but their strategies also followed the orthodoxy of Australian election campaigns. The campaigns were highly personalised, they drew on classic incumbent–challenger narratives and both presented their primary opponents as a danger to Australia's future. Given the ongoing fragmentation of the Australian political landscape, a significant question is whether this orthodoxy will continue to provide Australian voters sufficient motivation to support the major parties at a level where they can continue to expect to govern alone. The major parties are well aware of the problems they confront, but whether they are able or willing to respond to these broader forces in Australian politics remains to be seen.

References

Australian Electoral Commission (AEC). 2022. 'Demographic ratings'. *Political Party Name Abbreviations & Codes, Demographic Ratings and Seat Status*. Canberra: AEC. Available from: www.aec.gov.au/Electorates/party-codes.htm.

Bennet, Michael. 2022. 'The clan is still in full control: Why the Liberals lost WA'. *Australian Financial Review*, 6 June. Available from: www.afr.com/politics/the-clan-is-still-in-full-control-why-the-liberals-lost-wa-20220603-p5aqzh.

Bennister, Mark. 2007. 'Tony Blair and John Howard: Comparative predominance and institution stretch in the UK and Australia'. *British Journal of Politics and International Relations* 9: 327–45. doi.org/10.1111/j.1467-856x.2007.00292.x.

Bennister, Mark. 2008. 'Blair and Howard: Predominant prime ministers compared'. *Parliamentary Affairs* 61: 334–55. doi.org/10.1093/pa/gsm065.

Bennister, Mark. 2012. *Prime Ministers in Power: Political Leadership in Britain and Australia*. Basingstoke, UK: Palgrave Macmillan. doi.org/10.1057/978023 0378445.

Bittner, Amanda. 2011. *Platform or Personality? The Role of Party Leaders in Elections*. Oxford, UK: Oxford University Press. doi.org/10.1093/acprof:oso/9780199595365.003.0006.

Bittner, Amanda. 2021. 'The personalization of politics in Anglo-American democracies'. *Frontiers in Political Science* 3: 660607. doi.org/10.3389/fpos.2021.660607.

Campus, Donatella. 2010. 'Review of The Personalization of Politics: A Study of Parliamentary Democracies, by Lauri Karvonen'. *Political Communication* 27(4): 476–78. doi.org/10.1080/10584609.2010.517103.

Coorey, Phillip. 2022. 'Scott Morrison becomes a punching bag for Labor and Liberals alike'. *Australian Financial Review*, 7 April. Available from: www.afr.com/politics/federal/scott-morrison-becomes-a-punching-bag-for-labor-and-liberals-alike-20220407-p5abk3.

Coper, Ed. 2022. 'Secrets from the teals' digital war room: We created a direct line to voters and now TV political ads are dead'. *Sydney Morning Herald*, 6 June. Available from: www.smh.com.au/national/secrets-from-the-teals-digital-war-room-we-created-a-direct-line-to-voters-and-now-tv-political-ads-are-dead-2022 0605-p5ar5j.html.

Crossman, Richard. 1963. 'Introduction'. *The English Constitution*, 1–57. London: Fontana.

Davies, Anne. 2021. 'The 24-hour meme machine: What the US election can teach Australia about digital campaigning'. *The Guardian*, [Australia], 6 January. Available from: www.theguardian.com/australia-news/2021/jan/06/the-24-hour-meme-machine-what-the-us-election-can-teach-australia-about-digital-campaigning.

Dowding, Keith. 2012. 'The prime ministerialisation of the British Prime Minister'. *Parliamentary Affairs* 66(3): 617–35. doi.org/10.1093/pa/gss007.

Emerson, Craig and Jay Weatherill. 2019. *Review of Labor's 2019 Federal Election Campaign*. Canberra: Australian Labor Party. Available from: alp.org.au/media/2043/alp-campaign-review-2019.pdf.

Erickson, Paul. 2022. Address to the National Press Club, Canberra, 15 June. Personal communication.

Grattan, Michelle. 2022. 'The Liberals have a preselection mess in NSW—and it tells us something about Scott Morrison'. *ABC News*, 4 February. [First published on *The Conversation*]. Available from: www.abc.net.au/news/2022-02-04/liberals-election-scott-morrison-factional-infighting/100803848.

Katz, Richard and Peter Mair. 1993. 'The evolution of party organisations in Europe: The three faces of party organisation'. *American Review of Politics* 14(4): 593–617. doi.org/10.15763/issn.2374-7781.1993.14.0.593-617.

Kefford, Glenn. 2021. *Political Parties and Campaigning in Australia: Data, Digital and Field*. Basingstoke, UK: Palgrave Macmillan. doi.org/10.1007/978-3-030-68234-7.

Kelly, Sean. 2021. *The Game: A Portrait of Scott Morrison*. Melbourne: Black Inc.

Kolovos, Benita. 2022. 'Election losing machine: Ridiculed Victorian Liberal Party to keep targeting Dan Andrews'. *The Guardian*, [Australia], 24 May. Available from: www.theguardian.com/australia-news/2022/may/24/liberals-remain-steadfast-over-anti-andrews-strategy-in-victoria.

Mackintosh, J.P. 1968. *The British Cabinet*. London: Stevens.

McAllister, Ian. 2007. 'The personalization of politics'. In *The Oxford Handbook of Political Behavior*, edited by R. Dalton and H.-D. Klingemann, 571–88. Oxford, UK: Oxford University Press. doi.org/10.1093/oxfordhb/9780199270125.003.0030.

Mills, Stephen. 2014. *The Professionals*. Melbourne: Black Inc.

Murphy, Katharine. 2022. 'Even Scott Morrison is trying to distance himself from Scott Morrison now'. *The Guardian*, [Australia], 13 May. Available from: www.theguardian.com/australia-news/2022/may/13/even-scott-morrison-is-trying-to-distance-himself-from-scott-morrison-now.

Nielsen, Rasmus Kleis. 2011. 'Mundane internet tools, mobilizing practices, and the coproduction of citizenship in political campaigns'. *New Media & Society* 13: 755–71. doi.org/10.1177/1461444810380863.

Nielsen, Rasmus Kleis. 2012. *Ground Wars: Personalised Communication in Political Campaigns*. Princeton, NJ: Princeton University Press. doi.org/10.1515/97814 00840441.

Patrick, Aaron. 2022. 'Coalition ad agency has "dozens of ads" ready to go'. *Australian Financial Review*, 1 April. Available from: www.afr.com/politics/federal/coalition-ad-agency-has-dozens-of-ads-ready-to-go-20220330-p5a9ev.

Poguntke, Thomas. 2000. 'The presidentialization of parliamentary democracies: A contradiction in terms?'. Paper presented at the European Consortium for Political Research workshop The Presidentialization of Parliamentary Democracies?, Copenhagen, 14–19 April.

Poguntke, Thomas and Paul Webb. 2005. *The Presidentialization of Politics: A Comparative Study of Modern Democracies*. New York, NY: Oxford University Press. doi.org/10.1093/0199252017.001.0001.

Rahat, G. and T. Sheafer. 2007. 'The personalization(s) of politics: Israel, 1949–2003'. *Political Communication* 24(1): 65–80. doi.org/10.1080/10584600601128739.

Walter, James and Paul Strangio. 2007. *No, Prime Minister: Reclaiming Politics from Leaders*. Sydney: UNSW Press.

Worthington, Elise and Ariel Bogle. 2022. 'Liberal Party text alert warns voters about illegal boat interception'. *ABC News*, 21 May. Available from: www.abc.net.au/news/2022-05-21/liberal-text-alert-warns-of-illegal-boat-interception/101087650.

7

Media coverage of the campaign and the electorate's responses

Andrea Carson and Simon Jackman

Mainstream news coverage of the 2022 federal election campaign was widely criticised as pedestrian, lacking innovation and insight, light on substance and overly reliant on standard tropes of election coverage: from the vacuity of live coverage of Scott Morrison's journey to Yarralumla to request a dissolution of parliament to the televised debates, the campaign 'launches', the daily briefings, appearances and stunts by leaders and the resulting 'gotchas' and gaffes.

Anthony Albanese's failure to accurately recall the unemployment rate on the first day of the campaign encouraged journalists to seek 'gotcha' moments. Greens leader Adam Bandt told a journalist to 'Google it, mate' when asked a similar 'quiz'-like question. Angus and Bruns (2022) found a spike in the prevalence of the hashtag '#ThisIsNotJournalism' on Twitter and posts complaining about 'partisan bias, misrepresentation, shallow coverage, and absence of policy discussion' in the mainstream media. Prominent academic journalists Margaret Simons (2022) and Denis Muller (2022) wrote separate pieces questioning the quality of the election coverage, with Muller describing TV nightly election news as 'the most juvenile and uninformative in 50 years'. The night before election day, Albanese criticised mainstream media reporters: 'Some of the nonsense that's gone on from some journalists, thinking that the campaign was about them and gotcha moments, is one of the things that puts people off politics' (Sales 2022).

Likewise, Western Australian premier Mark McGowan accused the travelling press pack of 'bullying' Albanese and reporting 'lies' (Butler 2022).

These criticisms seem to go beyond the usual complaints from politicians about unfair media treatment or scholars bemoaning a dearth of substance in campaign coverage. We consider the validity of these criticisms by examining almost the *entirety* of media output over the course of the 2022 campaign, rigorously tracking the mix of topics presented in campaign coverage.

We do so by examining the front pages of the nation's leading print media, assessing the prevalence of election coverage, topics and tone. But we also employ a relatively new data source and methodology by analysing a corpus of *all* Facebook posts published by almost every Australian media organisation active on Facebook during the campaign (roughly 90,000 posts by more than 200 outlets). We contrast the prominence of election news and the topic mix in this online presentation of news with that of newspapers' front pages. We treat counts of user interactions with Facebook posts as proxy measures of mass interest and engagement with the posts' topic. Given the large size of Australia's Facebook user base, these proxies inform assessments about which elements of the media's presentation of the campaign resounded with the electorate and which did not, contrasting interaction counts relative to the media's *supply* of topics to the electorate.

To foreshadow one of our most important findings: 'hip-pocket' issues— led by housing affordability—were the single largest substantive focus of the media's election coverage, on front pages (Figure 7.2), in the media's promotion of content on Facebook and in user interactions (Figure 7.5), accounting for a massive one-third of the media's election-relevant posts. Nonetheless, Facebook users disproportionately engaged with content centred on individuals: the leaders, Independent candidates and the Katherine Deves/transgender athletes issue (Figure 7.9).

Politics, campaigns and the media: Australian exceptionalism

Unusually trenchant criticism of the media's coverage of the 2022 campaign is a key focus of our analysis. But we stress that the media's performance during an election campaign takes on added significance when we pause to consider the following elements of the Australian political and media landscape:

- First, the policy detail provided by Australian parties is typically thinner than in other countries (see Chapter 9, this volume) and is often released during the campaign itself, with news media the dominant vehicle of dissemination.

- Second, while less politically engaged citizens generally acquire information about politics and policy through passive media exposure rather than active searching, Australia's regime of compulsory voter turnout guarantees that this segment of the citizenry is a large proportion of the electorate.

- Third, Australian media ownership is highly concentrated. Ahead of the 2022 election, the combined audience of Australia's two major news companies, Nine Entertainment Co. (formerly Fairfax Media) and News Corp, was estimated to be 37.3 million monthly average reads. Moreover, eight of their mastheads featured in Australia's top 10 print and digital news brands (Roy Morgan 2022)—a dominance we confirm in our analysis of media presence on Facebook (see Table 7.1).

It should also be noted that Australian newspapers collectively hire more professional journalists than other media and their election reporting often informs television and radio coverage, making it a useful starting point for analysing mainstream reporting.

Mainstream media coverage

Newspaper front pages reveal editors' beliefs about which stories will draw public attention. These stories are replicated online and promoted through social media channels. This means that tracking page-one print stories provides an insight into the mainstream media's overall logic of what is considered 'newsworthy'. In other words, the newspaper front pages highlight the election issues to which Australia's major news outlets suggest their digital and print readers should pay attention. Whether they do or not is a separate matter, which we assess in later sections of this chapter.

Using the same method that we used in 2016 and 2019, we calculate how many front pages had at least one election story and the topic of the main story. We assess whether the story was positive, neutral or negative in the coverage of its subject. We find similar patterns to past years. Of 469 front pages available over the 41-day campaign,[1] 68 per cent carried an election story. In 2019, it was 69 per cent over the 37-day campaign.

In 2022, front-page election coverage increased during the five weeks, with a sharp rise when early voting opened on 9 May. However, coverage was not evenly spread across the nation's daily newspapers. The east coast mastheads and the country's two national papers, *The Australian* and the *Australian Financial Review*, recorded the most front-page election news stories. In contrast, the Northern Territory's *NT News* largely ignored the campaign on its front pages (see Figure 7.1).

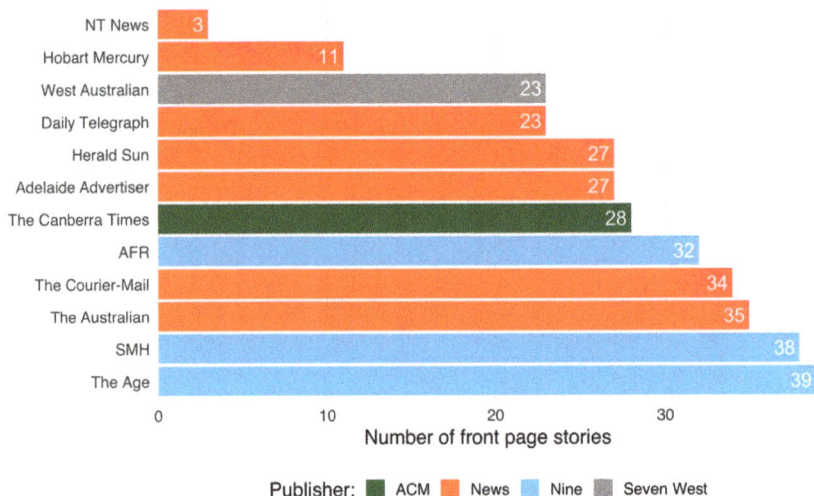

Figure 7.1 Front-page stories with election-relevant content, by masthead and publisher
Source: Data collected and analysed by the authors.

---

1   Some newspapers did not publish editions on the Easter or Anzac Day public holidays.

As in recent elections, the issues that attracted the most front-page coverage were offerings with polling commissioned by the media outlets themselves. Issues broadly related to the economy were far and away the most prominent page-one stories during the campaign and polls typically found the Coalition had an 'issue ownership' advantage in this domain (Konstantinidis 2008). Less prominently, national security also attracted considerable front-page attention—another domain in which the Coalition has historically enjoyed an issue-ownership advantage.

But in both these cases, the news over the course of the campaign— and leading up to it—was not favourable for the incumbent Coalition Government. Inflation, housing affordability and lacklustre wage growth were the major economic stories of the campaign. In response to inflationary pressure, the Reserve Bank of Australia (RBA) raised its benchmark interest rate on 3 May. This sounded an ominous portent: the last time the RBA had raised rates during a federal election campaign was when the Howard Government was defeated in 2007.

Likewise, the announcement of a security agreement between Solomon Islands and China was highly unwelcome; the decision had been a long time in the making, but the announcement mid campaign all but neutralised a traditional domain of political strength for the Coalition on national security—one that many expected would figure prominently in the Coalition's case for re-election.

Other prominent front-page stories featured reports on opinion polls, which consistently placed Labor ahead of the Coalition. Towards the end of the six-week campaign, stories appeared about the rise of the number of Independent candidates, particularly the subset referred to as the Teals, and speculation about their likely success.

Meanwhile, the Nine-owned mastheads *The Age* (Melbourne) and *Sydney Morning Herald* gave significant front-page coverage to Labor's promise to establish an integrity commission to stamp out corruption in politics, which was a promise Scott Morrison had turned his back on days before the campaign began (see Figure 7.2). The prominence of these stories could be considered setbacks for the Coalition.

Offsetting this coverage were numerous stories in News Corp mastheads reporting on criticisms of Opposition leader Anthony Albanese's competence. Examples included headlines in Brisbane's *The Courier-Mail* such as 'Amateur Albo' (16 April), the Sydney *Daily Telegraph*'s 'It's not so

Albaneasy' (12 April) and the Melbourne *Herald Sun*'s 'Don't count on me' (12 April). The last featured a large unflattering picture of Albanese with his tongue sticking out, photographed when he could not recall the nation's unemployment rate when under the pressure of the media spotlight. This story dominated the first week of the campaign coverage in the mainstream media and, as we show below, in the media's presentation of its content to its online audiences.

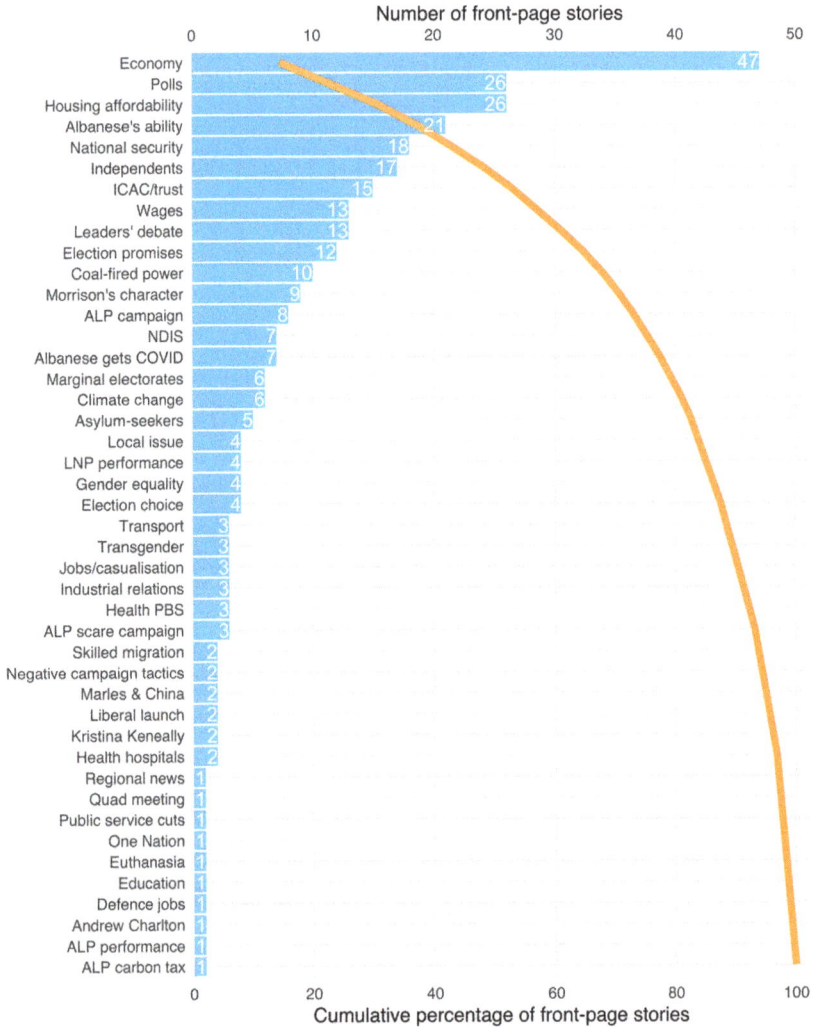

Figure 7.2 Topic prevalence in front-page newspaper stories with election content

Source: Data collected and analysed by the authors.

Some issues that media monitors found to have reached vast online audiences extending beyond newspapers and news coverage on Facebook were somewhat ignored in front-page legacy coverage. As an election issue, 'women/gender equality' was a prominent example of this divergence. This topic was ranked in the top four on social media platforms but failed to enter the top 10 issues covered in traditional media. The Covid-19 pandemic was also discussed much more prominently on social media compared with its conspicuous absence from the front pages of the mainstream press (McLintock 2022).

Partisan sentiment

As in previous campaigns, most front-page political stories were neutral in tone, but those conveying a negative overall sentiment tended to be directed at Labor. Many more negative stories about Labor were published in the News Corp papers (for example, *The Australian*, the *Daily Telegraph* and *The Courier-Mail*, comprising 38 stories) than in the Nine papers (10 stories), as displayed in Figure 7.3.

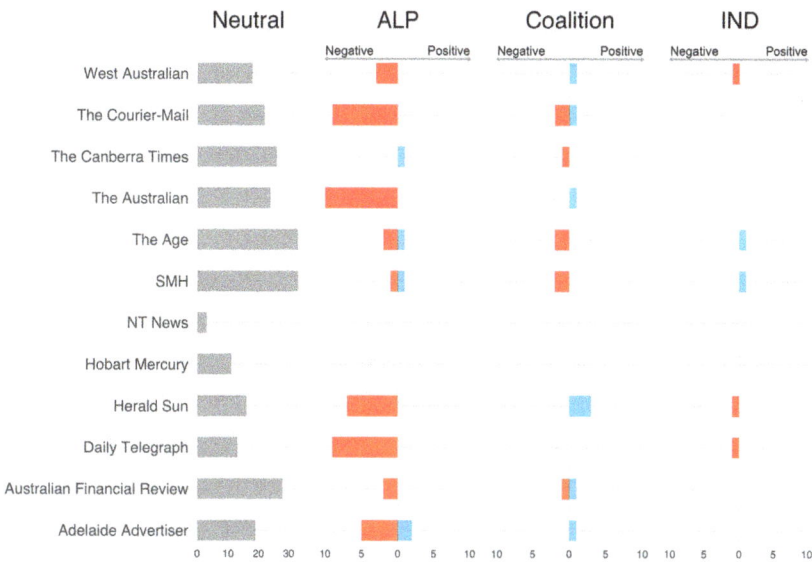

Figure 7.3 Sentiment of 320 front-page stories with election content, classified as neutral, positive or negative with respect to the indicated political parties, by masthead

Note: Bars indicate counts of stories.

Source: Data collected and analysed by authors.

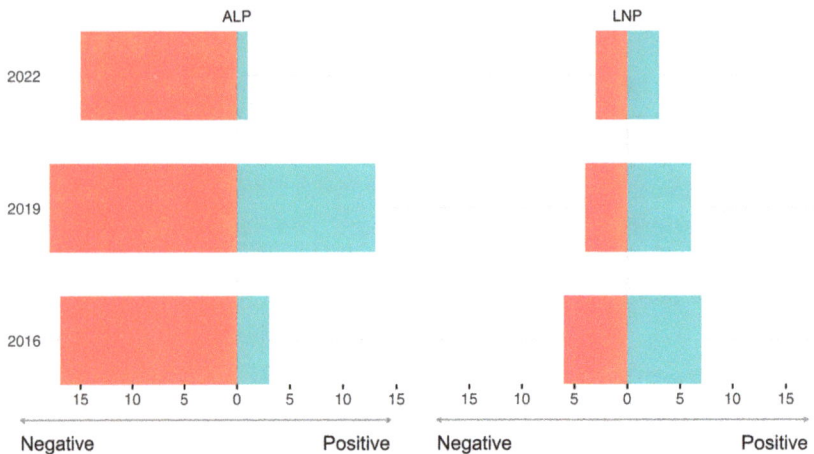

Figure 7.4 Sentiment of Monday to Saturday front-page election stories, towards the ALP and the Coalition, in the 2016, 2019 and 2022 election campaigns

Note: Bar lengths correspond to percentages of stories.

Source: Data collected and analysed by the authors.

This pattern is largely consistent with analyses of past federal election campaigns. In 2022, negative Labor stories constituted 15 per cent of front-page stories compared with 18 per cent in 2019 and 17 per cent in 2016. Interestingly, positive coverage of the Coalition was less apparent on the front pages of News Corp mastheads, making up only 3 per cent of stories in 2022 compared with 6 per cent in 2019 and 7 per cent in 2016 when the Coalition was victorious (see Figure 7.4).

Scare campaigns in mainstream media

Throughout the course of the campaign, two notable scare campaigns containing fake news (disinformation) emerged—one from each of the major parties.

The Coalition claimed that Labor, if elected, would introduce a new carbon tax by stealth—sometimes referred to as a 'sneaky carbon tax'. Prominent Liberal and Nationals politicians, including Senator Matt Canavan and Treasurer Josh Frydenberg, paid for dozens of ads on Facebook promoting the disinformation during the campaign. Midway through the campaign, Whitehaven coalmining chief Paul Flynn was quoted introducing the scare campaign into the mainstream media by accusing Labor of wanting to introduce a carbon tax by 'stealth'. Stories reporting Flynn's remarks ran on the front pages of *The Australian*, *The Age* and the *Sydney Morning Herald* on 27 April. The *West Australian* picked up the story on its front page two weeks later (Scarr 2022).

On the other side of politics, various State Labor branches, politicians and candidates alleged that the Coalition would introduce a cashless debit or welfare card aimed at pensioners that would limit their spending choices. Inspection of the Facebook Ad Library reveals that Labor or affiliated entities ran more than 100 ads with this message on Facebook. Some featured elderly narrators urging pensioners not to vote for Scott Morrison because, if re-elected, he would foist the cashless debit card on them.[2] This campaign also contained fake news and was called out on the front pages of News Corp's tabloid newspapers on four occasions in the second week of the campaign. Unlike the Liberal's carbon tax falsehoods, these press stories clearly labelled Labor's position as a 'lie' (Killoran 2022).

The online presentation of news during the campaign

Without the constraints of broadcast time or space on the printed page, there was a massive quantity of online campaign news in 2022. The media monitoring company Streem (McLintock 2022) calculated that online outlets accounted for 44.5 per cent of total federal election coverage, compared with television (21.3 per cent), radio (22.2 per cent) and print (12.1 per cent).

In addition to hosting their own websites, virtually every media organisation in Australia uses Facebook and other social media channels to promote their content. Further, the CrowdTangle platform makes it possible to record Facebook posts by media organisation and the number of interactions with each post (likes, shares and other reactions). The enormous reach of Facebook—perhaps as large as 70 per cent of the Australian population aged 13 and older (Kemp 2022)—makes analysis of user interactions with content a reasonable proxy for tracking dynamics in issue salience over the campaign.

---

2   Retrievable from the Meta Ad Library, available from: www.facebook.com/ads/library/?id= 736137650873992.

Facebook posts by media organisations

We used the CrowdTangle platform to collect 98,388 posts from 242 media organisations posted from the time the election was called on Sunday, 10 April 2022 until the close of polls at 6 pm AEST on 21 May 2022. At the time of our data collection shortly after the election, there were 34,898,854 user interactions associated with these posts; note, too, that CrowdTangle provides access to interaction counts per post, not to any data about individuals making the interactions.

Our corpus of media Facebook posts is not restricted to election-related news. This is because we: 1) did not wish to *a priori* constrain what content should count as election related or not; and 2) assessed the prominence of election-related content in the total corpus and in user interactions.

The set of media organisations in our corpus is large, spanning broadcast, print and online, metropolitan, regional and rural, large and small. Table 7.1 presents statistics on 30 of the media outlets contributing to our corpus, after ordering media organisations by total interactions, showing the top 10 highest and 10 random observations from the middle and lower terciles of media organisations ordered by total interactions.

Table 7.1 Details of 30 of 242 media entities in corpus of Facebook posts, grouped by total number of user interactions over the 2022 election campaign

Publisher	Posts	Subscribers	Interactions Total	Per post (median)	Per 1,000 subs (per post, median)
Top 10 by total interactions					
news.com.au	2,359	2,356,732	5,977,219	321	0.14
Sky News Australia	7,627	1,221,534	2,964,189	167	0.14
ABC News	2,746	4,561,406	2,002,949	296	0.06
9 News	1,256	2,945,316	1,656,813	562	0.19
7NEWS Australia	2,115	2,441,651	1,324,896	293	0.12
7NEWS Sydney	2,774	2,445,236	1,055,390	132	0.05
Sydney Morning Herald	2,008	1,230,593	1,043,701	240	0.20
9 News Melbourne	1,187	1,037,112	835,109	196	0.19
7NEWS Melbourne	2,010	1,857,843	806,824	171	0.09
The Courier-Mail	1,119	620,473	705,275	302	0.49

Publisher	Posts	Subscribers	Interactions		
			Total	Per post (median)	Per 1,000 subs (per post, median)
Sample of 10, middle tercile, by total interactions					
7NEWS Mackay	642	83,700	32,278	13	0.15
The Morning Bulletin	488	40,987	26,615	18	0.44
ABC Illawarra	166	68,746	25,339	68	0.98
Bendigo Advertiser	608	61,098	18,682	9	0.15
South Western Times	353	33,301	13,395	10	0.30
ABC South East NSW	103	59,749	10,781	48	0.80
Warwick Daily News	106	21,518	9,005	38	1.77
Wangaratta Chronicle	211	13,499	5,156	8	0.59
Maitland Mercury	254	48,623	4,811	12	0.25
Pilbara News	80	42,659	3,993	28	0.66
Sample of 10, lowest tercile, by total interactions					
Condobolin Argus	193	8,025	3,837	5	0.62
Blacktown Advocate	114	42,409	3,615	8	0.19
The Dubbo News	114	12,142	2,775	10	0.78
Merimbula News Weekly	64	17,611	2,393	30	1.73
Parkes Champion-Post	36	12,504	1,770	34	2.68
North West Telegraph	39	11,585	1,537	14	1.21
The Murray Valley Standard	46	16,271	1,211	16	1.01
Macleay Argus	65	11,596	1,136	7	0.60
The Ararat Advertiser	95	11,055	1,064	7	0.63
Southern Highlands Express	8	1,020	63	6	5.89

Just two print titles appear in the top 10 news media entities, the *Sydney Morning Herald* (Nine Entertainment) and Brisbane's *The Courier-Mail* (News Corp). The top 10 Facebook news media accounts by user interactions include three Seven West outlets, three News Corp outlets, three Nine Entertainment outlets and *ABC News*. The 18,372,365 interactions with these 10 accounts make up 53 per cent of all interactions with the media's campaign-period Facebook posts. Two News Corp–owned outlets, *news. com.au* and *Sky News*, sit at the top of this list, recording almost 9 million user interactions or more than one-quarter of all interactions. These counts of posts and interactions are not restricted to political stories but nonetheless reveal that the concentration of ownership and audience share in Australian news media is not restricted to print or broadcast.

The more Facebook posts made by a media organisation and the more subscribers to the Facebook account, the more interactions we should expect with the content of that media organisation. To help adjust for this 'volume' or 'supply'–driven feature of interaction counts, we also compute interactions per post normalised by the subscriber count for a given Facebook account, which are reported in the rightmost column of Table 7.1. This normalised metric plays an important role in our analysis below (see Figure 7.9). More localised or parochial media outlets perform well on this metric (for example, Brisbane's *The Courier-Mail*) or media serving regional or rural centres (for example, the *Parkes Champion-Post*, the *Merimbula News Weekly* or the *Warwick Daily News*)—often driven by locally focused, non-election content.

Classifying content into topics

We used machine-learning methods (Grootendorst 2022) to assign Facebook posts to topics. Our approach is iterative and initially agnostic with respect to the type and number of topics. Initial passes through the data reveal the demarcation between an election-relevant topic (ERT) and others. We then impose additional structure on the methods to better distinguish ERTs and to confidently assign posts to an ERT.

This analysis resulted in Facebook posts allocated to 22 mutually exclusive and exhaustive topics, 15 of them ERTs. In Figure 7.5, we report the prevalence of topics and interactions by topic.

A broad 'miscellaneous' topic is the single largest topic, ranging from lifestyle, pets, animals and shopping to Elon Musk's proposed takeover of Twitter. This category includes some political content insufficiently prevalent to constitute an ERT. Celebrity and entertainment news, sport and crime follow in both prevalence and user interactions. We should not forget that even during an election campaign, Facebook posts featuring trees with water gushing from their trunks (882,000 interactions), a gorilla's sixty-fifth birthday (235,000 interactions), sheep, dogs, babies, chickens and combinations thereof generate by orders of magnitude many more interactions on Facebook than election news.

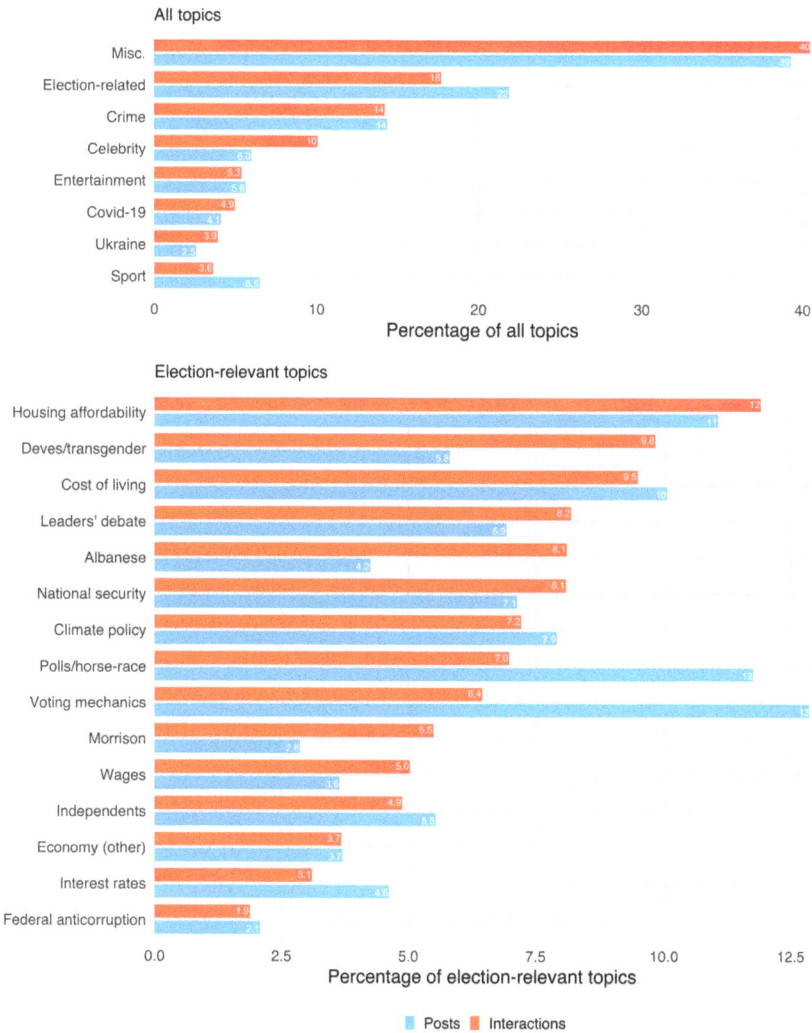

Figure 7.5 Share of Facebook posts and interactions, by topic, by media organisation during the 2022 Australian federal election

Note: Topics are separated into election-relevant topics (ERTs) and others and are sorted by their share of interactions.

Source: Data collected and analysed by the authors.

Nor should the viral character of popular Facebook posts be underestimated. The top 50 posts by user interactions accounted for 5.25 million or 15 per cent of all user interactions with almost 100,000 media Facebook posts; none was related to the election.

Even during an election campaign that resulted in a change of government, ERTs accounted for just 21.8 per cent of Facebook posts by media organisations during the campaign and 17.7 per cent of interactions (see Figure 7.5). This is a striking finding; generally, election news cannot compete for audience attention with more general non–election-related news items.

Hip-pocket issues

Among the 15 ERTs, housing affordability generated the most Facebook posts both by media organisations and by user interactions, accounting for 2.1 per cent of all posts (but 11 per cent of ERT posts) and 2.4 per cent of all user interactions (but 12 per cent of ERT posts), respectively. Other 'hip-pocket' issues also resonated strongly in terms of the supply of both content and user interactions. For example, posts about cost-of-living pressures generated 9.5 per cent of interactions with ERT posts, while posts promoting stories about wages and interest rates accounted for another 8.2 per cent of ERT posts and 8.1 per cent of interactions with ERT posts. The 'other' economic category picked up policy announcements or economic news such as the release of unemployment statistics, Labor's plans for reforming JobSeeker and a tax on multinational corporations, and the release of policy costings late in the campaign. Altogether, these accounted for another 0.8 per cent of Facebook posts by media organisations.

In total, economic matters accounted for one-third of Facebook posts on ERTs by media organisations during the campaign and one-third of interactions with ERT posts.

Election mechanics and the horserace

Media organisations also promoted stories about the election itself—what we dub the 'mechanics' of the election (the calling of the election, the close of rolls, the opening of early voting, how to find polling places and so on)—or 'horserace' stories, often relying on polls commissioned by media organisations, the likely role of preferences, seats 'in play' and 'pathways to victory'. These two topic areas are typically devoid of policy content, but account for 25 per cent of ERT posts. Despite this level of 'supply', Facebook users did not interact with these stories proportionately. Interactions with posts on election mechanics or 'horserace' stories accounted for a much smaller share of interactions with ERT posts—just 13.4 per cent.

Transgender athletes

Katherine Deves stood as the Liberal Party's candidate in Warringah after being hand-picked by Morrison. In the opening week of the campaign, Deves's signature issue—excluding transgender women from women's sports—was propelled into the campaign after Morrison said the issue was 'important' and that he shared Deves's views (see Chapter 5, this volume). Over the course of the campaign, Facebook posts by media organisations on this issue accounted for 5.8 per cent of all election-related posts. These posts generated a disproportionate number of interactions: 9.8 per cent of all interactions with posts on election topics.

Bulldozers, gaffes and debates: The leaders

Albanese's stumble on the first official day of the campaign—his inability to recall the unemployment rate—was the biggest story of the campaign's first week. But set against the totality of the flow of news over the campaign, posts about Albanese's personal strengths and foibles amounted to only 4.2 per cent of ERT posts by media. Nonetheless, Facebook users interacted enthusiastically with this content; posts centred on Albanese accounted for 8.1 per cent of interactions with media ERT posts.

A similar story holds for Morrison. Posts centred on Morrison became more prevalent towards the end of the campaign (as we detail below; see Figure 7.7). As is the case with Facebook stories about Albanese, Facebook users interacted with content about Morrison at almost twice the rate of the content's prevalence (5.5 per cent of all interactions with media ERT posts versus 2.8 per cent of posts).

Leaders' debates have become the key spectacles of recent election campaigns. The 2022 debates were no exception. While the debate hosted on Sky News was in 'town hall' format, the debates hosted by Nine and Seven were promoted aggressively as dramatic contests, with Morrison and Albanese to 'face off' in a 'showdown', with audiences invited to opine on 'who won'. The debates clearly disproportionately engaged Facebook users; interactions with Facebook posts by media about the debates accounted for 8.2 per cent of all interactions with media ERT posts.

Issue ownership and attention: National security contrasted with climate policy

Heading into the election campaign, national security was thought to be a strong issue for the Coalition. Early in the campaign, however, the news that Solomon Islands and China were announcing a security pact was seized on by Labor as the 'worst Australian foreign policy blunder in the Pacific since the end of World War II' (Wong 2022). The surge of media attention on this issue—plus a Chinese warship sighted close to the West Australian coast late in the campaign—resulted in national security accounting for 7.1 per cent of the media's ERT posts during the campaign.

Climate policy was slightly more prominent than national security during the campaign (7.9 per cent of media ERT posts). Its prevalence was less reactive to, say, international events or the release of economic statistics that drive salience for other topics. That said, in aggregate, Facebook users were less likely to interact with content about climate change than with national security; we stress that this finding warrants revision once we account for the volume of supply sources of posts below (see Figure 7.9).

The number, prominence and success of Independent candidacies were other key defining features of the 2022 election. That said, there were more Facebook posts from media organisations on the transgender athletes issue (5.8 per cent) than the emergence of the Community Independents (5.5 per cent) and twice the user interactions (9.8 per cent versus 4.9 per cent); but again, adjustments for the supply and source of Facebook posts on climate policy reveal it to be the most engaging substantive topic of the election campaign.

The topics less travelled

The salience of a federal anti-corruption commission lagged well behind other issues on Facebook. This topic was the least prevalent of the 22 topics we extracted with our analysis, represented in just 444 of 98,388 Facebook posts by media organisations.

Even less prominent were Facebook posts by media organisations on gender equality, the question of an Indigenous voice to parliament or issues of special relevance to First Nations people.

For instance, just 411 of 98,388 posts included *any* of the terms 'Indigenous', 'First Nations', 'Uluru Statement' or 'deaths in custody', and many of these were in a non-election context.[3] Only 148 posts contained any of the phrases 'equal pay', 'gender gap', 'gender equality', 'women's rights', 'glass ceiling', '#MeToo' (and variations), 'sexual/gender discrimination' or 'sexual harassment'.

The low prevalence of these topics meant that we assign posts on these topics to the broad 'Miscellaneous' category.

Topic salience over the campaign

Changes in topic salience over the campaign are the signatures of the interplay between competing campaign messages being advanced by parties and candidates, the media's appetite for reproducing, criticising or ignoring those narratives and the interests and tastes of the electorate.

Daily totals of interactions with media Facebook posts grouped by ERT appear in Figures 7.6 to 7.8; events corresponding to peaks in the daily time series are noted in the margin of each figure. It should be observed that policy announcements on matters of substance generated some of the highest daily interaction counts. Key among these were the parties' policies on housing affordability (1 May and 16 May) and Labor's calls for a rise in the minimum wage (11 May). There were also telling examples of the effects of news and events beyond the control of parties, candidates and the media such as the RBA's interest rate hike (3 May), the release of inflation statistics (27 April) and the presence of the Chinese naval vessel off the West Australian coast (13 May).

---

3   For example, warnings that a story might contain the name and images of a deceased Indigenous person, promoting tourism to venues 'celebrating Indigenous culture' and artist Blak Douglas winning the 2022 Archibald Prize.

Housing affordability

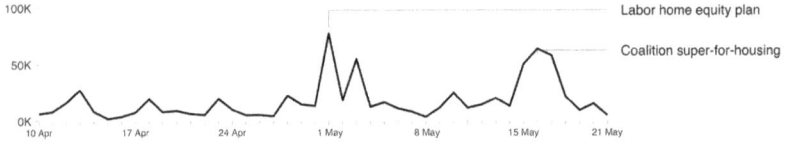

Deves/transgender

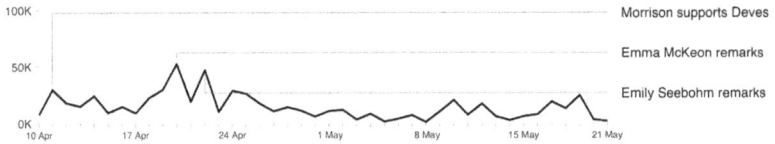

Cost of living

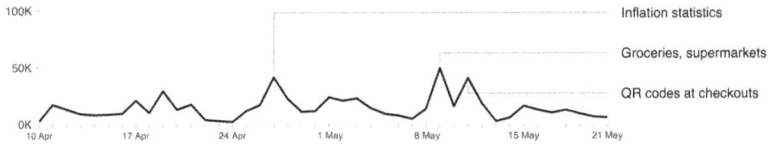

Leaders' debate

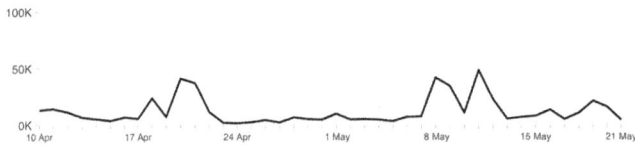

Albanese

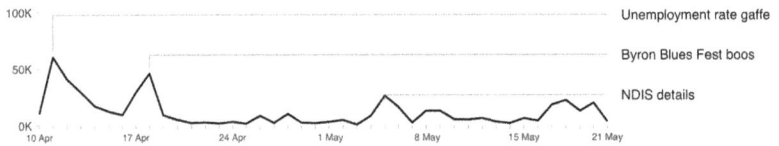

Figure 7.6 Interactions with Facebook posts by media entities, by topic and day, for ERTs ranked 1–5 by total interactions, during the 2022 Australian federal election campaign

Source: Data collected and analysed by the authors.

Nonetheless, campaign 'set pieces' remain staples of media coverage, perhaps none more so than 'co-productions' between the campaigns and media organisations such as the leaders' debates. As noted earlier, the combative character of these events—and aggressive cross-promotion by the sponsoring media organisations—helps propel the leaders' debates to be among the most engaging events of the campaign, at least as reflected in Facebook user interactions.

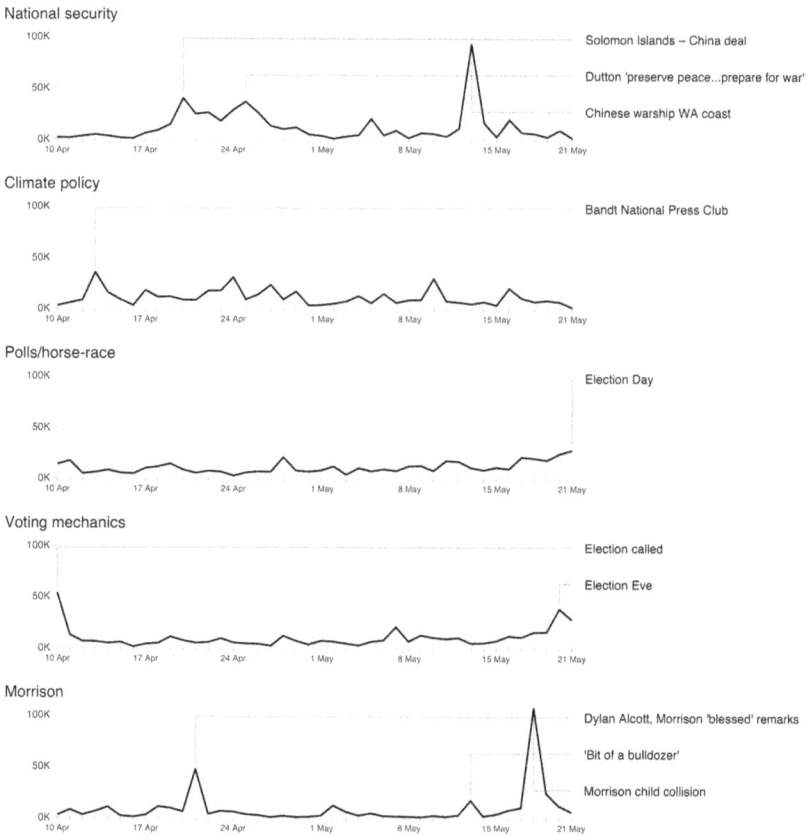

Figure 7.7 Interactions with Facebook posts by media entities, by topic and day, for ERTs ranked 6–10 by total interactions, during the 2022 Australian federal election campaign

Source: Data collected and analysed by the authors.

Albanese's gaffes at the start dominated the first week of the campaign but were replaced with an even more intense focus on Morrison by the end of the campaign. By the third leaders' debate (11 May), Morrison was promising a change of style, with his 'bit of a bulldozer' self-reflection on 13 May generating a minor uptick in the prevalence of stories focused on Morrison and in interactions with the accompanying Facebook posts. But Morrison's spectacular collision with a child on a soccer field on 18 May (just three days before election day) prompted the most user interactions we observed in a single day on any election topic: more than 106,000 interactions from only 77 Facebook posts. In contrast, the 80 Facebook posts by media organisations on Albanese's gaffe on 11 April generated just more than 60,000 interactions.

Wages

100K

Labor minimum wage rise

50K

0K
10 Apr   17 Apr   24 Apr   1 May   8 May   15 May   21 May

Independents

100K

50K

0K
10 Apr   17 Apr   24 Apr   1 May   8 May   15 May   21 May

Economy (other)

100K

Labor JobSeeker

Unemployment rate 4.0%

50K

Labor multinationals tax

0K
10 Apr   17 Apr   24 Apr   1 May   8 May   15 May   21 May

Interest rates

100K

RBA rate hike

50K

0K
10 Apr   17 Apr   24 Apr   1 May   8 May   15 May   21 May

Federal anticorruption

100K

Morrison remarks integrity commission

Labor national integrity commission

50K

0K
10 Apr   17 Apr   24 Apr   1 May   8 May   15 May   21 May

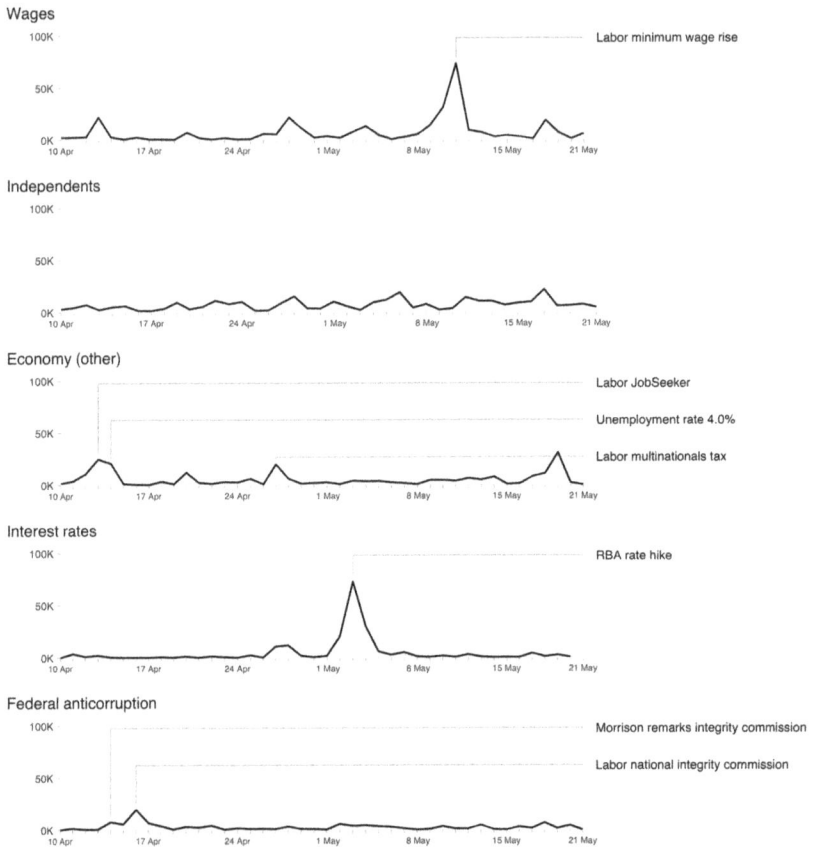

Figure 7.8 Interactions with Facebook posts by media entities, by topic and day, for ERTs ranked 11–15 by total interactions, during the 2022 Australian federal election campaign

Source: Data collected and analysed by the authors.

Interactions versus posts, engagement versus supply

Interaction counts reflect a sequence of distinct events: a content-generator publishing a Facebook post and users *encountering* the Facebook post and then interacting with the post (like, share, etcetera). Accordingly, the 'supply-side' choices by different media outlets—particularly those with large Facebook subscriber counts with particular political preferences—can distort the interpretation of interaction counts.

Given the huge volume of posts by some outlets (for example, *Sky News*, *news.com.au* and *ABC News*) and the large subscriber counts of some of these more prolific Facebook media accounts (see Table 7.1), we normalise interaction counts by the subscriber counts of the corresponding Facebook account. Specifically, for each post, we divide the count of interactions by the number of subscribers of the corresponding Facebook account (in thousands of subscribers); we then compute the median value of this quantity across all posts on a given topic, which we dub a normalised interaction count (NIC).

In Figure 7.9, we plot each topic's NIC against the volume of posts. In a crude sense, the media's supply of a topic is plotted on the horizontal axis and the public's engagement with that topic (NIC) is plotted in the vertical dimension; ERTs are plotted with a darker symbol and label. As we have already observed, even over the course of a federal election campaign, ERTs make up a modest proportion of the content generated by the media; to be sure, some ERTs are narrowly defined and hence small by volume of posts.

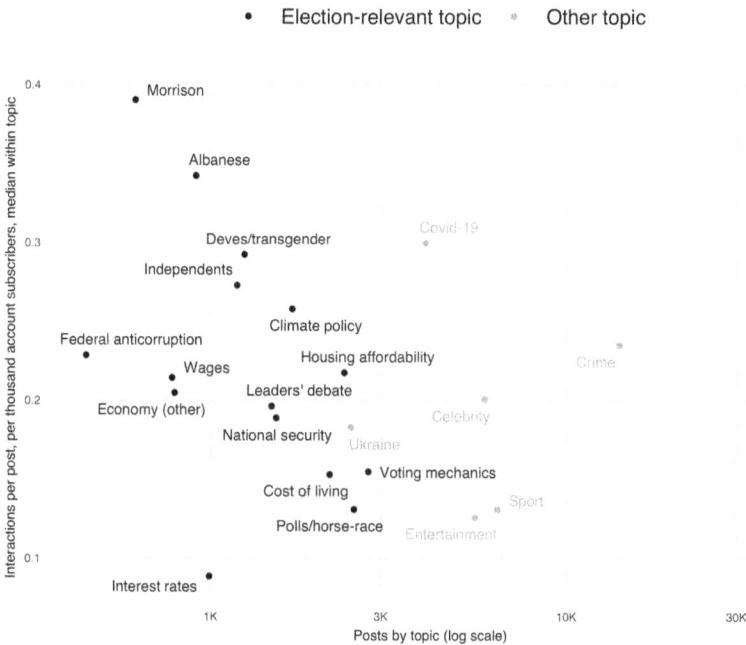

Figure 7.9 Interactions per post per thousand Facebook account subscribers, median within each topic (normalised interaction count), plotted against volume of posts per topic

Source: Data collected and analysed by the authors.

Among the set of ERTs, the 'Morrison' topic has the highest NIC, followed by the 'Albanese' topic. Stories about the leaders as individuals clearly animated the public out of proportion to the supply of those stories.

It has become commonplace to note the 'presidentialisation' of Australian politics (Kefford 2013; Gauja 2015), but media logics play no small role in this focus on leaders. Election campaigns are often storytelling deserts, lacking strong narratives or visuals. Publishers, editors and journalists are rewarded primarily for views, clicks and time spent on the site—a logic that leads to 'campaign as spectacle' for which producers and audiences demand *dramatis personae*. Housing affordability, inflation and climate policy affect all of us, perhaps profoundly, and are hardly irrelevant to the spectacle, but they lack speaking roles in the campaign drama.

In 2022, the *personae* obliged, supplying *dramatis* aplenty. Albanese's early and unexpected campaign gaffes thrust the spotlight on to his competence and suggested, at least for a while, a compelling storyline that, like in 2019, the Coalition would defy the polls and win on the back of Morrison being seen as a safer pair of hands.

But the dynamics of the last week of the campaign—with Morrison facing increasingly dire polls, a recognition that Morrison's own 'bulldozer' style was more a liability than an asset and the news editor's dream vision of his collision with the child on a soccer pitch—helped make Morrison himself *the* biggest surprise story of the election, as measured by NICs.

The analysis reported in Figure 7.9 also reveals that stories about Independents and the Katherine Deves/transgender issue generated high NIC scores—indicative of high levels of user interest and engagement. These, too, are topics with *people* more so than *issues* at their core: the upstart heroes and/or villains of the 2022 campaign drama.

Housing affordability sits at the NIC/post-volume frontier, driving high engagement and rating highly in the volume of posts. But climate policy generated more interest than any other substantive issue of the election, as assessed on the NIC metric. Still, issue-focused topics sit below the leaders, Independents and the Deves/transgender topic on the NIC metric.

Conclusion

Despite some justified criticisms of the media's performance in 2022, our analysis nonetheless finds that hip-pocket issues (housing affordability, cost of living, inflation, wages and interest rates) constituted the single largest source of content in the mainstream media's coverage of the campaign. While the 'gotcha' and 'gaffe' focus on Albanese generated opprobrium from critics, the volume of this coverage was small in the context of the entire volume of general content produced during the campaign.

Our novel analysis of interactions with Facebook posts by media organisations lets us assess—perhaps for the first time in studies of Australian election campaigns—the reaction of the public to the supply of content provided by the mainstream media. We discover that topics centred on personalities— the leaders, upstart Independents or controversial candidates—engage audiences disproportionately.

Given this outsized audience engagement with this more vivid, personalised type of political story, the better question to ask about election coverage is not why there is so much focus on the strengths and weaknesses of the leaders and their personalities, but why there is so little?

References

Angus, Daniel and Axel Bruns. 2022. '2022 Australian federal election: Update 5'. [Website post.] *Digital Media Research Centre*. Brisbane: Queensland University of Technology. Available from: research.qut.edu.au/dmrc/2022/05/20/2022-australian-federal-election-update-5/.

Butler, Josh. 2022. 'Mark McGowan accuses travelling press pack of "bullying" Anthony Albanese and reporting "lies"'. *The Guardian*, [Australia], 23 May. Available from: www.theguardian.com/australia-news/2022/may/23/mark-mcgowan-accuses-travelling-press-pack-of-bullying-anthony-albanese-and-reporting-lies.

Gauja, Anika. 2015. 'The presidentialization of parties in Australia'. In *The Presidentialization of Political Parties: Organizations, Institutions and Leaders*, edited by Gianluca Passarelli, 160–77. London: Palgrave Macmillan. doi.org/10.1057/9781137482464_9.

Grootendorst, Maarten. 2022. 'BERTopic: Neural topic modeling with a class-based TF-IDF procedure'. *arXiv*: 2203.05794v1. Available from: arxiv.org/abs/2203.05794.

Kefford, Glenn. 2013. 'The presidentialisation of Australian politics? Kevin Rudd's leadership of the Australian Labor Party'. *Australian Journal of Political Science* 48(2): 135–46. doi.org/10.1080/10361146.2013.786676.

Kemp, Simon. 2022. 'Digital 2022: Australia'. *DataReportal*, 9 February. Available from: datareportal.com/reports/digital-2022-australia.

Killoran, Matthew. 2022. 'PM slams ALP "lies"'. *The Courier-Mail*, [Brisbane], 20 April.

Konstantinidis, Ioannis. 2008. 'Who sets the agenda? Parties and media competing for the electorate's main topic of political discussion'. *Journal of Political Marketing* 7(3–4): 323–37. doi.org/10.1080/15377850802008350.

McLintock, Jack. 2022. 'The winds of electoral change were blowing on social media'. *Streem*, [Sydney], 24 May. Available from: www.streem.com.au/the-winds-of-electoral-change-were-blowing-on-social-media/.

Muller, Denis. 2022. 'How the "reality-distorting machinery" of the federal election campaign delivered sub-par journalism'. *The Conversation*, 25 May. Available from: theconversation.com/how-the-reality-distorting-machinery-of-the-federal-election-campaign-delivered-sub-par-journalism-183629.

Roy Morgan. 2022. 'Total news readership continues to grow—up 0.9 per cent for the 12 months to March 2022'. Press release, 23 May, Federal Poll Finding No. 8988. Sydney: Roy Morgan Research. Available from: www.roymorgan.com/findings/total-news-readership-continues-to-grow-up-0-9-per-cent-for-the-12-months-to-march-2022.

Sales, Leigh. 2022. 'Interview: Opposition leader Anthony Albanese'. *7.30*, [ABC TV], 20 May. Available from: www.abc.net.au/news/2022-05-20/interview:-opposition-leader-anthony-albanese/13891996.

Scarr, Lanai. 2022. 'Star WA Labor candidate linked to carbon tax'. *West Australian*, [Perth], 10 May.

Simons, Margaret. 2022. 'This is not journalism'. *Meanjin* 8(2)(Winter): 66–85.

Wong, Penny. 2022. 'Video: "Worst foreign policy blunder in the Pacific since the end of WWII": Penny Wong'. *ABC News*, 20 April. Available from: www.abc.net.au/news/2022-04-20/worst-foreign-policy-blunder-in-the-pacific-since/13847436.

8

Talking pictures (and cartoons, videos, memes, etcetera)

Lucien Leon and Richard Scully

On the morning of Sunday, 10 April 2022, viewers of ABC TV's weekly current affairs program *Insiders* received a very rude shock: the 'Talking Pictures' segment was dropped from its sacrosanct place in the last 10 minutes of the show. Mike Bowers' regular run-through of the week's cartoons and pictures was shunted in favour of footage of Scott Morrison in transit from Sydney to Yarralumla to ask Governor-General David Hurley to prorogue parliament and dissolve the House of Representatives and half the Senate. Thousands flocked to social media, where fans of all things cartoony could not only watch the unaired segment but also troll away to their hearts' content, questioning the national broadcaster's priorities.

It is easy to miss something significant here. The fact that viewers were able to catch up on the segment in this way—taking to the web to watch a free-to-air TV segment that consists of a photojournalist running through the best print-media cartoons while in conversation with a prominent commentator or cartoonist (in this case, cartoonist Cathy Wilcox)—tells us a great deal about the changed and changing landscape of political satire in twenty-first-century Australia. 'Talking Pictures' is a hybrid of old and new media forms and one that can now sit in an open browser window on the same desktop or tablet as the newest in politicised social media or a digitised newspaper. While *Insiders* first appeared in 2001 and, by 2008, ABC iView allowed easy perusal of 'Talking Pictures' and the like, by 2022—more so than in any previous federal election campaign—the Australian electorate was spoiled for choice when it came to satire and was able to access it via an often-bewildering array of media and social media platforms, in all manner of genres and forms.

That very sense of bewilderment was itself something palpable as the major and minor parties struggled to weaponise satire yet again. The Greens and the more progressive groups did well to realise the usefulness of TikTok; the Coalition manifestly failed to do so and retreated to Facebook and Twitter. Meanwhile, the Nine Entertainment, Seven West and Murdoch-employed cartoonists engaged in more traditional commentary, both in the papers and via Twitter or Patreon. And, by the time the campaign was properly up and running, even the right-of-centre cartoonists were hammering the Liberals and Nationals for their lack of engagement. This was a major shift from 'Morrison's miracle' of 2019, when the Coalition's apparent social media skill was a subject of reflection in the election washup.

Bewilderment also threatens the historian of the cartoon campaign: the quantum of visual satirical material produced is too vast to cover in encyclopaedic fashion. So, in this chapter, we examine how the satirical mosaic of cartoons, videos and memes circulating throughout the campaign responded to and illuminated a selection of key themes and events. In determining which images should be included for analysis, we have given preference to content with broad public reach (rather than the internal-party 'dark web'). Current newspaper readership and viewing figures validate the inclusion here of cartoons published in the editorial pages and webpages of the nation's metropolitan daily newspapers and video content broadcast or streamed on network media platforms. Also included are selected videos from independent satirists—for example, The Juice Media, The Chaser and Friendly Jordies all have subscriber bases that number in the hundreds of thousands. The sample also captured TikTok videos from political party accounts as well as content by citizen satirists identified by 'scraping' the top 100 results returned from each of the trending hashtags '#auspol', '#auspol2022', '#ausvotes', '#scomo' and '#albo'.

The memes that featured in the mainstream news media were sourced almost exclusively from a pool of 1,113 images mediated by nine Facebook groups: ALP Spicy Memes Stash, The Simpsons against the Liberals, Toilet Paper Australia, Australian Green Memes for Actually Progressive Teens, the Liberal Party of Australia, the ALP, the Greens, Young Liberals and Young Australian Greens. These have a combined subscriber base of more than 1.4 million, each of whom is a potential node in additional social networks.

The sharing and posting of memes, as well as their intermediation with legacy news media (traditional cartoons were also shared extensively), extend the reach of these images beyond their partisan base to a wider mainstream audience. The memes mediated by these groups provide a comprehensive cross-section of those proliferating online in discussion forums and Twitter, Instagram and Reddit feeds, and on this basis present a viable sample for analysis. In aligning the satirical responses with the election outcome, the images collectively frame a narrative of voters who, although underwhelmed by Labor's lack of vision, had lost patience with the incumbents' inaction on climate change, corruption and the cost of living.

The clock: TikTok-ing for the Coalition

If the visual campaign of the 2019 election was distinguished by the Coalition's successful weaponising of 'Boomer' memes on Facebook, the story of the 2022 campaign was the emergence of Gen Z videos on TikTok.[1] The 2020–21 Covid-19 pandemic lockdowns helped establish the online video-sharing platform as a social media staple for 32 per cent of Australians aged 16–64; with the 23.4 hours spent by Australians on the app each month representing an increase of 40 per cent over the course of 2021 (Kemp 2022). Leading into the pandemic, Australian TikTok users were predominantly young and female (Roy Morgan 2020).

Heading into the 2019 federal election, the Coalition engaged digital marketing agency Topham Guerin to manage their social media campaign. The agency's 'water dripping on a stone' strategy (Nehring et al. 2019) successfully prosecuted the Coalition's key slogan, 'The Bill Australia can't afford', via the production and dissemination of hundreds of low-quality memes. In reviewing their subsequent election loss, the ALP found their digital strategy wanting, observing that the content they produced 'was less engaging and made fewer impressions' with voters compared with 2016, while at the same time the Coalition had upped its game dramatically. Blaming Bill Shorten for Labor's lack of digital literacy, the review concluded that 'the party that develops a genuine "digital-first" culture will have a big advantage in the next campaign' (Emerson and Weatherill 2019: 79).

---

1   'Boomer' memes describe images disseminated predominantly on Facebook during the 2019 federal election campaign that were authorised by the Liberal Party and targeted at Baby Boomer voters (those born between about 1946 and 1964); Gen Z refers to the generation born between about 1997 and 2010.

Fast forward to 2022 and it is surprising that after such a strong social media performance in 2019 (Knaus 2019), the Coalition had largely disappeared from the meme space, both in its official messaging and in its non-affiliated 'fan' accounts. For example, the Young Liberals' Facebook page posted 70 per cent fewer meme images in 2022 than in 2019, while Innovative and Agile Memes—one of the more prolific and heavily subscribed 2019 aggregators of pro-Coalition memes—posted only a single meme on day one of the campaign before giving up entirely. Conversely, the progressively aligned Facebook accounts that featured prominently in the 2019 campaign maintained or increased their meme activity in 2022. The non-affiliated Australian Green Memes for Actually Progressive Teens (for which there is no conservative equivalent) churned out 698 memes to its 126,000 subscribers. This uptick in activity resulted in a dramatic increase in the proportion of memes critical of the Coalition. The comparative lack of interaction rates between pro-Coalition memes and others identified by Mark Rolfe (2022) could be attributable to the content itself: largely derivative of older, static meme formats and lacking any narrative (besides the economic threat posed by Labor).

Engagement on TikTok became an essential plank in the social media campaign strategy of all parties. TikTok provides a totemic reference for the impact of young voters and women on the election result, with Teal and Greens candidates stealing a march on the Coalition, wresting nine seats from the government. The Coalition evidently failed to understand the cultural features of TikTok that make it distinct from Facebook. For example, when Scott Morrison joined TikTok with a personal account in December 2021, his first posts were staid 'Seasons Greetings' and his profile was 'fortified' to disallow duets, stitches, mentions, saves and comments—staples of TikTok culture. By disabling these interactive elements and posting stage-managed content, Morrison's foray demonstrated a fundamental misunderstanding of TikTok audience engagement. Struggling with a growing public perception that Morrison engaged in excessive photo opportunities and led a corrupt government—exemplified in the oft-trending Twitter hashtags '#ScottyFromPhotoOps' and '#FederalICACnow'—a youth audience valuing authenticity and accountability witnessed Morrison's apparent aversion to both.

The Liberals' official TikTok account fell similarly flat. Created just three days before the start of the campaign, the content privileged quantity over quality. Despite posting at twice the rate of the ALP (129 uploads to 62), Liberal TikTok videos achieved fewer total views than Labor's (approximately 3 million views versus nearly 4.5 million) and fewer engagements with respect to likes, shares and comments (approximately 180,000 engagements versus 500,000). Labor's more successful strategy can be attributed to understanding the community better than the Liberals. They engaged in duets (split-screen videos that riff off other users' videos), stitches (videos that build on the videos of other users) and clap-backs (responses to critical comments or treatment) and employed ephemeral TikTok trends and humour notes familiar and specific to Gen Z. The Greens, Jacqui Lambie and Bob Katter also played a solid TikTok game, though the 'fan' accounts were the ones that produced the most original and engaging content and afforded greater insight into the electoral mood of young voters. Of the 100 most popular videos in the #auspol list, just seven came from official political accounts. A similar ratio applied to the other trending hashtags.

Heading into the campaign

Several graphic interventions in the leadup to the campaign telegraphed the lines of attack that would be employed by the major parties during the campaign proper. Australian Unions mobilised to gift and sell thousands of corflutes reminding voters that the prime minister 'doesn't hold a hose' (Plate 8.1). This throwaway line, ill-fatedly uttered by Morrison during the 2019–20 Australian bushfires, was subsequently exploited by Labor as shorthand for Morrison's apparent inaction on all fronts, including the Covid-19 vaccine rollout, provision of rapid antigen tests, Queensland's floods and the China–Solomon Islands security pact. Together with the even more cutting 'That's not my job' slogan and imagery (something Morrison had claimed repeatedly in various contexts since the late 2000s), this was a significant early mobilisation of satire. Meanwhile, conservative lobby group Advance Australia installed corflutes in several electorates depicting various Independents as closet Greens candidates (Plate 8.2): the opening salvo in a scare campaign that signalled Coalition concern about the rising popularity of Teal or 'Climate' Independents.

Plate 8.1 'Doesn't hold a hose' corflute by Australian Council of Trade Unions

Source: Australian Unions website (shop.australianunions.org.au/products/election-corflute-doesnt-hold-a-hose).

Plate 8.2 Corflutes by Advance Australia targeting Independents David Pocock and Zali Steggall

Sources: David Pocock's Facebook page (www.facebook.com/photo.php?fbid=549406 636551423); Zali Steggall's Facebook page (www.facebook.com/photo/?fbid=322362 170013232).

Advance Australia also sponsored mobile truck billboards to drive around Canberra, Melbourne and Perth, featuring Chinese president Xi Jinping casting a ballot for Labor (see Chapter 15, this volume). The defence minister, Peter Dutton, had in February primed for a 'khaki' election by accusing Albanese of being the Chinese Government's Manchurian candidate; he declared on Anzac Day—and again in his National Press Club debate with his opposition counterpart Brendan O'Connor—that Australia should 'prepare for war' with China and described a Chinese surveillance vessel's lawful navigation off the coast of Western Australia as an 'aggressive act'. Dutton's anti-China fervour was not only undermined by the announcement early in the campaign of China's security pact with Solomon Islands, but also prompted a warning that the hardline rhetoric could cost the Coalition votes in electorates with a high percentage of Chinese Australians. In the end, almost every area with greater than 10 per cent Chinese ancestry swung to Labor (Raue 2022).

A collaboration between comedian Dan Ilic and the Clean Energy Council saw tens of thousands of Australian suburban rubbish bins emblazoned with large-format stickers (Plate 8.3) featuring Scott Morrison wielding the lump of coal he famously used as a prop in parliament five years earlier. When Hornsby Shire Mayor and former Liberal heavyweight Philip Ruddock threatened to suspend rubbish collection unless residents removed the stickers, it merely served to increase sales. Ilic, well known for his crowd-funded billboards attacking Australia's climate credentials during the 2021 UN Climate Conference in Glasgow, led a team of writers, producers, directors and graphic designers in prosecuting the 'It's not a race' social media campaign (utilising yet another of Morrison's backfiring phrases). In addition to the bin stickers, the team targeted 'fossil-fuel' candidates with a series of memes and videos. Their video of Morrison's infamous *60 Minutes* ukulele performance, composited over a backdrop of footage from the 2019–20 Australian bushfires, was viewed more than 100,000 times within 48 hours of its Facebook and Twitter release.

Plate 8.3 Examples of bin stickers produced by the Smart Energy Council
Source: Twitter/Smart Energy Council.

Plate 8.4 Digitally edited billboard image on Twitter

Source: Twitter feed of Adrian Elton (@TheSurrealMcCoy).

Public satire was evident in other ways. Some of the $100 million that Clive Palmer is reputed to have paid in advertising went towards the installation of the distinctive, near-ubiquitous yellow billboards that many voters would recall from the 2019 campaign. While Adrian Elton's digital spoof 'Ikea' billboard image from three years earlier once again circulated widely on social media (Plate 8.4), several activist groups and citizens defaced dozens of real-life United Australia Party (UAP) billboards. The 'culture jammed' billboards presented voters with messages deriding UAP's stance

152

on climate policy and Covid-19 mandates, as well as personal attacks on Palmer (Plate 8.5). In the end, Palmer's UAP secured one Senate seat (in Victoria), but ultimately, the lesson of 2019 was even more compelling in 2022: money was not enough in the face of crowdsourced campaigning, and the billboard and corflute infrastructure made possible by vast outlays of funds was very vulnerable to defacing by activist groups and ridicule by fed-up voters.

Plate 8.5 Various examples of defaced UAP billboards on Twitter, 25 January – 20 February 2022

Sources: Twitter feeds of Extinction Rebellion South Australia (@XRSouthAus); Adjackers (@AdJackers); AdDistortion (@DistortedAd); Fraz (@Fraz9000).

Albo's gaffes

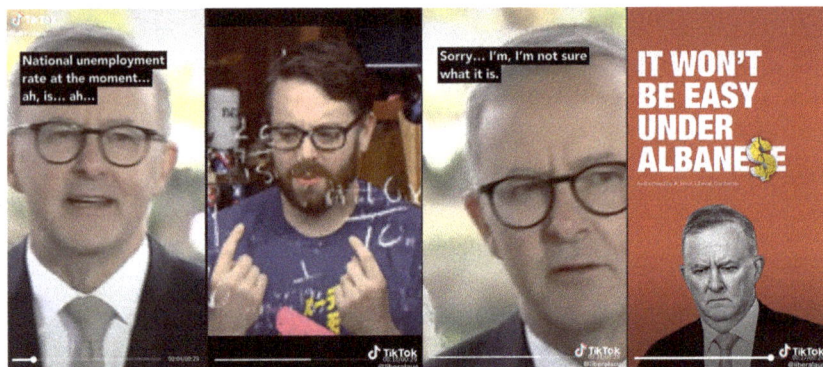

Plate 8.6 Still showing an image sequence from Liberal Party (@liberalaus) TikTok video

Sources: Liberal Party of Australia Facebook page, 21 April, 28 April, 7 May and 7 May 2022.

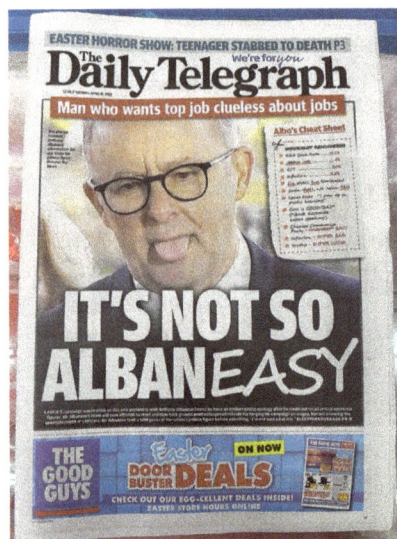

Plate 8.7 Front page, *Daily Telegraph* [Sydney]

Source: Liberal Party of Australia Facebook page, 12 April 2022.

The first day of the campaign was notable for Anthony Albanese's failure at a press conference to recall the national unemployment rate. This was the first of several stumbles by the Labor leader that punctuated the campaign and the Coalition attempted to frame Albanese's gaffes into a narrative that he was not across the policy detail. They prosecuted this relentlessly in their official and unofficial campaign messaging (Plate 8.6), ably supported by sections of the mainstream media (Plate 8.7), but this did not seem to cut through with voters. Neither did the tone-deaf attempt to make fun of Albanese's mellifluous surname nor the bizarre attempt to contrast the visibly fitter, healthier Labor leader (the fruits of a 'carb-free, grog-reduced 2021') with the more 'authentic' Morrison. In perhaps a telling failure to convince themselves of their own message, the Liberals' anti-Albanese billboards and messages invariably used images of the pre-2021, 18-kilogram heavier Labor leader.

As a gift to traditional cartoonists, the gaffe also featured in the mainstream media. In News Corp's *Herald Sun*, Mark Knight began his commentary on the election campaign with the image of the two leaders in 1950s Formula One cars—Morrison's visit to Yarralumla having coincided with the racing of the Australian Grand Prix in Melbourne (Plate 8.8). The gaffe then gave Knight the perfect metaphor to continue his theme the following day: Albanese (complete with 'L' plate) crashing out on 'Unemployment Rate Corner', while a smirking Morrison moves ahead (Plate 8.9). The more middle-of-the-road Nine Entertainment paper *The Age* saw John Shakespeare depict an ALP minder reassuring Albanese that he would be 'an unemployment expert in no time'; and *The Australian* used an unflattering press photo of the Labor leader as surrogate satire on its front page (12 April) as well as the traditional cartoon—by John Spooner (13 April)—to twist the knife. But these ultimately were more like wishful thinking on the part of the Coalition-aligned press. By the following Sunday, the cartoons downplaying the gaffe were the ones that dominated ABC TV's 'Talking Pictures' (including those by *Sydney Morning Herald/Age* cartoonist Megan Herbert, Alan Moir's self-published online effort, Jon Kudelka's for the Hobart *Mercury* and Brett Lethbridge for Brisbane's *The Courier-Mail*).

Plate 8.8 'And we're off' by Mark Knight
Source: *Herald Sun*, [Melbourne], 11 April 2022.

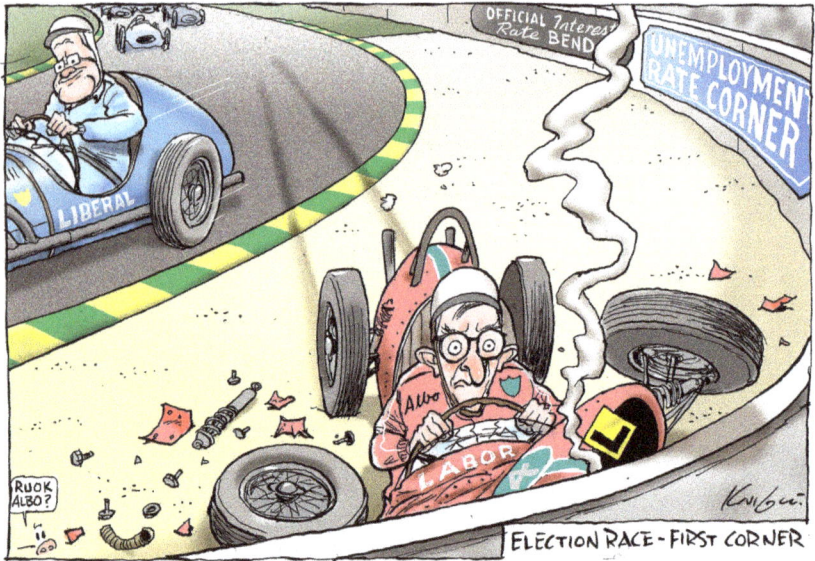

Plate 8.9 'Election race: First corner' by Mark Knight
Source: *Herald Sun*, [Melbourne], 12 April 2022.

No doubt, this change in perspective was helped by an ABC favourable to the ALP cause, but the impact of commentary in the intervening period was crucial. Lethbridge's cartoon relied for its effect on John Howard's 'So what?' comment on being quizzed about Albanese's gaffe. Reported in the mainstream media, the comment gained huge TikTok exposure via the likes of @belinduhpyne (248,500) and @ettigdirb (49,500). Greens leader Adam Bandt's comment to a journalist to 'Google it, mate' gained plenty of attention via the Young Greens and *The Guardian* on TikTok; and, within days, the pithy directive showed up on stickers, coffee mugs and T-shirts (including the one worn by Mike Bowers on *Insiders*' 'Talking Pictures' on 17 April). As such, follow-up gaffes-that-weren't by Albanese—on urgent care clinics not being formally costed (15 April) or the National Disability Insurance Scheme (NDIS) six-point plan (6 May)—received little attention from satirical commentators. David Rowe made the issue of the media reportage of gaffes itself a subject of comment. His typically grotesque rendering of a depressed Liberal–Nationals leadership sitting glued to the TV, hoping for a slip-up (Plate 8.10), was followed by a sequel: Morrison calling his now largely absent colleagues back to watch 'Albo's gaffe-ing again …', only to be told that they had all departed for their constituencies (or whereabouts unknown) (Plate 8.11).

Plate 8.10 'Politics now #247' by David Rowe

Source: *Australian Financial Review*, 1 May 2022.

Plate 8.11 'Guys! Albo's gaffe-ing again' by David Rowe

Source: *Australian Financial Review*, 5 May 2022.

Morrison's baggage

Rowe's image of Morrison sitting on the couch is typical of the approach taken by cartoonists and satirists in 2022, showing a prime minister now much more afflicted with the baggage of his term in office than in 2019. That largely 'clean' Morrison was better able to shape his own image, and cartoonists largely obliged in their depiction of a man garbed in all sorts of Cronulla Sharks merchandise. Come 2022, the merch was still there, but so, too, was the near-ubiquitous Hawaiian shirt, *lei* (or floral crown) and ukulele. Cathy Wilcox could scatter it throughout the background of her pre-election cartoon on 'authenticity' (Plate 8.12), throwing in Novak Djokovic, the Biloela family and a federal independent commission against corruption for good measure. Cartoonists and satirists also had plenty of recourse to the prime minister's own attempt to dress himself up as an ordinary bloke who cooked a curry every week—something first highlighted as far back as 2015 on Annabelle Crabb's *Kitchen Cabinet* for ABC TV and dissected by Sean Kelly (2021: 14–15). Morrison's 3 May Instagram post of what appeared to be a raw chicken curry spread virally (if not bacterially) and Wilcox used the trope to run through all the failings for which a curry was poor 'consolation' (Plate 8.13).

Plate 8.12 'Some people are saying you're racist …' by Cathy Wilcox
Source: *The Age*, [Melbourne], 5 April 2022.

Plate 8.13 'Consolation' by Cathy Wilcox
Source: *The Age*, [Melbourne], 3 May 2022.

The high-vis vest was now another pointer towards the style-over-substance critique that had dogged the prime minister for several years, and it was something shared by both disenchanted Coalition-leaning cartoonists and critics of Morrison and his government. Johannes Leak deployed the same pink-shirted, ponytailed 'Spin Doctor' he normally used to ridicule Albanese's image-making in one particularly cutting cartoon in *The Australian*. After being informed by a smug, high-vis–wearing and excavator-driving Morrison that 'having the courage of my convictions is a non-negotiable', the focus group research presented by the Spin Doctor prompts the prime minister to go from 'gravel' to 'grovel' mode, dumping his convictions as soon as he hears his message 'isn't resonating out there' (Plate 8.14).

Plate 8.14 'Having the courage of my convictions' by Johannes Leak
Source: *The Australian*, 16 May 2022.

Leak was not the only one to imagine a Coalition campaign being driven more by appearance than integrity. Matt Golding viewed the constant attempt by the Coalition to shift the election on to their preferred issues, resulting in constant rebuffs from the campaign manager: national security was countered by the China–Solomon Islands' pact, the climate 'scare' by Matt Canavan and the net-zero 2050 target and economic management by the seemingly endless list of 'inflation, cost of living, interest rates, wages, debt, deficit'. Golding's final panel, 'Character', results in the bemused apparatchik simply stating 'Um … you!'.

Meanwhile, Morrison's own gaffes seemed to amplify existing perceptions of his weaknesses. When he proclaimed that he and wife Jenny were 'blessed' not to have a disabled child, it exhibited a tone-deafness to those struggling with cuts to the NDIS. When he posted the apparently raw chicken curry to Instagram, it had a distinct '#ScottyfromPhotoOps' vibe about it, giving the lie to Morrison's carefully curated and confected public persona (Plate 8.15). Morrison's response to *A Current Affair* host Tracy Grimshaw's assertion that he had 'over-egged' his claim that he had 'saved the country' could hardly have been a stronger affirmation of his catalogue of failures. Clips of the interview popped up all over social media: TikTok user @candymoore remixed the exchange into an electronic dance music (EDM) 'banger' that was viewed more than 200,000 times (Plate 8.16). At the same time, Morrison's promise to change his leadership style from 'bulldozer' to something more palatable seemed to undermine his campaign pitch that voters 'knew who he was'—also allowing Albanese to frame his own identity in stark relief to Morrison: 'A bulldozer wrecks things. A bulldozer knocks things over. I'm a builder, that's what I am' (*ABC News*, 13 May 2022). Cartoonists of all persuasions were unimpressed. Warren Brown's 'Election shock therapy' showed a Morrison-faced bulldozer confessing to his psychologist, 'I've suddenly realized I identify as a bulldozer …' (*Daily Telegraph*, [Sydney], 13 May 2022). For a readership, a paper and a cartoonist not known for sympathy towards transgender people, this was doubly damning.

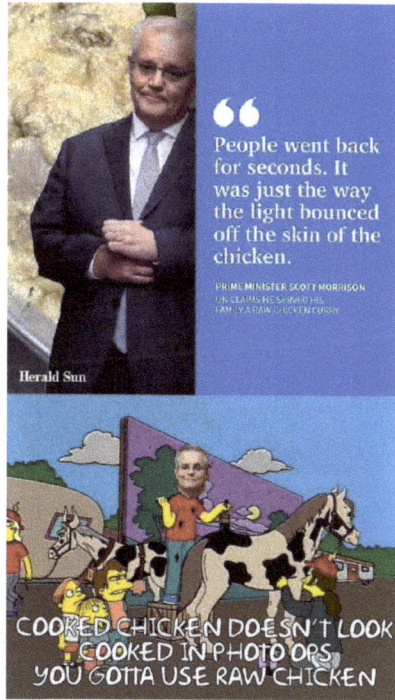

Plate 8.15 Meme by The Simpsons against the Liberals

Source: The Simpsons against the Liberals Facebook page (www.facebook. com/Simpsonsagainsttheliberals/photos/ 3228586707361720), 3 May 2022.

Satire was sometimes unnecessary: Morrison's clumsy tackle of a young child in a soccer game was instantly memed into a litany of things that Morrison had indeed knocked over (Plate 8.17). And it seemed too good to be true for the traditional press cartoonists, too, featuring in Dean Alston's *West Australian* work and David Pope's in *The Canberra Times* (both in the week 16–22 May). While Alston's Morrison was 'tackling anyone who might look like a Labor voter', Pope's victim was 'Wages'. Because of the production cycle of traditional cartooning, though, the endlessly recyclable memes were already clocking up the likes and shares well before Alston's and Pope's work appeared online or in print. Glen Le Lievre was able to be nimbler, via his Patreon account, showing Morrison decking Australia itself (19 May).

Plate 8.16 Still showing image sequence from @candymoore's TikTok video

Source: TikTok, @candymoore, 18 May 2022.

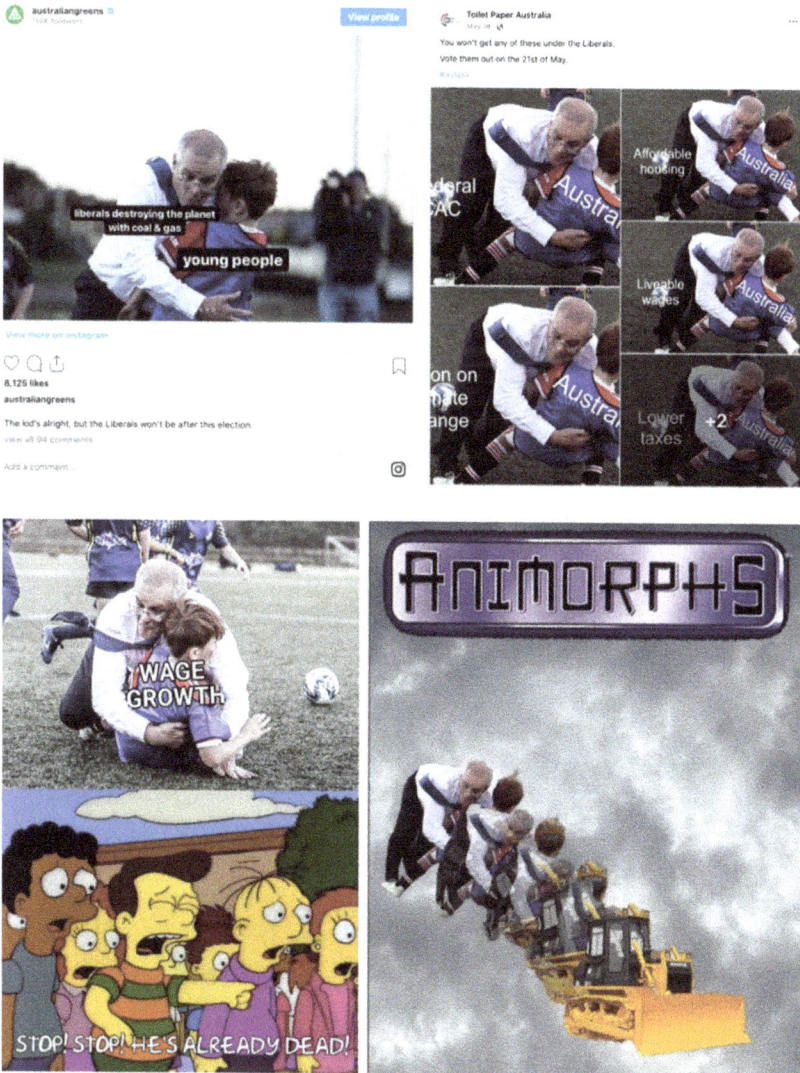

Plate 8.17 Morrison tackles child memes, 18–19 May 2022

Sources: (Clockwise from left) Greens Instagram page (www.instagram.com/p/CdsSP9 Dr6Fr/?hl=en); Toilet Paper Australia Facebook page (www.facebook.com/permalink. php?story_fbid=309940277996309&id=100069410160572); The Simpsons against the Liberals Facebook page (www.facebook.com/Simpsonsagainsttheliberals/photos/ 3241053366115054/); @bobkatters_crocodilefarm Instagram page (www.instagram. com/p/CduB-zfPW5e/?hl=en).

The most comprehensive account of Morrison's baggage was provided by The Juice Media's 1 May 'Honest government ad', laying out in excoriating detail the Morrison Government's perceived failures and shortcomings. The six-minute video (viewed more than 1.5 million times across all social media platforms) comprises a 35-item roll call of the Coalition's performance on ministerial ineptitude, climate change, cost of living, corruption, funding rorts, the treatment of women and First Nations peoples, the national Covid-19 response, aged care, the NDIS, natural disaster response, national security, 'Robodebt' and housing affordability. Thanks to the Coalition's largely presidential campaign style, Morrison's challenge was to convince voters that he was a caring, trustworthy, highly competent leader whose perceived failings were wholly attributable to global forces and events. After three years of getting to know Morrison, this was a big ask. In a TikTok video uploaded two days into the campaign, Jordan Shanks (aka Friendly Jordies) condemned the prime minister for cultivating a 'daggy dad' persona to effectively camouflage his government's poor policy record, declaring: 'ScoMo's family values schtick is not only getting old, it's become impossible to believe' (@friendlyjordies, *TikTok*, 12 April 2022).

Independents and minor parties

The fact that the Coalition's heavy election loss did not translate into a Labor landslide reflects the strong alternative voting patterns that a great many satirists pointed to before the election. The Greens' relative mastery of social media—so obvious in TikTok campaigning—also came through in other apps. Stephen Bates (Brisbane) used the gay dating app Grindr to employ several double-entendre ads that skirted the boundaries of satire (Plate 8.18) in a clear indication that he understood his constituency (he defeated his sitting LNP opponent with a two-party-preferred result of 53.7 per cent to 46.3 per cent).

While the Greens were a great success story, it was the 'Voices of' Independents movement that perhaps best spoke to a constituency focused more on the merits of local candidates than party affiliation. Satirists had trouble in such a context, with Mark Knight's assertion that the Teals were not so independent as all that (*Herald Sun*, [Melbourne], 1 May 2022) seeming to fall on deaf ears. The earlier Coalition insistence that voting Independent invited chaos or (worse) a Labor or Greens–dominated parliament received very little attention.

Plate 8.18 Stephen Bates' digital campaign stickers

Source: Australian Green Memes for Actually Progressive Teens Facebook page (www.facebook.com/GreenMemes/photos/7618581941545532), 28 May 2022.

Himself laid up at home with Covid-19, David Pope summed up so much of the crisis facing the Liberal heartland in a striking, self-published landscape of Kew's Junktion Hotel in Josh Frydenberg's Kooyong constituency (Plate 8.19). The minor controversy over Teal Independent candidate Dr Monique Ryan's posters being affixed to the dilapidated pub—even while the building itself sported enormous digital billboards urging voters to 'Keep Josh'—was reimagined for comic effect. 'Keep Josh—I could be PM! You fools, you maniacs!' replaced the more positive message of the real thing; there is graffiti on the pub exterior reading 'Barnaby' and 'Canavan' (referring to Nationals politicians) and Liberal Party posters are obscured by 'Sold' signs. In the finer details, the road signs show 'Climate' rising in the direction of 3°C+, an ICAC clearway and 'No Left Turn into Teal Street'.

Plate 8.19 'I could be PM' by David Pope
Source: Self-published, 6 May 2022.

With the Teals largely immune from outright caricature (not least because their gender posed a risk to the more cautious cartoonists post #MeToo), the minor parties were a safer bet for many. The calculated switch by George Christensen to contest a likely defeat for One Nation attracted a typically grotesque comment from David Rowe (*Australian Financial Review*, week of 11–17 April 2022), as did the reassignment of Coalition preferences to One Nation (@roweafr, week of 9–15 May 2022).

Women

The fact that the bulk of the Independent Teal candidates were women seemed to speak directly to the longstanding 'women problem' of the Liberals and Nationals. Just before the election, amid bitterly contested NSW preselections, David Rowe could burlesque the famous 1942 J. Howard Miller/Westinghouse poster 'We can do it!' to show Morrison ordering women: 'You will do it!' (Plate 8.20). In one of just three gender-themed TikTok videos, Labor stitched Deborah Knight's debate question ('Prime Minister, do you have a problem appealing to women, do you think?') together with reality TV star Kris Jenner, as Morrison proxy, declaring: 'It's really rare that I'm at a loss for words, but I don't know what to do and I'm pulling stories out of my—' (@australianlabor, *TikTok*, 8 May 2022). One fan-made video in the campaign's final hours, featuring Julia Gillard promising an Albanese Government would be one that 'cares about, values and includes women', was viewed more than 1.1 million times (@icacplz, *TikTok*, 20 May 2022). Otherwise, women featured relatively little in mainstream cartoons, broadcast comedy or social media satire, only reappearing in hindsight with Glen Le Lievre's teal-bathed 'morning after' cartoon from the *Australian Financial Review* (22 May 2022).

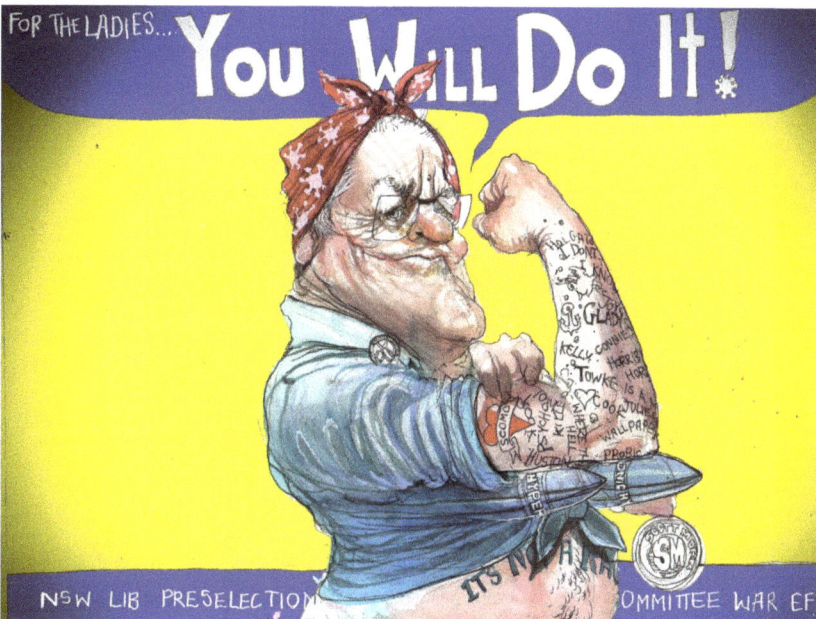

Plate 8.20 'For the ladies … You will do it!' by David Rowe
Source: *Australian Financial Review*, week of 10 April 2022.

Youth

Youth were also largely ignored by the satirists but were highly active in generating satirical content. They were not in the picture, so to speak, but making it. They embraced templates provided by Australian Green Memes for Actually Progressive Teens, creating dozens of scenarios explaining why ordinary voters 'won't be affected by the Greens' plan to tax billionaires and corporations' (Plate 8.21); these memes accounted for just more than 25 per cent of the total number of memes published by this group. Youth were highly engaged with TikTok during the pandemic, creating, sharing and liking content that reflected their concerns about climate change and an economy from which they felt excluded. The contempt expressed for the Coalition in these videos is palpable: apart from two Liberal Party videos, not a single video favoured the government. TikTok creator @mates.rates attracted more than 1.7 million likes for his videos taking aim at Morrison's character and the mainstream media's bias against Albanese (Plate 8.22). The Morrison in these clips is inauthentic and deceitful ('My favourite beer is Shark lager'), given to outrageous claims and subsequent revision ('My dad invented the pencil … I never said my dad invented the pencil') and unprepared to take responsibility for his mistakes ('It's not my responsibility to keep the ball in the court, that's not my job'). Albanese, on the other hand, is shown in these videos as a caring, decent bloke whose words and deeds are reframed in mock-hostile front-page headlines ('Albanese goes for a fist bump instead of a high-five … Will he fist the economy the same way?'). Deftly interwoven with these narrative structures are references to Morrison's Hillsong Church allegiance, inadequate response to natural disasters, fervour for fossil-fuel projects and disregard for education.

if your student diet consisted entirely of this, you will not be affected by the Greens plan to tax billionaires and corporations

if your phone has had a cracked screen for the past 3 months, you will not be affected by the Greens plan to tax billionaires and corporations

Plate 8.21 'Billionaire tax' memes from Australian Green Memes for Actually Progressive Teens

Source: Australian Green Memes for Actually Progressive Teens Facebook page (www.facebook.com/GreenMemes/photos/7443342875736107/), 21 April 2022.

Plate 8.22 Still showing image sequence from @mates.rates's TikTok video

Source: TikTok, @mates.rates, 18 May 2022.

Other prominent creators—@icacplz, @friendlyjordies, @tikyleaks and @genunited—challenged the narrative that the Coalition were inherently superior economic managers and railed against government pork-barrelling and rorting, housing affordability, stagnant wage growth, poor First Nations relations and Morrison's endorsement of anti-transgender candidate Katherine Deves. The nonpartisan content in the sample typically comprised informative videos explaining preferential voting and how to vote for candidates in both the House and the Senate. The high view, like and share counts for these videos indicate an inclination on the part of TikTokers to both inform and be informed about the participatory democratic process.

Cost of living

Inflation data released two weeks into the campaign revealed what voters intuited from the price of their groceries, petrol and home-building: the cost of living had risen more in the previous quarter than at any time in the previous two decades. Morrison's strategy was to convince the electorate that Australia was faring well in relative global terms and that, in 'uncertain times', it was best to stick with the Coalition's superior economic management. Fearmongering about Albanese's 'inexperience' and the prospect of 'higher taxes under Labor' was summed up in the Liberals' 'There's a hole in your budget' ad, which showed coins dropping into and then falling out of a rusty bucket to the tune of an earworm-worthy jingle. The advertisement featured prominently in print, broadcast and online, providing one of the very few successes for the Coalition in terms of audience reach and engagement. It was also one of the Coalition's few TikTok wins, with the original ad and a remixed EDM banger attracting more than 500,000 views (nearly four times the view count of the next most viewed video). The replies on TikTok and YouTube, however, should have concerned Liberal Party strategists. Viewers were impressed by the catchiness of the ad but remained focused on the perceived failings of the Morrison Government ('This song is so fire that I want to go to Hawai`i for a holiday').

Plate 8.23 'Knock knock' by David Rowe
Source: *Australian Financial Review*, 2 May 2022.

The interest rate rise was seen by cartoonists across the political spectrum as likely fatal to the Coalition: Warren Brown not only imagined a massive 'Interest Rates' freight train smashing through the front door of two ordinary Australians, but also a Frankenstein's monster appearing at the front door of Morrison and Frydenberg (*Daily Telegraph*, 3 May 2022); and the view from the other side of the door also saw David Rowe imagine Dutton, Morrison and Frydenberg cowering in fear of Reserve Bank of Australia governor Philip Lowe (Plate 8.23). The desperate vote-buying exercise of proposing Australians be able to tap into their superannuation to purchase property fell flat. Christopher Downes imagined a young couple cowering inside their now-empty piggybank (Plate 8.24), while Cathy Wilcox pointed out the obvious result of first homebuyers seeking to compete with 'downsizing boomers' on the property market (*The Age*, [Melbourne], 20 May 2022).

Plate 8.24 'Well, at least we have a roof over our heads' by Chris Downes
Source: *Mercury*, [Hobart], 18 May 2022.

Climate

If the Coalition's credibility in the climate arena was not already irreparably damaged after nine years of obfuscation, Morrison's job of convincing the electorate that his government was committed to the emissions reduction target formalised at Glasgow was made virtually impossible with Matt Canavan's 26 April intervention, when he told the media 'the net zero thing is all sort of dead' (ABC 2022). Labor seized gleefully on the split between inner-city Liberals and rural Nationals (Plate 8.25), while the Greens sought product differentiation by casting a pox on both the major parties' houses for their commitment to new fossil-fuel projects (Plate 8.26). The Liberals, after flirting briefly with a 'carbon tax' scare campaign that immediately ran out of steam (it turned out that the 'tax' was in fact a safeguard mechanism implemented by former prime minister Tony Abbott), retreated to familiar ground by avoiding any mention of the environment, talking up energy bills and accusing Albanese of walking both sides of the climate fence (Plate 8.27).

Plate 8.25 Meme by Australian Labor Party

Source: ALP Facebook page (www.facebook.com/AustralianLabor/), 27 April 2022.

Plate 8.26 Meme by Australian Green Memes for Actually Progressive Teens

Source: Australian Green Memes for Actually Progressive Teens Facebook page (www.facebook.com/GreenMemes/), 6 May 2022.

In addition to the stickers that colonised the nation's rubbish bins in the months leading up to the election, images of that lump of coal became a potent symbol on social media of the Coalition's disdain for the environment. TikTok creator @abitofpud paired Morrison's accompanying 'coalophobia' speech with images of recent natural disasters in a video viewed 800,000 times in the leadup to the campaign (@abitofpud, 9 March 2022). A piece of oratory designed to rally support for the coal industry had been effectively repurposed in condemnation of it. Then, on 22 April, The Chaser created a mash-up of Morrison's debate responses, posting it to Reddit, where a user suggested that it 'just needs a sick beat and some autotune'. The comedy team obliged, transforming an initially incoherent mash-up into a 90-second EDM banger of Morrison profanely proclaiming himself to be a corrupt and racist climate criminal driven by his love of coal (*The Chaser*, 23 April 2022). 'Coal makes me cum' was viewed 730,000 times across all social media platforms, with iTunes and Spotify downloads totalling more than 1 million (enough to see it take the number-one spot on the Australian iTunes chart in its first week of release). After so much said by Morrison's detractors, it was ultimately Morrison's own words that were weaponised against him.

Plate 8.27 Meme by Liberal Party of Australia

Source: Liberal Party of Australia Facebook page (www.facebook.com/
LiberalPartyAustralia/), 18 April 2022.

The outcome

Warren Brown (*Daily Telegraph*, [Sydney], 23 May 2022) was clear in his
view about who was responsible for Morrison's demise: burned at the stake
by an angry mob of mostly women holding 'Teal 1' posters.

Plate 8.28 Meme by Australian Green Memes for Actually Progressive Teens

Source: Australian Green Memes for Actually Progressive Teens Facebook page (www. facebook.com/GreenMemes/), 22 May 2022.

While Brown's take aligns with the popular wisdom throughout the campaign that presumed the crucial element would be disaffected Liberal voters drawn to the inner-city Independents, in the end, Labor won power on the back of a substantial tactical vote by left-wing voters (McAllister 2022). Youth might feel aggrieved at once again being left out of the picture, having helped the Greens snatch two seats from the Liberals to secure a record four House of Representatives seats and six Senate seats (Plate 8.33). Teals and Greens alike campaigned heavily on key issues of import to voters—most notably, climate change, gender equality and political integrity. Policy inertia in these areas—set against a backdrop of rising inflation, increasingly unaffordable housing and ill-conceived responses to natural disasters and the pandemic—sealed the government's fate. In the end, no promise of reinvention by Morrison would be enough to turn the Coalition ship around (Plate 8.34). In the campaign washup, Cathy Wilcox tweeted an ironic plea: 'Cartoonists of Australia will be engaging in a lot of soul-searching today. Please be understanding in our time of loss' (@cathywilcox1, 22 May 2022). The context was the departure of the cast of characters who had sustained satire for the past decade—Morrison and Frydenberg most notably.

Plate 8.29 Meme by Australian Green Memes for Actually Progressive Teens

Source: Australian Green Memes for Actually Progressive Teens Facebook page (www.facebook.com/GreenMemes/), 13 May 2022.

Conclusion

If a week is a long time in politics, three years is an eon in the digital age. The Coalition did not adapt their visual campaign to a social media environment that had moved on from ironic, low-quality memes built on slogans. Labor's visual content was seen by voters as more authentic, while the Greens exemplified how to engage voters via grassroots engagement with community social media pages, the production of meme templates and explainer videos. The Liberals ran pretty much the same social media campaign they did in 2019, but with far less intensity, and adopted an 'old school' and cynical approach to TikTok, demonstrating just how out of touch they were with youth. Apart from content produced by the Liberals themselves, pro-Coalition sentiment was wholly absent from TikTok. The voter content that achieved the highest engagement—measured in terms of views, likes, comments and shares—ran exclusively against the Coalition. Memes and videos told a story of a lot of anger in the electorate—particularly among young voters—towards the Morrison Government and Morrison in particular. Cartoonists from the still-mainstream (but only just) newspapers were more benign overall, but even the Murdoch and other Coalition-aligned artists were unimpressed with Morrison and his colleagues.

The beginnings of a long post-campaign realignment, and the difficulties in imagining the new landscape, bathed in the Teal wave (David Pope, *The Canberra Times*, 22 May 2022) was apparent from ABC TV's final *Insiders* episode of the campaign (29 May 2022). Fiona Katauskas joined Mike Bowers to review the work of Warren Brown, Matt Golding, Glen Le Lievre and others—happily, without interruption from breaking news.

References

Australian Broadcasting Corporation (ABC). 2022. *ABC News*, [ABC TV], 26 April.

Australian Electoral Commission (AEC). 2022. 'AEC launches campaign to combat disinformation'. Media release, 12 April. Canberra: AEC. Available from: www.aec.gov.au/media/2022/04-12.htm.

Emerson, Craig and Jay Weatherill. 2019. *Review of Labor's 2019 Federal Election Campaign*. 7 November. Canberra: Australian Labor Party. Available from: alp.org.au/media/2043/alp-campaign-review-2019.pdf.

Kelly, Sean. 2021. *The Game: A Portrait of Scott Morrison*. Melbourne: Black Inc.

Kemp, Simon. 2022. 'Digital 2022: Australia'. *DataReportal*, 9 February. Available from: datareportal.com/reports/digital-2022-australia.

Knaus, Christopher. 2019. 'Liberal Party also beat Labor on Facebook in 2019 Australian federal election'. *The Guardian*, [Australia], 4 June. Available from: www.theguardian.com/australia-news/2019/jun/04/liberal-party-also-beat-labor-on-facebook-in-2019-australian-federal-election.

McAllister, Ian. 2022. 'Unpopular leaders punished at the polls in 2022 election'. *Newsroom*, 24 June. Canberra: The Australian National University. Available from: www.anu.edu.au/news/all-news/unpopular-leaders-punished-at-the-polls-in-2022-election.

Nehring, Ron, Scott Hennig, Ben Guerin and Avens O'Brien. 2019. 'Using social media effectively'. Seventh ALS Friedman Liberty Conference, Sydney, 23–26 May. Available from: www.youtube.com/watch?v=0QeHsjnGcpg.

Raue, Ben. 2022. 'What happened with the Chinese-Australian vote in the big cities?'. *The Tally Room*, [Blog], 24 May. Available from: www.tallyroom.com.au/47839.

Rolfe, Mark. 2022. 'Election humour 2022: Can the major parties win votes with a funny marmot or a joke about Star Wars?'. *The Conversation*, 11 May. Available from: theconversation.com/election-humour-2022-can-the-major-parties-win-votes-with-a-funny-marmot-or-a-joke-about-star-wars-182292.

Roy, Morgan. 2020. 'Nearly 2.5 million Australians using TikTok—up over 850,000 (+52.4%) during first half of 2020'. Media release, 14 October, Federal Poll Finding No. 8538. Sydney: Roy Morgan Research. Available from: www.roymorgan.com/findings/8538-launch-of-tiktok-in-australia-june-2020-202010120023.

Part 2: Actors

9

The Australian Labor Party

Rob Manwaring and Emily Foley

In 2022, the ALP achieved something it had only previously secured four times in the previous seven decades: it won office from opposition. The 2022 result is a landmark event for Labor as Anthony Albanese matched what had only been achieved in 1972, 1983 and 2007. The 2022 result was striking for a range of reasons—notably, the rise of the Teal Independents, as documented throughout this collection—but the triumphant Labor result also obscures an underlying electoral fragility for the party and broader changes in Australia's party system.

In this chapter, we outline the distinctive factors that underpinned Labor's 2022 electoral performance and focus on the key transitions from the disappointing 2019 result under Bill Shorten. The chapter has three main sections. First, we outline Anthony Albanese's four-stage strategy, built on a process of review, vision-making, policy clearing/setting and the 'short' campaign. Second, we explore Labor's relations with its key stakeholders— notably, the business sector and the unions. Finally, we briefly situate Labor's win in the wider context of the electoral fortunes of the centre-left.

Overall, we offer three key arguments. First, we argue that describing Albanese's agenda as 'small target' misunderstands his policy agenda and pitch. Rather, we argue that the descriptor 'thin labourism' better captures the policy and ideological contours of Albanese's Labor. Second, we argue that Labor's 'pro-business' strategy reflects an effort to forge a consensual approach between capital and labour, but while it harks back to the Hawke neo-corporatist agenda, it is also distinctive. Third, we argue that, in part,

Albanese's win echoes that of other successful centre-left parties which have captured a distinctive post-Covid environment with something of a 'back to basics' agenda.

Labor's win in context

The electoral analysis of Labor's 2022 win is documented elsewhere in this volume (Chapters 16 and 17), but here we draw attention to three key developments. First, the structural support for Labor remains in decline, as evidenced by its declining primary vote—down to a record low of 32.6 per cent in 2022 (see Figure 9.1). This is part of the ongoing decline of the major parties' vote share—a trend common across many comparable democracies. Despite the win, Labor recorded an overall 0.8 percentage point swing against it. Second, in common with previous elections, Labor's vote share differed across the States and Territories, with Labor only increasing its primary vote in Western Australia, Queensland and the Australian Capital Territory. This is explored further in the section below on Labor's 'short campaign'. Third, there were seat-specific and localised issues for the party—notably, the miscalculation of running Kristina Keneally in the nominally safe seat of Fowler (Nguyen 2022). While Labor strategists may take comfort from the overall result and the implosion of the Liberals, the wider picture for Labor is one of a certain brittleness, fuelled by longer-standing electoral trends such as the rise of the minor parties and Independents, the decline of lifetime Labor voters and the rise of swing voters in a more pluralised party system (Cameron and McAllister 2019).

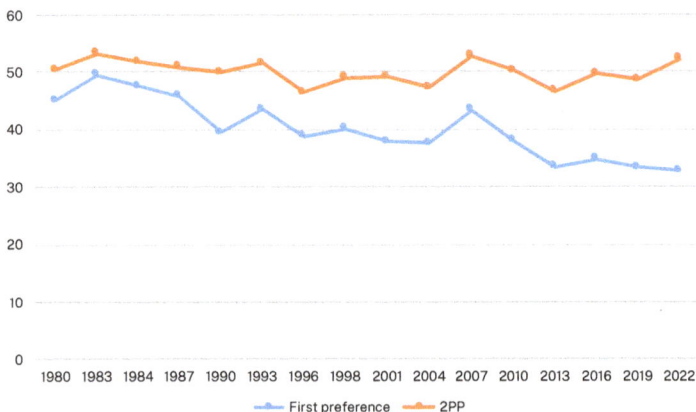

Figure 9.1 Labor's first-preference and two-party-preferred counts, 1980–2022

Source: Constructed by the authors from Australian Electoral Commission data.

Albanese's four-stage strategy

Albanese first contested the internal Labor Party leadership election against Bill Shorten in 2013. The voting system used combined the votes of party members and the federal caucus in equal proportion. Albanese won the rank-and-file vote but Shorten won heavily among MPs. After the 2019 loss, Albanese stood for the leadership again and was initially expected to face off against Chris Bowen, but Bowen withdrew. Albanese (from the party's Left faction) then assumed the leadership unopposed, with Richard Marles (from the party's Right faction) selected as deputy leader. Albanese faced a difficult period as Opposition leader that was marked by the global Covid-19 pandemic and Labor—in common with many other opposition parties—struggled to catch media attention. As one senior Labor figure reported to one of the authors, the ALP communicated with Keir Starmer's British Labour team, with both parties expressing the difficulty of achieving cut-through during the height of the pandemic. While Australia has a relatively positive story to tell in terms of its response to the pandemic—albeit largely helped by the luck of its remoteness and island status—Albanese was able to leverage a degree of valence politics against Morrison's Coalition Government. For much of the period, Albanese's Labor attacked the government's record on the slow purchasing of vaccines, the delayed vaccine rollout and the delays in setting up suitable quarantine facilities.

It is hard to overstate just how scarred the ALP leadership team was after the devastating 2019 federal election loss, and many of its renewal and policy choices stem from this defeat. Albanese adopted a four-stage strategy to win the 2022 election (Middleton 2022).

Stage one: Review

First, the party conducted a review of its 2019 campaign performance, which led to an important critical report (Emerson and Weatherill 2019). The post-election review offers a candid and strikingly honest take on the devastating 2019 loss, noting a 'cluttered' policy agenda, the unpopularity of the leader and, critically, internal institutional failures over the running of the campaign. A key element was Labor's spending agenda:

> Labor's tax policies did not cost the Party the election. But the size and complexity of Labor's spending announcements, totalling more than $100 billion, drove its tax policies and exposed Labor to

a Coalition attack that fuelled anxieties among insecure, low-income couples in outer-urban and regional Australia that Labor would crash the economy and risk their jobs. (Emerson and Weatherill 2019: 7)

Stage two: Vision

In the second stage of the campaign strategy, Albanese set out his 'vision' in a series of key speeches to a range of audiences. The collated speeches can be accessed on Albanese's website (Albanese 2020). These speeches arguably lack an overall coherence, but they champion a range of progressive, social-democratic and crucially labourist themes. They generally did not catch much media attention, but they were a key part of resetting Labor's agenda. In one of the early speeches, Albanese gave a brief overview of some of the core themes:

> The Labor Party is going to advance a progressive and practical agenda consistent with our values. Our policy agenda will be bold and clear. And by the time the next election comes about, Labor is going to be back as the party of growth, the party of aspiration, the party of social justice, the party of nation building, the party of the natural environment, the party of science and the party of the future. (Albanese 2020: 11)

It is striking that throughout the speeches, Albanese refers to Labor's core values but then does not go on to define them in much detail or give them sustained attention. For example, he references a core value of social mobility, but makes no references to it in later speeches nor any links to the emerging policy agenda around it. Figure 9.2 illustrates the frequency of the key words and themes from his vision speeches.

From the vision speeches, we can distil the Albanese approach around the following core themes and issues:

- economic growth
- fairness
- jobs and wages
- security
- nation-building and infrastructure
- aspiration.

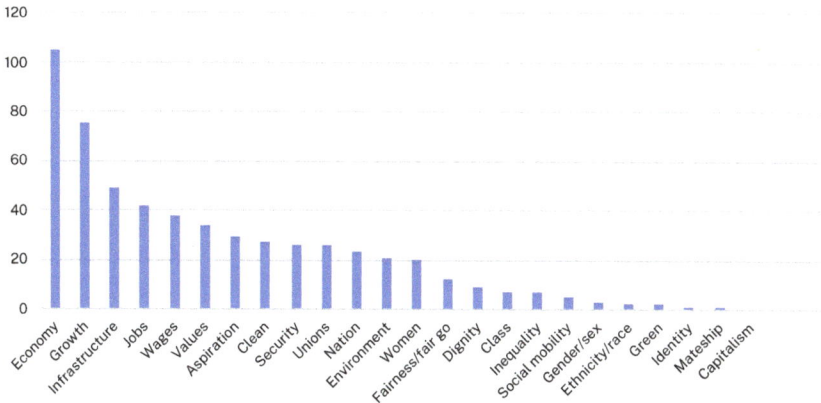

Figure 9.2 Keywords in selected speeches by Anthony Albanese, 2019–2020

Note: The figure reports keyword searches from a corpus of 11 key vision speeches, totalling 84 pages and 40,599 words.

Source: Compiled from Albanese (2020).

Albanese sets out a distinctively labourist approach in these speeches, giving centrality to the concepts of work, wages and conditions. Indeed, during the 'short' campaign, the rise in global interest rates, which included a mid-campaign rate rise by the Reserve Bank of Australia, drew further attention to the ongoing issue of wage stagnation in Australia.

Stage three: Policy clearing and policy renewal

Following the vision statements, the strategy shifted to the policy agenda. A key event was the Special Platform Conference held in March 2021 (ALP 2021a). This was critical because it was here that the factional trade-off over policy played out, with many of the key decisions made before the conference and by the key factional players (Remeikis 2021). Most importantly, Labor under Albanese abandoned several of Shorten's signature policies, including numerous tax concessions (see Table 9.1). There was a noticeable shift away from the technocratic tools for redistribution that characterised the Shorten period. A critical, yet largely overlooked, element of Labor's agenda was how it accepted and operated within the tax changes set out by the Coalition—arguably the most important was Labor's agreement to pass the highly regressive, so-called stage three tax cuts—the centrepiece of which was the removal of an entire income tax band (the 37 per cent band for those on incomes of $87,000 to $180,000 per annum) (ACOSS 2019).

Table 9.1 Albanese's policy agenda

Policy reversals/changes	Policy proposals
Reversal of policies on negative gearing and capital gains tax	Structural focus on improving capacity and productivity within the economy
Reversal of policy on 'franking' credits	Infrastructure investment in renewable energy; focus on local manufacturing ($1 billion National Reconstruction Fund); transport spending
Sign up to Coalition's stage three tax cuts — in effect, to remove the 37 per cent income tax band	Legislation on job security, wage theft and gender pay gap
Sign up to Coalition's Low to Median Income Tax Offset; fuel excise duty cut for six months	Push for universal childcare; expert panels on pay awards for care workers; reduce costs of medicines on the Pharmaceutical Benefits Scheme
	'Help to Buy' federal housing scheme (shared-equity scheme)
	Expansion of fee-free TAFE and university places

Source: Compiled by the authors.

The other significant policy development (and dilemma) for the ALP was the issue of climate change—a key issue for the whole election. In December 2021, Albanese revealed that the party would commit to a new target to reduce emissions by 43 per cent from 2005 levels by 2030, having already signed up to the Paris Agreement's overall strategy of net-zero emissions by 2050 (ALP 2021b; Morgan 2021; RepuTex 2021). Under its 'Powering Australia' plan, the ALP linked its climate strategy with its green jobs agenda and, in particular, its claim that the plan would create more than 600,000 jobs, many of which would be in the regions.

Politically, this position had two main impacts. First, it largely neutralised the issue—long a sore spot in the ongoing climate wars—for the ALP and placed further pressure on the Coalition's much weaker position. What also helped the ALP was the reversal of the stance of the Business Council of Australia (BCA) on Labor's climate policy. At the 2019 election, the BCA called Labor's then 45 per cent target 'economy wrecking'. Yet, with changing political and economic circumstances, the BCA undertook its own modelling and reversed its policy by pushing for a stronger, 46–50 per cent target by 2030 (Clarke 2021). While the BCA's position in 2019 arguably damaged Labor, its 2021 policy reversal added pressure on the Coalition. Second, for Labor, this was a classic compromise position, pulling Australia closer to allies like Japan (which has a 46 per cent by 2030 target), which was stronger than the Morrison Government's position but fell well short of the Greens' plans (see Chapter 12) and the broader scientific and stakeholder views that the target should be more ambitious.

Overall, Labor's new economic and tax policy agenda was shaped and constrained by the terms set by the Coalition and, as a result, sought to reduce its overall policy offerings, operate within strong fiscal constraints and strategically outflank the Coalition, especially on climate change.

Stage four: The short campaign

Labor needed to win at least seven seats to win a majority in the lower house, yet there were, in theory, several routes to office. At the time of the election, there were 15 Liberal seats held with margins of less than 5 per cent, and the ALP picked up six of these. What saw the ALP over the line was the perhaps unexpected win in Bennelong (NSW) and Labor's emphatic performance in Western Australia, which saw it win Hasluck, Pearce and Tangney, in addition to Swan. What was notable was the ALP's weak performance in Tasmania, which included two of the five most marginal Liberal-held seats.

Labor's short campaign, in our view, revolved around two main themes: a focus on the shortcomings of Scott Morrison's leadership and its own narrow, 'back-to-basics' labourist agenda. As Labor's campaign director Paul Erickson (2022) argued after the election, this approach was driven in part by Labor's qualitative fieldwork, which was showing a sense of 'change fatigue' among the electorate.

Labor focused on the centrality of leadership as a key campaign strategy, scrutinising the weaknesses of Morrison as a leader. A string of policy and leadership blunders by Morrison's government between 2019 and 2022—notably, around bushfires, the vaccine rollout and floods in Queensland and New South Wales—led some commentators to speculate that the campaign was Albanese's to lose (Grattan 2022; Keane 2022). The anti-Morrison strategy was fraught with risk, not least as opinion polling showed that while support for the ALP was relatively strong, Albanese's popularity as preferred prime minister was significantly weaker.

Labor's vision was 'for a better future' and focused on manufacturing, wage growth, gender pay parity and housing (Albanese 2022e). The early weeks of the campaign were tainted by a series of gaffes by Albanese, however, these did not appear to greatly affect Labor's overall short campaign performance.

In fact, it allowed key figures including Jason Clare and Katy Gallagher to promote Labor's agenda (Kenny 2022). However, while Albanese's gaffes did not sink the short campaign, an untested counterfactual is to ask whether a different leader might have improved Labor's overall result.

Despite the era-defining character of Labor's result, its performance in the lower house was mixed. The party secured an outright majority government and was clearly ahead in the two-party-preferred vote. Yet, Labor's countrywide performance was uneven and it made very little headway in Queensland and Tasmania.

A clear contributing factor to Labor's success in the federal election was the party's electoral dominance in Western Australia. The decision to have the ALP's campaign launch in Perth for the first time since the 1940s seemed to acknowledge the importance of the State from the very beginning of the six-week campaign. Labor now holds a majority of Western Australia's federal seats for the first time since 1990 (Phillimore 2022). More specifically, Labor's decision to use a separate advertising agency for its digital campaigning in the west, compared with the overall national strategy, created a successful grassroots-style campaign. It proved to be a long electoral night for ALP's 'true believers', as the overall swing to Labor did not look strong until the much later results from Western Australia rolled in.

Even accounting for 'change fatigue', Labor arguably underperformed electorally. While Labor's primary vote increased by a modest 0.8 per cent in Queensland, it failed to gain any lower house representation and, strikingly, lost the seat of Griffith (which it had held with a 2.9 per cent margin) to the Greens. After the election, only five of the 30 Queensland lower house seats belong to Labor. This has prompted Labor, post-election, to better understand the Queensland result, and Albanese and the new Cabinet travelled to Gladstone to unpick the lack of electoral traction (Milner 2022). The loss of Terri Butler in Griffith and Kristina Keneally in Fowler (NSW) injured the party, forcing Albanese to reshuffle his ministry after losing two key Cabinet members.

The Queensland result will be a disappointment to Labor, given that the State had been an electoral priority. Four months before the election, Albanese visited 20 towns throughout Queensland in 10 days and reassured the press and voters that Labor had learnt the lessons from its 2019 electoral defeat (Albanese 2022a). As early as January 2021, Albanese announced that Labor was targeting the seats of Leichhardt, Herbert, Flynn, Capricornia,

Longman, Petrie, Forde and Brisbane (Massola 2021). In relation to digital campaigning, the Queensland Labor Party spent $258,350 on political advertising on its Facebook and Instagram profiles between 21 March and 20 May 2022. The only Labor Party pages that spent more than Queensland on advertising were the national and Victorian Labor pages (Arya 2022: 7). Labor has a long history of Statewide electoral success in Queensland and looking to the 2025 election it may need to revisit its policy agenda, appeal and style of campaigning within that State (Crowley 2022).

New South Wales also produced mixed results for the ALP. Strikingly, it lost the 'safe' seat of Fowler in south-western Sydney, which it had held since 1984. The 'parachuting' in of Keneally as the Labor candidate for Fowler in late 2021 caused considerable controversy and criticism of the party machinery. The decision to run Keneally over Vietnamese-Australian lawyer Tu Le even led to some sitting federal Labor MPs like Anne Aly from Western Australia publicly condemning the decision as 'a huge failure for Labor on diversity' (Aly 2021).

While Labor may be delighted with the overall result, there is a fragility to its electoral base. In 2022, the focus of Labor's campaign was to position Albanese as a 'safe change' with a parliamentary party focused on 'renewal, not revolution' (Albanese 2022d).

'Thin' labourism under Albanese

If Labor either willingly accepted or felt forced to comply with the Coalition's regressive tax regime, its response was to build an agenda that pointed in a distinctly labourist direction. We use 'labourism' as a descriptor to refer to the tradition of a pragmatic social democracy that focuses narrowly on improving the pay and conditions of working people and seeking labour market activation strategies. Despite Albanese's own faith in progressive values, the agenda was steeped more in economic than in social forms of equality.

Albanese's thin labourism sought to address several systemic weaknesses within the Australian economy. A primary focus was the issue of wage stagnation—a policy setting deliberately marginalised by the Coalition. Labor's approach to deal with these structural economic weaknesses was to target its policy at specific groups and key vulnerable sectors. First, there was a raft of infrastructure spending, fuelled by the $10 billion National

Reconstruction Fund, which represented a potential second wave of stimulus spending in response to the Covid-19 pandemic. The infrastructure focus also tied into two other key elements in Labor's agenda. The infrastructure spending underpinned Labor's response to climate change through renewable energy technology. As Albanese also outlined in his campaign launch speech, the other element was a more nativist appeal to increase domestic manufacturing capabilities.

Second, Labor targeted key sectors and demographic groups, especially women, with a focus on affordable (and near-universal) childcare. As Albanese argued throughout the campaign, the focus on childcare was not a welfare strategy but a key plank of the ALP's economic renewal plan (Curtis 2020). This was also linked to key workers in other 'care' sectors. The third plank was a traditional centre-left focus on training and education with key pledges around expanding fee-free places in the TAFE/vocational sector. Taken together, these strategies were arguably more internally consistent, or mutually supporting, than perhaps the more redistributive agenda under Shorten's leadership.

We argue that it is better to describe this approach as 'thin labourism' than 'small target'. Small target implies both ideological convergence with the Coalition and a less expansive spending program. This does not adequately describe Labor's approach; it was not 'Coalition-lite', despite clear policy agreements on issues such as offshore detention. But why 'thin' labourism? Here, Freeden's concept of ideological morphology is instructive. Freeden (1996) identifies ideologies as revolving around a set of core, adjacent and peripheral values and ideas. In his 1996 treatment of socialism, Freeden identifies a range of key values that dovetail with Heywood's (2021) account. Without systematically mapping these out against Albanese's agenda, we can see that the key values traditionally associated with the social-democratic tradition are downplayed, marginalised or organised. Notably, we note the downgrading of class politics, the critique of capitalism and collective forms of action. Some of these are, of course, implicit in Albanese's agenda, but it is a thin labourist approach in that the core of the agenda is a revalorising of the central concept of work—not, for example, the concepts of equality or welfare. The term 'thin' is used here not necessarily as a normative critique, although of course it can be used that way, but rather as a conceptual approach to better understand the pragmatic dimension of Albanese's Labor. Supporters of Labor's agenda might prefer a term such as 'strategic labourism' or 'new labourism'.

We can also see how Albanese brings in other ideological strains and values—nativism and environmentalism, for example—to buttress this 'work-first' agenda. It is striking, too, how in the Australian context the Labor Party is unable or unwilling to have a public discussion about its welfare policies. There has been a longstanding neoliberal assault on the Australian welfare system, which has historically had a much more targeted (rather than universal) character. Since John Howard's Coalition Government in the 1990s, a range of key benefits have not been significantly increased or had positive legislated increases (Whiteford and Redmond 2018). For example, as part of its 2018 'Raise the Rate' campaign, the Australian Council of Social Service noted that the Newstart (now JobSeeker) allowance had not increased above the consumer price index since 1994 (ACOSS 2018: 2).

If we use Keman's (2017) typology of welfare clusters (social-democratic, universal welfare and social safety), we could argue that Australia has shifted from an atypical 'social-democratic' cluster to a much more minimalist 'safety net' approach. Neither Shorten's technocratic social democracy nor Albanese's thin labourist approach has sought to radically refurbish the fundamentals of Australia's welfare state. The thin labourist approach is instructive in not just what it seeks to valorise, but also what it ignores, downplays and marginalises. And what of its electoral success? Party strategists might argue that Albanese's thin labourist approach was electorally more successful than Shorten's, but there was not necessarily a ringing endorsement of Labor at the 2022 polls (Soutphommasane 2022).

A new consensual politics? Labor's relationships with key stakeholders

Albanese sought to position his leadership of the ALP in a Bob Hawke 'consensus' style of approach (Murphy 2022). In a speech leading up to the election campaign, Albanese called for a rediscovery of Hawke's 'spirit of consensus that … used to bring together governments, trade unions, businesses and civil society around their shared aims of growth and job creation' (Albanese 2022f). This consensus refers to not just the trade union movement and the business sector, but also Commonwealth and State governments, given they ultimately share the same interests: a stronger economy, increased productivity and 'more good jobs' (Albanese 2022b). The new consensus revolved around three key issues within industrial relations policy: wages, insecure work and gender inequality.

Throughout the short campaign, and in his vision speeches, Albanese highlighted his commitment to facilitating mechanisms for the collaboration of the trade union movement and the business sector. Labor's Powering Australia Plan, for example, was touted as having the support of the BCA, the Australian Chamber of Commerce and Industry, the Australian Industry Group, the National Farmers' Federation and the Australian Council of Trade Unions (ACTU) (Albanese 2022f). This was linked to Labor's promise to hold an employment summit with the trade unions and business to tackle problems relating to wage growth and economic productivity (Albanese 2022b: 34). This approach appears to be supported by some bodies within the business sector, like the BCA (2022), who welcomed Labor's election victory as 'a chance to seize the opportunity and end the deadlock on workplace relations, restore the Hawke–Keating enterprise bargaining system to lift productivity and let Australians earn more'. The summit also seemed to placate the needs of the business sector—specifically, the need for solutions to skills shortages (Bonyhady 2022).

Albanese's shift towards a 'safe' centrist path for Labor, whereby not appearing anti-business while not exclusively talking about the trade unions, aided the party in communicating values of fairness and security (Manwaring et al. 2022). At the same time, through the assistance of the trade union movement, Labor was able to launch a campaign on job security and wages, while presenting a more consensual solution than that of the Coalition.

There was a clear contrast between the approach of former leader Shorten and that of Albanese in working with business. Company directors were reportedly supportive of Albanese and other key shadow Cabinet figures like Jim Chalmers and Richard Marles and their 'pro-business' rhetoric compared with Shorten's more 'pragmatic' approach to the private sector that sought to target the 'big end of town' in pursuit of tackling economic inequality (Boyd 2022: 40; Manwaring 2020: 282).

Despite this friendlier approach to the private sector, Labor and the trade union movement presented similar messaging, with both seeking to target Australia's rising costs of living, wage stagnation and insecure work. The ACTU and State-based trade union councils such as Unions NSW and the Victorian Trades Hall Council ran two separate campaigns in the 2022 federal election. The first was based on industrial relations reform—specifically, wages and job security. The ACTU focused its social media campaigns on childcare, costs of living, wage growth, job security, an integrity commission and a raise in minimum award wages of 5.5 per cent.

Plate 9.1 Victorian Trades Hall Council corflute attacking Scott Morrison
Source: Emily Foley.

The second—which received the most coverage during the short campaign—was an attack campaign to persuade voters against voting for Morrison's Coalition Government (Haselmayer 2019) (see Plate 9.1). Other unions campaigned on policy areas to strengthen attacks on the Coalition. The Australian Education Union, for example, focused on increased funding for public schools while the Australian Nursing and Midwifery Federation supported Labor's plan to fix the crisis in the aged care sector.

While not overtly supporting the ALP, Australian Unions and the ACTU maintained a strong anti-Coalition message leading up to and after the election. The capacity for third-party interest groups like the unions to push negative or attack styles of campaigns was beneficial to Labor, which was able to focus on the positive promotion of jobs and growth. In this area, Labor and the trade union movement promoted similar messaging in their pursuit of industrial relations reform, secure jobs and wage growth. Labor's and the unions' 'parallel' campaigning (rather than mutually reinforcing campaigning as in the 2007 anti-WorkChoices campaign) arguably reflects something of an ongoing distancing between the party and the wider union movement, driven by the declining union density in many sectors. This distancing and pragmatism place the union movement and the party on different footings than in the past.

The ALP in comparative context

Finally, we situate the performance of the ALP in a wider comparative context. Much recent scholarship of the centre-left has catalogued the declining electoral fortunes of the longstanding family of centre-left social-democratic and labour parties. Since a highpoint in the mid 1990s, many centre-left parties have taken a third-way turn and, since the 2000s, electoral fortunes have suffered—although this also reflects a more general decline for all major parties in comparable countries. After the Global Financial Crisis (GFC) of 2008–09, there was speculation that the left might recover its fortunes, but in many cases, this failed to materialise. The ALP, for example, was barely electorally rewarded for its generally well-received stimulus response to the GFC. However, more recently, there has been some limited revival of the centre-left (see Table 9.2). With some caveats, we can make some observations about the overall performance of the centre-left.

Table 9.2 Centre-left party performance in 12 selected countries

Country	Centre-left party	Recent electoral performance	Vote share most recent election (%)
United Kingdom	British Labour	Out of office: Lost 2010, 2015, 2017 and 2019 elections.	32.1 (2019)
Netherlands	Partij van de Arbeid (PvdA; Labour Party)	Out of office: Sixth placed in 2021. In coalition 2012–17 (24.8% in 2012; 5.7% in 2017).	5.7 (2021)
France	Parti socialiste (PS)	Out of office: Won the presidential election in 2012, but lost in 2017 and 2022. Now part of the New Ecological and Social People's Union (left alliance).	1.7 (2022 presidential election)
Austria	Sozialdemokratische Partei Österreichs (SPÖ; Social Democratic Party of Austria)	Out of office: SPÖ and Austrian People's Party (OVP) in grand coalition, 2008–17.	21.2 (2019)
Belgium	Parti socialiste (PS; Francophone) Flemish Socialist Party (SP.A)	In office (part of 'Vivaldi' four seasons, seven-party coalition): Instability in party system; six governments from 2019 to 2020. Right coalition (four parties from 2014 to 2019). Centre-left led six-party coalition from 2011 after 2010 election.	PS, 9.46; SP.A, 6.71 (2019)
Germany	Sozialdemokratische Partei Deutschlands (SPD; Social Democratic Party of Germany)	In office ('traffic-light' coalition from 2021): Junior partner in grand coalition with Christian Democratic Union of Germany, 2013–21; in opposition, 2009–13.	25.7 (2021)
Spain	Partido Socialista Obrero Espanol (PSOE; Spanish Socialist Workers' Party)	In office since 2018 (current coalition with Podemos): First-placed party in April 2019 election; lost in 2016 to People's Party but ousted them in 2018.	28 (November 2019)
Portugal	Partido Socialista (PS)	In office (majority): In coalition with left block, communists and Greens since 2015.	41.4 (2022)
Sweden	Sveriges Socialdemokratiska Arbetareparti (SAP; Swedish Social Democratic Party)	Out of office, losing 2022 general election. Was in office as minority government (2014–22).	28.3 (2018)

Country	Centre-left party	Recent electoral performance	Vote share most recent election (%)
Norway	Arbeiderpartiet (AP; Labour Party)	In office (minority government since 2021): Centre-right government with wins in 2013 and 2017 elections.	26.3 (2021)
Aotearoa New Zealand	New Zealand Labour Party	In office (majority): Won 2021 as majority, after 2017 win in coalition with New Zealand First. Previously in opposition nine years.	48.7 (2021)
Australia	ALP	In office (majority): Had not won a majority of seats since 2007, lost 2013, 2016 and 2019 elections.	32.6 (2022)

Source: Compiled by the authors.

First, some centre-left parties have not recovered from their downturn in fortunes after the GFC. The cases of the French Parti socialiste (PS), the Dutch Partij van de Arbeid (PvdA; Labour Party) and of course the end of the Panhellenic Socialist Movement (PASOK) in Greece are instructive. Either party system changes or exogenous political shocks have fundamentally destabilised the centre-left. In a country like Belgium with two centre-left parties, they remain part of an incredibly fractured political system and have relatively strong footholds in some regions.

Elsewhere, the parties have recovered. For example, there was a resurgence across Scandinavia, with a number of centre-left governments taking office in Norway and elsewhere. There are leading examples of relatively strong centre-left performers—notably, the Partido Socialista (PS) in Portugal (and their remarkable success as a 'contraption' coalition) and the Jacinda Ardern–led Labour Government in Aotearoa New Zealand. In this respect, the ALP's return to office reflects this wider, limited return of the centre-left.

It is worth making a few observations about the state of the left more generally. First, many of the left's parties are recording historically low vote shares, even when they win office (for example, the Swedish Social Democratic Party). Generally, many European countries have coalition governments and the ALP's win also reflects the general shift away from mainstream parties. The centre-left is holding on to 20–30 per cent of the electorate and government formation dynamics reflect whether they can achieve power.

We can also make some comparative judgements about the reorientations of the centre-left, especially since the third-way era. In many respects, the parties have moved 'left' and, in Europe in particular, have placed a stronger emphasis on rebuilding their welfare states. This arguably stands in contrast with the cases of Aotearoa New Zealand and Australia (Manwaring 2021). In several comparable cases, we can also see how the centre-left is appealing to certain values to underpin its agenda. Common themes such as 'dignity' and 'security' are part of the electoral pitch of the centre-left in the United Kingdom, Aotearoa New Zealand and Germany. Moreover, as with Albanese's labourism, we can also see a strong shift to the parties adopting significant decarbonisation and climate change strategies in their economic plans, while consistently seeking to remain 'pragmatic' and 'fiscally responsible'.

A snapshot comparison with Olaf Scholz's win in Germany gives a strong insight into how the parties are winning back the electorate, especially after long periods of centre-right rule. Scholz's Sozialdemokratische Partei Deutschlands (SPD; Social Democratic Party) was losing in the polls but managed to win with 25.7 per cent of the vote after Angela Merkel left the political stage. Scholz's leadership agenda had a valence/competence theme: 'Which person do we want to run the country?' (Chazan 2021). Crucially, like Albanese, the SPD concentrated its policy agenda on core issues close to the party's heart. Chazan (2021) notes that Scholz 'ran an uncluttered campaign based on simple promises: a higher minimum wage, stable pensions, more affordable housing and a carbon-neutral economy'.

This appears to be a common thread among a few of the more successful centre-left parties—coalescing their appeal on a core number of 'back to basics' claims: improved wages, addressing cost-of-living and housing issues and so forth. The electoral situation for the centre-left is brittle and uncertain but a thin or 'new' labourism has helped the parties address, in part, their ideological positions from the third-way heyday.

Conclusion

In 2022, the ALP managed to exorcise some of the ghosts of the harrowing 2019 result, recalibrating its agenda around a thin labourism—making clear and steady appeals to the electorate on issues of competence but also making pitches based on incremental economic gains, along with a concerted effort to address climate change—long neglected by the Coalition. Their successful win does, however, rest on an electoral brittleness and there are wider future dilemmas such as the distancing from the unions. Yet, the ALP remains a striking case of how the centre-left has sought to recalibrate its identity and policy agenda.

References

Albanese, Anthony. 2020. *Labor's Vision for Australia: Speeches from the Labor Party Leader*. Canberra: ALP.

Albanese, Anthony. 2022a. 'Better future for Queensland; Novak Djokovic debacle; Scott Morrison; Government advertising; Labor caucus'. [Transcript]. Doorstop interview, Brisbane, 15 January.

Albanese, Anthony. 2022b. 'Australia's best days are ahead'. Address to the National Press Club, Canberra, 25 January. Available from: anthonyalbanese.com.au/media-centre/australias-best-days-are-ahead.

Albanese, Anthony. 2022c. 'Labor will tackle wage stagnation'. *Australian Financial Review*, 27 January. Available from: www.afr.com/policy/economy/labor-will-tackle-wage-stagnation-20220126-p59rge.

Albanese, Anthony. 2022d. 'Budget reply 2022: Working together, we can build a better future'. Speech, Parliament of Australia, Canberra, 31 March. Available from: anthonyalbanese.com.au/media-centre/budget-reply-2022.

Albanese, Anthony. 2022e. 'Vote for a better future: Australian Labor Party federal election campaign launch'. Speech, Perth, 1 May. Available from: anthonyalbanese.com.au/media-centre/vote-for-a-better-future-2022-campaign-launch.

Albanese, Anthony. 2022f. 'Time to advance'. Speech to Australian Financial Review New Platform for Growth Conference, Sydney, 9 March. Available from: anthonyalbanese.com.au/media-centre/time-to-advance-afr-conference.

Aly, Anne. 2021. 'Huge failure for Labor on diversity: Anne Aly slams own party over Kristina Keneally lower house'. *NewsRadio*, [ABC], 11 September. Available from: www.abc.net.au/news/2021-09-11/this-is-a-huge-failure-for-labor-on-diversity:/13537704.

Arya, Prachi. 2022. *Political Advertising on Social Media Platforms during the 2022 Federal Election*. Report, June. Canberra: The Australia Institute. Available from: australiainstitute.org.au/wp-content/uploads/2022/06/Political-advertising-on-social-media-platforms-WEB.pdf.

Australian Council of Social Service (ACOSS). 2018. 'Raise the rate: Increase Newstart and related payments'. *Explainer*, March. Canberra: ACOSS. Available from: www.acoss.org.au/wp-content/uploads/2018/03/Raise-the-Rate-Explainer-1.pdf.

Australian Council of Social Service (ACOSS). 2019. *The Government's Tax Cuts: Who Gains? What Do They Cost?* ACOSS Briefing Note, June. Canberra: ACOSS. Available from: www.acoss.org.au/wp-content/uploads/2019/06/ACOSS -briefing-note_tax-cuts_who-gains_what-do-they-cost_final.pdf.

Australian Labor Party (ALP). 2021a. *ALP National Platform: As Adopted at the 2021 Special Platform Conference*. March. Canberra: ALP. Available from: alp.org.au/media/2594/2021-alp-national-platform-final-endorsed-platform.pdf.

Australian Labor Party (ALP). 2021b. *Powering Australia*. Canberra: ALP. Available from: www.alp.org.au/policies/powering-australia.

Bonyhady, Nick. 2022. 'Unions, business, lay out priorities for incoming Albanese government'. *Sydney Morning Herald*, 22 May. Available from: www.smh.com.au/business/workplace/unions-business-lay-out-priorities-for-incoming-albanese-government-20220522-p5anht.html.

Boyd, Tony. 2022. 'Albo's got business onside'. *Australian Financial Review*, 27 May. Available from: www.afr.com/chanticleer/albo-s-got-business-onside-20220527-p5ap58.

Business Council of Australia (BCA). 2022. 'Business welcomes an Albanese Labor government'. Media release, 23 May. Melbourne: BCA. Available from: www.bca.com.au/business_welcomes_an_albanese_labor_government.

Cameron, Sarah and Ian McAllister. 2019. *Trends in Australian Political Opinion: Results from the Australian Election Study 1987–2019*. Canberra: ANU.

Chazan, Guy. 2021. 'Merkel's natural heir: How Olaf Scholz won Germany's election'. *Financial Times*, [London], 28 September. Available from: www.ft.com/content/de7669b5-da22-4fe1-bf33-a11eb50885d6.

Clarke, Tyrone. 2021. 'Key industry group says "a lot has changed" since rubbishing Labor's 2030 emissions reduction target'. *Sky News*, 3 November. Available from: www.skynews.com.au/australia-news/politics/key-industry-group-boss-says-a-lot-has-changed-since-rubbishing-labors-2030-emissions-reduction-target/news-story/c9ccc8bd7c730780b6e266870e29d8fd.

Crowley, Kate. 2022. 'Good timing and hard work: Behind the election's "Greenslide"'. *The Conversation*, 24 May. Available from: theconversation.com/good-timing-and-hard-work-behind-the-elections-greenslide-183719.

Curtis, Katina. 2020. 'Anthony Albanese defends childcare plan, says subsidies for wealthy families are not welfare'. *Sydney Morning Herald*, 9 October. Available from: www.smh.com.au/politics/federal/anthony-albanese-defends-childcare-plan-says-subsidies-for-wealthy-families-are-not-welfare-20201009-p563o9.html.

Emerson, Craig and Jay Weatherill. 2019. *Review of Labor's 2019 Federal Election Campaign*. Canberra: ALP. Available from: alp.org.au/media/2043/alp-campaign-review-2019.pdf.

Erickson, Paul. 2022. 'Campaign director's address to the National Press Club'. Speech, National Press Club, Canberra, 15 June.

Freeden, Michael. 1996. *Ideologies and Political Theory: A Conceptual Approach*. Oxford, UK: Oxford University Press. doi.org/10.1093/019829414X.001.0001.

Grattan, Michelle. 2022. 'Grattan on Friday: It's Albanese's to lose, as Morrison looks for some momentum'. *The Conversation*, 12 May. Available from: theconversation.com/grattan-on-friday-its-albaneses-to-lose-as-morrison-looks-for-some-momentum-182953.

Haselmayer, Martin. 2019. 'Negative campaigning and its consequences: A review and a look ahead'. *French Politics* 17(3): 355–72. doi.org/10.1057/s41253-019-00084-8.

Heywood, Andrew. 2021. *Political Ideologies: An Introduction*. London: Bloomsbury Publishing.

Keane, Bernard. 2022. 'Albanese's in the box seat with just a fortnight to go'. *Crikey*, 9 May. Available from: www.crikey.com.au/2022/05/09/labor-albanese-election-lead-polls/.

Keman, Hans. 2017. *Social Democracy: A Comparative Account of the Left-Wing Party Family*. London: Routledge. doi.org/10.4324/9781315166247.

Kenny, Mark. 2022. 'Half-time results are in: Who's having a good election campaign, and who isn't?'. *The Conversation*, 5 May. Available from: theconversation.com/half-time-results-are-in-whos-having-a-good-election-campaign-and-who-isnt-182122.

Manwaring, Rob. 2020. 'The Australian Labor Party'. In *Morrison's Miracle: The 2019 Federal Election*, edited by Anika Gauja, Marian Sawer and Marian Simms, 277–93. Canberra: ANU Press. doi.org/10.22459/MM.2020.13.

Manwaring, Rob. 2021. *The Politics of Social Democracy: Issues, Dilemmas and Future Directions for the Centre-Left*. London: Routledge. doi.org/10.4324/9780429027109.

Manwaring, Rob, Charlie Lees and Grant Duncan. 2022. 'Centre-left parties worldwide have struggled to reinvent themselves: What kind of ALP is fighting this election?'. *The Conversation*, 5 April. Available from: theconversation.com/centre-left-parties-worldwide-have-struggled-to-reinvent-themselves-what-kind-of-alp-is-fighting-this-election-181601.

Massola, James. 2021. 'With his back to the wall, Albanese comes out swinging with target seats, slogan, IR policy plan'. *Sun Herald*, [Sydney], 31 January. Available from: www.smh.com.au/politics/federal/with-his-back-to-the-wall-albanese-comes-out-swinging-with-target-seats-slogan-ir-policy-plan-20210129-p56xwk.html.

Middleton, Karen. 2022. 'The four-quarter plan: Inside Albanese's strategy to win'. *The Saturday Paper*, 14–20 May. Available from: www.thesaturdaypaper.com.au/news/politics/2022/05/14/the-four-quarter-plan-inside-albaneses-strategy-win/165245040013876.

Milner, Cameron. 2022. 'Federal Labor down and out in the Sunshine State'. *The Australian*, 24 June. Available from: www.theaustralian.com.au/subscribe/news/1/?sourceCode=TAWEB_WRE170_a_GGL&dest=https%3A%2F%2Fwww.theaustralian.com.au%2Fcommentary%2Ffederal-labor-down-and-out-in-the-sunshine-state%2Fnews-story%2F72029fdbd507e8a3c625b52b514fe429&memtype=anonymous&mode=premium&v21=dynamic-groupa-test-noscore&V21spcbehaviour=append.

Morgan, Wesley. 2021. 'Labor's 2030 target betters the Morrison government, but Australia must go much further, much faster'. *The Conversation*, 3 December. Available from: theconversation.com/labors-2030-climate-target-betters-the-morrison-government-but-australia-must-go-much-further-much-faster-173066.

Murphy, Katharine. 2022. 'Anthony Albanese to embrace Labor luminary Bob Hawke's consensus style if ALP wins election'. *The Guardian*, [Australia], 9 March. Available from: www.theguardian.com/australia-news/2022/mar/09/anthony-albanese-says-he-will-follow-bob-hawkes-lead-to-boost-wealth-for-all-australians.

Nguyen, Cat-Thao. 2022. 'A lesson for Labor: Why the people of Fowler rejected Keneally'. *Sydney Morning Herald*, 24 May. Available from: www.smh.com.au/national/a-lesson-for-labor-why-the-people-of-fowler-rejected-keneally-20220522-p5aneg.html.

Phillimore, John. 2022. 'Swing when you're winning: How Labor won big in Western Australia'. *The Conversation*, 22 May. Available from: theconversation.com/swing-when-youre-winning-how-labor-won-big-in-western-australia-183599.

Remeikis, Amy. 2021. 'Labor finalises energy platform for next election – as it happened'. *The Guardian*, [Australia], 31 March. Available from: www.the guardian.com/australia-news/live/2021/mar/31/alp-national-conference-2021-live-updates-news-anthony-albanese-federal-election-chris-bowen-energy-platform-australian-labor-party.

RepuTex. 2021. *The Economic Impact of the ALP's Powering Australia Plan*. Report, 3 December. Melbourne: RepuTex Energy. Available from: www.reputex.com/research-insights/report-the-economic-impact-of-the-alps-powering-australia-plan/#:~:text=Investment%20unlocked%20by%20the%20ALP's,4%25%20to%20the%20Transport%20sector.

Soutphommasane, Tim. 2022. 'Labor's win in Australia isn't decisive—but it marks a reshaping of politics'. *New Statesman*, 23 May. Available from: www.new statesman.com/world/australasia/2022/05/labors-win-in-australia-isnt-decisive-but-it-marks-a-major-political-shift.

Unions NSW. 2022. 'Send Morrison packing'. Campaign. Sydney: Unions NSW. Available from: www.unionsnsw.org.au/campaign/send-morrison-packing/.

Victorian Trades Hall Council. 2022. *2022 Federal Election*. Melbourne: Victorian Trades Hall Council. Available from: www.weareunion.org.au/2022_federal_election.

Whiteford, Peter and Gerry Redmond. 2018. 'Election FactCheck Q&A: Is it true Australia's unemployment payment level hasn't increased in over 20 years?'. The Conversation, 16 May. Available from: theconversation.com/election-factcheck-qanda-is-it-true-australias-unemployment-payment-level-hasnt-increased-in-over-20-years-59250.

10

The Liberal Party of Australia

Marija Taflaga

After three prime ministers and three terms in office, the Liberal Party of Australia (LPA) lost the 2022 election. It suffered a 5.7 per cent swing against it and lost 19 seats, many of which the party had held since their creation. The government limped into the campaign after 14 torrid months, wracked by a series of scandals and policy missteps. The campaign did not appear decisive: voters were focused on the government's record and, given its lack of a positive future agenda, the government again resorted to negative attacks on Labor and a selective appraisal of its own record. Against hope, Prime Minister Scott Morrison could not change voters' negative perceptions of his character or overturn the belief that his government was tired and lacked vision for the future.

Morrison resigned as party leader during his concession speech but did not quit parliament. This defeat represented one of the worst the LPA has faced and has rebalanced the Coalition. Queensland became the new locus of power within the LPA, with the Liberal National Party of Queensland (LNP) the dominant grouping. The Nationals now make up one-quarter of the joint party room and the LPA has lost most of its moderate/left faction MPs in the southern States.

The federal context

Since the 2019 election, the Liberal Party has faced several challenges, illustrating the ongoing organisational drift (Barry 2020) within the party's State divisions. The federal organisation of Australia's party system means that events at the subnational level affect the party's capacity to mobilise for national campaigns. A series of poor results in State polls demoralised the party and played into negative media coverage that fed a perception (real or imagined) of the federal government's unpopularity. The West Australian division was devastated in the March 2021 State election, losing all but two of its lower house seats and their party leader. Part of the popular explanation for this crushing result was the federal government's support of Clive Palmer's legal challenge to Western Australia's strong closed border during the pandemic and the ongoing popularity of Labor premier Mark McGowan (Hastie 2022). The Country Liberal Party and LNP, respectively, failed to unseat Labor governments in the Northern Territory and Queensland elections despite long-lived governments and much criticism of Queensland's Covid-19 management by the federal government. The only positive news was the return of the Tasmanian Liberal Government in May 2021, which fed perceptions that Tasmania would be a strength for the Morrison Government come the federal poll, despite the volatility of some of its northern seats. However, it was the unexpected landslide loss of the first-term Liberal Government in South Australia just a month before the federal poll that reinforced a building narrative about voters' impatience with the federal government's Covid-19 response and an unwillingness to grant second chances (Butler 2022a).

Internal party matters and candidate selection

Internal organisational scandals erupted in the Liberal Party's two largest divisions. In the aftermath of the 2019 Victorian election, that State's division reckoned with its lengthy and expensive litigation battle with its financial backer, the Cormack Foundation. Worth more than $70 million, the foundation was established in 1988 to provide funding for the Liberal Party, especially in Victoria. Liberal powerbrokers were eager to secure more of Cormack's funds and opposed the board's decision to give donations to other right-leaning political forces including Family First and the Institute of Public Affairs. Then Victorian LPA president Michael Kroger launched legal action challenging the foundation's independence, which the LPA lost (Hewett 2018).

In 2021, a branch-stacking scandal revealed the alleged use of taxpayer-funded staff to recruit among Melbourne's Christian and South Asian communities, which resulted in the preselection loss of long-serving conservative MP Kevin Andrews (Harris and Sakkal 2020). The scandal saw questions raised about factional powerbrokers Michael Sukkar and Marcus Bastiaan, with the latter choosing to resign from the Liberal Party. The party launched a forensic audit of its membership lists, finding multiple irregularities, including third-party payment of membership fees (for 170 of its 12,000 members or 1.5 per cent), warehousing of members and inappropriate accessing of membership details (Rollason and Willingham 2020). Victoria's Independent Broad-based Anti-corruption Commission assessed the case, but did not proceed with an investigation, possibly due to a lack of resources (Sakkal and McKenzie 2020). Sukkar, a federal minister, was investigated by the federal Department of Finance about the potential misuse of government staff, but the department concluded there was insufficient evidence to warrant further action (Curtis 2020). Finally, a perception of crisis enveloped the division after incendiary and extreme rhetoric on Covid-19 lockdowns and protests, which precipitated yet another change of leadership for the State party (ABC News 2021).

In New South Wales, the preselection process was thrown into chaos as a result of ongoing warfare between all three of the party's factions: the (hard) Right, the Hawke/Centre-Right and the Moderates/Left.[1] The origins of the conflict lie in the passing of the 2017 'Warringah Motion', which was the culmination of a long-running campaign to increase internal party democracy within the NSW division. The motion itself was championed by Tony Abbott, in part as revenge against the factional forces that had destroyed his prime ministership. The motion received narrow majority support from the party membership. It proposed three important changes: 1) it established plebiscites as the default mode for candidate selection,

---

1   'The Right' is the preferred name of that faction, but their opponents call them 'the Hard Right'. Likewise, the 'Moderates' is the preferred name of that faction, but their opponents call them 'the Left'. The Centre-Right is often called the 'Hawke Right', which reflects the hostility of both the Right and the Moderates towards this middle faction. Many within the Right and Moderates often claim the Hawke Right/Centre-Right does not have an 'ideological base' and is instead a patronage network led by Alex Hawke (leader of the NSW Centre-Right). Others argue it is a vehicle for evangelical Christianity and therefore has a substantive basis.

replacing the existing delegate model, which was relatively easy for factional warlords to control; 2) it increased the threshold from 70 to 90 per cent of votes required out of the 30-member state executive in order to override normal candidate selection procedures; and 3) it curtailed the powers of the state director to circumvent normal candidate procedures (Clennell 2018).

Rather than receiving the approval of the State executive, which was required to enact a constitutional change, a deal between the Left and the Right saw the reforms watered down with the 'Bennelong Motion'. The compromise saw plebiscites reserved for lower house seats only, alongside some continued State executive involvement. In addition, the introduction of plebiscites as a matter of practice was deferred until the 2022 federal and 2023 State election cycles (Clennell 2018; Barry 2020).

Plebiscites were unwelcome news to several sitting NSW MPs, including Centre-Right factional chief Alex Hawke and Trent Zimmerman, co-convenor of the Left/Moderates. The shock resignation of NSW premier Gladys Berejiklian prompted an unlikely powersharing deal between the Moderates (the largest faction) and the Right, which saw the Right's Dominic Perrottet become premier. With both federal and State governments vulnerable, competition for the available talent threatened to destabilise the minority State government as Morrison attempted to poach sitting State MPs to run federally. Any resulting by-elections could have seen the State government fall. This created the conditions in which the Perrottet Right was motivated to broker a deal over the NSW preselections. This deal, however, was controversial as it involved demoting sitting senator Concetta Fierravanti-Wells (Right faction), who had strong support among the membership. Therefore, a small number of dissidents on the State Council were able to block the factional agreement because it could not receive the 90 per cent majority vote to overturn normal plebiscite candidate selection procedures. This produced a stalemate (Robertson 2022a).

In response, Hawke, leader of the Centre-Right, used an act of administrative creativity. In New South Wales, a representative of the prime minister sits on the candidate selection committee. Hawke—Morrison's factional ally—was also his representative on this committee. Hawke refused to attend any of the scheduled committee meetings for 10 months and turned a representative role into a procedural break. The tactic would either place sufficient pressure on the State Council to pass the factions' deal or force a federal intervention in the NSW branch. An intervention would empower the factional chiefs to override the membership and endorse their favoured candidates. Conveniently for the Right and Moderate factions, the public furore over the growing crisis allowed both to shift all the blame on to Hawke and the Centre-Right and, by proxy, Morrison.

This tactic forced several emergency meetings of the LPA's Federal Executive in March–April 2022. Dominated by representatives from the State divisions, the executive was reticent to intervene in New South Wales because it ran counter to the party's ethos of divisional independence and the concern that it would set an unwelcome precedent. With time running out and previous orders for the NSW division to settle its internal affairs, the federal executive granted Morrison his desired intervention. A three-person committee of Morrison (Centre-Right), Premier Dominic Perrottet (Right) and former party president Chris McDiven (previously seen as a Moderate) re-endorsed three sitting members and selected six candidates to run in the remaining seats (Osborne 2022).

The six newly selected candidates had only a few weeks to establish their campaigns before the poll. One of these 'captain's pick' candidates, Katherine Deves (Warringah), was controversial on several fronts. Deves gained preselection despite not technically qualifying due to insufficient time as a party member. Many within the party questioned her suitability to try to win back the seat from Independent Zali Steggall given her discriminatory attitudes towards transgender people. Indeed, Deves's selection marked a sharp contrast in strategy from Morrison's previous preferred candidate, former NSW premier Gladys Berejiklian, whom he had spent weeks publicly encouraging to run (Patrick 2022).

The saga's final act involved a legal challenge to the administrative probity of the preselection decisions by Right faction member Matthew Camenzuli, in the name of internal party democracy. This challenge further diminished Morrison's tactical agility and his standing as prime minister. The NSW Supreme Court ruled in favour of the NSW division and the preselection decisions stood. The High Court refused leave to appeal. It was speculated that the court proceedings forced the prime minister to delay calling the election until these legal matters were resolved (Robertson 2022b). The resulting compromise did not meet Abbott's goal of taking the factional players out of politics. If anything, these democratic reforms and the overhaul of central authority changed only enough to make both unworkable. For some powerbrokers, the compromise provided an opportunity to accentuate their powers like never before (Robertson 2022c).

Women and representation

The Liberal Party was unable to shift the public perception that it struggled to represent, make policy for and understand the needs of women. Attempts by the Morrison Government to address this perception via policy initiatives proved ineffective and even counterproductive (Doran 2021). Despite having the highest number of female Cabinet ministers, Morrison and his government remained deaf to women's distinct needs in their policymaking, budgets and management of the Covid-19 pandemic. The pandemic underscored chronic underfunding and poor pay and conditions within the care sector, a workforce that is dominated by women. The government's support for male-dominated sectors of the economy (construction) and relative neglect of female-dominated industries (early learning) revealed its priorities (Hayne 2020). Moreover, the masculine tone of the government was also reflected in how power was distributed within its overwhelmingly male inner circle (Benson and Chambers 2019).

Most damaging of all was Morrison's clumsy political response to a series of scandals in 2021 that highlighted the treatment and safety of women in politics specifically and women in society generally (see further Chapter 5, this volume). Eventually, a positive response was the commissioning of what became a landmark review of the parliamentary workplace. Thanks to the leadership of Sex Discrimination Commissioner Kate Jenkins, this resulted in the most ambitious of the numerous parliamentary reports into harassment and bullying commissioned internationally after the globalisation of the #MeToo movement (Jenkins 2021). Less successful was the establishment of a Cabinet working group, led by the most senior Liberal woman, Marise Payne, focused on women's policy needs (Martin 2021). During the year, women frontbenchers were regularly sent out to defend the poor conduct of men (Sales 2021), adding to the perception that the Liberal Party was ill equipped to progress this agenda.

Despite the depth of the political crisis, little progress was made in altering the underlying conditions retarding women's representation within the LPA. Morrison expressed an openness to consider gender quotas (Curtis 2021), but he took no specific action to pressure the State divisions to change candidate selection rules and procedures. Instead, Morrison defended the chaotic candidate selection process in New South Wales as a means of getting more women selected (Bourke 2022). As for incumbent Liberal women, the failure to place two conservative women senators, Amanda

Stoker (Queensland) and Fierravanti-Wells (NSW), in winnable spots underscored the party's inability to make progress. In the case of Fierravanti-Wells, it personally damaged Morrison and torpedoed his attempt to reset the political debate with his election-eve budget. As noted, Fierravanti-Wells was the victim of a factional deal to settle the NSW Senate ticket. In retaliation, Fierravanti-Wells gave an extraordinary speech in the Senate describing herself as a 'marked woman' and outlining the machinations that saw her own faction betray her, in conjunction with an excoriating attack on Morrison's character. She argued that Morrison had 'lost the faith of the party', was 'an autocrat and a bully who has no moral compass' and concluded that he 'is not fit to be Prime Minister' (Senate Hansard, 29 March 2022: 426). Further damaging his standing, Morrison was attacked by another NSW Liberal Party woman, this time from the Moderate faction: upper house member Catherine Cusack. Cusack accused Morrison of politicising the Northern Rivers flood response by allocating resources in accordance with partisan considerations. In addition, she accused him of attempting to radically change the character of the party by recruiting among religious evangelicals. She resigned from the LPA arguing that it was no longer ideologically 'liberal' and publicly attacked Morrison during the campaign (Park 2022).

The campaign

The Morrison Government entered the campaign in a weak position. Unlike in 2019, the prime minister was now a known—and unpopular—quantity (ANU News 2022). Speculation about the government's re-election strategy centred on an early election in late 2021, off the back of a successful vaccination rollout via the federally funded GP network that would minimise the role of the States (Probyn 2021). A series of policy failures undid the original rollout plan, resulting in months-long lockdowns in both Sydney and Melbourne during 2021. Negative perceptions of the federal government were compounded both by a failure to secure sufficient rapid antigen tests during the 2021–22 summer and by a perceived slow response to major flooding disasters along the east coast. On a personal level, Morrison's character came under repeated attack: he was publicly accused of lying by the French president over Australia's abandonment of a submarine contract (Muller 2022); leaked text messages from Deputy Prime Minister Barnaby Joyce referred to Morrison as 'a hypocrite and a liar'; and texts from Berejiklian called Morrison a 'horrible, horrible person' (Murphy 2022).

The prime minister called a six-week campaign in the hope that it would give him time to regain ground. Morrison toured the outer suburbs and regions in a tightly disciplined and message-focused campaign. The strategy aimed to produce arresting images for the national nightly news and bespoke targeted grants for local media (Knott 2022a). He favoured commercial media, all but refusing to appear on the ABC. The government's campaign headquarters was again in Brisbane and the campaign team appeared to be heavily male dominated; one journalist reported that the local barbershop did a roaring trade (Benson 2022). As for campaign innovations, the party set up several websites, including LaborLies.com.au and WeakLeadership. com.au, alongside an explicit 'mythbusting' team designed to head off any Labor scare campaigns. This mythbusting team counted the stillborn Labor scare campaign that pensioners would be placed on the cashless welfare card as a win (Hutchinson and Brook 2022).

An early stumble by Albanese gave the government hope, but as the campaign unfolded, events blindsided and buffeted them: the China–Solomon Islands security agreement (Kaiku 2022), worse than expected inflation figures (Butler 2022b) and an unwelcome interest rate rise (Coorey and Mizen 2022). Reflecting his weak position, Morrison agreed to three leaders' debates. He tied the first but narrowly lost the next two. While Morrison believed until the final moments of the campaign that he could win, his advisers and ministers were preparing for defeat. However, none of them expected the extent of the loss (Markson 2022).

A personalised campaign

As if to underscore the lack of policy substance in the campaign, it overwhelmingly focused on the character of the two rivals. Morrison's main theme attempted to reprise his 2019 tactic of attacking Labor as inexperienced and incompetent. The Liberals' tagline 'Life won't be easy under Albanese' was an echo of 'The Bill you can't afford' from 2019. Yet, despite Albanese's repeated stumbles, Morrison struggled to find a fruitful line of attack.

Morrison's campaign appeared to be targeting males in outer-suburban and regional seats that were either Labor voters or would consider voting Labor. The images he worked so hard to craft were overwhelmingly coded masculine, emphasising worksites, tradies and high-visibility gear, and contrasted sharply with Labor's care-focused campaign (see Chapter 5, this volume). This crafted image of an 'ordinary bloke' complemented Morrison's repeated return to the candidacy of Deves—a women's sport and anti-trans advocate. Morrison would tactically reignite the debate over Deves's candidacy, attempting to demonstrate his concern for women's rights, religious minorities and the stifling pall of political correctness in public debate (Maiden and Foster 2022). Conservatives within the party claimed it had reinvigorated the volunteer base in New South Wales, but key Moderates were furious, arguing it was damaging their chances in their traditional heartland seats (Markson 2022). Reporting revealed that non-Christian faith leaders in western Sydney had not heard of trans women in women's sport (Knott 2022b), suggesting that the tactic was unlikely to flip traditional Labor strongholds in the outer suburbs.

Labor welcomed a campaign focused on Morrison's maleness and character and targeted his inability to take responsibility. In the final week, Morrison claimed he could 'change', admitting he was 'a bit of a bulldozer' (Grattan 2022). The admission saw journalist Tracy Grimshaw (Mimis 2022) forensically interrogate the prime minister on the sincerity of his claim, while revisiting his failures since 2019. Albanese also pounced, declaring that a bulldozer 'wrecks things' and contrasted himself as 'a builder' (Butler 2022c). The next day, Morrison accidentally crash-tackled a child during a campaign event at a soccer game (Humphries 2022), reinforcing all his negatives for hostile audiences and engendering sympathy among voters who felt the prime minister should be cut some slack given the circumstances of the previous three years.

The Teal Independents

The masculine, outer-suburban and regional focus of the prime minister's campaign contrasted starkly with the contest in the Liberal Party's traditional heartland of wealthy seats in the big cities. Morrison avoided the inner suburbs of Sydney, Melbourne and Brisbane and the party was forced to run two campaigns: one targeting Labor and the other against the Teal Independents—mostly women running in the Liberal Party's blue-ribbon metropolitan seats. The Teals forced the redirection of party resources to safe seats and tied down government ministers—most notably, Treasurer Josh Frydenberg, preventing him from campaigning across the country (Fyfe 2022).

The Independents' campaigns were structured around the climate crisis, integrity in politics and women's place in society—three significant government weaknesses and three personal weaknesses of the prime minister (Wahlquist 2022). Many of these candidates were partly funded by Climate 200, an advocacy group seeking to progress pro-climate policies in Australia. Liberal volunteers in the most high-profile Teal seats were dramatically outnumbered and could not match the grassroots organising and energy of the insurgents (see Chapter 14, this volume). The Liberals struggled to accurately gauge sentiment in the Teal seats, which were not included in their overnight tracking poll. Indeed, the party's Labor-focused polling showed the contest narrowing (Benson 2022). While many expected to be defeated, the Liberal Party's campaign team was blindsided by the extent of the swings and losses in their traditional heartlands. The result was a resounding rebuke of both Morrison and his party from communities that had voted non-Labor since 1901.

Party policy and ideology

The Morrison Government did not develop a major policy agenda to take to the 2022 election. Policy, such as it was, was largely framed by the budget, which focused on cost-of-living relief for targeted voter groups, such as cheaper medicines for pensioners and the suspension of the petrol excise until September 2022 (Coorey 2022). The government pursued piecemeal policies around boosting onshore manufacturing and apprenticeship training. It also pledged more money for the care economy but was outbid by Labor, and the messaging was muddied by Morrison's rhetorical pivot away from government capacity to influence Australians' lives for the better (Scarr 2021).

Climate policy was important and the government was desperate to neutralise the issue before the election. Morrison spent his term in government crab-walking to a new position on climate, eventually securing agreement before the climate summit in Glasgow for a 2050 target, though not before gruelling negotiations with the Nationals. In exchange for endorsing a 2050 target, the government promised billions in spending projects for the regions (Coorey 2021; see further Chapter 11, this volume). The government had no concrete plan for how it would achieve the goal beyond the slogan of 'technology, not taxes'. The government hoped to re-prosecute its attack on Labor's climate plans, but the combination of repeated flood disasters—some within Sydney itself—the high-profile campaigning of the Teals, Labor's message discipline and a shift in support from the business community all combined to make this a negative policy domain for the Coalition.

Instead, the government opted to focus on fiscal policy, attempting to attack Labor on its spending plans, particularly its support for higher wages in the upcoming national minimum wage case, and to link this to rising inflation. However, this became confusing for the government due to its own large income-support spending pledges and the huge debt accumulated during the pandemic. The prime minister's previously stated virtue of being 'non-ideological' and a pragmatist had significantly undermined the Liberals' brand of fiscal rectitude, especially when it was revealed that the government had given up to $38 billion to profitable businesses as part of its wage subsidy scheme (Conifer 2021). While business opposed large wage increases, the campaign focus on the cost of living made opposition to the modest pay increase of $1 an hour unseemly. If anything, the contest over wage policy appeared to backfire for the government and energised Albanese's campaign, creating a point of differentiation between the two leaders.

On integrity and corruption (see further Chapter 3), the Morrison Government cemented negative perceptions about its commitment to transparency and accountability when it withdrew from its promise to legislate a Commonwealth integrity commission. The government blamed Labor for failing to support its bill, but without even attempting to legislate it (Visentin 2022a). This bizarre political tactic summed up the shameless attitude of the government when scandals broke over its overtly politicised distribution of grant programs.

At the Liberals' campaign launch, Morrison declared a 'new era of opportunity', with a housing affordability plan that would allow first homebuyers to access their superannuation for a deposit. Unfortunately, Jane Hume, the relevant minster, undermined the policy the next day when she pointed out that such a policy would lead to price rises (Visentin 2022b). The government attempted to walk back the claim about price rises, arguing instead that the impact would be minimal because it was such a small scheme. This raised the question, what good would it really do? The policy was seen as a contrasting approach to Labor's shared-equity scheme. Morrison attacked this policy and was unfazed when it was later revealed he had supported such a policy only a few years earlier (Maiden 2022).

Perhaps the government's clearest agenda item was to increase defence spending and capability in the face of a more insecure and uncertain world. The government struck a new security partnership with the United Kingdom and the United States, which saw it junk its contract for French-designed submarines and embark on Australia's third submarine design in a decade (Hartcher 2022). As noted, the government was blindsided by the announcement of a security deal between China and Solomon Islands, which gave Labor ammunition to claim the government's Pacific step-up was a failure and to point to tangible consequences for Australia's policy settings on climate change. This did not stop the government from attempting to revive an earlier scare campaign about Labor being China's preferred candidate, by releasing information about a Chinese surveillance boat off the West Australian coast in the final week of the campaign (Greene 2022). In the government's desperation to shift the focus on to its preferred topics, it also released information—in violation of its own 'on-water matters' principle—about a refugee boat on the high seas in an attempt to launch a last-minute scare about the ALP (Opray 2022).

The result

The result was the worst in the LPA's history and its magnitude took party insiders by surprise. The Liberals lost seats across the country and, devastatingly, blue-ribbon seats, some of which they had held since Federation. Through a combination of tactical voting by both Labor and Greens voters and a partial (greater than 15 per cent) collapse in support among their own partisans (Cameron et al. 2022), the party lost seats in Sydney, Melbourne and Perth to the Teal Independents and Labor (see further Chapter 16, this volume). It lost to the Greens in Brisbane and, incredibly, its ACT Senate spot (with a required quota of 33.3 per cent) to the Independent David Pocock. The party did not win a single lower house seat.

The party performed particularly poorly in Victoria, New South Wales and Western Australia. In Victoria—once the jewel in the LPA crown—the party was reduced to eight (of 39) seats in the House of Representatives and four senators. The party lost blue-ribbon seats in Melbourne, including Kooyong (Frydenberg) and Higgins (Katie Allen). The party held on to Deakin (Michael Sukkar), Aston (Alan Tudge) and Menzies (Keith Wolahan), reducing these long-held seats to marginal status. While some large swings (as high as 7 per cent) were achieved in parts of outer Melbourne, Labor held these seats with margins of more than 10 and 15 per cent.

The party was devastated in New South Wales, retaining only nine (of 47) lower house seats, comparing poorly with the Nationals' seven. The party just held Bradfield and suffered greater than 5 per cent swings in very safe seats such as Berowra (Julian Leeser), Cook (Morrison) and Mitchell (Hawke). Underscoring the party's poor performance, the largest swing (2.4 per cent) towards the government was in Gilmore, where popular former State government minister Andrew Constance narrowly lost.

The party lost five seats in Western Australia—most to Labor. This result came as a surprise to party insiders and added to the devastation of that division. In South Australia, Boothby was lost to Labor and the Liberals failed to regain Mayo from the Centre Alliance. In Queensland, the party lost Brisbane and Ryan to the Greens, in an echo of the Teal wave further south. Only in Tasmania did the party hold its seats.

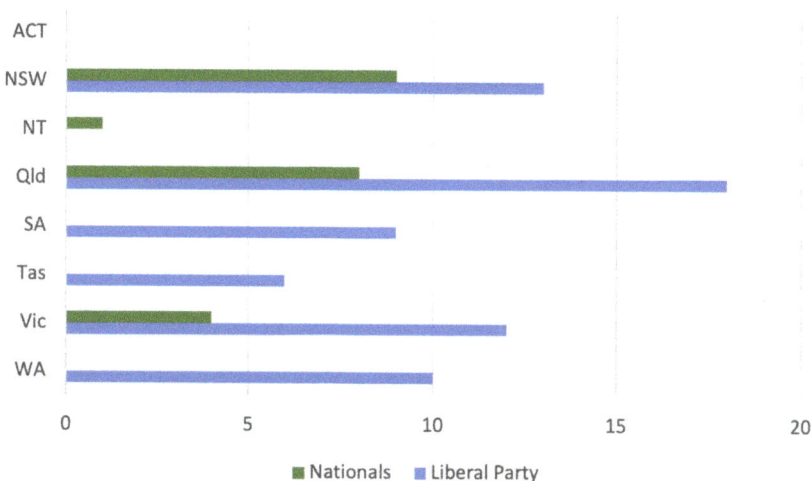

Figure 10.1 Balance of Coalition seats, House of Representatives and Senate combined

Note: The Coalition comprises four parties: the Liberal Party of Australia (LPA), the Nationals (NP), the Liberal National Party of Queensland (LNP) and the Country Liberal Party of the Northern Territory. All federal politicians must choose to sit in the LPA or NP party rooms. The figures above reflect those choices.

Source: Compiled by the author.

The result saw the Queensland LNP, especially its outer-suburban and regional members, form the largest block within the Liberal Party, shifting the centre of power decisively north (Figure 10.1). Disappointingly, the Liberal Party went backwards on female representation for another successive election, mirroring the long-running decline in the LPA's female vote. Men continued to vote for the LPA in its traditional strongholds and swings towards the Coalition in Labor's outer-suburban seats point to a long-running trend of Labor's blue-collar base switching to the Coalition. Indeed, the overall results appeared to reflect the government's strategy of targeting the outer suburbs, regions and male voters—albeit with mixed success. The Coalition failed to win in coal-belt seats, lost outer-suburban seats such as Robertson in New South Wales and failed to pick up any of Labor's outer-suburban seats.

Unsurprisingly, older voters continued to support the Liberal Party (see further, Chapter 18, this volume). Some have raised concerns about a potential demographic challenge for the party, but a bigger issue is perhaps the Coalition's failure to address declining homeownership or to rebalance the tax system away from those already holding significant assets and superannuation. Combined, these policy settings have delayed many Australians' entry into the property/wealth-owning class, which is correlated with a greater propensity to vote for conservatives (Ratcliff et al. 2020).

Relations within the Coalition and the road ahead

The result left relations between the Coalition partners frayed. National Party leader Barnaby Joyce disowned any responsibility for Liberal losses in the inner cities. Indeed, he appeared to abandon the Coalition, effectively saying it was not his job to help the Liberals win (Ransley 2022); he was deposed as leader shortly after the poll. In the aftermath of defeat, Morrison floated the idea of the Liberal–Nationals parties becoming the brand of conservatism in Australia, with a new party taking up the mantle of 'liberal' Australia (Markson 2022). If adopted, it would see the Liberals permanently forgo their heartland seats, refocus their powerbase in the regions and outer suburbs and commit to a new coalition based on potentially different faultlines. Of course, this would depend on the (unlikely) agreement of the National Party.

References

ABC News. 2021. 'Matthew Guy touts COVID recovery plan after toppling Michael O'Brien as Victorian Liberal leader'. *ABC News*, 7 September. Available from: www.abc.net.au/news/2021-09-07/victorian-liberal-leadership-michael-obrien-matthew-guy/100439184.

ANU News. 2022. 'Unpopular leaders punished at the polls in 2022 election'. *ANU News*, 24 June. Canberra: The Australian National University. Available from: www.anu.edu.au/news/all-news/unpopular-leaders-punished-at-the-polls-in-2022-election.

Barry, Nicholas. 2020. 'The Liberal Party'. In *Morrison's Miracle*, edited by Anika Gauja, Marian Sawer and Marian Simms, 295–311. Canberra: ANU Press. doi.org/10.22459/MM.2020.14.

Benson, Simon. 2022. 'Party over: The moment Libs knew'. *The Australian*, 28 May.

Benson, Simon and Geoff Chambers. 2019. 'The power list: Inside Morrison's inner circle of trust'. *The Australian*, 6 December. Available from: www.theaustralian. com.au/nation/politics/the-power-list-inside-scott-morrisons-inner-circle-of-trust/news-story/44a59bd4a183fce3ef540909a894e9b4.

Bourke, Latika. 2022. '"I stood up for women": PM defends captain's picks in federal seats'. *Sydney Morning Herald*, 5 April. Available from: www.smh.com. au/national/i-stood-up-for-women-pm-defends-captain-s-picks-in-federal-seats-20220405-p5ab40.html.

Butler, Josh. 2022a. 'South Australia election: Labor win should have Morrison Government "trembling", ALP says'. *The Guardian*, [Australia], 20 March. Available from: www.theguardian.com/australia-news/2022/mar/20/south-australian-state-election-labor-win-should-have-morrison-government-trembling-says-alp.

Butler, Josh. 2022b. 'Federal election briefing: Bombshell inflation figure adds fuel to cost of living fire—plus Albanese shows he's all business and no party'. *The Guardian*, [Australia], 27 April. Available from: www.theguardian.com/australia-news/2022/apr/27/federal-election-briefing-bombshell-inflation-figure-adds-fuel-to-cost-of-living-fire-plus-albanese-shows-hes-all-business-and-no-party.

Butler, Josh. 2022c. 'Builders and bulldozers: Anthony Albanese rubbishes Scott Morrison's late attempts at change'. *The Guardian*, [Australia], 13 May. Available from: www.theguardian.com/australia-news/2022/may/13/builders-and-bulldozers-anthony-albanese-rubbishes-scott-morrisons-late-attempts-at-change.

Cameron, Sarah, Ian McAllister, Simon Jackman and Jill Sheppard. 2022. *The 2022 Australian Federal Election: Results from the Australian Election Study.* [Computer file]. Available from: australianelectionstudy.org/wp-content/uploads/The-2022-Australian-Federal-Election-Results-from-the-Australian-Election-Study.pdf.

Clennell, Andrew. 2018. 'The Liberal peacemakers'. *The Australian*, 20 February.

Conifer, Dan. 2021. 'At least $38b in JobKeeper went to companies where turnover did not fall below thresholds, data finds'. *7.30*, [ABC TV], 2 November. Available from: www.abc.net.au/news/2021-11-02/38b-in-jobkeeper-went-to-companies-where-turnover-did-not-fall-/100586310.

Coorey, Phillip. 2021. 'Nationals to get billions for net zero'. *Australian Financial Review*, 17 October. Available from: www.afr.com/politics/federal/nationals-to-get-billions-for-net-zero-20211017-p590n4.

Coorey, Phillip. 2022. 'PM splashes cash in dash to the polls'. *Australian Financial Review*, 29 March. Available from: www.afr.com/politics/federal/pm-s-audacious-8-6b-election-bid-20220329-p5a8zz.

Coorey, Phillip and Ronald Mizen. 2022. 'Interest rate rise is "above politics", PM insists'. *Australian Financial Review*, 2 May. Available from: www.afr.com/politics/federal/interest-rate-rise-is-above-politics-pm-insists-20220502-p5ahp7.

Curtis, Katina. 2020. 'Department clears Liberal MPs of misuse of taxpayer funds for staff'. *The Age*, [Melbourne], 14 October. Available from: www.theage.com.au/politics/federal/department-clears-liberal-mps-of-misuse-of-taxpayer-funds-for-staff-20201014-p564y3.html.

Curtis, Katina. 2021. '"We tried it the other way": Morrison and ministers push Liberals to adopt quotas'. *Sydney Morning Herald*, 23 March. Available from: www.smh.com.au/politics/federal/we-tried-it-the-other-way-morrison-and-ministers-push-liberals-to-adopt-quotas-20210323-p57ddd.html.

Doran, Matthew. 2021. 'Government dumps plan to allow domestic violence victims to withdraw superannuation'. *ABC News*, 22 March. Available from: www.abc.net.au/news/2021-03-22/government-dumps-domestic-violence-victims-superannuation-plan/13268294.

Fyfe, Melissa. 2022. '"I ain't no Bambi": How a paediatrician ended up in politics'. *Good Weekend*, [*The Age*], [Melbourne], 23 July. Available from: www.theage.com.au/national/i-ain-t-no-bambi-how-a-paediatrician-ended-up-in-politics-20220608-p5as9v.html.

Grattan, Michelle. 2022. 'Morrison confesses to being a "bulldozer", suggests he'll change "gears"'. *The Conversation*, 13 May. Available from: theconversation.com/morrison-confesses-to-being-a-bulldozer-suggests-hell-change-gears-183030.

Greene, Andrew. 2022. 'Defence Minister Peter Dutton says a Chinese spy ship has been seen near secretive naval facility off Western Australia'. *ABC News*, 13 May, [Updated 14 May]. Available from: www.abc.net.au/news/2022-05-13/chinese-spy-ship-spotted-near-naval-facility-western-australia/101064538.

Harris, Rob and Paul Sakkal. 2020. 'How the Victorian Liberals' conservative warlords tore the party apart'. *The Age*, [Melbourne], 29 August. Available from: www.theage.com.au/politics/federal/how-the-victorian-liberals-conservative-warlords-tore-the-party-apart-20200828-p55q9z.html.

Hartcher, Peter. 2022. 'Radioactive: Inside the top-secret AUKUS subs deal'. *Sydney Morning Herald*, 14 May. Available from: www.smh.com.au/politics/federal/radioactive-inside-the-top-secret-aukus-subs-deal-20220510-p5ak7g.html.

Hastie, Hamish. 2022. 'The inside story of how Labor conquered the western front'. *Sydney Morning Herald*, 25 May. Available from: www.smh.com.au/national/the-inside-story-of-how-labor-conquered-the-western-front-20220523-p5antl.html.

Hayne, Jordan. 2020. 'Free child care to end in July after minister says it did its job during Coronavirus'. *ABC News*, 8 June. Available from: www.abc.net.au/news/2020-06-08/free-childcare-coronavirus-support-to-end-july/12332066.

Hewett, Jennifer. 2018. 'Kroger loses the pot in the battle with the Cormack Foundation'. *Australian Financial Review*, 14 June, [Updated 15 June]. Available from: www.afr.com/opinion/kroger-loses-the-pot-20180614-h11ed2.

Hill, Jess. 2021. 'The reckoning: How #MeToo is changing Australia'. *Quarterly Essay 84*, November. Available from: www.quarterlyessay.com.au/essay/2021/11/the-reckoning.

Humphries, Alexandra. 2022. 'Prime Minister Scott Morrison crashes into a child during soccer training in Tasmania on campaign trail'. *ABC News*, 18 May. Available from: www.abc.net.au/news/2022-05-18/scott-morrison-crashes-over-child-on-soccer-pitch-campaign-trail/101078710.

Hutchinson, Samantha and Stephen Brook. 2022. 'Liberals fire up their "Mythbuster" machine for election campaign'. *Sydney Morning Herald*, 4 May. Available from: www.smh.com.au/national/liberals-fire-up-their-mythbuster-machine-for-election-campaign-20220503-p5ai9g.html.

Jenkins, Kate. 2021. *Set the Standard: Report on the Independent Review into Commonwealth Parliamentary Workplaces (2021)*. Canberra: Australian Human Rights Commission. Available from: humanrights.gov.au/set-standard-2021.

Kaiku, Patrick. 2022. 'PNG and the Solomon Islands–China security agreement'. *The Interpreter*, 23 May. Available from: www.lowyinstitute.org/the-interpreter/png-and-solomon-islands-china-security-agreement.

Knott, Matthew. 2022a. 'Miracle seeker'. *Sydney Morning Herald*, 7 May.

Knott, Matthew. 2022b. 'How are faith communities responding to Katherine Deves?'. *Sydney Morning Herald*, 15 May.

Maiden, Samantha. 2022. 'Unearthed clip shows Scott Morrison backing shared equity scheme during GFC'. *News.com.au*, 2 May. Available from: www.news.com.au/finance/economy/australian-economy/unearthed-clip-shows-scott-morrison-backing-shared-equity-scheme-during-gfc/news-story/4aaae251f8c38f5afa6d6d6f840843f5.

Maiden, Samantha and Alexandra Foster. 2022. 'Morrison says he still supports Katherine Deves despite her retracted apology for trans comments'. *News.com.au*, 10 May. Available from: www.news.com.au/national/federal-election/morrison-says-he-still-supports-katherine-deves-despite-her-retracted-apology-for-trans-comments/news-story/cf4a3c6ebbef545462fcf04da14804ad.

Markson, Sharri. 2022. 'Re-elect PM? Some not so Kean'. *The Australian*, 11 June.

Martin, Sarah. 2021. 'Women's Cabinet Taskforce discusses "practical" budget measures in first meeting'. *The Guardian*, [Australia], 6 April. Available from: www.theguardian.com/australia-news/2021/apr/06/womens-cabinet-taskforce-discusses-practical-budget-measures-in-first-meeting.

Mimis, Sheri. 2022. 'Tracy Grimshaw asks Prime Minister Scott Morrison the tough questions you want answered'. *9Now*. Available from: 9now.nine.com.au/a-current-affair/federal-election-tracy-grimshaw-interviews-scott-morrison/49594146-0a92-427a-97c5-e2a91dedeeec.

Muller, Denis. 2022. '"I don't think, I know": How 5 words from the French President triggered a ruinous run on Morrison's character'. *The Conversation*, 21 May. Available from: theconversation.com/i-dont-think-i-know-how-5-words-from-the-french-president-triggered-a-ruinous-run-on-morrisons-character-179755.

Murphy, Katharine. 2022. 'Barnaby Joyce called Scott Morrison "a hypocrite and a liar" in leaked text message'. *The Guardian*, [Australia], 4 February. Available from: www.theguardian.com/australia-news/2022/feb/04/barnaby-joyce-called-scott-morrison-a-hypocrite-and-a-liar-in-leaked-text-message.

Opray, Max. 2022. 'Probe into election day boat stunt'. *Post*, [*The Saturday Paper*], 25 May. Available from: www.thesaturdaypaper.com.au/post/max-opray/2022/05/25/probe-election-day-boat-stunt.

Osborne, Paul. 2022. 'Federal Liberals step in over NSW stoush'. *The New Daily*, 4 March. Available from: thenewdaily.com.au/news/politics/australian-politics/2022/03/04/federal-liberals-nsw-stoush/.

Park, Andy. 2022. '"They have travelled so far from what we believe": Liberal infighting continues'. *RN Drive*, [Radio National], 18 April. Available from: www.abc.net.au/radionational/programs/drive/liberal-infighting-continues-over-anti-trans-comments/13844618.

Patrick, Aaron. 2022. 'How a gender warrior hijacked the 2022 election'. *Australian Financial Review*, 20 April. Available from: www.afr.com/politics/federal/how-a-gender-warrior-hijacked-the-2022-election-20220419-p5aehz.

Probyn, Andrew. 2021. 'Scott Morrison risks facing political danger in post-coronavirus vaccine Australia'. *ABC News*, 2 February, [Updated 5 February]. Available from: www.abc.net.au/news/2021-02-02/scott-morrison-political-dilemma-election-covid-19-vaccine/13109674.

Ransley, Ellen. 2022. 'Barnaby Joyce says not his fault Liberal Party lost 19 seats'. *News.com.au*, 23 May. Available from: www.news.com.au/national/federal-election/barnaby-joyce-says-not-his-fault-liberal-party-lost-19-seats/news-story/3555c9f6b8bd07f2a20bcc5ae1261ed4.

Ratcliff, Shaun, Jill Sheppard and Juliet Pietsch. 2020. 'Voter behaviour'. In *Morrison's Miracle*, edited by Anika Gauja, Marian Sawer and Marian Simms, 253–74. Canberra: ANU Press. doi.org/10.22459/MM.2020.12.

Robertson, James. 2022a. 'The decline of Scott Morrison spells trouble for allies'. *The New Daily*, 7 February, [Updated 8 February]. Available from: thenewdaily.com.au/news/politics/2022/02/07/scott-morrisons-decline-trouble/.

Robertson, James. 2022b. 'Morrison accused of using public resources to fight Liberal factional war'. *The New Daily*, 31 March, [Updated 1 April]. Available from: thenewdaily.com.au/news/politics/australian-politics/federal-election-2022/2022/03/31/morrison-liberal-factional-war/.

Robertson, James. 2022c. 'Revenge served cold for Liberal blamed for election wipeout'. *The New Daily*, 2 June, [Updated 3 June]. Available from: thenewdaily.com.au/news/politics/2022/06/02/liberal-kingpin-blamed-election-wipeout/.

Rollason, Bridget and Richard Willingham. 2020. 'Victorian Liberal Party branch-stacking investigation finds 170 memberships paid by someone else'. *ABC News*, 18 December. Available from: www.abc.net.au/news/2020-12-18/victorian-liberal-party-branch-stacking-review-handed-down/12996900.

Sakkal, Paul and Nick McKenzie. 2020. 'IBAC to assess allegations of Liberal rorts likened to "red shirts" affair'. *The Age*, [Melbourne], 15 October. Available from: www.theage.com.au/national/victoria/ibac-to-assess-allegations-of-liberal-rorts-likened-to-red-shirts-affair-20201015-p565dc.html.

Sales, Leigh. 2021. 'Industry Minister Karen Andrews speaks on the non-inclusive culture at Parliament House'. *7.30*, [ABC TV], 23 March. Available from: www.abc.net.au/7.30/industry-minister-karen-andrews-speaks-on-the-non/13270254.

Scarr, Lanai. 2021. 'Scott Morrison: PM wants government to butt out of people's lives as Australia opens up'. *West Australian*, [Perth], 13 December. Available from: thewest.com.au/news/coronavirus/scott-morrison-pm-wants-government-to-butt-out-of-peoples-lives-as-australia-opens-up-c-4930727.

Visentin, Lisa. 2022a. 'Morrison walks from federal integrity commission, blames Labor'. *Sydney Morning Herald*, 14 April. Available from: www.smh.com.au/politics/federal/morrison-walks-away-from-integrity-commission-promise-without-labor-support-20220414-p5adgd.html.

Visentin, Lisa. 2022b. 'Liberal minister admits super-for-housing policy could "bump" home prices'. *Sydney Morning Herald*, 16 May. Available from: www.smh.com.au/politics/federal/liberal-minister-admits-super-for-housing-policy-could-bump-home-prices-20220516-p5alml.html.

Wahlquist, Calla. 2022. 'Teal Independents: Who are they and how did they upend Australia's election?'. *The Guardian*, [Australia], 23 May. Available from: www.theguardian.com/australia-news/2022/may/23/teal-independents-who-are-they-how-did-they-upend-australia-election.

11

The National Party of Australia

Anika Gauja

Rural and regional electorates in Australia are increasingly complex spaces owing to population changes, greater levels of disadvantage compared with urban areas, infrastructure challenges, the evolving nature of primary industries and resources and the particular—if not differential—impacts of broader issues such as climate change. As the traditional party of rural and regional Australia, the Nationals have been under electoral pressure for some time as the party continues to search for broader relevance, having let go of once core values such as country-mindedness, rural exceptionalism and agrarian collectivism (Botterill and Cockfield 2015). While the party has also faced increased levels of political competition from minor parties and Independents, the 2019 Australian federal election saw the Nationals hold all its lower house seats, once again illustrating that it has been able to stem the tide of electoral losses that affected the party in the early 2000s (Cockfield 2020; Curtin and Woodward 2012; Cockfield and Botterill 2011; Woodward and Curtin 2010).

The 2022 election result continued this pattern of relative stability, particularly compared with the performance of the party's Coalition partner, the Liberals. Once again, the Nationals held on to their existing parliamentary representation. The party's approach to the election was to hold what ground it could, rather than seek any significant electoral expansion. As in recent federal elections (see, for example, Cockfield and Curtin 2018), the Nationals' 2022 campaign was characterised by a small-target, locally focused strategy that was built on a war-chest of pre-election infrastructure and spending promises, but it was conducted in the context of a broader fragmentation within the party and its supporter base over climate change policy, as well as significant electoral challenges from Independent candidates with progressive environmental policies. The electoral challenge from the Community Independent movement (see Chapter 14, this volume) replaced the former populist threat from parties such as Pauline Hanson's One Nation (PHON) and the Shooters, Fishers and Farmers Party in New South Wales and Victoria, which was prominent in previous elections (Cockfield and Curtin 2018), and exposed tensions within the party over its policy on climate change.

The National Party has a distinctive structure that has evolved as the party's support base has contracted. The party is registered federally and in New South Wales, Victoria, South Australia and Western Australia. In Queensland and the Northern Territory, the National Party has amalgamated with the Liberal Party under the banner of the Liberal National Party of Queensland (LNP) and the Country Liberal Party (NT).[1] This organisational context has significant implications for evaluating the party's election campaigns. In terms of the analysis contained in this chapter, Nationals candidates are identified as those endorsed by the State parties in New South Wales, Victoria, South Australia and Western Australia. In Queensland and the Northern Territory, Nationals candidates running for the LNP and the Country Liberals have been positively identified from the Nationals' federal website. To examine levels of support for the party in the House of Representatives, I look at the Nationals and the LNP separately after 2008 (when these parties amalgamated). Given the limited scope of the party's campaign, I also look more closely at the results for the individual seats contested to give a better indication of trends in support. The situation in the Senate is also complex, with the Liberal and National parties running joint tickets in all States and Territories, except South Australia, where the party ran independently of the Liberals. The Nationals did not field Senate candidates in Western Australia, Tasmania and the Australian Capital Territory.

---

1   The party is commonly referred to as both 'The Nationals' and the 'National Party (of Australia)'. This reflects attempts to rebrand the organisation over time. In 2003, the federal conference agreed that 'The Nationals' should be used for campaigning purposes and, in 2006, this became the party's official name. In 2013, the federal council agreed that while 'The Nationals' should continue to be used for campaigning, the constitutional name of the party should revert to 'The National Party of Australia' (Nationals 2022a).

Candidates and preselections

The party contested 22 House of Representatives seats, which was down from the 26 seats contested in 2019. This represented a tighter concentration of resources in campaigning for winnable and 'must-hold' seats. The highest numbers of seats were contested in New South Wales (nine), followed by Queensland (six) and Victoria (four). In these States, the Nationals contested most seats as the incumbent party. The only seats in these States in which the Nationals were looking to make electoral gains were in Hunter (NSW), Richmond (NSW) and Indi (Victoria) and all three campaigns were unsuccessful. Only one seat was contested by the Nationals in each of South Australia, Western Australia and the Northern Territory—all unsuccessfully. The party's strategy was one of consolidating resources and looking to hold on to existing seats, rather than electoral expansion.

Table 11.1 Nationals' MPs and senators after the 2022 federal election

Name	Electorate (State)	Primary swing (%)	Main challenger
House of Representatives			
David Littleproud	Maranoa (Qld)	+0.3	ALP
Kevin Hogan	Page (NSW)	–4.0	ALP
Barnaby Joyce	New England (NSW)	–2.4	ALP
Andrew Gee	Calare (NSW)	+3.0	Ind. (Kate Hook)
Michael McCormack	Riverina (NSW)	–13.4	ALP
Pat Conaghan	Cowper (NSW)	–7.6	Ind. (Caz Heise)
Michele Landry	Capricornia (Qld)	–1.2	ALP
Anne Webster	Mallee (Vic.)	+22.7	ALP
Mark Coulton	Parkes (NSW)	–1.4	ALP
Sam Birrell	Nicholls (Vic.)	–25.1	Ind. (Rob Priestly)
Colin Boyce	Flynn (Qld)	–1.0	ALP
Darren Chester	Gippsland (Vic.)	+0.1	ALP
David Gillespie	Lyne (NSW)	–5.8	ALP
Llew O'Brien	Wide Bay (Qld)	–3.6	ALP
Keith Pitt	Hinkler (Qld)	–3.9	ALP
Andrew Willcox	Dawson (Qld)	+0.4	ALP
Senate			
Perin Davey	NSW	Not up for election in 2022	
Ross Cadell	NSW	Elected	

Name	Electorate (State)	Primary swing (%)	Main challenger
Bridget McKenzie	Victoria	Re-elected	
Susan McDonald	Queensland	Not up for election in 2022	
Matt Canavan	Queensland	Re-elected	
Jacinta Nampijinpa Price	Northern Territory	Elected	

Source: AEC (2022).

In three seats, the party did not have the advantage of an incumbent candidate due to retirements and one resignation. Both Damien Drum (MP for Nicholls in Victoria) and Ken O'Dowd (MP for Flynn in Queensland) retired. George Christensen, who held the Queensland seat of Dawson, resigned from the party in April 2022 to contest a Senate seat for PHON.

Colin Boyce, a former State parliamentarian elected to represent the seat of Callide in the Queensland Legislative Assembly in 2017, was preselected to contest Flynn for the party. In Nicholls in Victoria, the party selected Sam Birrell, CEO of the Committee for Greater Shepparton. In Dawson in Queensland, the party preselected Whitsunday mayor and third-generation farmer Andrew Willcox. Willcox had been mayor since 2016. While each of these candidates has a connection to farming communities, their backgrounds are more diverse. Boyce, for example, worked in the coal-seam gas industry as a high-pressure pipe welder and Birrell has a background as an agronomist. This is illustrative of the party's candidate profile shifting over the longer term, from farmers to regional small business owners and those with a primary occupation outside agriculture. The backgrounds of all three successful candidates demonstrate the importance of existing local profiles, whether this is in the community sector, politics or business.

In addition to recontesting the House of Representatives seats it previously held, the Nationals preselected candidates who ran in the seats of Indi (Victoria, Liz Fisher), Hunter (NSW, James Thomson), Richmond (NSW, Kimberly Hone), Lingiari (NT, Damien Ryan), Barker (SA, Jonathan Pietzsch) and Durack (WA, Ian Blayney). Of these, only Pietzsch is a farmer. With a background in finance and having moved to the country after meeting her husband, Fisher's biography highlighted her community links and volunteer work with local schools. Thomson's professional background is in community advocacy, with a rural connection provided through his parents' farm-contracting business, while Hone and Ryan are small business owners. Blayney was previously the Nationals' member for the WA Legislative Assembly seat of Geraldton but was defeated in the 2021 State election by Lara Dalton from the ALP.

Table 11.2 Additional House of Representatives seats contested by the Nationals at the 2022 election

Name	Electorate (State)	Primary swing (%)	Main challenger
Elizabeth Fisher	Indi (Vic.)	–5.7	Ind.
James Thomson	Hunter (NSW)	+4.0	ALP
Kimberly Hone	Richmond (NSW)	–13.5	ALP
Damien Ryan	Lingiari (NT)	–2.2	ALP
Jonathan Pietzsch	Barker (SA)	–0.3	Lib.
Ian Blayney	Durack (WA)	+2.5	Lib.

Source: AEC (2022).

Candidates for the House of Representatives are preselected by electoral councils comprising party members and elected parliamentarians in each electorate. While the party's central council retains the right to refuse to endorse a preselected candidate, this method of selection is more internally democratic than those of the two major parties, who typically combine membership votes with that of the central office in their decision-making processes (Cross and Gauja 2014). Indeed, the Nationals have been a leader among Australian parties in experimenting with open primary votes (or community preselections) for the selection of its candidates (Gauja 2012), although this was not used for the 2022 federal election.

Only four of the party's 22 lower house candidates were women. The two incumbent women MPs, Anne Webster and Michelle Landry, were re-elected. The women who contested Indi and Richmond were not elected. The candidate for Indi, Elizabeth Fisher, claimed that a late preselection in February left her with little time to build support in the electorate (Bunn 2022). The Nationals' preselected candidate for the northern NSW seat of Richmond, Kimberly Hone, was discredited when controversial statements she had previously made on social media about religion, race, gender and climate change came to light. Local party members wrote to leader Barnaby Joyce with the concern that Hone had not been upfront about her past and underlying motivations when seeking preselection (Smee 2022).

The Nationals' Senate candidates were more balanced in terms of sex, with six women and four men appearing on Coalition/Nationals tickets across Australia. Of note was the preselection of Jacinta Nampijinpa Price, an Indigenous woman and Deputy Mayor of Alice Springs, who replaced incumbent Sam McMahon as the party's candidate for the Northern Territory Senate seat. McMahon subsequently resigned from the party and unsuccessfully contested the Senate for the Liberal Democrats. Across both the House and the Senate, there was no net gain for women's representation in the party. While the party established a Federal Women's Council in 1959, which is designed to guide women's policy and support the preselection of women candidates, the 2022 campaign was still dominated by male figureheads such as Joyce, Matt Canavan and David Littleproud.

Policies and campaigning

The party's national policy platform contained five key planks, which provided a tailored variation on the Liberal Party's campaign message. The policy statement began with the recognition that 'because of COVID, regional populations are growing, bringing challenges but also great opportunity' (The Nationals 2022b). The Nationals' policy platform had the following key elements:

1. Strengthening the economy to deliver more jobs and more apprentices and working towards unemployment below 4 per cent.
2. Tackling cost-of-living pressures through a reduction in fuel costs, increasing housing affordability and reducing tax for regional workers and their families.
3. Greater investment in regional infrastructure to create long-term opportunities and growth to underpin regional prosperity.
4. Building a better health system to provide more GPs and health specialists in the regions and towns where they are needed.
5. Bringing back manufacturing to Australia to reduce reliance on others while creating local jobs in regional communities. (The Nationals 2022b)

The synergy between the two Coalition parties, at least in the framing of the campaign nationally, was so apparent that Joyce began his campaign speech at the National Press Club by lauding the Coalition's credentials and criticising the ALP and Independent candidates, rather than establishing his party as a distinctive voice for rural and regional Australia. Indeed, the National Party was not mentioned once (Joyce 2022).

One notable omission from this list of policy positions that featured prominently in the campaign was climate change. During the previous parliament, Joyce had led the Nationals to support the Liberal Party's policy of net-zero emissions by 2050 in return for an additional Cabinet position and extra financial support for transitioning rural and regional economies. The deal, however, was fractious within the party: a tally of party room votes that was made public revealed that 12 MPs supported the policy and nine opposed (Martin and Murphy 2021). Littleproud, Darren Chester and Bridget McKenzie were supporters of the deal, whereas Queensland MPs Canavan and Llew O'Brien were vocal opponents. Joyce also revealed that he did not support the deal.

The deal the Nationals had made to support the 2050 targets provided the party with a war-chest of funding announcements and infrastructure promises that it was able to use across the campaign. This included more than $20 billion worth of projects including inland rail, dams and road repairs, much of it slated for seats in northern Australia. However, the campaign also highlighted continuing disagreements about the policy. Canavan, for example, declared the policy was 'sort of dead' and Colin Boyce, the party's candidate for Flynn, suggested that net zero by 2050 was a 'flexible plan. It leaves us with wriggle room as we proceed into the future' (Murphy 2022). While this disagreement created confusion and uncertainty about the party's true position on the issue, which arguably negatively impacted on the Coalition's performance, different Nationals MPs were able to speak about their own support for the policy, which resonated more positively with Nationals' voters in the southern States. Chester, MP for Gippsland, described the party as a 'loose coalition of independents ... a whole bunch of people from right across regional Australia representing quite diverse communities all thrown together in the one room' (quoted in Barbour and Sullivan 2022). Chester had been one of the most vocal Nationals in publicly declaring his support for action on climate change (Murphy and Hurst 2021).

The party's ability to conduct parallel national and local campaigns and to mould itself according to the image and needs of its local candidates becomes more apparent when looking at individual key-seat contests. As in 2019, Joyce kept a relatively low profile, campaigning—almost exclusively—in the Northern Territory, Queensland and northern New South Wales. This tactic reflected his relative unpopularity with the electorate at large: data from the 2022 Australian Election Study showed that Joyce ranked the most unpopular among the party leaders with survey respondents. On a scale of one to 10, Joyce's approval rating was 3.2, ranking below Scott Morrison (3.8), Greens leader Adam Bandt (4.1) and Anthony Albanese (5.3) (Cameron et al. 2022: 13–14). Joyce made one visit to Nicholls (Victoria), beginning the Nationals' 2022 campaign at the launch of the Echuca–

Moama bridge project. At a press interview, the party's local candidate, Sam Birrell, was asked whether Joyce would hurt or help his chances. Birrell replied, distancing himself somewhat from Joyce and the party: 'They all help. But essentially this is a local campaign. It's the people of Nicholls deciding which candidate can best continue on the delivery' (quoted in Whinnett 2022). The Independent candidate for Nicholls, Rob Priestly, provided a nice summation of the Nationals' dilemma in the seat when he lauded the retiring Nationals member as a 'good bloke', but noted that 'his party's interests just don't align with that of the area' (quoted in Francis 2021). Birrell's campaign was local in its orientation, featuring policy announcements such as rail infrastructure and support for a community wellbeing centre.

In the Queensland electorate of Flynn, a seat characterised by the prominence of mining and the resources sector, Boyce became (in)famous for his electioneering comment that 'net zero' was flexible—a view that he stood by after winning the seat: '[T]he road to [net zero] is not a straight lineal road, given the world events and what's happening in the world, and the fact that the world is, in my view, in a precarious position' (quoted in Peel 2022). This provided substantial differentiation from the ALP, which was the other key party contender in the seat (contested by Gladstone Mayor Matt Burnett). Boyce also campaigned on increased local funding for mental health services and $10 million promised to connect the inland rail to the Port of Gladstone. With six lower house members identifying as Nationals (see Table 11.1), regional Queensland remains a relative stronghold for the party, perhaps reflecting a more coordinated approach to campaigning in this State by virtue of the amalgamated party. However, with the Nationals' recording primary vote swings against all but one of these members, Labor appears to have made some inroads with a strategy of deploying Queensland senator Murray Watt to forge closer links and campaign within regional Queensland communities (Hines and McGhee 2022).

In the NSW seat of Cowper, Pat Conaghan campaigned on a platform of providing more housing in the region, particularly for vulnerable individuals and groups. Conaghan faced strong competition from Independent Voices 4 Cowper candidate, Caz Heise, who campaigned on a platform of climate action. In Mallee in Victoria, Anne Webster acknowledged the diversity of the electorate, but flagged health care and access to services as the number-one issue in the region, followed by roads and infrastructure and the Murray–Darling Basin rail project (Brissenden 2022).

While the Nationals' campaign strategy is driven largely by appealing to local communities, the party is also constrained compared with its Coalition partner in terms of public funding that can be used for electoral expenditure. Given the party's relative size and vote share, the Nationals received only a fraction of the election funding allocated to the Liberal and Labor parties. Excluding Queensland, where the Liberals and Nationals have amalgamated as a single party, the Nationals received $2.9 million in reimbursements from the AEC, compared with $27.6 million for the Liberals and $24.6 million for Labor (AEC 2020). This means the party relies on locally targeted television, print and media advertising, public events that gather local news coverage and traditional canvassing by local volunteers. Compared with the expenditure of the ALP and the Liberals, as well as prominent Independent candidates (see Chapter 13, this volume), the party's social media spending was very modest. Data from the Meta Ad Library, for example, show that from the beginning of April to election day, the federal National Party spent just $30,100 on 25 paid advertisements (Meta 2022).

Results

The Nationals were able to hold all their House of Representatives and Senate seats. This, as noted, continues a period of relative stability for the party in terms of parliamentary representation. However, as demonstrated in Figure 11.1, the relative decline of their primary-vote share continues, while the gap between vote share and seat share is widening. In 2022, the party's primary vote declined to just 3.6 per cent nationally (not including the LNP), which was down from 4.5 per cent in 2019. With the party's share of lower house seats steady, the result increases the discrepancy between the Nationals' vote share and its parliamentary representation, further indicating the geographic concentration of its vote. As we explain in the key-seat analysis below, this overall trend hides mixed results in individual seats, though it could be indicative of the strong challenge posed by the Independents movement to many traditionally Nationals-held seats across regional and rural Australia, which was a key theme in mainstream media commentary (see, for example, Cowie and Preiss 2022).

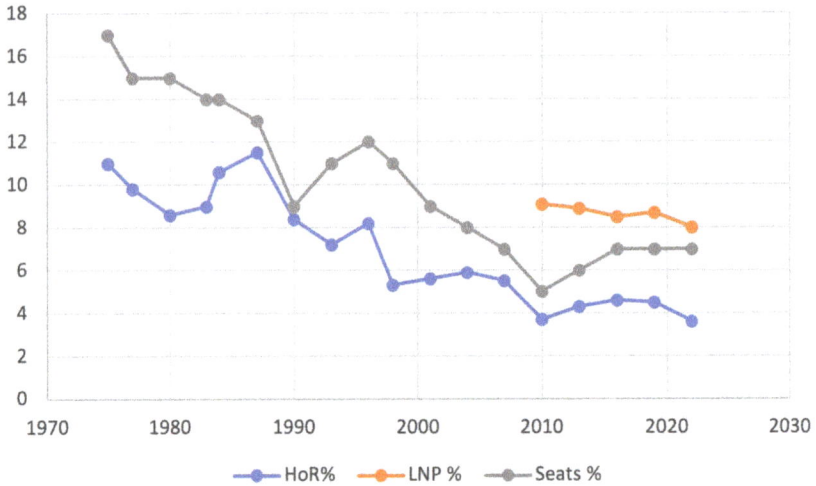

Figure 11.1 Nationals' vote and seat share, 1975–2022
Sources: AEC (2022, 2019); UWA (2018).

Using original data from the Australian Cooperative Election Survey, we can also examine broader trends in the Nationals' vote. The survey was collected through the YouGov online panel during the campaign (2–18 May). This is a sample of 5,988 respondents, which used a set of demographic, geographic and political quotas to ensure it was representative of the Australian electorate (with a rural oversample that produced 2,219 respondents in rural and provincial electorates).

The Nationals' relative shares of votes in 2019 and 2022 are depicted in the two Sankey charts in Figures 11.2 and 11.3. Figure 11.2 contrasts the National Party vote among survey respondents in the 2019 federal election for the House of Representatives (left column) with how they intended to vote for the 2022 election at the time the survey was conducted. The flows between the two columns depict voters switching, or maintaining, their votes. Thicker lines represent a greater volume of votes. The graph aligns with the overall decline in the Nationals' vote seen in the official primary count. However, we see the party vote redistributed across the political spectrum—flowing not just to Independent candidates but also to the Coalition, Labor, the Greens and PHON. One possible explanation for this is a population shift away from the seats the Nationals contested—and/or the fact they contested fewer seats overall—leaving fewer voters with the option to vote for the party in 2022.

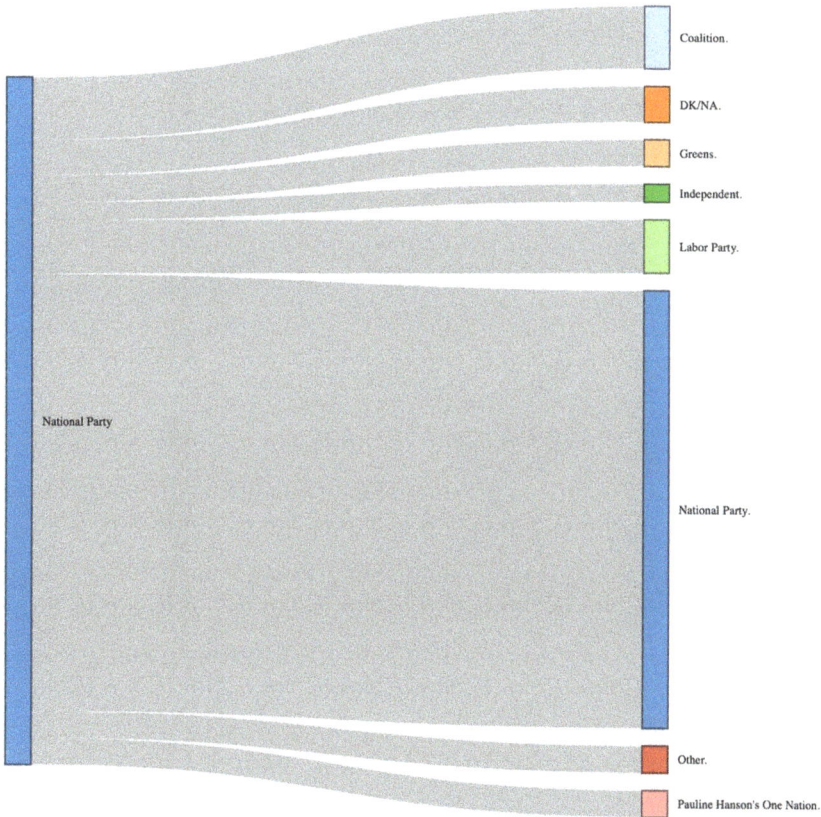

Figure 11.2 Change in the vote for the Nationals, 2019 vote versus 2022 voting intention—all respondents

DK/NA = don't know/not applicable

Source: Gauja and Halpin (2022).

However, if we restrict the analysis to respondents in rural electorates only, we see that the magnitude of the party's vote increased slightly from 2019 to 2022, and it was able to hold on to most voters. Again, those who chose to switch their allegiance directed their votes across the political spectrum, not simply to Independent candidates.

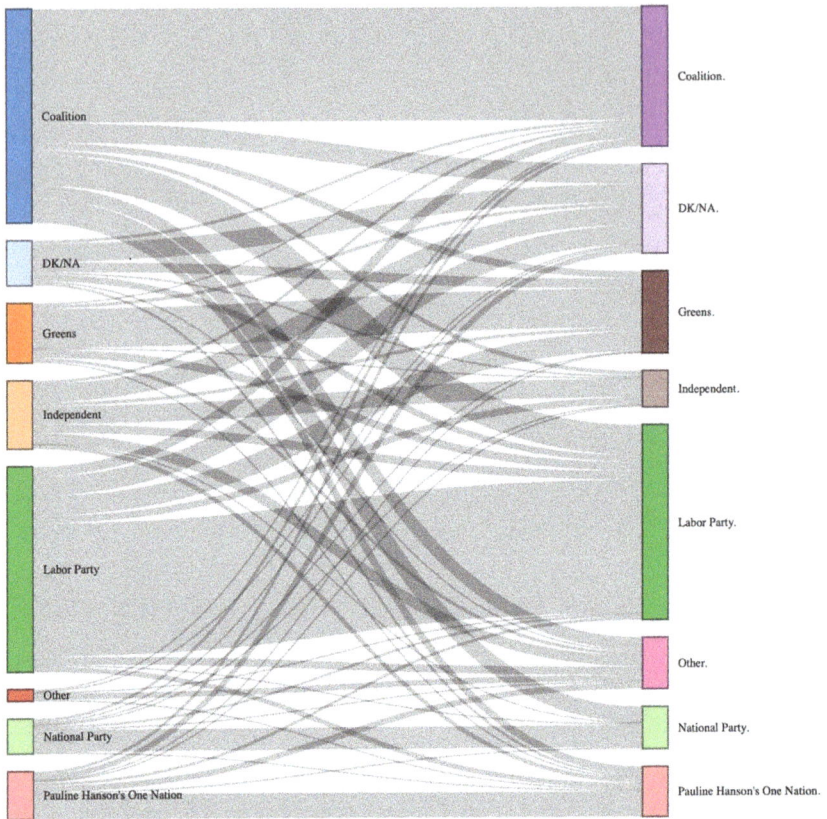

Figure 11.3 Change in vote for the Nationals and other parties, 2019 vote versus 2022 voting intention — rural respondents only

DK/NA = don't know/not applicable

Source: Gauja and Halpin (2022).

As noted, however, the party's national result obscures some of the trends in individual seats. In the three key seats in which the incumbents had retired or resigned (Flynn, Nicholls and Dawson), the party was able to hold on with varying margins. In Dawson, Andrew Willcox saw a slight increase in the primary vote but suffered a 4.2 per cent decrease in the two-party-preferred margin. In Flynn, Boyce was elected but with a 4.8 per cent two-party-preferred swing against him. Voters swung away from the Nationals and back to Labor in coalmining towns such as Moura and Blackwater in Queensland, but the Nationals polled much more strongly in that State's agricultural towns such as Theodore, Rolleston and Capella (Peel 2022). Birrell narrowly defeated Independent Rob Priestly in Nicholls, but the party recorded a 25 per cent fall in its primary vote.

In the non-incumbent seats where the party tried to make electoral gains, the results were mixed. In Indi, Barker and Durack, the Nationals also faced competition from the Liberal Party, which effectively lowered the former's vote and pushed the party out of contention (in each of these three seats the Liberal Party finished in either first or second place after the allocation of preferences). In seats where the party did not face a three-cornered contest, the result was more positive, with the party finishing second after the distribution of preferences in Hunter, Richmond and Lingiari.

In other electorates where the Nationals faced strong Independent candidates, they lost ground. In Cowper, for example, Conaghan's primary vote dropped by almost 8 per cent against Independent Caz Heise. The Nationals continued to lose support in Indi, where they polled less than 4 per cent, losing further ground to Helen Haines, and were also outpolled by PHON. In Calare, Andrew Gee was able to hold the seat with a modest increase in his primary vote against Independent Kate Hooke, but considering the Shooters, Fishers and Farmers Party did not field a candidate, his vote should have been significantly higher. Gee's relatively strong performance could be attributed to his deviation from the Coalition line on several key issues, including the federal integrity commission, climate change and his threat to resign from the party over the handling of veterans' affairs (Chan 2022).

A strong swing was also recorded against former Nationals leader Michael McCormack in Riverina. Ann Webster, MP for Mallee, was the only Nationals candidate to gain significant ground. The swing in her favour could, however, be attributed to the fact that the Liberal Party did not contest the seat (it was a three-cornered contest in 2019). Overall, the results suggest that while the party's electoral strategy of holding seats rather than maximising vote share is working to secure a reasonably consistent level of parliamentary representation, the party continues to lose support across Australia. This support is not just flowing to Independent challengers but is also spreading more broadly across the political spectrum, highlighting the increasing policy and population complexity of regional areas, as well as the continued fragmentation of the party system.

Conclusion: Implications for the Coalition and the way forward

The Nationals held a leadership vote to elect their leader at the first party room meeting after the election. The party traditionally spills the leadership after each election, so this was a routine contest. The ballot was contested by three candidates: Barnaby Joyce, David Littleproud and Darren Chester. Littleproud was elected leader, while Senator Perin Davey was elected deputy leader, which has provided some gender balance within the party's leadership. With these choices, the party room has signalled its intention to align the party's policy positions more with the middle ground of politics—particularly with respect to climate change. As Littleproud noted: '[W]e have made a sensible decision to be part of the global community; the global community asked us to sign up to net zero by 2050' (Sullivan and Evans 2022). With the Liberals' poor performance, the Nationals now make up a much more significant proportion of the Coalition but, given the divisions that exist within the party room, there is doubt that they will be able to leverage this to articulate a stronger position within the Coalition.

We saw some of these tensions emerge in the first few months of the forty-fifth parliament with the passage of the Labor Government's Climate Change Bill 2022, which legislated Australia's climate change targets as a 43 per cent reduction from 2005 levels by 2030 and net zero by 2050. All National Party parliamentarians voted against the legislation, but this was based on their objection not to the targets themselves but to enshrining them in law. The ambiguity of this position does little to resolve the ongoing debate within the party room about how climate change should be addressed and its effect on rural communities. With the ALP holding a majority in the House of Representatives and the Greens, the Jacqui Lambie Network and David Pocock holding the balance of power in the Senate, the Nationals' position on the issue was a moot point. The party's greatest challenge going forward will be to demonstrate that it can continue to represent and provide a voice for diverse rural communities from opposition.

References

Australian Electoral Commission (AEC). 2019. 'House of Representatives results'. *Tally Room: 2019 Federal Election*. AEC: Canberra. Available from: results.aec. gov.au/24310/Website/HouseResultsMenu-24310.htm.

Australian Electoral Commission (AEC). 2020. *Election Funding and Disclosure Report: Federal Election 2019.* AEC: Canberra.

Australian Electoral Commission (AEC). 2022. 'House of Representatives—Final result'. *Tally Room: 2022 Federal Election.* AEC: Canberra. Available from: results. aec.gov.au/27966/Website/HouseDefault-27966.htm.

Barbour, Lucy and Kath Sullivan. 2022. 'Barnaby Joyce's leadership tested as National Party fights to retain all seats this election'. *ABC News*, 11 May. Available from: www.abc.net.au/news/2022-05-11/federal-election-test-barnaby-joyce-leadership -of-nationals-/101026070.

Botterill, Linda and Geoff Cockfield. 2015. 'From "unstable" to "stable" minority government: Reflections on the role of the Nationals in federal Coalition governments'. *Australian Journal of Politics & History* 61(1): 53–66. doi.org/ 10.1111/ajph.12086.

Brissenden, Neve. 2022. 'Mallee MP sets out election agenda'. *The Stawell Times-News*, [Victoria], 25 February: 8.

Bunn, Anthony. 2022. 'Down, down, down—Nats plunge again'. *The Border Mail*, [Albury, NSW], 23 May.

Cameron, Sarah, Ian McAllister, Simon Jackman and Jill Sheppard. 2022. *The 2022 Australian Federal Election: Results from the Australian Election Study.* Canberra: ANU.

Chan, Gabrielle. 2022. 'Barnaby Joyce says all is well with the Nationals' vote—but a deeper dive suggests trouble lies ahead'. *The Guardian*, [Australia], 24 May. Available from: www.theguardian.com/australia-news/2022/may/24/barnaby-joyce-says-all-is-well-with-the-nationals-vote-but-a-deeper-dive-suggests-trouble-lies-ahead.

Cockfield, Geoff. 2020. 'The National Party of Australia'. In Anika Gauja, Marian Sawer and Marian Simms (eds), *Morrison's Miracle: The 2019 Australian Federal Election*, 313–28. Canberra: ANU Press. doi.org/10.22459/MM.2020.15.

Cockfield, Geoff and Linda Botterill. 2011. '"Back from the brink"? The National Party after the 2010 election'. *Australian Journal of Political Science* 46(2): 341–51. doi.org/10.1080/10361146.2011.568935.

Cockfield, Geoff and Jennifer Curtin. 2018. 'The National Party of Australia's campaign: Further "back from the brink"'. In Anika Gauja, Peter Chen, Juliet Pietsch and Jennifer Curtin (eds), *Double Disillusion: The 2016 Australian Federal Election Campaign*, 317–34. Canberra: ANU Press. doi.org/10.22459/DD.04. 2018.14.

Cowie, Tom and Benjamin Preiss. 2022. '"One of the most likely to fall": Independent push gathers steam in regional Victoria'. *The Age*, [Melbourne], 14 May. Available from: www.theage.com.au/politics/victoria/one-of-the-most-likely-to-fall-independent-push-gathers-steam-in-regional-victoria-20220512-p5akou.html.

Cross, William and Anika Gauja. 2014. 'Designing candidate selection methods: Explaining diversity in Australian parties'. *Australian Journal of Political Science* 49(4): 611–25. doi.org/10.1080/10361146.2014.958979.

Curtin, Jennifer and Dennis Woodward. 2012. 'Rural and regional Australia: The ultimate winners?'. In Marian Simms and John Wanna (eds), *Julia 2010: The Caretaker Election*, 239–47. Canberra: ANU Press. doi.org/10.22459/J2010. 02.2012.20.

Francis, Gianni. 2021. 'Independents warning as Nicholls contest begins'. *Daily Telegraph*, [Sydney], 8 December.

Gauja, Anika. 2012. 'The "push" for primaries: What drives party organisational reform in Australia and the United Kingdom?'. *Australian Journal of Political Science* 47(4): 641–58. doi.org/10.1080/10361146.2012.731490.

Gauja, Anika and Darren Halpin. 2022. 'Rural Politics Module'. In Shaun Ratcliff, Ariadne Vromen, Darren Halpin and Campbell White, *Australian Cooperative Election Survey.*

Gazy, Matt. 2022. '"Humbled": Conaghan retains Cowper after close call'. *Coffs Coast Advocate*, [Coffs Harbour, NSW], 24 May.

Hines, Jasmine and Rachel McGhee. 2022. 'Regional Queensland voted for the Liberal National Party. What do they make of the Labor government and the "Greenslide"?'. *ABC Capricornia*, [*ABC News*], 25 May. Available from: www. abc.net.au/news/2022-05-25/country-city-divide-voting-results-federal-regional-qld/101090822.

Joyce, Barnaby. 2022. 'Address (Deputy Prime Minister)—National Press Club'. Speech, National Press Club, Canberra, 11 May. Available from: nationals.org. au/address-deputy-prime-minister-national-press-club/.

Martin, Sarah and Katharine Murphy. 2021. 'Nationals agree to net zero target by 2050 despite Barnaby Joyce's opposition'. *The Guardian*, [Australia], 24 October. Available from: www.theguardian.com/australia-news/2021/oct/24/nationals-agree-to-net-zero-target-by-2050-despite-barnaby-joyces-opposition.

Meta. 2022. *Ad Library*. [Online]. Menlo Park, CA: Meta. Available from: www. facebook.com/ads/library/?active_status=all&ad_type=political_and_issue_ads& country=AU&sort_data[direction]=desc&sort_data[mode]=relevancy_monthly _grouped&media_type=all.

Murphy, Katharine. 2022. 'Coalition candidate says net zero by 2050 is a "flexible plan that leaves us wriggle room"'. *The Guardian*, [Australia], 25 April. Available from: www.theguardian.com/australia-news/2022/apr/25/coalition-candidate-says-net-zero-by-2050-is-a-flexible-plan-that-leaves-us-wiggle-room.

Murphy, Katharine and Daniel Hurst. 2021. 'Frontbencher Darren Chester warns Nationals not to sideline themselves in climate debate'. *The Guardian*, [Australia], 11 February. Available from: www.theguardian.com/australia-news/2021/feb/11/frontbencher-darren-chester-warns-nationals-not-to-sideline-themselves-in-climate-debate.

The Nationals. 2022a. 'Key dates in the party's development'. *Our History*. Canberra: The Nationals. Available from: nationals.org.au/about/our-history/key-dates-and-events/.

The Nationals. 2022b. *Our Plan for Regional Australia*. Canberra: The Nationals. Available from: nationals.org.au/election-2022/.

Peel, Charlie. 2022. 'Net zero up in air, says winning Nat'. *The Australian*, 26 May: 5.

Smee, Ben. 2022. 'NSW Nationals candidate tells congregation of her aim to "bring God's kingdom" to politics'. *The Guardian*, [Australia], 21 April. Available from: www.theguardian.com/australia-news/2022/apr/21/nsw-nationals-candidate-tells-congregation-of-her-aim-to-bring-gods-kingdom-to-politics.

Sullivan, Kath and Jake Evans. 2022. 'David Littleproud elected to lead the Nationals in opposition after post-election leadership vote'. *ABC News*, 30 May, [Updated 31 May]. Available from: www.abc.net.au/news/2022-05-30/barnaby-joyce-out-david-littleproud-elected-to-lead-nationals/101109494.

University of Western Australia (UWA). 2018. *Australian Politics and Elections Archive 1856–2018*. [Online.] Perth: UWA. Available from: elections.uwa.edu.au/index.lasso.

Whinnett, Ellen. 2022. 'Election 2022: The Deputy PM ain't no city slicker'. *Gold Coast Bulletin*, [Qld], 18 April: 6.

Woodward, Dennis and Jennifer Curtin. 2010. 'Rural and Regional Australia'. *Australian Cultural History* 28(1): 113–19. doi.org/10.1080/07288430903165337.

12

The Greens' campaign: Google it, mate

Stewart Jackson and Josh Holloway

More than a year before the 2022 election, the Australian Greens made their basic electoral strategy clear. In a press release, leader Adam Bandt outlined the party's targets: to win nine House of Representatives seats and expand its Senate representation to 12 through gains in New South Wales, Queensland and South Australia (Zhou and Remeikis 2021). Beyond re-electing Bandt in Melbourne, the Greens' targets in the lower house spanned Liberal and Labor seats in east coast capitals and the 'rural' NSW seat of Richmond. Changes in 2016 to the Senate electoral system that removed group voting tickets, as well as a consolidating voter base, made gains in the Senate contest more likely. For the House, there were hopes that (and active campaigns for) several of the Greens' target divisions could be in play. While the Greens' vote had certainly risen in opinion polling over the two years before the election, winning these seats was no easy feat. Most had well-known major-party incumbents, including frontbenchers like Labor's Terri Butler in Griffith (Qld).

The Greens sought to meet their electoral goals with a model of campaigning and style of policy platform both long in development. The party placed greatest emphasis on grassroots organising, waging 'ground' campaigns in several key seats that were of unprecedented scale and duration for a minor party—and, indeed, campaigns that either major party would likely struggle to match. The Queensland Greens coupled this with 'mutual aid' programs, embedding themselves in communities to provide, for instance, aid packages and cleanup assistance after floods. On policy, the Greens advocated a distinctly green-centred social democracy. Campaign appeals spoke of climate action holistically, but also gave prominence to classic left-redistributionist policies, such as expanding the welfare system, building public housing, increasing taxes on big business and including dental health in Medicare.

What transpired on election night began to be called a 'Greenslide' as the party looked to be winning or highly competitive in seven lower house seats (Courty et al. 2022). This later changed to Queensland being renamed (somewhat euphemistically) 'Greensland', as it became clear that the Greens were in the running for three seats: Ryan, Griffith and Brisbane. Despite the Greens' clearly stated aims for the election and favourable polling through the campaign, immediate media commentary about the party's gains expressed 'shock' at the result (Wordsworth 2022). This was not a universal response, however. Among the small handful of media outlets that had dedicated time to covering the Greens and inner Brisbane's contests, analysis instead rightly pointed to a result years in the making (for example, Smee 2022). Early vote tallies held the prospect of the Greens again holding the balance of power in both houses, with a Labor minority government needing to negotiate agreement on legislation. Although Labor struggled on the night, it was clear that the Coalition had lost the election, with a swing of 3 per cent against it and a loss of 18 seats. Further vote counting delivered Labor a slim majority, but a significant benefactor, along with the emerging bloc of Teal Independents, was the Greens.

The campaign moment

Three days into the official election campaign—a campaign marked by gaffes and half-truths from the Opposition leader and the prime minister—Greens leader Adam Bandt stood in the National Press Club ready to receive questions on his party's platform. Key to the Greens' policy prescriptions were addressing climate change with a just transition for coal and gas workers, a treaty with First Nations people, environmental justice and combating the falling wages of workers amid rising costs of living. The question he received from *Australian Financial Review* journalist Ronald Mizen centred on Bandt's comments on the disparity between wages and inflation and ended with a 'gotcha': 'What is the wage price index?' Bandt's response resonated across the media: 'Google it, mate.'

The invective underscoring the word 'mate' made it clear that Bandt was not going to play this journalistic game. He went on to explain that 'gotcha' questions were why the public had lost faith in both politicians and the media. Media coverage, according to Bandt, should instead focus on revealing and discussing details of policy, such as addressing pressing issues like affordable housing, student debt and expanding Medicare—but particularly the increasing disparity between wages growth and inflation. 'When you've got wages growth at about two-and-a-bit per cent and inflation at three-and-a-half per cent that is part of the problem' (Bandt 2022). On the day, wages growth was 2.3 per cent and inflation was at 3.5 per cent, demonstrating that Bandt was entirely aware of the answer to Mizen's question, but not prepared to indulge the questioner.

By the time Bandt addressed the press club, the election campaign was well under way. Indeed, the 'phony campaign' had been in operation since February and had hit full swing by the time of the budget and budget reply speeches of the major parties on 29 and 30 March, respectively. The budget itself was two months early, to accommodate the expected election in mid May. The Greens had their own, barely covered, reply to the budget and were now voicing a concern felt by many: election coverage was deviating from policy discussion to a fact-checking exercise. But how had we come to this point?

Early in the campaign, 29 per cent of Australians surveyed by the ABC's *Vote Compass* said that climate change was the issue that mattered most to them (Baker 2022), pointing to the possibility that climate action would be at the centre of party appeals and media coverage. Yet, climate change was a problem both Labor and the Coalition preferred to say little about (Kilvert 2022). While the Liberal National Party of Queensland (LNP) senator Matt Canavan claimed that 'net zero is dead' (Maiden 2022), this was not echoed or discussed by either Scott Morrison or Anthony Albanese.

In contrast, the Greens proffered a fully costed plan to reach net-zero emissions by 2035, with an immediate freeze on all new fossil-fuel projects, rapid transition to 100 per cent renewable energy, a just transition for coal and gas workers and development of green manufacturing industries. When the ABC asked climate scientists to rate the various parties, the Greens were the resounding winner in terms of the right policies for Australia (Kilvert 2022). The question remained, however, whether this would have any effect on the Greens' vote amid the determination of competitors (apart from the Teal Independents) to suppress the attention afforded to climate action.

That the Greens were struggling for attention, particularly relative to the Teal Independents, was a common refrain among media commentators (for example, Crowe 2022). This overlooks, of course, the power of media actors themselves in determining who or what is covered, when and how. This power applies to coverage not just of parties, but also of policy issues. Late-campaign analysis comparing surveyed voters' concerns with media coverage showed considerable misalignment in priorities between the public and the press (Nicholas et al. 2022). Press coverage of aged care, education and, especially, climate change was neglected—despite being of high importance to voters and, for the Greens, core campaign issues. For the Greens to stand out among a crowded electoral field and reinforce such policy issues as decisive matters for voters, the party and its candidates would need to be creative in their campaigning.

Candidates

The Greens ran in all 151 seats across Australia and in all Senate elections, as they had done for the previous seven federal elections. There were 32 Senate candidates, of whom only one was standing for re-election after the 2016 vote (Peter Whish-Wilson in Tasmania). Two sitting candidates had replaced retiring senators during the previous term: Lidia Thorpe replacing former party leader Richard Di Natale in Victoria and Dorinda Cox replacing Rachel Siewert in Western Australia. Of the five remaining Senate competitions, three were serious target seats for the Greens: South Australia, Queensland and New South Wales. Perhaps most interestingly, the Greens ran 17 Indigenous candidates across the nation, including three as lead Senate candidates, comprising almost 10 per cent of their candidates. This also marks a serious break with the underrepresentation of Indigenous candidates in electoral contests, given that since 2001 the ALP and the Coalition have between them nominated just 32 Indigenous candidates in federal elections (Evans and McDonnell 2022).

In the House of Representatives, the Greens nominated 77 women, 71 men and three nonbinary candidates, achieving a near-equal gender split between men and women. This compares well against Labor (43.7 per cent), the Coalition (29 per cent), the United Australia Party (UAP; 35.8 per cent) and Pauline Hanson's One Nation (PHON; 32.9 per cent) (see further Chapter 5, this volume). The gender parity represents an improvement for the Greens from their 2019 low of 43 per cent women nominated for the lower house. The list of target seats for the Greens diversified for this election, too. It included key Brisbane electorates (Ryan, Griffith and Brisbane) as well as Macnamara, Higgins and Kooyong in Victoria, Richmond in New South Wales and the Australian Capital Territory. Beyond these targets, high-priority areas for campaigning encompassed additional capital-city seats, such as Cooper (Victoria) and Grayndler and Sydney (NSW). Several of these priority seats appeared unrealistic to win, held as they were by high-profile incumbents or host to popular Independent campaigns. Collectively, however, the seats represent a 'heartland' territory for the Greens, where maximising the Senate vote was realistic, even if the odds for lower house representation were slim. Of the remaining target seats, those in Queensland and Victoria represented an opportunity to expand the Greens' vote and, with the right preference flows, to pull off unlikely victories.

Results

The results, as noted above, came as somewhat of a shock to much of the media and other parties, despite signs in the preceding months that the Greens could do well in some of their target seats. However, it was in the Senate that the Greens were able to achieve all their aims bar a second, far less likely goal of electing a senator from the Australian Capital Territory. The Senate contests this time included three sitting senators (Cox in Western Australia, Thorpe in Victoria and Whish-Wilson in Tasmania). The other five seats—three in the States and two in the Territories—were contested by a mixture of experienced and novice campaigners. In all but the Australian Capital Territory and South Australia, the Greens saw swings to them of between 2 and 3 per cent, representing a significant consolidation of their vote (see Table 12.1).

The change in the Greens' vote can in part be attributed to their extensive campaigning during the previous three years, but also noteworthy is the continuing impact of changes made to electoral laws in 2016, removing group voting tickets and creating sufficient barriers to micro-parties. Certainly, several such parties have been either deregistered or merged to create more viable entities. This led to a decline in the number of Senate tickets generally, but particularly in New South Wales, where the number of tickets reduced from 35 in 2019 to 23 in 2022. In effect, there are fewer peripheral parties to divert the first-preference votes of less-committed supporters away from the Greens. Conversely, the effect of a crowded electoral contest likely explains some of the relative underperformance of the Greens' Senate swing in South Australia. In that State, the Rex Patrick Team, Animal Justice Party and Legalise Cannabis Party each polled roughly 2 per cent while both major parties comfortably maintained primary votes above 30 per cent. The SA Greens fared far better in the House, receiving the largest Statewide swing.

Table 12.1 The Greens' primary votes and swings in the House of Representatives and Senate, 2022

	House of Representatives		Senate	
	Vote	Swing	Vote	Swing
NSW	10.0	+1.3	11.5	+2.7
Vic.	13.7	+1.9	13.9	+3.2
Qld	12.9	+2.6	12.4	+2.5
WA	12.5	+0.9	14.3	+2.5
SA	12.8	+3.2	12.0	+1.1
Tas.	12.0	+1.9	15.5	+2.9
ACT	18.7	+1.8	10.3	−7.4
NT	13.1	+2.9	12.3	+2.0
National	**12.3**	**+1.9**	**12.7**	**+2.5**

Source: AEC (2022a).

Table 12.1 also demonstrates the dramatic fall in the ACT Senate vote. This appears to be largely due to the presence of high-profile Independent candidate David Pocock, who was particularly well known in the Territory as a former member of the Canberra-based rugby union team the Brumbies and had more recently dedicated his time to conservation work. His campaign was seen to be riding high on the surge of Independents nationally, but in the relatively small ACT community his personal profile provided a significant headstart. His primary vote of 21 per cent was double the Greens' vote and sufficient to win the ACT Senate seat from the Liberal Party. Further, both major-party groupings also saw a fall in their primary vote, with respectable showings from both the UAP and PHON. However, the UAP and PHON were shown to be more paper than actual threats in terms of swinging large numbers of votes, with PHON losing just over 1 per cent of its vote and the UAP gaining just over 1 per cent.

Though the Greens received their highest aggregate lower house votes in the Australian Capital Territory and Victoria, examining primary votes in individual seats shows a more nuanced story (Table 12.2). What is immediately obvious is the dramatic rise of the Greens' vote in the party's targeted Queensland divisions. While Melbourne remains the Greens' strongest seat, with a primary vote now almost 50 per cent, the party achieved swings of more than 12 per cent in Griffith and close to 10 per cent in Ryan. Both Macnamara and Cooper saw a more than 6 percentage point rise in the vote, but in both cases, this was arguably a product of recent underperformance. This explanation is especially likely in Cooper, where the Greens' vote crashed from 36 to 21 per cent between 2016 and 2019 after party infighting over preselection and the dumping of popular local candidate Alex Bhathal. The selection of an Indigenous unionist candidate, Celeste Liddle, appears to have begun the recovery of the Greens' vote in Cooper, albeit not to a level that seriously risks the re-election chances of former ACTU president Ged Kearney for Labor.

Table 12.2 The Greens' primary votes and swings in key House of Representatives seats, 2016–2022

	2022		2019		2016	
	Vote	Swing	Vote	Swing	Vote	Swing
Melbourne	49.6	+0.3	49.3	+5.5	43.8	+1.1
Griffith	34.6	+11.0	23.6	+6.5	17.1	+6.8
Ryan	30.2	+9.9	20.3	+1.6	18.7	+4.3
Macnamara	29.7	+5.5	24.2	+0.6	23.8	+3.6
Wills	28.3	+1.7	26.6	−4.2	30.8	+8.6
Cooper	27.4	+6.3	21.1	−15.1	36.2	+9.8
Brisbane	27.2	+4.8	22.4	+3.0	19.4	+5.1
Richmond	25.3	+5.0	20.3	−0.1	20.4	+5.1
Canberra	24.7	+1.4	23.3	+4.6	14.9	+1.9
Sydney	23.0	+4.9	18.1	−0.7	18.8	+0.5
Higgins	22.7	+0.2	22.5	−2.8	25.3	+8.5
Perth	22.2	+3.3	18.9	+1.8	17.1	+5.1
Grayndler	22.0	−0.5	22.5	+0.3	22.2	+0.2
Adelaide	20.1	+4.4	15.7	+5.8	10.4	+0.3
National	**12.2**	**+1.8**	**10.4**	**+0.2**	**10.2**	**+1.6**

Source: AEC (2022a).

Also of note is the relative flatness of the Greens' vote in inner Sydney over successive elections, some of which can be put down to the seats of Grayndler and Sydney being held by Anthony Albanese and Tanya Plibersek, respectively. Both are respected and popular Labor MPs, with

Albanese serving as Opposition leader (now prime minister) and Plibersek long a fixture on the ALP frontbench. But it is worth also considering that the underlying State seats are principally held by Greens and Independent MPs. This raises the prospect that, should Albanese or Plibersek resign from parliament, a Greens or Independent challenger could win these seats. Another possibility is that voters in these electorates, while generally green-leaning, are looking for a different kind of MP to those whom the Greens have so far selected. In contrast with inner Sydney, seats centred on Perth and Adelaide have seen sustained growth in the Greens' vote. Though both Perth and Adelaide currently maintain Greens support significantly below what would be required for the party to win, they are also divisions that have received comparatively less attention and fewer resources in election campaigns thus far.

Table 12.3 shows the impact of prominent Independent candidates backed by well-organised campaigns. The listed seats are for the electorates in which Teal candidates (or those broadly associated with them, such as Zali Steggall, Kerryn Phelps and Rebekha Sharkie) were successful. Each shows a significant drop in the Greens' vote—although at different elections, depending on when an Independent candidate first emerged. Further, the Greens' vote does not tend to quickly or fully recover after an Independent is elected. This is exemplified by the seats of Wentworth and Warringah, where Independents emerged earlier. A similar pattern can be found in the South Australian seat of Mayo, where a previously high Greens vote remains significantly reduced after being nearly halved in the 2016 victory of Sharkie (Nick Xenophon Team; Centre Alliance) over the Liberal candidate.

Table 12.3 The Greens' primary votes and swings in 'Teal' seats, 2016–2022

	2022		2019		2016	
	Vote	Swing	Vote	Swing	Vote	Swing
Mayo	11.8	+2.5	9.3	+1.2	8.1	−6.1
Curtin	10.4	−4.9	15.3	+1.3	14.2	−0.6
North Sydney	8.6	−5.0	13.6	+0.6	13	−2.5
Wentworth	8.3	+0.8	7.5	−7.3	14.9	+0.8
Goldstein	7.8	−6.3	14.0	−1.9	15.9	0.0
Warringah	7.4	+1.3	6.1	−6.1	12.2	−3.3
Kooyong	6.3	−14.9	21.2	+2.7	18.9	+2.3
Mackellar	6.1	−5.4	11.5	−2.5	14.1	−0.1
National	**12.2**	**+1.8**	**10.4**	**+0.2**	**10.2**	**+1.6**

Source: AEC (2022a).

It appears that, at least in some electorates, the Greens vote is relatively 'soft', with a considerable number of supporters willing to abandon the party to vote strategically in defeating a sitting or challenging Liberal (a tendency shared with some Labor voters). Certainly, the continued strengthening of a reliable vote in Melbourne bodes well for the future re-election of the new Greens MPs in Griffith, Ryan and Brisbane. The volatility in seats such as those in Table 12.3, however, points to strategic weaknesses for the party in building a reliable base of support from which to seriously challenge incumbent major-party MPs. More broadly, much has been made of the 'demise' of two-party dominance in Australian politics after the 2022 election (for example, Probyn 2022), with the Greens' success a key facet of this development. Yet, there remains the potential for the major parties to reassert their prevailing positions, reversing trends towards multi-party politics—as has occurred in similar democracies such as the United Kingdom (Prosser 2018).

Campaign focus and strategy

The Greens have rarely articulated a definitive ideological orientation beyond reference to their 'four pillars' of ecological sustainability, grassroots democracy, social justice, and peace and nonviolence. The party is, after all, a confederation of subnational branches, each with varied origins, membership and ideological tendencies. Yet, in his National Press Club address in April 2022, Bandt clearly positioned his party as defenders of Australian social democracy. Bandt asserted the role of government in fixing the inequality crisis—a role he claimed the Liberals had no intention of occupying and that Labor had abandoned:

> With Labor siding with the Liberals to rip $184 billion out of the public purse to fund tax cuts for the wealthy, $69 billion in handouts to push up housing costs and $98 billion for coal and gas subsidies, social democracy is headed for the chopping block unless more Greens are elected. (Bandt 2022)

Political parties in Australia tend not to adhere to a single set of coherent ideological principles; the Greens are no different in this respect. There are also undoubtedly members and supporters alike who are more radical, or more moderate, than the positions expressed by Bandt (Gauja and Jackson 2016). Nonetheless, Bandt's comments reflect an increasing consolidation of the party's policy platform on a green social democracy. The party continues to afford matters of the environment—on which much of the public's knowledge and the standing of the party are based—high priority. The Greens, however, are ecologically centred, not focused. The party has increasingly sought to occupy left-redistributive policy space partly vacated by Labor, connecting issues of inequality, housing, workers' rights and public services with its environmental and climate objectives (Holloway et al. 2019). Bandt and Greens candidates pitched much of their redistributive agenda as a remedy for the increasing costs of living—a key issue as the election campaign wore on.

The party's emphasis on cost-of-living measures appears to be key to its success in Queensland in particular. Indeed, the Queensland branch often gave top billing to traditional social-democratic proposals in campaign communications: free childcare, free education and including dental health in Medicare—paid for by increased taxes on billionaires. Attention to climate change and the environment was by no means absent, however. For the Queensland Greens, the 2022 election was also a test for a years-long experiment in which a field campaign of unprecedented scale for the party entailed not just doorknocking, but also a program of community mutual aid. Thus, while the party claims to have knocked on more than 90,000 doors in the seat of Griffith alone, it had also been embedded in the community, delivering among other initiatives relief packages and cleanup assistance after Queensland's devastating floods (Smee 2022). It created a context in which the Greens' messages on urgent climate action—but also a broader point about the disconnect of the major parties from local communities—were likely much more compelling.

Campaigning in the 'air' and on the 'ground'

The Greens have tended to eschew large-scale television campaigning, principally due to the cost of advertising in the capital cities. Although the party's 2020–21 annual return showed receipts for the party of some $16 million, this includes both the national organisation and State branches (AEC 2022b). The structure of Australian Greens campaigns is such that two-thirds of expenditure occurs at the State level, with a commensurately smaller amount for national campaigning. The fact that election campaigning draws heavily on volunteers holds for Australian parties generally, but is especially the case for the Greens, who lack the financial resources of their primary competitors. What the party cannot achieve or afford through advertising must be made up for through more labour-intensive electioneering.

There is ongoing debate among scholars and practitioners alike about the relative effectiveness of the air (for example, advertising) and ground (for example, doorknocking) modes of campaigning. The academic literature—albeit mostly focused on the United States—suggests that the 'ground game' of field campaigning and doorknocking voters has little capacity to change voters' minds and is more effective at increasing turnout (Kalla and Broockman 2018). Australian scholars tend to remain open to the notion of ground campaigns shifting votes, albeit cautiously so (Mills 2014; Kefford 2021). After the 2022 election, it would be difficult to convince the Greens that field campaigns hold no prospects of electoral gain. Indeed, at face value, the tens of thousands of doors knocked on and the community-level mutual aid programs appear to be critical to the party's recent and future successes.

The Greens' achievements on the ground raise questions about the efficacy of an advertising- or 'air'-dominated approach. We need only look at the UAP's reputed advertising spend of some $80 million to realise that carpet-bombing the electorate with party messaging does not appear to be as persuasive as some argue. In the online space specifically, the UAP spent roughly three times as much as the Greens on social media advertising for limited electoral return (Arya 2022). But the Greens' spending, too, reveals interesting results. The party allocated roughly $600,000 to social media ads and in some target seats (such as Macnamara and Richmond) even outspent the major parties. Yet, it was precisely these seats that the Greens failed to secure, while those such as Brisbane were won despite minimal reliance on online advertising. It is worth noting that Stephen Bates's successful campaign for Brisbane did entail some of the more creative online ads, including on dating app Grindr (Farmilo 2022). Further, advertising and field campaigning are complementary—part of an integrated campaign of increasing the number of contacts a potential voter receives from a party.

Creating a movement

The impact of the ground campaign in the three Brisbane seats is particularly important. The Queensland Greens' campaign was noted for its continuous approach (Smee 2022). From 2016, local party branches made a point of engaging with local communities when adverse weather or the Covid-19 pandemic made it impossible for some community members to access services they required, with embedded party members providing transport, acting as couriers, delivery drivers, helpers and generally assisting where possible within their community. This is not to say that members of other parties, whether the ALP or the LNP, were not involved in such activities—many were—but the Greens branded themselves and were visible and organised.

Of course, the Greens have a long history of involvement in social movement activities, whether on the environment generally (particularly climate, forest preservation and land-clearing campaigns), feminist and LGBTQIA+ issues, or on questions of democracy, nonviolence and governmental transparency. Party members' involvement in and engagement with rallies and protests are well established (Jackson and Chen 2012, 2015; Gauja and Jackson 2016), and continued campaigning means the Greens retain something of a political monopoly of association on some policy issues.

Yet, the Greens' mutual aid efforts reflect an evolution in their campaigning and style of presence in the electorate. To the extent that mutual aid could promote greater contact between more and less privileged groups in a community, there is the potential for the generation of the kind of intergroup solidarity—especially along class and ethnic lines—that is at the core of the Greens' emerging social-democratic messaging. Community mutual aid can also be a source of new party members and encourage more sustained activism (Spade 2020). Where the party's efforts offer locals aid and help alleviate reliance on traditional institutions—institutions the party argues have been weakened and warped by decades of neoliberalism—the Greens could also harness persistent 'anti-politics' sentiment among some of the public. Max Chandler-Mather's first speech in the House of Representatives is the clearest indication of this growing acknowledgement (or, perhaps, reassertion of an earlier belief temporarily lost to professionalised politics) within the Greens of the importance of 'acting collectively' towards 'improving people's lives outside the cycle of electoral politics' (Chandler-Mather 2022).

Party competition

A point of growing contention between party activists is the increasing number of three-cornered races for the House of Representatives in which Greens candidates with favourable preference flows risk dislodging incumbent Labor MPs. Three-cornered races were traditionally considered those instances where both the Liberal and the National parties, as well as

Labor, ran candidates in an electorate. Green (2020) notes that the number of such contests has declined significantly over the past 40 years, from a high of 72 in 1987 to only 11 in 2016 and 2019. In 2022, the number of seats in which the Nationals ran against the Liberals fell to just three. With a decline in the two main conservative parties running against each other, genuinely competitive multi-party dynamics at the electorate level have become less of a feature in federal politics. However, the increasing Greens vote—and a vote increasingly concentrated in urban electorates (Table 12.2)—coupled with a dramatic rise in support for Independents, challenges this trend. That is, competitive three-cornered contests are re-emerging, albeit of a significantly different character than in the past.

In 89 electorates in the 2022 election, Greens candidates were among the final three contenders remaining as preferences were distributed. Of course, the Greens were far from likely winners in the majority of these 89 seats—and this figure in fact represents a decline from earlier elections, such as 2010 (135 seats). But as Raue (2022) shows, the median Greens vote among these three-cornered contests has steadily increased across successive elections to roughly 18 per cent as of 2022, again reflecting a concentration of the Greens vote as well as a livelier contest within the non–major-party vote. What is more, the typical gap between the second and third-placed candidates in three-candidate-preferred counts has significantly reduced over time (Raue 2022). Among the tightest of such counts are targeted Greens seats, including those won (Brisbane) and narrowly lost by a few hundred votes (Macnamara).

Contests that had the ALP ahead of the Greens in three-candidate-preferred counts were by far the majority, with the ALP winning the seat in every occurrence. However, there is a smaller subset of cases where the Greens ended up ahead of the ALP at the penultimate round of the count and in those instances went on to win the seat (Brisbane, Griffith, Melbourne and Ryan). In a further subset of seats, the Greens came ahead of the Liberal Party but behind the ALP, with Liberal preferences ensuring an ALP win. In those seats (Canberra, Cooper, Grayndler, Sydney and Wills) there existed, at least in theory, an opportunity for the Greens to win the seat. That the Greens have now wrested seats from the LNP (Brisbane and Ryan) ought to blunt a common complaint from Labor activists that the Greens are a net negative for 'progressive' politics by only targeting Labor votes and Labor-held electorates. Yet, continued victories in Melbourne and now Griffith—as well as meaningful challenges in Macnamara, Wills and Cooper—make this unlikely. The absence of a Labor–Greens rapprochement in the electoral arena likely has implications for legislative dynamics between the two parties, with climate and emissions reduction legislation thus far the clearest indication of considerable enduring antagonism.

Relevant to the Labor–Greens relationship, too, is the leadership of Bandt, who has been a consistent advocate of the benefits—and necessity—of greater cooperation between the two parties. As early as the 2013 election—Bandt's first after winning the seat of Melbourne—he sought to highlight the policy outcomes of agreement negotiated to ensure Greens support of the minority Gillard Labor Government, even as both Labor and broader Greens campaign material downplayed the partnership (Holloway 2019: 204). This stance has held, as evidenced in Bandt's repeated promotion of powersharing prospects through the 2022 election campaign (McIlroy 2022). Second, Bandt's leadership thus far has coincided with far greater internal party unity than demonstrated under his predecessors, particularly the tenure of Di Natale. Bandt has less baggage from previous significant internal disputes and has credibility even among more radical elements of the party membership. This arguably gives Bandt some greater, though perhaps temporary, leeway in negotiating outcomes with Labor that could fall short of stated Greens policy goals.

Conclusion

Increasingly, the Greens are in direct competition with the ALP for what was once considered core Labor territory—both geographically and in the progressive policy space. There will be further ALP–Greens contests in the future, which may not always be beneficial for the two parties' capacities to work together after hard-fought campaigns. The potential exists at that point for a hung parliament, with the ALP opting to govern in minority rather than going into coalition with the Greens or striking a more formalised support agreement as in the forty-third parliament. This could risk constructive and stable progressive government. Notwithstanding apparently good relations between Bandt and Albanese, the very real question that must be answered by the Greens and the ALP is whether the current pattern of antagonistic interparty relations in electoral contests will continue, and how this will play out in post-campaign (and, especially, legislative) interactions. There are potential solutions. Internationally, for instance, there are examples of cooperative electoral pacts (such as that between New Zealand Labour and Greens) aimed at improving these parties' collective abilities to defeat conservative parties and generate ongoing mutual trust.

The same question could be raised about the rise of Community or Teal Independents. The Greens had long held hopes of winning seats such as Wentworth in New South Wales and Higgins in Victoria on the basis that only they could attract a strong enough vote to beat incumbent Liberals. In none of the two-party (ALP–Liberal) preferred counts in the seats won by Independents would the ALP have been successful, no matter how close it may have come. This suggests that the Greens' strategy of preferencing Independent candidates over the ALP in those seats was the correct decision. But the emergence of these successful Independents does render these former Liberal heartland seats well out of reach for the Greens, as well as the ALP.

References

Arya, Prachi. 2022. *Political Advertising on Social Media Platforms during the 2022 Federal Election*. Canberra: The Australia Institute. Available from: australia institute.org.au/wp-content/uploads/2022/06/Political-advertising-on-social-media-platforms-WEB.pdf.

Australian Electoral Commission (AEC). 2022a. 'House of Representatives: Final results'. [Updated 1 July.] *Tally Room: 2022 Australian Federal Election*. Canberra: AEC. Available from: results.aec.gov.au/27966/Website/HouseDefault-27966.htm.

Australian Electoral Commission (AEC). 2022b. 'Political party returns 2020–21'. *AEC Transparency Register*. Canberra: AEC. Available from: transparency.aec. gov.au/AnnualPoliticalParty.

Baker, Emily. 2022. 'Vote Compass data shows climate change, cost of living and the economy are the big election issues, but voters still split along party lines'. *ABC News*, 22 April. Available from: www.abc.net.au/news/2022-04-22/vote-compass-federal-election-issues-data-climate-change-economy/101002116.

Bandt, Adam. 2022. 'The fight for the future'. Speech, National Press Club, Canberra, 13 April. Available from: www.youtube.com/watch?v=FcWvseAGlpA.

Chandler-Mather, Max. 2022. 'First speech—Max Chandler-Mather'. House of Representatives, Parliament of Australia, Canberra, 1 August. Available from: greensmps.org.au/articles/first-speech-max-chandler-mather.

Courty, Audrey, Melanie Vujkovic and Staff. 2022. 'Greens celebrate "shifting tectonic plates" in Queensland politics as losing rival candidates go to ground'. *ABC News*, 22 May. Available from: www.abc.net.au/news/2022-05-22/qld-federal-election-lnp-regroup-as-greens-celebrate-major-win/101083852.

Crowe, David. 2022. 'Greens struggle for attention as independents fight to change game'. *Sydney Morning Herald*, 8 April. Available from: www.smh.com.au/politics/federal/greens-struggle-for-attention-as-independents-fight-to-change-the-game-20220407-p5abn6.html.

Evans, Michelle and Duncan McDonnell. 2022. 'More partisans than parachutes, more successful than not: Indigenous candidates of the major Australian parties'. *Australian Journal of Political Science* 57(4): 346–67. doi.org/10.1080/10361146.2022.2065968.

Farmilo, Kathleen. 2022. 'The Greens' Brissy candidate put campaign ads on Grindr & they're topping Morrison's photo-ops'. *Pedestrian*, 27 April. Available from: www.pedestrian.tv/federal-election-australia/the-greens-brisbane-candidate-grindr-campaign-ads/.

Gauja, Anika and Stewart Jackson. 2016. 'Australian Greens party members and supporters: Their profiles and activities'. *Environmental Politics* 25(2): 359–79. doi.org/10.1080/09644016.2015.1104803.

Green, Antony. 2020. 'The decline of three-cornered contests at federal elections'. *Antony Green's Election Blog*, 17 December. Available from: antonygreen.com.au/the-decline-of-three-cornered-contests-at-federal-elections/.

Holloway, Josh. 2019. Measuring minor party impact: The Australian Greens in a changing party system. Unpublished PhD thesis, Flinders University, Adelaide.

Holloway, Josh, Narelle Miragliotta and Rob Manwaring. 2019. 'Issue competition between green and social democratic parties in majoritarian settings: The case of Australia'. *Australian Journal of Political Science* 54(1): 18–36. doi.org/10.1080/10361146.2018.1529228.

Jackson, Stewart and Peter Chen. 2012. 'Understanding Occupy in Australia'. *Journal of Australian Political Economy* 69: 1–24.

Jackson, Stewart and Peter Chen. 2015. 'Rapid mobilisation of demonstrators in March Australia'. *Interface: A Journal for and about Social Movements* 7(1): 98–116.

Kalla, Joshua L. and David E. Broockman. 2018. 'The minimal persuasive effects of campaign contact in general elections: Evidence from 49 field experiments'. *American Political Science Review* 112(1): 148–66. doi.org/10.1017/S0003055417000363.

Kefford, Glenn. 2021. *Political Parties and Campaigning in Australia: Data, Digital and Field*. Cham, Switzerland: Palgrave Macmillan. doi.org/10.1007/978-3-030-68234-7.

Kilvert, Nick. 2022. 'Climate change is being buried this election. We asked scientists to rate the major parties' policies'. *ABC Science*, [*ABC News*], 10 May. Available from: www.abc.net.au/news/2022-05-10/climate-change-election-policies-scientists-give-verdicts/101020002.

Maiden, Samantha. 2022. 'Climate change war erupts as Nationals MP Matt Canavan declares net zero is "dead"'. *News.com.au*, 26 April. Available from: www.news.com.au/national/federal-election/climate-change-war-erupts-as-nationals-mp-matt-canavan-declares-net-zero-is-dead/news-story/7018e748ff20ea64d7204171ee8a5df8.

McIlroy, Tom. 2022. 'Greens bid to govern alongside Labor'. *Australian Financial Review*, 10 April. Available from: www.afr.com/politics/federal/greens-bid-to-govern-alongside-labor-20220410-p5acdt.

Mills, Stephen. 2014. 'Rules for radicals comes to Carrum'. *Inside Story*, 5 December. Available from: insidestory.org.au/rules-for-radicals-comes-to-carrum/.

Nicholas, Josh, Nick Evershed, Kahled Al Khawaldeh and Johanna Lewis. 2022. 'Revealed: How the top issues voters care about are not getting aired in election campaign'. *The Guardian*, 18 May. Available from: www.theguardian.com/news/datablog/2022/may/18/how-often-do-voters-top-concerns-feature-at-election-campaign-press-conferences-and-in-the-media.

Probyn, Andrew. 2022. 'After his election win, Albanese's next challenge starts now— bringing the cross bench and a third of voters with him'. *ABC News*, 23 May. Available from: www.abc.net.au/news/2022-05-23/albanese-challenge-convince-voters-the-right-man-for-the-job/101089966.

Prosser, Christopher. 2018. 'The strange death of multi-party Britain: The UK general election of 2017'. *West European Politics* 41(5): 1226–36. doi.org/10.1080/01402382.2018.1424838.

Raue, Ben. 2022. 'Understanding 3CP trends'. *The Tally Room*, 27 June. Available from: www.tallyroom.com.au/47966.

Smee, Ben. 2022. 'How knocking on 90,000 doors delivered Queensland Labor heartland to the Greens'. *The Guardian*, [Australia], 23 May. Available from: www.theguardian.com/australia-news/2022/may/22/how-knocking-on-90000-doors-delivered-queensland-labor-heartland-to-the-greens.

Spade, Dean. 2020. *Mutual Aid: Building Solidarity during This Crisis (and the Next)*. London: Verso Books.

Wordsworth, Matt. 2022. 'The shock federal election result in Queensland that was hiding in plain sight'. *ABC News*, 22 May. Available from: www.abc.net.au/news/2022-05-22/queensland-federal-election-greens-politics-analysis/101088630.

Zhou, Naaman and Amy Remeikis. 2021. 'Potential date for trans-Tasman bubble to be announced—As it happened'. [Live blog], *The Guardian*, [Australia], 22 March. Available from: www.theguardian.com/australia-news/live/2021/mar/22/senate-estimates-veteran-suicide-royal-commission-morrison-albanese-politics-live?page=with:block-6057c8c78f08131c2e529e6b&filterKeyEvents=false.

13

Independents and minor parties

Jill Sheppard

In an election with unprecedented media and public attention on non–major-party candidates across the country, that light focused heavily on a small number of Teal, Climate 200–sponsored and 'Voices For'–endorsed individuals in marginal electorates. Away from the spotlight, Independent, minor-party and micro-party candidates continued to chip away at the major parties' long-term electoral dominance. However, only a few of these disparate and less well-organised efforts bore fruit: former local deputy mayor Dai Le beat a high-profile ALP candidate in the seat of Fowler, former rugby union player David Pocock was elected to the Senate in the Australian Capital Territory, UAP candidate Ralph Babet sneaked into the final Senate seat in Victoria and Tammy Tyrrell from the Jacqui Lambie Network beat longstanding Liberal senator Eric Abetz to the final Senate spot in Tasmania. Pauline Hanson retained her Senate seat, which she has held since 2016.

Elsewhere, Independent candidates failed to coordinate—with public consequences. In the NSW seat of Hughes, Georgia Steele and Linda Seymour competed for the non–major-party vote. In the Australian Capital Territory, Pocock and Kim Rubenstein contended for third-party endorsement, with Pocock prevailing in both endorsements and electoral success (see also Chapter 17, this volume). Narratives of the 2022 election will undoubtedly focus on the 'Teal wave' and the demise of the two-party system, but beneath that surface, much of the campaigning typified the scrappy battles engaged in by Independent candidates for many decades.

For every Zoe Daniel, Zali Steggall or Pauline Hanson there are literally hundreds of candidates whose names will never be known beyond their friends and family. They campaign with few resources or volunteers, juggling full-time employment with part-time electioneering, and they have traditionally not campaigned with any idea of winning. To that end, 2022 presents a watershed election, with seven new Independent candidates elected, forming a House of Representatives crossbench of 16 members. This chapter examines the strategies of those Independent and other candidates outside the major organised groups in 2022, their successes and failures and their future place in the Australian political landscape. For further detail on the organisation and strategies of the 'Voices For' groups that successfully backed candidates across the country, see Chapter 14 in this volume. For discussion of third-party actors and their role in campaigns across the country (including Climate 200), see Chapter 15.

Independents in the Australian political system

Independent candidates have traditionally fared poorly in Australian federal elections, for two deeply entwined reasons. First, the method of alternative (or instant runoff) voting used for election to the House of Representatives, combined with single-member districts, means that a well-funded, well-known candidate from either of the two established major parties can usually see off less well-resourced challengers. The ALP and Liberal–National Coalition have, as in similar countries around the world, effectively worked in concert to prevent the entry of insurgent parties or candidates (Miragliotta and Errington 2012; Ghazarian 2015). Indeed, movements like Climate 200 have explicitly sought to disrupt major-party dominance by replicating party-style coordination. Second, Australian voters have until recently been satisfied with the candidates offered to them at election time, happily supporting whichever of the two (or three) major-party candidates they prefer. Australians have among the highest rates of partisan identification in the world and party labels make the choice on election day simple for most moderately engaged voters (McAllister et al. 2015).

By way of evidence, the Howard Government's election to a majority of seats in both the House of Representatives and the Senate in 2004 is now viewed as more of an albatross than a gift (Bean and McAllister 2009). For the first time in most voters' lives, the government won control of both houses of parliament and implemented policies (primarily the industrial relations package labelled WorkChoices) that indulged its ideological bent while alienating voters, due largely to the lack of checks and balances of an oppositional Senate. However, in the days after the 2004 landslide—before WorkChoices—voters were largely content. Satisfaction with democracy and the state of the political system was the highest on record and John Howard was a historically popular prime minister (Cameron and McAllister 2019).

Of course, by 2007, the Howard Government was tired, struggling to defend the WorkChoices reform package and grappling with internal turmoil after the release of the 'McLachlan note' that revealed a (subsequently ignored) 1994 agreement between Howard and his deputy, Peter Costello, to transfer leadership to Costello after one and a half terms in office. Combined with the surge of media darling Kevin Rudd—leader of the Opposition ALP, former diplomat and Mandarin speaker—Howard and his government were on the ropes and were beaten soundly at the 2007 election.

Why is any of this relevant to a chapter on Independent candidates? Howard and Rudd were remarkably popular leaders (indeed, perhaps Rudd is one of the few challengers who could have beaten Howard in 2007) who set Australian democracy on an upward trajectory from 2004. The 2010 election stopped this in its tracks. There are two plausible explanations for this: one is that Australian voters did not and could not accept a woman prime minister in Julia Gillard (despite voting for enough of her ALP candidates to ensure she stayed prime minister); the other is that Australian voters could not abide a hung parliament.

Australian voters have tended to prefer stable majority (federal) governments to minority ones. Gillard was a moderately popular leader—much better liked than Tony Abbott (then leader of the Liberal Party) and almost as popular as her predecessor, Rudd, in 2010 (Cameron and McAllister 2019). The concept of a hung parliament, and the idea that Independent candidates could 'hold a government to ransom', was foreign and worrying to most 2010 voters. Certainly, satisfaction with and trust in the political system have declined since 2010, according to the Australian Election Study. How, then, did we get from the nadir of 2010 to the Independents' high point of 2022?

In just over 10 years, Australian voters have learnt to love (at least the idea of) minority government. The driving force for this shift is the continuing decline in the perceived performance of both the leaders and the parties of Australian government. The revolving-door leadership dramas of 2010 to 2018 have surely contributed to decreasing voter satisfaction (Cameron 2020), but compulsory voting and the system of single-member districts and alternative voting provide the necessary conditions. In a country in which most adults are required to vote and the electoral choices are increasingly unsatisfactory, viable alternatives must surely thrive eventually. So it was in 2022.

Who did not join the Independent movements and why?

Of course, thriving as a viable alternative to an established political party is easiest when you have money and time at your disposal, but both resources are famously scarce. Two key differences in 2022 from previous elections were the presence of an established national 'Voices For' movement with a track record of training and nurturing successful House of Representatives candidates in the Victorian electorate of Indi (see Chapter 14, this volume) and the newly formed Climate 200 movement that funded pro-climate candidates across the country (Chapter 15, this volume). The emergence of Simon Holmes á Court—heir of one of the country's richest families—as the key figure behind Climate 200 changed the financial calculus of running for many would-be challengers to major-party incumbents. For the first time in recent history, Independent candidates could compete on a similar footing to established parties and privately wealthy candidates, bucking the cartelisation trend among the two major parties.

However, even social movements and billionaire patrons have limited funds and many Independent candidates in 2022 remained hamstrung by personal financial and family constraints. These candidates can be grouped into three categories: the voluntarily Independent, the involuntarily Independent and the minor or micro-party aligned. The first group contains those candidates who did not (openly, at least) seek patronage from a wealthy benefactor. One example is Dr Li Fuxin, a candidate for the ACT Senate who has contested several previous elections at the State and federal levels on a platform of 'speaking for all and standing for harmony', and who has purported connections to the Chinese Communist Party (Hui and Welch 2022). At the other end of the spectrum, Drew Pavlou ran for the Queensland Senate on a notably anti-communist platform entirely unrelated to any of the organised Independent movements (Parnell 2022).

Other Independent candidates occupied a grey area: seeking the 'independence' inherent in this kind of candidacy, but with policy goals overlapping those of the 'Voices For' and Climate 200 movements. Two Senate candidates in the Australian Capital Territory—the country's most reliably progressive jurisdiction, but one tightly held by the two major parties—fulfill this profile: former Australian rugby union representative David Pocock and constitutional law professor Kim Rubenstein. While Pocock did accept some funding from Climate 200, he did not embrace the 'united front' branding of the Victorian or NSW Teal candidates. He spoke in equal measure about rugby, growing up in Zimbabwe and his affection for Canberra and about his key concerns of climate change, integrity and social justice. Rubenstein similarly emphasised her background in legal scholarship, credentials as an expert on citizenship rights and concerns about political integrity and transparency. Unlike other Teal candidates who challenged allegedly impotent Liberal 'moderates', Rubenstein and Pocock set their sights on one of the Liberal Party's most conservative representatives in Senator Zed Seselja.

However, small differences wash out during a hectic election campaign. Voters may have conflated Pocock and Rubenstein—as well as further-flung candidates such as Rob Priestly in the rural Victorian seat of Nicholls—with the professionally organised movements of Teal and 'Voices For' candidates. It is impossible to quantify how—or whether—candidates like Pavlou or Pocock benefited from national media coverage of Independents in Sydney and Melbourne. Much will depend on how the large crossbenches in both the House of Representatives and the Senate organise and cooperate: will pre-election alliances turn into happy parliamentary coalitions or will this new generation of legislators prefer to break out on their own? If nothing else, the 2022–25 parliament is a welcome boon for students of Australian legislative behaviour frustrated by decades of party discipline.

Minor and micro-parties

Small political parties have long inhabited the fringes of Australian politics, usually manifesting in the form of radical right-wing candidates (Pauline Hanson) or more populist candidates (Clive Palmer and former acolytes Jacqui Lambie and former rugby league player Glenn Lazarus). Otherwise, Independent candidates have often formed micro-parties to maximise their success under the electoral system: Glenn Druery famously wrangled a 'Minor Party Alliance' to get Bob Day (Family First) and Ricky Muir (Australian Motorist Enthusiast Party) elected to the Senate under the group voting ticket rules operating in 2013, just as Rubenstein and Pocock created shell parties to ensure they were listed 'above the line' on the 2022 Senate ballot paper.

For the purposes of this chapter, I examine parties that have existed beyond the course of one election. This therefore includes Clive Palmer's UAP, which was initially a coopted rebranding of Joseph Lyons' (and later Robert Menzies') Depression-era party and more recently a Trumpesque populist party centred on nativism and Covid-19 scepticism. It also includes Pauline Hanson's One Nation (PHON), the Jacqui Lambie Network, Katter's Australian Party and the Centre Alliance.

At the 2022 election, these parties largely retained their status quo position. Hanson was returned to the Senate after a knife-edge preference distribution that saw her sneak into the sixth Queensland vacancy. The Jacqui Lambie Network—formed primarily to keep Lambie above the line on the Senate ballot paper—doubled its presence in the Senate to two, Katter was elected to the seat of Kennedy for the eleventh time, while the South Australian Centre Alliance retained its sole House of Representatives seat (Rebekha Sharkie in Mayo, who notionally stood as a party candidate but joined other Community Independents in accepting funding from Climate 200), but lost Stirling Griff and Rex Patrick from the Senate before 2022.[1]

Despite their ostensibly average performance in 2022, Australia's minor and micro-parties have an outsized effect on the country's electoral politics. Palmer spent up to $100 million on the UAP's 2022 campaign (Martin 2022), for the return of one Victorian Senate seat and disproportionate levels of media and public attention. Before and after the election, Palmer was the subject of almost twice as many Google searches as Zoe Daniel (and fellow Teals such as Monique Ryan and Allegra Spender) despite Daniel's quite exceptional victory over Tim Wilson in the Liberal's Melbourne heartland of Goldstein (Figure 13.1).

---

1   Both senators defected from the Centre Alliance during their terms and neither was re-elected under their new party tickets in 2022.

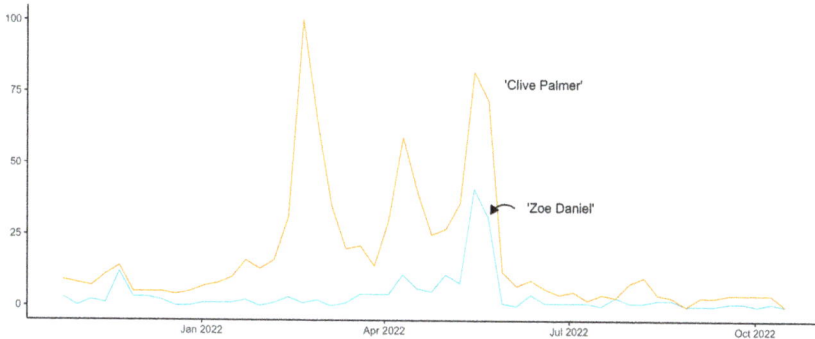

Figure 13.1 Google Trends data showing trends in searches for 'Zoe Daniel' and 'Clive Palmer' by Australian internet users, October 2021 to October 2022

Note: The Y-axis represents an index score of the number of searches, benchmarked to all searches on all topics within Australia.

Source: Google Trends data analysed by author.

The Teal and other Independent and micro/minor-party candidates enjoyed a symbiotic relationship in 2022. Many stalwarts of the Australian political fringe—Katter, Palmer, Andrew Wilkie, Nick Xenophon and his successors in South Australia, and Brian Harradine, among others—chipped away at the major parties' support bases for decades. Their persistence has normalised the concept of Independent candidates in Australia, regardless of their electoral success. This bore fruit in the community-organised campaign of Cathy McGowan in the Victorian seat of Indi in 2013 (and subsequently Helen Haines, leading to the export of their grassroots-based strategy across the country).

In the other direction, non-Teal Independents likely benefited from the normalisation of Independent victories in 2022. Two factors contributed to the idea that Independents were viable electoral prospects: first, the intensive media coverage of candidates such as Daniel in Goldstein and Spender in Wentworth; second, the publication of YouGov's multilevel regression post-stratification (MRP) analysis of polling on 10 May (11 days before the election). MRP analyses incorporate electorate-specific characteristics (the percentage of tertiary-educated voters, the percentage of first-generation migrants, etcetera) to predict local candidates' electoral prospects, rather than using national-level results as a blanket prediction (White and Ratcliff 2022). YouGov's findings—specifically that Daniel was polling ahead of Liberal incumbent Wilson—further normalised the idea that Independent challengers could win Liberal-held seats. For a national electorate accustomed to a two-party system and previously nervous about minority governments, this news surely had an effect.

Voters' responses to Independent candidates

Indeed, at some point between 2010—when Gillard was elected prime minister with the support of Independent crossbench MPs, to the dissatisfaction of many voters used to majority federal governments—and 21 May 2022, Australian voters learned to love minority government. Perhaps it was on 10 May 2022, but more likely it was when Gillard navigated her minority government through a widely praised term of parliament (Curtin 2015). Since 2010, the rate of first preferences cast for major-party candidates in the House of Representatives has continued its long-term decline (see Chapter 16, this volume).

However, we should not overstate the electoral decline of the major parties. The ALP managed to form majority government in 2022. There was no rise in the number of Independent candidates standing nationally between 2019 and 2022, and the electoral swing from major parties to Independent candidates was larger between 2016 and 2019 than between 2019 and 2022 (see Chapter 16, this volume). If anything, the more important 'Independent-quakes' occurred in 2010 and consistently thereafter; 2022 instead represented the consolidation of decades of electoral neglect into one particularly well-resourced movement.

I finish by reflecting on the eight Independent and micro-party candidates who achieved electoral success in 2022 from outside the 'Voices For' and Teal movements: Babet, Hanson, Katter, Le, Pocock, Sharkie, Tyrrell and Wilkie.

Ralph Babet (UAP, Victoria, Senate)

Ralph Babet was elected to the sixth Victorian Senate vacancy under the UAP mantle based on strong preference flows from other Independent and micro-party candidates (Green 2022; Chapter 17, this volume). We know little about Babet, beyond his experience as a real estate agent and belief that the 'World Economic Forum is carrying out a globalist takeover of the country's sovereignty' (Wilson 2022). Since being elected, Babet has expressed views that align with the right wing of the Liberal–National Coalition, including the following tweets:

> The sacrifices we've made to be here are massive. Financially. Socially. Mentally. We're not doing this because we want to but because we have to. Our country needs us. Public service has no tangible reward, history and doing what is right is [*sic*] the only reward. (Babet 2022a)

> Sometimes I drink champagne. But I never drink the Kool-Aid. We must reduce the size and power of not only the Government but the bureaucracy which surrounds it. I believe in limited Government & free market principles. #koolaid #freethinker #nocultshere #biggovernmentsucks (Babet 2022b)

These few traces of ideological bent suggest that Babet will vote with the Coalition on most key issues. He was not visible during the official campaign period, either in person or on social media. Indeed, the UAP generally was uncharacteristically quiet throughout the 2022 campaign: the party released an economic statement in April 2022 that targeted offshore investments, government debt and the decline of onshore manufacturing industries as its key concerns (UAP 2022).[2] Through the month before the election, Palmer's public statements warned that China had gained control of the World Health Organization, that a UAP government would instruct the Reserve Bank of Australia to cap interest rates and that the Chinese Government was covertly buying swathes of land in Western Australia. These sclerotic policy positions received little media attention; only Palmer's accusations that AEC staff were stealing ballots attracted sustained coverage. As of October 2022, the party appears more concerned with its ongoing battles with the AEC than with engaging in legislative or policy debate.

Pauline Hanson (PHON, Queensland, Senate)

Pauline Hanson, first elected to the federal parliament as the Member for Oxley in 1996 and a senator since 2016, continues to embrace populist and nativist rhetoric to little policy effect. Indeed, political scientists have argued that her inability to lead a cohesive party has and will continue to

---

2   This statement mentioned Craig Kelly, the former Liberal MP and notional leader of a UAP parliamentary party. Kelly was not returned to the House of Representatives as a UAP candidate in 2022.

undermine her political impact (see, for example, McSwiney 2021). On the other hand, she continues to be re-elected and the party named for her continues to see intermittent success at the State level.

In late 2021, PHON commissioned a series of web cartoons that largely framed the two major parties as out of touch, other minor parties and candidates (such as Bob Katter) as irrational and untrustworthy and Hanson as the only voice of reason (Wilson 2021). Few of the 28 videos referred to positive policy commitments or a coherent platform; the only common thread was a deeply populist message that 'politicians' do not care for voters, but Hanson and her party are not really politicians (see also Chapter 4, this volume). In early May 2022, the AEC requested that the party remove the videos from YouTube on account of false information about voter fraud and insufficient authorisation information (Worthington and Workman 2022); Hanson subsequently used this request to emphasise her status as a lone voice against government overreach. Beyond these semi-regular cartoons, Hanson used her time in parliament to capitalise on voters' frustrations with Covid-19–related lockdowns and vaccine mandates. In practice, this strategy probably had little effect other than to consolidate existing PHON supporters (particularly in Queensland, which experienced among the least restrictive Covid policy responses of all the States and Territories). As it stands, Hanson was re-elected to the Senate due largely to preferences flowing from UAP voters (Green 2022).

Bob Katter (Katter's Australian Party, Kennedy, House of Representatives)

Elected to the federal parliament as the Nationals candidate for the Queensland seat of Kennedy (formerly held by his father) in 1993, Bob Katter quickly established himself as an arch social conservative. In 2001, he quit the Nationals to oppose free trade, economic rationalism and immigration (Waterford 2001). His idiosyncratic approach to representation has since seen him returned easily at all but the 2013 federal election, when the LNP's Noelene Ikin got to within 2 per cent (two-candidate-preferred) of winning the seat. Like many of his Independent counterparts, Katter has established his own micro-party (Katter's Australian Party, or KAP) to support like-minded candidates at the Queensland and federal levels. The KAP has achieved reasonable success at the State level, with three members sitting in the Queensland Parliament as of 2022, but it failed to replicate Katter's success at the federal level.

In 2022, Katter won 63 per cent of the final vote to continue holding off LNP challengers. Like Wilkie in Tasmania, he has leveraged the benefits of incumbency with exceptional results. While it is notoriously difficult to estimate the extent of a 'personal vote' in isolation from the many factors that contribute to an election result—economic context, performance and name recognition of challengers, effects of national leaders, etcetera—Katter seems to have cultivated a personal following that does not easily extend beyond Kennedy's borders.[3]

Nonetheless, Katter's resilience in the face of LNP challengers and an increasingly progressive national electorate suggest there is a place for nationalist agrarian politics in Australia. Katter's 2022 election campaign leaned heavily on his core issues: country-of-origin labelling on meat and horticultural products, infrastructure for primary industries and restrictions on foreign ownership of Australian land. Whether this policy platform can outlive Katter—coming up to 30 years as the local member—remains to be seen. The KAP's failure to launch outside Kennedy suggests probably not.

Dai Le (Independent, Fowler, House of Representatives)

Member for Fowler Dai Le's pre-parliamentary career is ostensibly conventional—journalist for local media and latterly the ABC, repeat candidate for the NSW Liberal Party and decade-long member of Fairfield City Council (including a stint as deputy mayor)—but for the four pivotal years she spent in refugee camps between her mother fleeing South Vietnam in 1975 and arriving in Sydney in 1979. When political scientists talk about descriptive representation and the need for greater diversity in parliament, we wave our metaphorical hands towards people like Le: lived experience of forced migration, war and domestic upheaval and the need to rebuild lives, family and community in an alien country. On the other hand, we tend to value (implicitly, if not always explicitly) a new legislator's ability to 'hit the ground running' on being sworn in (Lupia and McCubbins 1998).

In other words, Le is a political scientist's ideal candidate in almost every way. She is equipped with both political and personal experiences (including surviving breast cancer) that should engender empathy with marginalised and underrepresented constituents and perspectives that differ from

---

3   See Lucas et al. (2022) on the role of the 'personal vote' in the absence of party cues.

the majority of her new parliamentary colleagues. This poses immediate challenges both for Le herself, with tremendous expectations on her shoulders from the communities she represents and from the commentariat (including political scientists), and for the real-life validity of our normative ideals of democratic representation. Le has declared on her website (daile. com.au/) that she 'will continue to be the local candidate who faces the same challenges we all do' and is 'applying [her] extensive experience in dealing with the issues we face'. Her tenure will prove a fascinating Australian test case for theories of descriptive and substantive representation.

The circumstances of Le's rise to national prominence and eventual election reflect many of the problems facing Australian politics more broadly. The NSW branch of the ALP—required by the party's gender quota to nominate women candidates and protect those already in parliament—faced the prospect of demoting either Deborah O'Neill or Kristina Keneally from a winnable position on the ALP Senate list. To protect Keneally—a prominent senior woman in the party (with a national profile since her time as NSW premier from 2009 to 2011)—party factions agreed to nominate her in the electoral division of Fowler, which was more than 40 kilometres from her primary home and a community with which she had little connection or experience. Most notably, Fowler is home to among the highest concentration of Vietnam-born Australians in the country. Before Keneally's entry to the preselection contest, local party members and the retiring member had supported Tu Le's nomination for the seat. The expectation that a second-generation Vietnamese-Australian would give way to a white (United States–born) woman from Sydney's Northern Beaches seemed to encapsulate the indifference of the major parties to diversity, local representation and young candidates from outside the 'political class' (see, for example, McGowan 2022).

With both local and national media deriding the ALP's decision to nominate Keneally in Fowler, Dai Le capitalised on the situation. More than any of the Teal or Climate 200 candidates,[4] or Pocock in the Australian Capital Territory, Le campaigned on a platform of local infrastructure and services: better roads, better hospitals, support for manufacturing jobs and housing affordability (daile.com.au/). In short, she campaigned as though asking

---

4 On her election, Le immediately distanced herself from the cohort of successful Teal and Climate 200 candidates: 'The teal independents—I'm a real independent' (in Parkes-Hupton and Kozaki 2022). However, since being sworn into the House, she has been regularly photographed with other members of the parliamentary crossbench.

to be returned as deputy mayor, yet she won the seat with a 21 per cent swing towards her on the two-candidate-preferred count. In an election in which 'localness' was particularly salient, the jurisdiction for which Le was running seems not to have mattered; her campaign platform would surely have looked the same had she been contesting a State seat. Whether Fowler voters will hold her to account on her promises remains to be seen.

David Pocock (David Pocock for the ACT, ACT, Senate)

David Pocock was elected to represent the Australian Capital Territory in the Senate after receiving 21 per cent of the primary vote (0.64 of a quota) and preferences from both the Greens (0.31 of a quota) and Kim Rubenstein (0.13 of a quota), who were excluded in earlier rounds of counting. At the end of calculations, Pocock easily unseated the Liberals' Zed Seselja, breaking the major-party stranglehold on the Territory's two Senate seats. Although Pocock was initially approached to nominate on behalf of a 'Voices For'– like group of Canberran political activists ('ProACT'), on announcing his nomination, he instantly distanced himself from any third-party actors or movements. That he accepted $856,000 in donations from Climate 200 was only revealed via the AEC's annual financial disclosure report in February 2023 (Barlow and Jervis-Bardy 2023).

Certainly, few Canberrans would have been unaware of Pocock when he announced his candidacy in December 2021. He first moved to the Territory in 2013 to play professional rugby union for the ACT Brumbies. While professional athletes come and go in a town like Canberra, Pocock was immediately distinguished by his regular media appearances, enthusiasm for life in Canberra and ostensible interest in the local community and politics. His subsequent campaigning successfully leveraged his longstanding credibility in the community: even a very minimally engaged voter would probably have been able to identify Pocock as an athlete of some sort who was worried about climate change and famously refused to marry his female partner until same-sex marriage was legalised. On the back of eight years in the Canberra spotlight, his official campaign could afford to be relentlessly optimistic and strategically vague.

Pocock's campaign—even more so than the pro-integrity campaign run by Rubenstein—spoke to voters' frustration with 'politics as usual' and promised a 'new way of politics'. This is, of course, the conceit of any 'outsider' candidate; Katter continues to self-describe as a political maverick after 29 years in the House of Representatives. To the extent that Pocock offered a policy platform, he promised to pursue a federal anti-corruption body 'with real power', 'truth in advertising' laws for federal election campaigns and limits on political donations (Pocock 2022b). More parochially, he threw his support behind the Territory's right to legislate on voluntary assisted dying without threat of being overridden by federal laws and the development of a new stadium and convention centre in central Canberra (Pocock 2022a). In general, Pocock's campaign platform strongly resembled the broadly pro-integrity, pro-climate rhetoric of most 'Voices For' candidates and every Climate 200 candidate, despite his reluctance to be discussed alongside them.

Yet, despite his large public profile—and ability to raise funding, recruit volunteers and attract national media attention without significant third-party support—it is difficult to predict the kind of legislator Pocock will become. His trajectory—from son of a Zimbabwean family whose farm was requisitioned under the Mugabe regime to teenage migrant, professional rugby union player with 78 test caps for Australia, climate activist once arrested for blockading construction on a coalmine, to federal senator—is simultaneously well known and bafflingly complex. What are the legacies of Pocock's Zimbabwean upbringing, the influence of his family, who left the country after losing their farm, and his Christian education? What can Canberran voters expect from a new senator with almost zero formal experience in politics? Does his transition from unusually well-read professional athlete to senator carve a new path for similar personalities (succeeding where Lazarus and others floundered) or will the constraints of formal politics prove too frustrating? Perhaps his 2012 reflections on Jungian psychology can be used to predict his approach to representative politics:

> 'I was trying to come to terms with my motives for being the best,' he explains. 'Is it just because I want people's approval or want people to like me, and I want to be famous, for want of a better word? Or was it because I enjoy challenging myself and it was something I love doing? I realised those things are in everyone. It's a little bit of both.' (Pocock, quoted in Maley 2012)

Tammy Tyrrell (Jacqui Lambie Network, Tasmania, Senate)

Tammy Tyrrell's election to the Senate in Tasmania is undoubtedly a reflection of the personal popularity of her employer, Senator Jacqui Lambie, and more obliquely, the legacy of former senator Nick Xenophon. As a senator for South Australia from 2008 to 2017, Xenophon parlayed his own electoral success into a micro-party, the Nick Xenophon Team (NXT). The six-year parliamentary terms afforded senators from the States meant that in election years when Xenophon did not need to stand, he nominated trusted colleagues under the aegis of NXT and encouraged his personal support base to vote for them. This led to the election of three senators in the 2016 double-dissolution election (Xenophon, Stirling Griff and Skye Kakoschke-Moore), as well as Rebekha Sharkie's surprise victory in the lower house seat of Mayo. Three years later, support for NXT collapsed, the party renamed itself the Centre Alliance and both Griff and Patrick stood (unsuccessfully) under different micro-party labels.

NXT's brief—but unexpectedly large—success has provided a template for personally popular, notionally Independent senators such as Lambie. Asking her personal support base to vote for a trusted colleague—in this case, her office manager and long-time employee—has instantly doubled her influence in the federal parliament. While the Jacqui Lambie Network will likely never be a political party as we commonly conceive them, it does fit the mould of a 'personal party'—one designed to support a leader's personal vision, not designed to last and with little ideological or organisational coherence (Kefford and McDonnell 2016).

We know little about Tyrrell beyond her occupational background, and what we do know points to a very close relationship with Lambie. The job title 'office manager' tends to underemphasise one's importance to a legislator: the office manager often oversees their boss's professional life, from their diary to their correspondence, and generally knows and judges every person who comes into the legislator's orbit. On that front, Tyrrell should be as well connected and knowledgeable about Senate processes as any incoming senator. On the other hand, she has no discernible political ideology beyond her personal allegiance to Lambie. In political science terms, she claims to be an archetypical delegate model of representative: 'There's no closed doors, it's all about opening doors. I'll talk to anybody, I am not scared to have a chat' (Tyrrell, quoted in Bovill 2022).

For someone in Lambie's position, seeking to expand her parliamentary influence while not being usurped by her new colleague in Canberra, Tyrrell seems a perfect choice. Whether she can expand the network's support base in Tasmania is less clear.

Andrew Wilkie (Independent, Clark, House of Representatives)

Andrew Wilkie won his fifth election in the Tasmanian seat of Clark (formerly Denison) in 2022 with a slight swing against him (4.5 per cent at the primary-vote level and 1.3 per cent after preferences). Nevertheless, his two-candidate-preferred vote share is still 71 per cent—larger than Bob Katter's hold on Kennedy and the second-safest seat in the country. Yet, Wilkie commands relatively little attention outside Tasmania; an average mainland voter would likely not recognise his name or picture.

Originally nominating for the Greens in 2004 (standing against then prime minister Howard in the seat of Bennelong), Wilkie first won election in Denison in 2010, benefiting from both Greens and Liberal preferences against the Labor incumbent. Immediately thrown into the national spotlight when neither major party secured a majority of seats in the House of Representatives, Wilkie shunned his potential 'kingmaker' role and very quickly supported Gillard's ALP to form government. Although he originally came to national prominence (and Greens candidature) on the back of his whistleblower campaign to prevent Australia's involvement in the second Gulf War, once elected, Wilkie focused mainly on problem gambling (particularly the proliferation of poker machines).

Unlike many of his crossbench colleagues, Wilkie demonstrates a coherent ideological outlook: protection for whistleblowers (particularly on humanitarian issues), urgent action against climate change, restrictions on gambling companies and greater accountability and transparency in politics. To the extent that he campaigned in 2022, it was on these issues (broadly defined). His platform would fit easily within the Australian Greens—the party he publicly denounced in 2008. Indeed, he has effectively chosen a path of fewer party-supplied resources (and no party label to boost his vote at election time) but unlimited freedom to pursue his own interests as the Member for Clark. If we are to pigeonhole Wilkie's approach to legislating and campaigning, it is the opposite to fellow Tasmanian Tyrrell: he is a classic Burkean, wielding his personal judgement not only on how to vote in the parliament but also on which causes to pursue. Perhaps more than any other recent Independent parliamentarian, Wilkie's approach will provide the template for the incoming Teal legislators.

Conclusion

The ostensibly seismic result by Independent candidates at the 2022 election was built on decades of work by unaligned, often disorganised Independent and minor-party challengers spending their own time and money to offer an alternative to the major parties. This election proved to be an ideal culmination of pent-up dissatisfaction with the Coalition and the ALP, an influx of resources for pro-climate candidates and enough belief in the viability of these candidates that major-party voters could confidently shift to an Independent or minor-party candidate without wasting their vote.

Outside those candidates supported by third-party movements such as Climate 200 or the 'Voices For' groups, Independents and successful minor-party candidates in 2022 represented a diverse group of established parliamentarians (Hanson, Wilkie and Katter), micro-party beneficiaries of well-known leaders (Babet and Tyrrell) and well-known locals with deep roots in their community (Pocock and Le). Only Pocock has much in common with the more prominent incoming members of the crossbench, but despite his shared focus on climate change and political integrity, he has so far sought to distance himself from their more organised movement. Although they will not necessarily enjoy the resources or imprimatur of the rest of the crossbench, this group represents the longer Australian tradition of non–major-party politicians with the ability to have an outsized impact on politics in the country.

References

Babet, Ralph. 2022a. Tweet, 23 June, 8.55 am. @senatorbabet, *Twitter*. Available from: twitter.com/senatorbabet/status/1539743791577694210.

Babet, Ralph. 2022b. Tweet, 23 June, 11.37 pm. @senatorbabet, *Twitter*. Available from: twitter.com/senatorbabet/status/1539965832151072768.

Barlow, Karen and Dan Jervis-Bardy. 2023. 'Simon Holmes a Court's Climate 200 revealed as David Pocock's biggest donor in expensive ACT Senate run'. *The Canberra Times*, 1 February, [Updated 2 February]. Available from: www.canberratimes.com.au/story/8067709/the-war-chest-which-helped-a-rugby-star-blast-zed-seselja-out-of-parliament/.

Bean, Clive and Ian McAllister. 2009. 'The Australian Election Survey: The tale of the rabbit-less hat. Voting behaviour in 2007'. *Australian Cultural History* 27(2): 205–18. doi.org/10.1080/07288430903165360.

Bovill, Monte. 2022. 'Who is Tasmania's likely new senator, Tammy Tyrrell?'. *ABC News*, 30 May. Available from: www.abc.net.au/news/2022-05-30/who-is-tammy-tyrrell-likely-tasmanian-senator/101108328.

Cameron, Sarah. 2020. 'Government performance and dissatisfaction with democracy in Australia'. *Australian Journal of Political Science* 55(2): 170–90. doi.org/10.1080/10361146.2020.1755221.

Cameron, Sarah M. and Ian McAllister. 2019. *Trends in Australian Political Opinion: Results from the Australian Election Study, 1987–2019*. Canberra: The Australian National University. Available from: australianelectionstudy.org/publications/.

Curtin, Jennifer. 2015. 'The prime ministership of Julia Gillard'. *Australian Journal of Political Science* 50(1): 190–204. doi.org/10.1080/10361146.2015.1010481.

Ghazarian, Zareh. 2015. *The Making of a Party System: Minor Parties in the Australian Senate*. Melbourne: Monash University Press.

Green, Antony. 2022. '2022 Queensland Senate election'. *Antony Green's Election Blog*, 4 June. Available from: antonygreen.com.au/2022-queensland-senate-election/.

Hui, Echo and Dylan Welch. 2022. 'ACT Senate candidate Li Fuxin linked to Chinese Government's foreign influence arm'. *ABC Investigations*, [*ABC News*], 14 May. Available from: www.abc.net.au/news/2022-05-14/act-senate-candidate-li-fuxin-linked-to-china-influence-arm/101065860.

Kefford, Glenn and Duncan McDonnell. 2016. 'Ballots and billions: Clive Palmer's personal party'. *Australian Journal of Political Science* 51(2): 183–97. doi.org/10.1080/10361146.2015.1133800.

Lucas, Jack, R. Michael McGregor and Kim-Lee Tuxhorn. 2022. 'Closest to the people? Incumbency advantage and the personal vote in non-partisan elections'. *Political Research Quarterly* 75(1): 188–202. doi.org/10.1177/1065912921990751.

Lupia, Arthur and Mathew McCubbins. 1998. *The Democratic Dilemma: Can Citizens Learn What They Need to Know?* Cambridge, UK: Cambridge University Press.

Maley, Jacqueline. 2012. 'Code of honour'. *Sydney Morning Herald*, 10 November. Available from: www.smh.com.au/sport/rugby-union/code-of-honour-201211 05-28sto.html.

Martin, Sarah. 2022. 'Clive Palmer's massive advertising spend fails to translate into election success for United Australia Party'. *The Guardian*, [Australia], 22 May. Available from: www.theguardian.com/australia-news/2022/may/22/clive-palmers-massive-advertising-spend-fails-to-translate-into-electoral-success.

McAllister, Ian, Jill Sheppard and Clive Bean. 2015. 'Valence and spatial explanations for voting in the 2013 Australian election'. *Australian Journal of Political Science* 50(2): 330–46. doi.org/10.1080/10361146.2015.1005005.

McGowan, Michael. 2022. 'Tu Le says Labor "learned the hard way" after Kristina Keneally loses safe seat'. *The Guardian*, [Australia], 23 May. Available from: www.theguardian.com/australia-news/2022/may/23/tu-le-says-labor-learned-the-hard-way-after-kristina-keneally-loses-safe-seat.

McSwiney, Jordan. 2021. 'Social networks and digital organisation: Far right parties at the 2019 Australian federal election'. *Information, Communication & Society* 24(10): 1401–18. doi.org/10.1080/1369118X.2020.1757132.

Miragliotta, Narelle and Wayne Errington. 2012. 'Legislative recruitment and models of party organisation: Evidence from Australia'. *The Journal of Legislative Studies* 18(1): 21–40. doi.org/10.1080/13572334.2012.646708.

Parkes-Hupton, Heath and Danuta Kozaki. 2022. 'Candidate who beat Keneally says she'll be a "real independent", not a Teal one'. *ABC News*, 23 May. Available from: www.abc.net.au/news/2022-05-23/dai-le-says-labor-took-fowler-for-granted-in-federal-election/101090766.

Parnell, Sean. 2022. 'Meet the anti-communist activist behind the Kim Jong-Un stunt'. *Sydney Morning Herald*, 13 May. Available from: www.smh.com.au/politics/federal/bull-in-a-china-shot-drew-pavlou-s-anti-communist-senate-campaign-20220513-p5al35.html.

Pocock, David. 2022a. 'Making Canberra count'. Campaign website. Available from: www.davidpocock.com.au/making_canberra_count.

Pocock, David. 2022b. 'Restoring integrity'. Campaign website. Available from: www.davidpocock.com.au/restoring_integrity.

United Australia Party (UAP). 2022. 'United Australia Party outlines economic plan for freedom and prosperity'. Media release, 7 April. Gold Coast, Qld: UAP. Available from: www.unitedaustraliaparty.org.au/united-australia-party-outlines-economic-plan-for-freedom-and-prosperity/.

Waterford, Jack. 2001. 'And all the rest: Jack Waterford's Election File: Part Two'. *Eureka Street* 11(8): 17–19.

White, Campbell and Shaun Ratcliff. 2022. 'Explainer—MRP: A new way of polling'. *The Australian*, 10 May. Available from: www.theaustralian.com.au/nation/politics/mrp-a-new-way-of-polling/news-story/393a33b7c671f254db1b215 15528c215.

Wilson, Cam. 2021. 'Pauline Hanson's cartoons got a lot of attention. But are they effective?'. *Crikey*, 20 December. Available from: www.crikey.com.au/2021/12/20/hansons-cartoons-got-attention-but-are-they-effective/.

Wilson, Cam. 2022. 'Meet Ralph Babet, Clive Palmer acolyte and Victoria's newest senator'. *Crikey*, 20 June. Available from: www.crikey.com.au/2022/06/20/meet-ralph-babet-clive-palmer-acolyte-and-maybe-victorias-newest-senator/.

Worthington, Elise and Michael Workman. 2022. 'AEC warns Pauline Hanson's One Nation over false voter fraud claims in cartoon attacking Labor'. *ABC Investigations*, [*ABC News*], 29 April. Available from: www.abc.net.au/news/2022-04-29/aec-warns-pauline-hanson-one-nation-over-voter-fraud-video/10 1026812.

14

The rise and impact of Australia's movement for Community Independents

Carolyn M. Hendriks and Richard Reid

On election night 2022, Zoe Daniel, Community Independent candidate for the bayside Melbourne electorate of Goldstein, declared: 'What we have achieved here is extraordinary. Safe Liberal seat, two-term incumbent— independent' (Daniel 2022). Daniel was celebrating her defeat of the Liberal incumbent and junior minister Tim Wilson with 33,815 first-preference votes and 52.76 per cent of the two-candidate-preferred vote. And so it was that the Liberal Party was defeated by a Teal Independent in six inner-city electorates, in Melbourne, Perth and Sydney: Curtin, Goldstein, Kooyong, Mackellar, North Sydney and Wentworth. Yet, the full story of the Community Independent candidates at the 2022 election, and the movement that supported them, is more complicated than suggested by the caricature of affluent metropolitan electorates preferring professional female Independents over 'moderate' Liberal incumbents.

The rise in support for Community Independents is a national phenomenon. It was spurred by growing voter frustration with the Morrison Government's lack of action on climate change and political integrity and boosted by community organising efforts that channelled this frustration into attractive political alternatives. This was an election in which many Australians shifted away from political parties as their preferred vehicle of political representation, opting instead for a locally engaged, place-based Community Independent candidate. Indeed, more than 470,000 Australians put a Community Independent first in 2022.

In this chapter, we examine the diverse local groups and individuals powering this national movement. We explore the rise of 'Voices For' groups as well as local Community Independent candidate groups, drawing attention to the multiple ways they engaged in the 2022 election. We also examine the electoral campaigns of 22 Community Independent candidates and offer reasons why some were elected and others not. To conclude, we reflect tentatively on the democratic impact and future of Australia's Community Independent movement.

Our discussion draws on multiple data sources, including: more than 40 semi-structured interviews with organisers and convenors of local 'Voices For' and Community Independent candidate groups, Community Independent candidates and campaign managers; participant observation of multiple community events, campaign efforts and public meetings; AEC election results; and relevant media and digital resources including webinars, websites and social media.

Our research finds that the movement for Community Independents is a loose network of placed-based groups, each carving out its own local pathway for improving political representation. The place-based variation across community groups is an important nuance that has been overlooked in the national media, both by those celebrating the 'Teal wave' and by those critiquing the 'party-like' behaviour of the movement (see, for example, Campion 2021). In what follows, we show that there is considerable diversity within the movement: some local groups selected or endorsed a Community Independent candidate in the 2022 election, while others chose not to follow this path and instead facilitated broader community engagement with all the local candidates. There was also much diversity in the scale and style of the Community Independent campaigns.

An 'explosion' of community groups working for democratic renewal

An important seed for the Community Independents movement was the successful community organising efforts of Voices for Indi (V4I), a local group that formed in 2012 to re-energise and improve democratic representation in the federal seat of Indi in north-eastern Victoria. A central part of V4I's democratic repair effort involved selecting and supporting an Independent candidate, Cathy McGowan, who was successfully elected in 2013 and again in 2016 (see Hendriks 2017; McGowan 2020). When McGowan announced that she would not contest the 2019 election, V4I ran an extensive community selection process, from which Helen Haines emerged as the preferred community candidate (see Hendriks et al. 2020: Ch. 4). Haines was successfully elected in 2019 and re-elected in 2022 on a significantly increased margin (58.94 per cent, up from 51.39 per cent).

The idea that this community-driven approach to electoral change was a 'rural story' was debunked in 2019 when Community Independent Zali Steggall defeated former prime minister Tony Abbott in the seat of Warringah, centred on Sydney's Northern Beaches (see Curtin and Sheppard 2020). In the wake of the 2019 election, people interested in democratic renewal around Australia reflected in awe on what the communities of Indi and Warringah had achieved. Frustrated and dismayed by the re-election of the Coalition, individuals and communities began to discuss ways to renew democracy and affect change in the culture of political representation and to pursue action in substantive policy areas, particularly climate change.

Plate 14.1 2022 Indi campaign
Source: Richard Iskov.

Some communities began to organise local groups with the aim of improving democratic representation and engagement in their federal electorate. Many of these adopted the label of 'Voices For' or 'Voices of' combined with the name of their federal electorate. Also emerging were a few community groups focused on the Senate and on building a broader regional identity (for example, ProACT in the Australian Capital Territory and its selection of David Pocock as an Independent Senate candidate for the 2022 election). The goals of these 'Voices For' groups vary but a common thread is the aspiration to 'do representative democracy better' in their federal electorate. They seek a local MP who is answerable to their community and not beholden to a political party—a representative who listens to the local community and is trustworthy and engages with constituents.

A key focus for many 'Voices For' groups—as their name suggests—is to explore views and values across the electorate and communicate these to their local MP. Many groups use 'kitchen table conversations' (KTCs) as a participatory method to engage local people in discussions about their views on key issues in the electorate and their democratic expectations. Centred on listening, KTCs are small in-person or online groups that engage in dialogue guided by a set of questions and a moderator. The aim is to share and hear rather than to agree and form a consensus (see Crooks and McPherson 2021). Many 'Voices For' groups collated what they had heard at the KTCs into a community report, which they published on their website and distributed via social media (see Plate 14.2). In the leadup to the 2022 election, many groups also presented (or sent) their report to the sitting local member and, in some cases, to all candidates.

In some electorates, communities established a specific group to find and endorse a Community Independent—for example, Hughes Deserves Better, Mackellar Rising, North Sydney's Independent, Kooyong Independent and Curtin Independent. These Community Independent candidate groups are distinct from the 'Voices For' groups in that they are specifically focused on finding local people who are willing to stand as a Community Independent in their electorate. Typically, 'Voices For' groups have a broader remit centred on strengthening political representation; they work to engage and mobilise local people in conversations about how to improve democracy. Unlike Community Independent candidate groups, not all 'Voices For' groups selected or endorsed a Community Independent candidate for the 2022 election. In some electorates (for example, Kooyong and North Sydney), the candidate groups coexisted with local 'Voices For' groups, while in other electorates, such as Curtin, no 'Voices For' group emerged.

Plate 14.2 Community report from Voices of Boothby

Source: Voices of Boothby, designer Amanda Hassett.

Between 2020 and 2021, many 'Voices For' and Community Independent candidate groups formed in preparation for the 2022 election, especially in New South Wales and Victoria. During this period communities endured successive waves of Covid-19 with strict lockdowns and other social distancing measures. Consequently, most groups shifted their community organising and engagement efforts to online platforms such as Zoom. Several groups we interviewed commented on how well online engagement worked for them; they were able to connect with many people from across the electorate (especially the time-poor) without requiring them to leave home. Online engagement was particularly helpful in larger rural and regional seats where vast distances can make it difficult to form community connections across the electorate.

In the six months leading up to the 2022 election, there were more than 40 groups publicly listed (in various ways), only 33 of which were what we classify as 'active'—that is, groups that regularly updated their websites and posted on their social media accounts, convened public events and were publicly engaged with the 2022 election. Figure 14.1 shows the increasing number of active groups based on the date they joined Twitter.

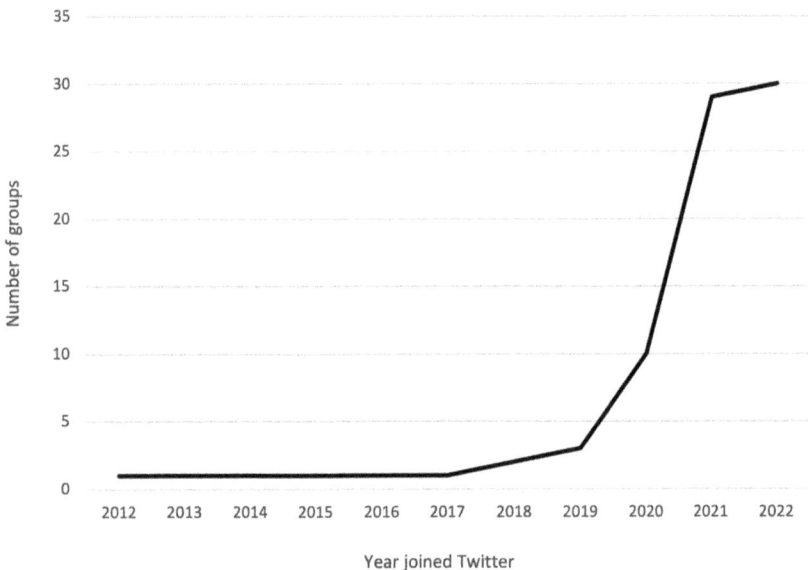

Year joined Twitter

Figure 14.1 Active 'Voices For' and Community Independent candidate groups, 2012–2022
Source: Data collected and analysed by the authors.

Most active groups are in south-eastern Australia (27, or 82 per cent in New South Wales and Victoria), with three in Queensland, two in Western Australia and one in South Australia. There are also State and Territory government–based groups in the Australian Capital Territory, Tasmania and Victoria. Most active groups have emerged in Coalition-held seats, with most in seats with Liberal MPs, followed by Nationals MPs, with only two in seats held by Labor at the 2019 election (Voices of Corangamite and Voices for Wollongong).

Australia's movement for Community Independents

The rise of these community groups working on democratic renewal began to attract national media attention in the 12 months before the 2022 election. Different narratives circulated in the media framing the rise in groups variously as, for example, a failure of the Liberal and National parties to speak to moderate Liberals, a revolt by professional women or a symptom of disaffection with political parties. There was also a significant amount of critical analysis of the groups as pseudo-parties or 'fake' Independents who used the label as a cover for a broad movement of the left—which was the preferred line of attack from the Coalition parties (see Millar 2022).

Although commentators disagreed on the reasons these community groups emerged, collectively, they were framed as a 'movement', with labels such as 'the voices movement' or 'the Independents movement' and, later in the election, 'the Teal wave'. The 'movement' label drew attention to the growing momentum around the nation of communities self-organising to do representative politics differently through community listening and engaged political representation. It also drew attention to two issues of growing popular concern: improving integrity and trust in politics and acting on climate change. However, the 'movement' label had the effect of obfuscating the significant diversity of the local groups and individuals involved.

Informal networking and mentoring

From 2013, individuals and groups began to network informally, often beginning through connections made by members of Voices for Indi. V4I convened several in-person networking events, including the Indi Shares Summit on participatory grassroots campaigns in 2014, which was attended by more than 70 people (Chan 2014), another in 2015 with a focus on the 2016 federal election and the Getting Elected to Represent Your Community workshop in 2018. All these events provided a strong catalyst for networking and action in other electorates. After 2019, this networking was expanded by individuals and groups associated with Steggall's campaign in Warringah and work by 'Voices for AU' led by Denis Ginnivan, Lesley Howard and Phil Haines (see Howard and Ginnivan 2022). By the end of 2021, several loose networks around the nation had formed to share resources and advice. Much of this networking and advice-sharing occurred behind the scenes via in-person and online meetings and social gatherings, and through digital platforms such as Slack and WhatsApp. Covid-19 and various lockdowns during 2020 and 2021 meant there were periods when only online networking within and between communities was possible.

With communities becoming more accustomed to engaging and networking online, advocates within the movement began to organise web-based public events to generate a national conversation on Community Independents—something that would have been challenging and expensive to organise face-to-face. The first of these was a national online convention, Community Independents—Getting Elected, which was held in February 2021, attracting 300 participants from across 78 electorates. After the convention, the Community Independents Project (CIP) was established by Cathy McGowan, Alana Johnson and Jill Briggs (from Indi) and Tina Jackson (from Warringah) to support Community Independents by facilitating networking and knowledge-sharing (see Cohen 2022). Throughout 2021 and early 2022, the CIP ran eight 1.5-hour evening Zoom sessions for interested members of the public to share information and network. Some of these events were well attended, such as the webinar panel discussion with Malcolm Turnbull, Kevin Rudd and Kerry O'Brien on 14 February 2022 that was attended by more than 2,800 people from 88 electorates (see Plate 14.3).

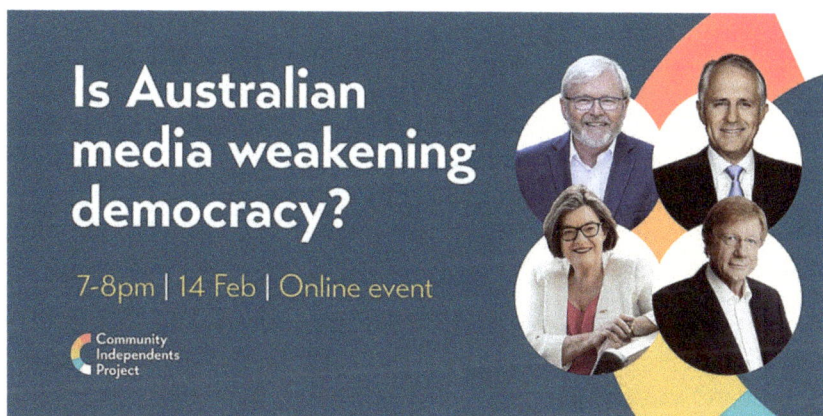

Plate 14.3 Advertisement for an online event by the Community Independents Project

Source: Community Independents Project.

Plate 14.4 Cathy McGowan at a workshop for campaign volunteers for Community Independent candidate for Cowper, Carolyn Heise

Source: Reproduced by permission of the Australian Broadcasting Corporation — Library Sales. Erin Semmler © 2022 ABC.

McGowan's role in forming and promoting the Community Independent movement deserves mention. As one of the founders of the CIP, McGowan established herself within the movement as the wise matriarch of all things 'Independent'. She individually mentored a number of Community

Independent candidates (especially in regional electorates) and held workshops for local volunteers in many electorates (see Plate 14.4). Externally, McGowan became an unofficial spokesperson for the movement, appearing regularly in the national media—particularly in the final weeks of the campaign (see, for example, ABC 2022; Cohen 2022)—narrating a cohesive story about the power of Community Independents and rebutting criticisms from the major parties that Independents would cause parliamentary dysfunction or were part of a pseudo-party.

Incumbent Community Independent MP for Warringah, Zali Steggall, also played a high-profile role within the Community Independents movement, acting with McGowan as something of a spokesperson. A similar public role was not assumed by Haines, Community Independent MP for Indi, who chose instead to support community groups and Independent candidates behind the scenes. There were many other individual community leaders and campaigners who worked backstage within the movement to connect people and coach or mentor them in their local democratic repair efforts.

Finding, selecting or endorsing Community Independent candidates

During the 2022 election, community groups travelled varied paths. Some 'Voices For' groups selected or endorsed an Independent candidate and then remained formally separate from the campaign (for example, Voices 4 Cowper). Other 'Voices For' groups selected, endorsed and then helped coordinate a large community-led election campaign (for example, those in Bradfield, Calare and Goldstein). Then there were 'Voices For' groups that either chose to or were unable to stand a candidate and instead participated in their election processes in other ways, such as organising a candidates' forum (for example, in Bennelong and Nicholls). In other cases, an original 'Voices For' group laid the groundwork for the establishment of what we have termed a Community Independent candidate group that separately focused on selecting and endorsing a local candidate (for example, in Mackellar and North Sydney). Finally, there were groups that did not use the 'Voices For' label that were set up with the sole intention of identifying and supporting a Community Independent (for example, in Curtin). The distinction between these and some of the 'Voices For' groups that were also focused on candidate selection was not always significant and reflects the difficulties of drawing boundaries between the group types. Importantly, for all, the candidate assumed control of the campaign. As well as a diversity of approaches, there was diversity in the electoral impact of Community Independents; some achieved considerable swings while others appear to have had minimal impact on their local electoral outcome.

Among the groups that selected a local Independent candidate themselves, the selection processes varied considerably. Some candidates emerged from the community organising work in their 'Voices For' groups (for example, Kate Hook in Calare and Sophie Scamps in Mackellar). In other cases, the group sought prospective candidates from outside the initial group by advertising for expressions of interest in local newspapers (for example, Kooyong Independent, Voices for Cowper and Voices of Wannon) (see Plate 14.5). In electorates where multiple candidates had stepped forward, the relevant group went through a selection process to identify the final candidate to be endorsed. In some electorates, the candidate was selected through an interview process with key members of the organising committee (for example, North Sydney's Independent, Voices of Goldstein and Voices of Mornington Peninsula), while in other cases selection was put to the community through either a deliberative process or a community vote (for example, Voices for Cowper, Voices for Indi and Voices for Monash).

Plate 14.5 Part of the newspaper advertisement placed by Voices of Wannon
Source: Voices of Wannon.

In some electorates, more than one community-minded candidate emerged. Two examples of this were in the south-western Sydney seat of Hughes and in Flinders, based on the Mornington Peninsula in Victoria. In the case of Hughes, two Independents, Linda Seymour and Georgia Steele, ran competing campaigns, with tensions between the candidates due to concerns about voter confusion and vote-splitting. In Flinders, the Voices of Mornington Peninsula–endorsed candidate, Claire Boardman, withdrew after it emerged that another former member of the group and former mayor, Despi O'Connor, planned to run as an Independent (Norington 2022). Voices of Mornington Peninsula then endorsed Sarah Russell to replace Boardman.

Several 'Voices For' groups did not stand a candidate at the 2022 federal election—for two main reasons: they were unable to find a suitable candidate or they intentionally decided not to. Both Voices of Bennelong and Voices for Durack had sought to endorse a candidate for the election. As Voices of Bennelong (2022) tweeted:

> Here in Bennelong we suffer from candidate envy. If only we could find our Nicolette Boele … To all those in Bradfield—we hope you know how lucky you are! What we would do to find a quality candidate to vote for and get behind.

Of those groups that decided not to stand a candidate, these can be further divided into those who felt it was premature and plan to run a candidate at the next federal election and others who decided not to select or endorse an Independent candidate because it would limit the breadth of their community engagement; in the words of Voices of Wentworth (2022: 2), not endorsing a candidate enables them to engage 'with as many constituents as possible, from all parts of the political spectrum'. Groups that did not associate themselves with an Independent candidate were able to participate more broadly in the election (for example, Voices of Bennelong, Voices of North Sydney and Voices of Wentworth).

Community Independent candidates in the 2022 election

The diversity of local community groups supporting or endorsing candidates in the 2022 election presents some analytical challenges. Indeed, deciding exactly who is a 'Community Independent' candidate is not straightforward. While most community candidates had been selected or endorsed by a community group, there were some, such as Rob Priestly (Nicholls) and Allegra Spender (Wentworth), who were not formally supported or endorsed by a public 'Voices For' or Community Independent group, yet both had been associated in the media, and self-identified in their campaigns, as part of the broader Community Independent movement. For this reason, we have included Priestly and Spender in our analysis, but they remain an important manifestation of the lack of clear boundaries in such a loose movement.

Another central puzzle in identifying Community Independents is whether they differ from other Independents and, if so, how. It would be uncommon to find an Independent who did not embed themselves firmly in a rhetoric of 'community', as Dai Le (successful Independent candidate in Fowler) does on her website: 'your Local independent' (daile.com.au/). Le's attempt to distance herself from the Teal Independents was clear in the election and for this reason we have decided not to include her in our analysis in this chapter (but see Chapter 13, this volume). However, Le's strong local campaign raises analytical questions about when an Independent is to be considered a 'Community Independent'.

In the discussion below, we focus on 22 Community Independent candidates—11 in inner and outer metropolitan seats: Boothby, Bradfield, Curtin, Goldstein, Hughes (two candidates), Kooyong, Mackellar, North Sydney, Warringah and Wentworth; three in provincial seats: Cowper, Groom and Hume; and eight in rural seats: Calare, Casey, Flinders, Indi, Monash, Nicholls, Page and Wannon. As shown in Table 14.1, all the electorates were Coalition-held seats or had Independent incumbents. In addition, all the candidates considered in our analysis (except Alex Dyson and Rob Priestly) were women with professional backgrounds. During the campaign, the national media focused particular attention on these three characteristics of the Community Independent candidates: urban, professional women contesting Coalition-held seats.

Table 14.1 Community Independent candidates

Candidate	Electorate	Type of electorate	Incumbent party
Penny Ackery	Hume	Provincial	Liberal
Nicolette Boele	Bradfield	Metropolitan	Liberal
Kate Chaney	Curtin	Metropolitan	Liberal
Zoe Daniel	Goldstein	Metropolitan	Liberal
Jo Dyer	Boothby	Metropolitan	Liberal

Candidate	Electorate	Type of electorate	Incumbent party
Alex Dyson	Wannon	Rural	Liberal
Claire Ferres Miles	Casey	Rural	Liberal
Helen Haines	Indi	Rural	Incumbent
Carolyn Heise	Cowper	Provincial	Nationals
Suzie Holt	Groom	Provincial	LNP
Kate Hook	Calare	Rural	Nationals
Deb Leonard	Monash	Rural	Liberal
Hanabeth Luke	Page	Rural	Nationals
Rob Priestly	Nicholls	Rural	Nationals
Sarah Russell	Flinders	Rural	Liberal
Monique Ryan	Kooyong	Metropolitan	Liberal
Sophie Scamps	Mackellar	Metropolitan	Liberal
Linda Seymour	Hughes	Metropolitan	Liberal/UAP
Allegra Spender	Wentworth	Metropolitan	Liberal
Georgia Steele	Hughes	Metropolitan	Liberal/UAP
Zali Steggall	Warringah	Metropolitan	Incumbent
Kylea Tink	North Sydney	Metropolitan	Liberal

Source: Authors' original research.

The campaigns of the Community Independents

The processes of candidate selection and the unknown timing of the election made it difficult for local community groups to know how best to plan and resource their campaigns. Some Community Independent campaigns were in place some six to 12 months before the election was called. There were, however, many groups that selected candidates much closer to the election. Some communities strategically held off announcing their candidate as late as possible to prevent attacks from incumbents but for others the selection processes took that long to complete. Most launches of the Community Independent candidates were large public events with lots of colour, supporters, volunteers and media.

Plate 14.6 Campaign launch for Penny Ackery (Hume), 13 November 2021
Source: Alex Tewes.

The Community Independent candidates' use of colour deserves mention because in the months leading up to the election the word 'Teal' became synonymous with the movement in the media and subsequently in public discourse. Teal was Steggall's winning campaign colour in Warringah in 2019, but in 2022, it also came to be associated with Community Independent candidates appealing to voters through a mix of moderate 'blue' (liberal) values and 'green' issues, such as acting on climate change (see Murphy 2022). Although 'Teal' was widely used in the media throughout the election, some in the movement we interviewed do not identify with the 'Teal' label. For them, it simply represents lazy journalism—a shorthand to describe what is otherwise a diverse movement of different communities, groups and individuals.

While the 'Teal' label may not resonate with all in the movement, it was nevertheless the campaign colour adopted by almost half the 22 Community Independent candidates we consider in this chapter. Others chose conservative blues (light or sky-blue), sometimes combined with a splash of pink (for example, Kylea Tink in North Sydney and Kate Hook in Calare) or lemon (Sophie Scamps in Mackellar). Bold, bright, fresh orange was used by Helen Haines, Rob Priestly and Georgia Steele. A few candidates

(Jo Dyer, Linda Seymour and, on occasion, Penny Ackery) used purple—a colour associated with the women's movement in Australia and globally (Sawer 2007). The only Queensland Community Independent candidate, Suzie Holt from Groom, selected a mix of dark green and white—signalling her autonomy and independence from the southern and urban Community Independents. Overall, there does not appear to be a single unifying colour across the Community Independent movement (see Plates 14.7 and 14.8). Instead, colours were selected for specific purposes in each electorate, where they carried their own local meaning and significance.

Plate 14.7 Campaigning in Calare for Independent candidate Kate Hook
Source: Kate Hook.

Plate 14.8 Local hub in Alexandra, in the Victorian seat of Indi
Source: Helen Haines campaign team.

The campaigns of the Community Independents varied considerably—
not just because some electorates had much larger campaign funding than
others. Each campaign took its own local approach to campaigning and
working with volunteers, adapting to the particularities of the electorate, its
geography, the nature of the electoral contest and the non-financial resources
of the group. Several campaigns, particularly those in rural and regional
seats, established 'hubs' in shopfronts in main streets across their electorate
as a place for volunteers to meet and interact with the broader community
(see Plate 14.8). Modelled after the successful Indi campaigns, local hubs
enabled the central campaign team to delegate volunteer coordination
to local areas. Social media was an important part of all the Community
Independent campaigns, but some teams were unable to do targeted social
media campaigning due to lack of funds, staff or skills.

Building and managing a large volunteer base were crucial for all the
Community Independents. All the campaigns had a dedicated 'volunteer
manager', while well-resourced electorates invested in software such
as NationBuilder to help coordinate and task volunteers. Some of the
most successful campaigns claimed they had some 2,000 volunteers,
although most of the candidates had core groups of volunteers in the low

hundreds who did most of the campaign work. Some campaign teams (with backgrounds in community organising) wrestled with how best to coordinate and engage their volunteers. Volunteer empowerment thrives with more decentralised leadership, but there is always the temptation to control the campaign from the top—as parties do. In some electorates, tensions emerged between the expectations and desires of the volunteers and the messaging and decisions of the central campaign team. Balancing the energy, enthusiasm and expectations of the community volunteers with the campaign team's strategies, goals and messaging was challenging for many of those we interviewed.

Independent candidates also needed to strike a balance between performing as a local, 'real' and 'authentic' candidate and appearing sophisticated, professional and 'representative-worthy'. They also had to be 'from here' but not perceived as only 'from there'—that is, they needed to be from the local community but not too strongly associated with a particular suburb, beach or town within the electorate. This was a particular challenge for Community Independent candidates in regional and rural electorates where strong roots in one town or regional centre made it more challenging to build an identity and trust in other localities that could be up to three hours' drive away.

Funding became a significant election issue, with media and Coalition attention focusing on the role of Climate 200, which provided funding support to most, although not all, of the Community Independents (see Holmes à Court 2022). C200 provided campaigns varying amounts, with Independent candidates in the most 'winnable' electorates receiving significantly more than others. Independent candidates in rural and regional seats (such as Calare, Cowper and Hume) received significantly less support from Climate 200 than some of their metropolitan counterparts. Climate 200 funding allocation was piecemeal and unpredictable; candidates accepting their donations would receive initial seed funding and then, depending on polling data, would be given more. In several electorates, the significant donations from Climate 200 did not arrive until the last weeks of the campaign by which time some teams felt it was too late. The support of Climate 200 was emphasised in Coalition attacks and added to the claims that the Community Independents were just like a political party and not Independents at all (see Millar 2022).

Climate 200 funding was important for many candidates but all were keen to ensure it was not a majority of their funding. To our knowledge, Climate 200 was not the majority funder of any Community Independent campaign;

all were reliant on broader fundraising efforts, particularly from within their electorates. Some campaigns chose not to accept large sums from certain individuals or groups so as not to fuel attacks about the influence of donors. Most importantly, however, the range of campaign spending by Community Independents, based on AEC declarations, was significant—from $54,324 to $2,124,058 (AEC 2022).

The narrative of Community Independents as urban elites beholden to wealthy businessman Simon Holmes à Court and climate activists (via Climate 200) negatively impacted several campaigns in rural and regional seats. Indeed, in some country areas, the 'Teal' label was picked up quickly by Liberal and Nationals campaigns and used to discredit Community Independent candidates, regardless of whether they accepted Climate 200 funding. To counter claims of outside influence, candidates such as Suzie Holt (Groom) chose not to take any funding from Climate 200 and accepted campaign donations only from within Queensland.

Plate 14.9 Co-campaign event by, from left, Kylea Tink, Allegra Spender, Sophie Scamps and Zali Steggall

Source: Allegra Spender Instagram, 17 May 2022.

The claim that Community Independents were part of a pseudo-party was also fuelled by the co-campaigning that took place between some Community Independent candidates. A clear example of this was the occasional joint campaign events between Sydney-based Community Independent candidates, particularly Zali Steggall (Warringah), Allegra Spender (Wentworth), Kylea Tink (North Sydney) and Sophie Scamps (Mackellar) (see Plate 14.9). The joint appearances of such Community Independent candidates attracted media attention and were seen to benefit the new candidates through association with the popular Steggall.

Election outcomes

The results for the Community Independent candidates can be grouped into three: those who won their seat (Table 14.2); those who were the closest competitor to the incumbent party—that is, were present in the final distribution of preferences (Table 14.3); and those who were not electorally competitive (Table 14.4). The candidates listed in Table 14.2 were also those who received the most national media attention during the campaign. It should be noted that some of those in Table 14.4 received higher first-preference votes than, for example, Suzie Holt in Groom, but were not in the final distribution due to the nature of preference flows in their electorate. In addition, some of those listed in Table 14.2 proved significant challengers in traditionally very safe Coalition seats.

Table 14.2 Successful Community Independent candidates

Electorate	Candidate	Winning margin (no. of votes)	2CP (%)
Curtin	Kate Chaney	2,657	51.26
Goldstein	Zoe Daniel	5,635	52.87
Indi	Helen Haines (incumbent)	18,158	58.94
Kooyong	Monique Ryan	6,035	52.94
Mackellar	Sophie Scamps	4,955	52.50
North Sydney	Kylea Tink	5,666	52.92
Warringah	Zali Steggall (incumbent)	20,450	60.96
Wentworth	Allegra Spender	7,449	54.19

2CP = two-candidate-preferred

Source: Australian Electoral Commission.

Table 14.3 Community Independent candidates in second place

Electorate	Candidate	Margin from winning (no. of votes)	2CP (%)
Bradfield	Nicolette Boele	–8,190	45.77
Calare	Kate Hook	–20,775	40.32
Cowper	Caz Heise	–5,172	47.68
Groom	Suzie Holt	–13,220	43.11
Nicholls	Rob Priestly	–7,251	46.19
Wannon	Alex Dyson	–7,933	46.08

2CP = two-candidate-preferred
Source: Australian Electoral Commission.

Table 14.4 Community Independent candidates not in final distribution of preferences

Electorate	Candidate	First-preference vote
Boothby	Jo Dyer	7,441 (6.54%)
Casey	Claire Ferres Miles	8,307 (8.34%)
Flinders	Sarah Russell	5,189 (5.25%)
Hughes	Linda Seymour	3,138 (3.24%)
Hughes	Georgia Steele	13,891 (14.33%)
Hume	Penny Ackery	16,045 (15.32%)
Monash	Deb Leonard	10,372 (10.72%)
Page	Hanabeth Luke	13,734 (13.13%)

Source: Australian Electoral Commission.

Community Independents were only elected in Coalition-held seats—indeed, only seats held by the Liberal Party. In addition, none of the provincial and rural Community Independent candidates was elected, except in Indi, where McGowan and then Haines have built strong voter support (in 2022, Haines received just more than 40 per cent of first preferences, up from about 32 per cent in 2019). It should also be noted that while the media focused on the challengers to Liberal 'moderates', the victories of Kate Chaney over Celia Hammond and Monique Ryan over Josh Frydenberg, in addition to the previous victories of Steggall and McGowan against Abbott and Sophie Mirabella, respectively, provide potential counterexamples (on the challenge to Liberal 'moderates', see Harvey 2022). In addition, the political 'moderateness' of some incumbent MPs was undermined by their adoption of quite aggressive campaign strategies.

Plate 14.10 Some of the Community Independent MPs in the forty-seventh parliament (from left): Zoe Daniel, Sophie Scamps, Zali Steggall, Allegra Spender, Kylea Tink and Monique Ryan

Why some Community Independent candidates were electorally successful and others were not is likely due to a mix of national and local factors. In the absence of survey data on the relevant electorates, we offer some conjectures about potentially important factors, noting that this is an area for further research. First, some campaigns were more successful than others at tapping into popular frustration with the Morrison Government, particularly on climate change and integrity. Community Independent candidates in some rural and regional seats did not run as hard on climate change as their city counterparts—for fear of being labelled 'Green'. Further explanations include: candidates were selected and launched their campaigns late; they were unable to raise as much financial support (both from Climate 200 and other sources); they faced strong campaigns from incumbents, especially promises on local infrastructure projects, which were a significant concern in regional and rural electorates; or they were unable to build their volunteer base into the thousands that were seen in some of the successful campaigns. Many of the Independent candidates in metropolitan seats were standing against high-profile incumbents and this aided name recognition and helped raise funds from donors outside the electorate (as in Indi in 2013 and Warringah in 2019). In some electorates, two Independents stood (for example, Hughes and Flinders) and this potentially divided voter attention. Finally, the popularity, campaigning style or approach of the incumbent could have been a factor in resisting the swing to a Community Independent.

Conclusion

The growth of 'Voices For' and Community Independent candidate groups over the past decade demonstrates that local grassroots community organising and participation are alive and well in many parts of the country. While many groups did not produce the electoral outcomes they had hoped for, they have tapped into a growing desire for improved political representation. For roughly 20,000 people to volunteer and support Community Independents suggests there is a strong demand for more localised and participatory ways of 'doing democracy'. Many local communities around the country remain committed to the goal of successfully electing an Independent local member who is engaged, responsive and unencumbered by a political party. Paradoxically, the pathway for communities to realise this goal is to travel through a competitive electoral process that thrives on the kind of 'old-style' politics that they reject: money-fuelled election campaigns with excessive advertising, limited policy content and slick, polished public performances. The election results show that some communities and their candidates were better skilled and resourced than others to successfully travel through this competitive electoral process.

Once the dust from the 2022 election settles, it will be fascinating to observe what happens not just in parliament but also in electorates around Australia. In ongoing research, we are observing the development and evolution of 'Voices For' and Community Independent candidate groups and their effect on how MPs (whether Independent or not) engage with their constituents. For those community groups that now have an elected 'community voice' some tricky conversations and decisions lie ahead. For while they have helped to bring 'their' Independent candidate into power, for future electoral success, the new MP will need to engage with a broader set of constituents and local groups. The examples of McGowan, Haines and Steggall will no doubt present models for ways forward. Communities that were not successful in electing an Independent will reflect on the experiences of the 2022 election and use these to inform future directions and strategies. An important lesson for many has been the need to invest more time, skills and resources in the campaign effort and in building the profile of their candidate. Others are keen to ensure that their ongoing community organising and engagement efforts reach more diverse groups, including the young and marginalised.

The national conversation on the need to improve political representation and engagement in Australia is set to continue. There is strong resolve among key players in the movement to continue supporting and inspiring Community Independents and broader community engagement, with further events already planned. The presence of eight Community Independents in the House of Representatives and David Pocock in the Senate provides a formal institutional platform for the movement and their performance will be a key test for it. Ultimately, it will depend on the effort, engagement and activity of communities around Australia—something that will continue as long as they demand a new politics, both in style and in substance.

References

Australian Broadcasting Corporation (ABC). 2022. 'The final countdown'. *Q+A*, [ABC TV], 19 May. Available from: www.abc.net.au/qanda/2022-19-05/1387 9188.

Australian Electoral Commission (AEC). 2022. *AEC Transparency Register*. Canberra: AEC. Available from: transparency.aec.gov.au/.

Campion, Vikki. 2021. 'Let's not kid ourselves, the Voices sound like a party'. *Daily Telegraph*, [Sydney], 18 December.

Chan, Gabrielle. 2014. 'Voices for Indi give political minorclass where everyone is welcome'. *Bush Mail*, [*The Guardian*], 16 June. Available from: www.the guardian.com/news/bush-mail/2014/jun/16/voices-for-indi-give-political-minor class-where-everyone-is-welcome.

Cohen, Janine. 2022. 'An independent woman: Cathy McGowan'. *Australian Story*, [ABC TV], 16 May, [Updated 21 July]. Available from: www.abc.net.au/austory/ independent-woman-cathy-mcgowan/13879412.

Cohen, Janine and Matt Henry. 2022. 'How former member for Indi Cathy McGowan could be secret weapon for "teal independents" in federal election'. *Australian Story*, [ABC TV], 16 May. Available from: www.abc.net.au/news/2022-05-16/ the-godmother-of-the-independents-cathy-mcgowan/101052838.

Crooks, Mary and Leah McPherson. 2021. *Kitchen Table Conversations: A Guide for Sustaining Our Democratic Culture*. Melbourne: Victorian Women's Trust.

Curtin, Jennifer and Jill Sheppard. 2020. 'The Independents'. In *Morrison's Miracle: The 2019 Australian Federal Election*, edited by Anika Gauja, Marian Sawer and Marian Simms, 357—71. Canberra: ANU Press. doi.org/10.22459/MM. 2020.18.

Daniel, Zoe. 2022. 'Independent Zoe Daniel defeats Liberal Tim Wilson in Goldstein'. [Video], *ABC News Australia*, 21 May. Available from: www.youtube. com/watch?v=qvEDcej5tYc.

Harvey, Claire. 2022. 'Progressive warriors bombarded from the left'. *The Weekend Australian*, 14 May.

Hendriks, Carolyn M. 2017. 'Citizen-led democratic reform: Innovations in Indi'. *Australian Journal of Political Science* 52(4): 481–99. doi.org/10.1080/103611 46.2017.1374345.

Hendriks, Carolyn M., Selen A. Ercan and John Boswell. 2020. *Mending Democracy: Democratic Repair in Disconnected Times*. Oxford, UK: Oxford University Press. doi.org/10.1093/oso/9780198843054.001.0001.

Holmes à Court, Simon. 2022. *The Big Teal*. Melbourne: Monash University Publishing.

Howard, Lesley and Denis Ginnivan. 2022. 'A positive politics: Community Independents and the new wave of political engagement'. *Arena Quarterly* 11(September). Available from: arena.org.au/a-positive-politics-community-independents-and-the-new-wave-of-political-engagement/.

McGowan, Cathy. 2020. *Cathy Goes to Canberra: Doing Politics Differently*. Melbourne: Monash University Press.

Millar, Royce. 2022. 'A secret party? Immoral? Explaining who the "teal" independents really are'. *The Age*, [Melbourne], 6 May. Available from: www.theage.com.au/ politics/federal/a-secret-party-immoral-explaining-who-the-teal-independents-really-are-20220505-p5aio4.html.

Murphy, James. 2022. 'Fifty shades of teal'. *Pursuit*, 18 May. Melbourne: University of Melbourne. Available from: pursuit.unimelb.edu.au/articles/fifty-shades-of-teal.

Norington, Brad. 2022. 'Climate 200 felt like a party to us, say snubbed independents'. *The Weekend Australian*, 30 April: 5.

Sawer, Marian. 2007. 'Wearing your politics on your sleeve: The role of political colours in social movements'. *Social Movement Studies* 6(1): 39–56. doi.org/10.1080/14742830701251294.

Voices for Indi. 2023. *The Indi Way: How a rural community sparked a social and political movement.* Scribe: Melbourne.

Voices of Bennelong. 2022. Tweet, 21 February, 9.40 am. @VoicesBennelong, *Twitter.* Available from: twitter.com/VoicesBennelong/status/14958911273202 64707?cxt=HHwWhoCqqcDDvMIpAAAA.

Voices of Wentworth. 2022. Wentworth Cares: Community Engagement Report 2022. Available from: www.voicesofwentworth.org/_files/ugd/b05b27_3ed6c 5793d5a46238fb0ffb4f2818a7e.pdf.

15

Third-party campaigning organisations

Ariadne Vromen and Serrin Rutledge-Prior

Whether or not we view the 2022 federal election as a win for Labor or a loss for the Liberals, we must recognise the prominence of campaigning organisations—most notably, Climate 200—in the leadup to the election as a victory for third parties. In Australian electoral law a third party is defined as an individual or entity that is not a political party–associated entity or a parliamentarian and that incurs regular electoral expenditure of more than about $15,000 per annum. Traditionally within Australian politics, third parties have tended to be industry or business-oriented interest groups and unions that choose to spend money supporting candidates, parties or ideas during an election campaign. Over the past 10–15 years, new organisations have emerged as active third parties, including environmental, animal rights, human rights and religious organisations and, in particular, GetUp!, which is featured in this chapter. During the same period, concerns about the influence of money and fundraising donations in politics have heightened, leading to several new iterations of regulations around the actions and fundraising activities of third parties. Arguably, electoral law has been changed to try to curtail the emergence of new organisations, as well as make both their fundraising activities and their political activities much more transparent.

In this chapter, we focus on the activities of four campaigning organisations that were active as third parties during the 2022 election campaign. We argue that while some tactics were shared across the groups, particularly their use of digital campaigning via social media and Facebook advertising, they differed in their emphasis on a range of campaign issues, tactics and overall influence on the campaign discourse. Comparing GetUp!, Climate 200, the Australian Christian Lobby (ACL) and Advance (formerly Advance Australia), we can see that both progressive and conservative actors are now clearly active and visible in the third-party space. We can also see that there is an interdependency in the campaigning work of these third parties in their capacity to fundraise large amounts of money to spend during the campaign, as well as the organic reach of their brand of ideas. Of the four organisations, Climate 200 had the highest profile due to its success in raising funds for the campaigns of successful Independent Teal candidates. The influence of the other three organisations can be seen mainly in their capacity to shape discourse on campaign issues and disrupt the election campaign with notable tactics or stunts.

Background

Third-party campaigning organisations, like political parties, adapt and change over time. From one election to the next, third-party action is shaped by the electoral competition and the policy context of the organisation and the campaign. The 2022 election is important in that, in similarity with 2019, there were several active third parties and all were influenced by new trends within hyperlocal campaigning and targeting individual electorates for direct voter contact, rather than aiming at the general Australian voting population (Mills 2020). Third-party campaigns were also underpinned by targeted social media advertising, especially on Facebook. This was not the first election to use these tactics, as they emerged in Australia in 2016 (Vromen 2018), growing out of the email mobilisation of the 2007 election (Vromen 2017), but in 2022 all organisations were using digital tactics and they are now more or less mainstream. The other important influence on the emergence of local groups doing campaign work is the 'Voices For' movement, which is covered in Chapter 14. It is sufficient to say here that the legacy of a new form of grassroots organising to bring *to* politics people who would generally be considered outsiders and not insiders in major-party political networks is an important discursive feature of third-party campaigning as well.

The existing research on digital campaigning organisations demonstrates that they are proliferating and that the tactics used have diffused from progressive to conservative organisations in recent times (Hall 2022). They tend to be driven by multiple issues rather than overtly partisan and use crowdsourced digital tactics and storytelling. Most have low organisational overheads but focus on managing strategic multichannel communications, not only to persuade their supporter base to act but also to capture mainstream media attention to establish the legitimacy of their ideas (Karpf 2012, 2016).

The four organisations and their issues

As noted above, there have been recent changes in electoral law that have defined and reshaped the actions and influence of third parties. This is partly in response to public concern about the undue influence of interest groups, or third parties, on politics in Australia (see Cameron and Wynter 2018). The term 'third party' itself is confusing, as many interpret it to mean another group or party standing for election that is not one of the two major-party groupings. Rather, in electoral law, 'third party' is designated to a group that is not an election contestant or registered party and is separate from, but connected to, election campaigns. Third parties need to make financial disclosure declarations to the AEC when they spend more than $14,500 on election-specific activities in a financial year. They will then be on the AEC's *Transparency Register* for at least three years.

After creating a new disclosure and registered category of 'political campaigner' in late 2018, Australian electoral law was changed again in late 2021 to label mainly the same organisations as 'significant third party' organisations. This status applies when:

- electoral expenditure is more than $250,000 in a financial year, or any one of the previous three years
- electoral expenditure is equal to the disclosure threshold during that financial year and electoral expenditure during the previous financial year was at least one-third of the revenue of the person or organisation for that year
- during the financial year the person or organisation operates mainly for electoral expenditure fundraising (AEC 2022b).

As of July 2022, 36 organisations were registered with the AEC as significant third parties, including all four organisations analysed in this chapter. Other organisations on the list include unions, business lobbyists, environmental organisations and nine organisations formed specifically to fundraise for local campaigns for Independent election candidates. In comparison, in the financial year ending July 2019 that covered the 2019 election, 24 organisations were registered as 'political campaigners', including GetUp! and Advance. The ACL was only registered as a third party in that year and Climate 200 had not yet emerged.

GetUp!

GetUp! was formed in 2006 with an explicit aim of campaigning in the 2007 election to unseat the long-term Coalition Government and to draw attention to it having a majority in both houses of parliament at that time. GetUp! pioneered digital campaigning in Australia—first, using email supporter lists, online petitions and crowdfunding, and more recently, using social media advertising to mobilise supporters and create political change (Vromen 2017). These are now standard digital tactics for any political organisation or interest group involved in campaign work.

GetUp! has been active in the five subsequent Australian elections (see Vromen 2018) but arguably in 2022 they purposefully kept a lower profile in light of criticism after the 2019 election of their campaign work against 'hard-right politicians' as well as the emergence of new players supporting Independent campaigns on some of their core issues of concern. GetUp!'s five overarching campaign areas were: economic fairness, environmental justice, media and democracy, First Nations justice and human rights. Of these, First Nations justice was at the foreground of GetUp!'s 2022 campaign, with an emphasis on action on climate change, federal protection for cultural heritage, electoral participation and reducing inequality. GetUp! also targeted electorates in the major cities that were most likely to see challengers unseat incumbent conservative politicians.

Climate 200

Climate 200 formed in 2019 and, like GetUp!, is a progressive, born-digital organisation that uses similar digital tactics but has a particular focus on crowdfunding and fundraising for Independent candidates focused on climate change mitigation. Climate 200 was started by wealthy philanthropist

Simon Holmes à Court and its main election campaign issues were climate change, electoral and political integrity and gender equity. Climate 200 provided election campaign donations to 23 Independent candidates, of whom six were elected and four re-elected to the House of Representatives and one elected to the Senate.

Advance

Advance (formerly Advance Australia) formed in 2018 as a conservative response to GetUp! and its first election campaign was in 2019 (Zhou 2019). Initially funded by several businesspeople, the organisation received $1 million in the 2020–21 financial year from the business holdings of Western Australia–based couple Simon and Elizabeth Fenwick (AEC 2022a; Karp et al. 2022). It is another born-digital organisation that uses similar digital tactics to GetUp! but has a focus on core ideals of freedom, security and prosperity. During the election campaign, it focused on climate change policies and the influence of China and provided a counter voice to Independent candidates supported by Climate 200, especially targeting the campaign of ACT Senate candidate David Pocock. The newly elected Country Liberal Party senator for the Northern Territory, Jacinta Nampijinpa Price, was previously a spokesperson for Advance.

The Australian Christian Lobby

The ACL was formed in 1995 and while it has been active in politics and elections as a third party, it is also a registered charity. This status limits its political activities and advocacy role (Seibert 2021; Maddison and Carson 2017). The ACL gained a high public profile by opposing marriage equality reform in Australia in 2017, largely due to the advocacy of then leader Lyle Shelton (Watson 2021). During the 2022 election campaign, the main issues on which it campaigned included religious freedom, education, abortion and the sexualisation of society. The ACL used digital tactics including Facebook advertising and focused campaigning materials such as leaflets and billboards in marginal Coalition seats. It promoted its election-specific YouTube interviews, conducted by managing director Martyn Iles and politics director Wendy Francis, with prominent socially conservative candidates in the Coalition and minor parties.

Table 15.1 Reach of third parties: Donations and social media followers

	GetUp!	Climate 200	Advance	ACL
Fundraising	$10.1 m	$12 m	n.a.	$9 m
Donors in past year	44,000	11,200		
AEC declaration after 2019 election	$13.7 m	n.a.	$2.4 m	$62,000
Facebook followers	502,000	4,200	90,000	302,000
YouTube subscribers	28,000	100	730	100,000
Instagram followers	46,000	5,900	n.a.	14,000

n.a. = not available

Sources: Websites and Facebook, YouTube and Instagram pages of organisations (as of June 2022); AEC (2022a).

Table 15.1 contrasts the four organisations in terms of their reach (defined as their capacity to raise money), how much money we know they are spending during election campaigns and their social media followers across Facebook, YouTube and Instagram. The table shows that the progressive organisations raised a significant amount of money leading up to the 2022 campaign. While Advance does not publicly reveal the same data on its webpage, it is unlikely to be anywhere near as much as both GetUp! and Climate 200. The ACL has similarly high annual revenue (about $10 million) but only declared $62,000 in electoral expenditure in 2019. This is an important point of comparison between the ACL and the three other organisations, which are much more overtly political. While the ACL is an influential lobby group, it has been less visibly active during elections, probably to maintain its status as a charity and a deductible gift recipient.

The other way of comparing the four organisations is via their social media reach. This is important for understanding who is using organic social media posts as well as explaining what they spend on social media advertising—especially on Facebook—to try to reach a broader audience. Relative to the other three organisations, GetUp! has by far the largest group of followers on Facebook and Instagram, both of which are important sites for sharing campaign and issue-driven posts. Climate 200 has not invested a lot of time in growing its supporter base on social media; the candidates it supports have done this work instead. However, the organisation did post throughout the campaign and paid for advertising on Facebook. The ACL is notable here in its use of videos on YouTube, where it has easily the largest base of the four with more than 100,000 subscribers.

Campaign strategies and online presence

All four of the third parties used some form of local electorate direct voter contact campaigning as well as digital tactics during the election campaign. We contrast what the organisations were doing and how they were reported on in the media. From this, we can see that the *novelty* of the campaign tactics often drives media attention.

Key campaign tactics

As reflected in our analysis of the legacy media's coverage of the four organisations (see 'Media attention' below), each organisation used a key tactic(s) distinct from that of the others (Figure 15.1).

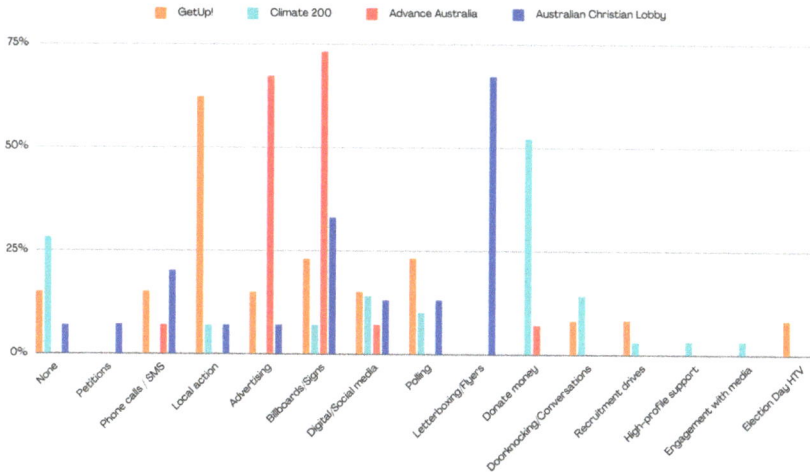

Figure 15.1 Reportage of election campaign tactics (percentage of articles)

HTV = how-to-vote

Sources: Third-party articles in Australian news outlets, sourced via Factiva and ProQuest, 9 April 2022 to 4 June 2022 (n = 72).

GetUp! and local action

The tactic most associated with GetUp! in the 2022 media coverage was local action, involving campaigning and events in communities, which featured in 63 per cent of articles. Several articles mentioned GetUp!'s campaigning presence in the rural seat of Leichhardt in far north Queensland, where the organisation attracted the ire of incumbent Coalition MP Warren Entsch. Entsch accused GetUp!, which had been handing out food alongside how-to-vote cards, of attempting to 'coerce First Nations people with bananas' (Calcino 2022). After local action, the next most common strategy was the use of billboards, signs and polling (each mentioned in 23 per cent of articles). This represents a shift in reported tactics since the 2016 election, in which election-day leafletting and donations/fundraising were the most widely reported strategies (see Table 15.2).

Table 15.2 Comparison of GetUp!'s tactics reported in the media in 2016 and 2022 election campaigns

Tactic	Percentage of articles	
	2022	2016
Petitions and digital/social media	15	10
Phone calls/SMS	15	8
Local action	62	7
Donations	0	26
Advertising and billboards/signs	38	14
Election-day actions (including how-to-vote cards)	8	29
Doorknocking/conversations with voters	8	17
Polling	23	0
Recruitment drives	8	0
None	15	0

Note: Certain categories have been merged to facilitate comparisons across the two years of measurement.

Sources: Third-party articles in Australian news outlets, sourced via Factiva and ProQuest, 9 April 2022–4 June 2022 (n = 72).

While not mentioned as frequently in the media coverage relative to 2016, GetUp!'s efforts in leafleting and letterboxing were mentioned frequently in their 16 emails to supporters over the campaign period. In general, GetUp!'s emails focused heavily on the various kinds of actions in which GetUp! supporters had been involved during the campaign, with an emphasis on those involving local communities and person-to-person interactions. This community-oriented framing was extended to email recipients, who were addressed as 'friend' throughout the emails. The nine emails that featured a call to action included requests for donations (referred to as 'chipping in') and more active ways to participate in the 'movement': by taking part in calling parties, watching and sharing campaign videos on social media and completing GetUp!'s post-election survey.

Climate 200 and donations

The tactic most associated with Climate 200 in the news media was the donation of money—both small and large online donations from members of the public *to* Climate 200 and *from* Climate 200 to selected Independent candidates. This campaign tactic was mentioned in 52 per cent of articles featuring Climate 200.

Advance and billboards

Advance's use of 'provocative billboards' (Napier-Raman 2022) to attack candidates in their electorates was prominent both on public streets and in the media coverage. Of the articles in our media analysis that covered Advance, 73 per cent mentioned the use of billboards and signs—notably, Advance's 'Green superman' billboards—while 67 per cent of articles mentioned Advance's use of digital tactics such as targeted Facebook advertising. The 'Green superman' billboards, which targeted Independent ACT Senate candidate David Pocock and Independent MP for Warringah (NSW) Zali Steggall, featured doctored photographs of each candidate in a superman-style pose, revealing an outfit with the Greens logo beneath their civilian clothing.

Advance also invested in billboards featuring images of Steggall and three Australian champion female swimmers alongside the words 'Women's sport is not for men'. These billboards, which included a quote from Steggall suggesting that the exclusion of trans women from competitive sport would be 'transphobic', were intended to denigrate Steggall. However, the media noted that they were not necessarily perceived as such by passers-by—many of whom interpreted the billboards as an endorsement of Steggall's position (Knox 2022). Beyond its focus on individual Independent candidates, Advance also targeted the Labor Party with its 'Xi Jinping truth trucks'— mobile billboards showing a doctored image of Chinese president Xi Jinping voting for the Labor Party, alongside the words 'CCP says vote Labor' (Elias 2022).

The issues raised in these billboards (the 'green threat' posed by Independents, trans women in sport and Labor's supposed connections with the Chinese Communist Party) also featured heavily in Advance's campaign emails to supporters. One such email suggested recipients show their support on the Facebook page of Liberal candidate for Warringah Katherine Deves for her critical stance on trans women athletes competing against cis-women.

As reflected in their calls to 'help fill the election war-chest', Advance's emails to supporters tended to frame the organisation as 'fighting for' their supporters against the threats of job losses, 'wokesters' in Labor, the Greens and GetUp!, and cuts to national defence spending.

The ACL and letterboxing

The tactic most associated with the ACL in the media was more traditional localised direct voter contact via letterboxing and leafletting. The ACL campaigned against several Independent MPs and the five Liberal MPs who crossed the floor to vote with Labor in favour of legislation to provide greater protection to LGBTIQ+ students. Among other tactics, the campaign featured the local distribution of flyers that depicted target MPs in bulldozers, knocking down a building marked 'Faith-based schools' (Harris 2022).

Digital tactics: Social media posts and targeted advertising

Social media campaigns: Facebook and YouTube

Facebook remains the primary social media platform for digital campaigning as it is where most Australians—in particular, persuadable voters—are likely to have an account. An analysis of the organisations' Facebook activities in the four weeks before the election and two weeks after indicates that Advance was the most active, with 215 posts, while Climate 200 was the least active, with 88 posts (see Table 15.3). The same pattern can be seen in follower engagement, with Advance's Facebook followers arguably the most engaged of the four organisations and those of Climate 200 the least engaged. Advance received the highest average comments per post (the most active form of engagement of those listed in Table 15.3) and the second-highest average number of post shares and 'likes'. Advance also received a much higher average number of 'ha-ha' reactions to their posts than the other organisations, perhaps reflecting the tendency in many of their posts to use humour to deride disfavoured candidates or parties.

Table 15.3 Follower engagement on organisations' Facebook pages, 10 April – 4 June 2022

Organisation	Comments	Shares	Average engagement							Total posts
			'Like'	'Love'	'Wow'	'Ha-ha'	'Sad'	'Angry'	'Care'	
GetUp!	153	221	829	94	6	75	23	76	16	**117**
Climate 200	23	8	81	16	0	5	0	1	1	**88**
Advance	328	201	722	40	7	174	9	46	2	**215**
ACL	148	159	783	151	2	5	16	5	11	**112**

Note: Greatest engagement across organisations highlighted in italics.

Source: Crowdtangle (www.crowdtangle.com/).

Table 15.4 Top-10 election posts by engagement, per organisation, 9 April – 4 June 2022

Organisation	Post topic	Date	Engagement
GetUp!	Celebrating Eric Abetz's electoral loss	31/5/2022	11,189
	Celebrating election result and criticising Morrison Government	22/5/2022	7,189
	Claiming the election represented a 'vote for climate justice'	23/5/2022	6,547
	Associating Scott Morrison with fossil-fuel industry	3/5/2022	5,342
	Suggesting that Scott Morrison is racist	13/5/2022	5,080
	Celebrating Scott Morrison's birthday with the 'gift' of an 'early retirement' party	13/5/2022	4,200
	Indigenous rights and representation	23/5/2022	4,025
	Accusing Katherine Deves of transphobia	16/5/2022	4,004
	Celebrating election of First Nations representatives to parliament	25/5/2022	3,868
	Reminding people to check their enrolment with the AEC	17/4/2022	3,698

Organisation	Post topic	Date	Engagement
Climate 200	Celebrating Climate 200–supported women candidates elected to parliament	23/5/2022	894
	Calling on people to 'fix our democracy'	15/5/2022	377
	Supporting Teals' campaigns as a 'community movement'	27/5/2022	324
	Sharing story of community rallying around Dr Monique Ryan	16/5/2022	309
	Sharing story of Allegra Spender's conversation at pre-poll station with Simon Baker	20/5/2022	269
	Supporting Dr Monique Ryan	4/5/2022	258
	Celebrating David Pocock's predicted unseating of Liberal senator Zed Seselja	1/6/2022	257
	Calling on voters to 'restore democracy' (by voting for an Independent)	5/5/2022	253
	Support for Teal Independents	7/5/2022	251
	Celebrating Kate Chaney's election to Curtin	27/5/2022	230
Advance	Sharing an image that suggests the hypocrisy of Teal voters	22/5/2022	8,382
	Suggesting Greens candidates are unfit for office	5/5/2022	6,686
	Celebrating election of Jacinta Nampijinpa Price	22/5/2022	6,599
	Opposing trans women in sport and the MPs who have voiced support for trans rights	20/4/2022	6,266
	Sharing a meme that makes fun of green movement	10/5/2022	5,279
	Suggesting Scott Morrison should show firmer support for coal and nuclear power	30/4/2022	5,191
	Calling on Zali Steggall to apologise for her comments suggesting those who oppose trans women in sport are transphobic	24/4/2022	4,599
	Sharing meme targeted at Labor supporters	11/5/2022	4,422
	Opposing trans women in sport and the MPs who have voiced support for trans rights	21/4/2022	4,349
	Sharing Advance's full-page ad in the *Herald Sun* [Melbourne] that suggests Labor is 'in the pocket' of the Chinese Government	18/5/2022	4,201

Organisation	Post topic	Date	Engagement
ACL	Calling on people to pray for Australia	20/5/2022	10,586
	Congratulating Anthony Albanese on election win	22/5/2022	3,225
	Informing people about the ACL billboards targeting 'rogue Liberal MPs' who voted to repeal s.38 of the Sex Discrimination Act	26/4/2022	2,529
	Sharing a video message from managing director Martyn Iles about the election result	23/5/2022	2,031
	Sharing a video discussing whether the 'freedom friendly minor parties' should be supported	28/4/2022	1,453
	Sharing article about the how the ACL has criticised the Liberal MPs who crossed the floor to support amendment to the Sex Discrimination Act	15/4/2022	1,428
	Sharing video about which candidates are Christians	7/5/2022	1,379
	Sharing images from ACL-hosted public election forum	11/4/2022	1,334
	Sharing video that ranks parties from 'extreme woke left' to 'right-wing conservative'	10/5/2022	1,146
	Sharing election Q&A video featuring response to question about whether voting for Christians matters if their parties do not permit conscience votes	17/4/2022	1,069

Source: Crowdtangle (www.crowdtangle.com/).

317

An examination of the most popular Facebook posts from each of the four organisations (see Table 15.4) reveals different campaign issues being prioritised as well as a different focus on either negative or positive campaigning language. Climate 200's posts were the most conventional, with most of the top posts focused on showing support for its chosen candidates and several mentioning campaign tactics such as local actions and gaining support from high-profile individuals. This could be a way of reassuring the Teal Independents' supporter base that while their candidates aimed to 'do politics differently', they would adhere to parliamentary representative traditions. At the same time, the near absence of posts across the sample of 88 that mentioned the billionaire founder of Climate 200, Simon Holmes à Court, could reflect the awareness that some of its supporters were less likely to warm to reminders of the organisation's elite leadership.[1]

In contrast to Climate 200's top posts—all of which are positive reinforcements of support for core candidates and issues—GetUp! displays a mixture of both positive posts (for example, those celebrating the achievements of First Nations candidates in the election) and negative (for example, those critical of Scott Morrison and his government). GetUp!'s most popular Facebook posts also reflect its core campaign issues, including climate change, Indigenous representation and voting against conservative politicians.

Advance's top posts are the most negative, with most posts focused on criticism of their adversaries: the environmental movement, the Greens and Labor, trans women athletes and the MPs who have shown support for trans rights. In contrast with GetUp!, however, Advance is more likely to use humour and memes to get its messages across, seeming to learn and borrow from GetUp!'s success in negative, meme-driven campaign posts in the 2016 election and earlier (Vromen 2018).

Finally, the ACL's top posts are the least overtly political, with many of those with the greatest engagement consisting solely of an image featuring a Bible verse. This overt focus on the (positive) teachings of Christianity and the Bible arguably explains the higher number of average 'love' reactions received by ACL posts during the campaign period than was received by any of the other three organisations. The ACL's election-oriented posts were

---

1   One post does quote Holmes à Court from an interview with the *Australian Financial Review* (Durkin 2022), in which he uses language that arguably seeks to show his solidarity with everyday Australians: '[W]e've been gas-lit by the government' and 'Australia is doing a *sh*t* job on emissions reductions' (emphasis added).

more earnest and information-heavy, contrasting with the mocking tone and memes/images of many of the Advance posts. Among the 10 top posts, five shared videos featuring Iles discussing the election and candidates and one was an article about ACL's criticisms of the Liberal MPs who crossed the floor to support an amendment to the *Sex Discrimination Act* preventing faith-based schools from discriminating against students based on their gender identity.

Targeted advertising

We also collected data from the Meta Ad Library as targeted Facebook ads generate a larger audience than organic Facebook posts on organisations' pages alone. They also provide impression data that Crowdtangle does not, as well as the amount of money the organisation spent on each advertisement. Both political and third parties use targeted advertising to reach a predefined audience on social media in a way that traditional advertising through broadcast, print or household leafletting is less able to (Dommett and Power 2019).

Table 15.5 lists the paid social media ads with the highest impressions for each organisation. The ACL spent most on a single ad on one of their key campaign issues: the religious freedom of parents to choose an education for their children that was in line with their values ($25,000–$30,000). However, this ad ran over six months, before and after the election period, so this amount does not accurately reflect their election campaign spending. Advance seemed to be the biggest spender on ads, spending between $10,000 and $25,000 on each of their top-five ads, all of which had a consistent message equating a vote for Labor with a vote for the Greens.

Spending a lot does not necessarily equate to impressions or views. For example, GetUp! did not spend nearly as much as other organisations on its 10 most successful ads, but it had the highest impressions per dollar. Nearly all its top ads were targeted *against* the incumbent government in support of GetUp!'s core campaign issues of climate change, Indigenous rights and gender and social equity; this meant its paid high-impression ads were overall more negative than its organic posts. Climate 200's approach to paid Facebook ads is important as they were clearly targeted at particular electorates in support of the campaigns of individual Independent candidates and achieved significantly large impressions. The individual campaigns of the Climate 200–backed candidates also spent a significant amount on Facebook advertising (Barlow 2022). Only one of Climate 200's top-10 ads mentioned donations (contrasting with the media's reportage).

Table 15.5 Top-five Facebook/Instagram election ads by number of impressions, 9 April – 4 June 2022

Organisation	Post topic	Dates active	Impressions	Cost	Impressions per dollar	Which groups saw the ad most?
GetUp!	Coalition's treatment of women	4/5/2022 – 9/5/2022	900,000 – 1,000,000	$6,000 – 7,000	128–67	Women 25–34 years old NSW
	First Nations representation in government	3/5/2022 – 8/5/2022	600,000 – 700,000	$4,500 – 5,000	120–56	Women 25–44 years old NSW
	Critical of Morrison Government's response to First Nations housing and land issues	9/5/2022 – 21/5/2022	450,000 – 500,000	$5,000 – 6,000	75–100	Women 25–34 years old NSW
	Critical of Morrison Government's claims about funding of the NDIS	3/5/2022 – 21/5/2022	450,000 – 500,000	$2,500 – 3,000	150–200	Women 24–44 years old NSW
	Coalition's 'problem with men'	9/5/2022 – 11/5/2022	400,000 – 450,000	$2,500 – 3,000	133–80	Women 24–34 years old NSW

Organisation	Post topic	Dates active	Impressions	Cost	Impressions per dollar	Which groups saw the ad most?
Climate 200	Vote for climate-focused Independent to address climate change	6/4/2022 – 22/4/2022	900,000– 1,000,000	$10,000– 15,000	60–100	Women 25–34 years old ACT
	Vote for pro-climate Independents (i.e., Allegra Spender)	4/5/2022 – 21/5/2022	400,000– 450,000	$6,000– 7,000	57–75	Women 25–34 years old NSW
	Vote for pro-climate Independents (i.e., Kylea Tink)	4/5/2022 – 21/5/2022	300,000– 350,000	$6,000– 7,000	43–58	Women 25–34 years old NSW
	Vote for pro-climate Independents (i.e., Sophie Scamps)	4/5/2022 – 21/5/2022	300,000– 350,000	$6,000– 7,000	43–58	Women 35–54 years old NSW
	Vote for pro-climate Independents (i.e., Zoe Daniel)	4/5/2022 – 21/5/2022	300,000– 350,000	$6,000– 7,000	43–58	Women 25–34 years old Vic.

Organisation	Post topic	Dates active	Impressions	Cost	Impressions per dollar	Which groups saw the ad most?
Advance	If you vote Labor, you'll get Greens	12/4/2022 – 5/5/2022	700,000– 800,000	$15,000– 20,000	35–53	Men 65+ years old NSW
	If you vote Labor, you'll get Greens and lose Australia Day	12/4/2022 – 5/5/2022	700,000– 800,000	$20,000– 25,000	28–40	Men 65+ years old NSW
	If you vote Labor, you'll get Greens and face new taxes	12/4/2022 – 5/5/2022	600,000– 700,000	$15,000– 20,000	30–47	Men 65+ years old Qld
	If you vote Labor, you'll get Greens and weakened national security	12/4/2022 – 5/5/2022	600,000– 700,000	$10,000– 15,000	40–70	Men 65+ years old Qld
	If you vote Labor, you'll get Greens and weakened national security	9/4/2022 – 2/5/2022	450,000– 500,000	$10,000– 15,000	30–50	Men 65+ years old NSW

Organisation	Post topic	Dates active	Impressions	Cost	Impressions per dollar	Which groups saw the ad most?
ACL	Religious freedom in faith-based schools	2/2/2022– 2/8/2022	> 1,000,000	$25,000– 30,000	> 33	Women 65+ years old NSW
	Interview with Queensland senator Amanda Stoker critical of vaccine mandates	9/5/2022– 21/5/2022	350,000– 400,000	$10,000– 15,000	23–40	Men 35–44 years old Qld
	Donating to ACL's election campaign	14/4/2022– 10/5/2022	250,000– 300,000	$3,500– 4,000	63–86	Women 65+ years old Qld
	Critical of Bridget Archer's voting record on faith-related bills	28/4/2022– 21/5/2022	175,000– 200,000	$7,000– 8,000	28–21	Women 65+ years old Tas.
	Critical of Fiona Martin's voting record on faith-related bills	28/4/2022– 13/5/2022	175,000– 200,000	$6,000– 7,000	25–33	Men 25–44 years old NSW Women 65+ years old NSW

Source: Meta Ad Library (www.facebook.com/ads/library/?active_status=all&ad_type=political_and_issue_ads&country=AU&media_type=all).

As shown in Table 15.5, the top ads by impressions for both GetUp! and Climate 200 were targeted most heavily at women, with those living in New South Wales and aged 25–34 years most likely to see the ads. By contrast, Advance's top ads were targeted most strongly at men aged over 65, living in New South Wales or Queensland. Meanwhile, the ACL's top ads were targeted mostly at women aged over 65 and men 35–44 years old. All the ads that the ACL targeted most heavily at older women were on the topic of religious freedom in faith-based schools, while the only ad that was not targeted at this group was one critical of vaccine mandates.

Media attention

It is important to the success of the influence of third-party organisations for their ideas to be covered in mainstream media including newspapers and television. This attention obviously expands the potential audience that can be persuaded about their ideas, but it also legitimates their role as political actors within the campaign. We have analysed 72 news articles in which our third parties were a feature, meaning that they were included in either the headline or the lead paragraph. Note that there were many more than this number of articles that incidentally mentioned Climate 200 as the source of funding for a number of Independent candidates in the election, but these are not included in the analysis as they are not primarily about the actions of Climate 200.

Who reports on whom?

We find that left-leaning media outlets reported more frequently on the two conservative campaign organisations, while the same is true of the right-leaning media outlets in relation to the more progressive campaign organisations. As can be seen in Table 15.6, of the articles featuring Climate 200 and GetUp!, 76 per cent and 69 per cent, respectively, came from a News Corp–owned outlet. By contrast, News Corp was responsible for only 13 per cent and 20 per cent of the articles featuring Advance and the ACL, respectively. Advance was featured most frequently by the ABC (27 per cent of articles) and Australian Community Media (33 per cent)—specifically its subsidiary, *The Canberra Times*. Nine Entertainment, owner of the *Sydney Morning Herald* and *The Age*, was the single umbrella company responsible for the greatest proportion of articles covering the ACL (27 per cent).

Table 15.6 News articles on third-party organisations by owner of media outlet

Organisation	Articles by media outlet (%)					Total articles (n)
	ABC	Australian Community Media	News Corp	Nine Entertainment	Other	
GetUp!	8	0	69	15	8	**13**
Climate 200	0	0	76	10	14	**29**
Advance	27	33	13	7	20	**15**
ACL	7	13	20	27	33	**15**

Sources: Factiva and ProQuest, 9/4/22–4/6/22 (n = 72).

The collection of just 13 articles that focused on GetUp!'s campaign represents a substantial decrease in traditional media coverage since 2016 (when 42 news articles covered GetUp!) and a continuation of the decrease in coverage seen since the 2010 election (115 articles) (Vromen 2018). There are several potential explanations for this, including the fact that there is now a crowded field of third parties involved in election campaigns, thus reducing GetUp!'s novelty and attention; the other is that GetUp! purposefully ran a very localised and low-profile campaign in 2022, after extensive criticism of its less successful campaigning against hard-right politicians in 2019 (Grattan 2019). Notably, Paul Oosting, GetUp!'s national director since 2015, resigned soon after the 2022 election.

Campaign issues

As suggested by the media's coverage, there was relatively little overlap across the four groups in terms of their key campaign issues (see Table 15.7). The greatest similarity could be seen—perhaps unsurprisingly—between GetUp! and Climate 200, with the most frequently reported campaign issue for both organisations being climate change (mentioned in 62 per cent and 69 per cent of articles, respectively). However, there was relatively little overlap otherwise. The next most prominent issues featured in the media's coverage of GetUp! were natural disasters and Indigenous rights, while the Climate 200 coverage focused on the issues of integrity in politics and gender equity.

Table 15.7 Reportage of third-party organisations' campaign issues

Campaign issue	Percentage of news articles				
	GetUp! (2022)	GetUp! (2016)	Climate 200	Advance	ACL
Climate change (pro-action)	62	19	69	0	0
Climate change (anti-action)	0	n.a.	0	13	0
Natural disasters	38	n.a.	0	0	0
Covid-19 pandemic	15	n.a.	0	0	0
Indigenous rights/issues	31	n.a.	0	0	0
Housing	23	n.a.	0	0	0
Environment	8	n.a.	0	0	0
Jobs/economy	0	n.a.	7	0	0
Health care	15	7	0	0	0
Integrity in politics	0	n.a.	48	0	0
Gender equity	0	n.a.	21	0	0
China (anti)	0	n.a.	0	47	0
Liberal Party/government (anti)	31	43	14	0	0
Labor (anti)	0	n.a.	0	47	0
Greens (anti)	0	n.a.	0	87	0
David Pocock (anti)	0	n.a.	0	73	0
Zali Steggall (anti)	0	n.a.	0	67	0
Transgender rights (anti)	0	n.a.	0	27	80
Religious freedoms	0	0	0	0	47
General campaign	8	21	7	0	0
No campaign issues mentioned	31	n.a.	21	0	13

n.a. = Data not available.

Note: In the 2016 campaign, it was found that 'hard-right politicians' was the issue most reported on in relation to GetUp! (Vromen 2018). This category has been merged with 'Liberal Party/government (anti)' here, for ease of comparison.

Sources: Factiva; ProQuest.

That Advance received as much primary media coverage as GetUp! reflects its use of controversial but novel visual stunts and the reactionary nature of its campaign issues. The top three issues associated with the organisation were opposition to the Greens (87 per cent of articles), opposition to David Pocock (73 per cent) and opposition to Zali Steggall (67 per cent)—all of which are a manifestation of Advance's climate scepticism (an issue that was mentioned directly in 13 per cent of the Advance articles). With Advance's 'Green superman' billboards and signs suggesting that Pocock and Steggall were 'secret' Greens, the implication was clear: a vote for Pocock and Steggall was a vote for the Greens and a radical climate agenda. Roughly one-quarter of the articles on Advance also referred to the organisation's anti-transgender-rights leanings—a position also strongly associated with the ACL in the media's reportage (80 per cent of articles). For Advance, the issue was trans women in sport, while for ACL, it was its campaign against Independent MP Rebekha Sharkie and Liberal MPs who crossed the floor to vote in support of proposals to change the Sex Discrimination Act to prevent religious schools from discriminating against transgender students. Otherwise, there was no overlap in the reported campaign issues of Advance and the ACL; the latter's only other key campaign position was reported to be that of support for religious freedoms (47 per cent of articles).

Article orientation

None of the articles in the sample was overtly positive in its coverage of any of the organisations—a finding that is not surprising given that media outlets tended to focus on those organisations to which they are less ideologically aligned. Instead, the orientation of articles tended to be negative (see Table 15.8). Two-thirds of the articles on both Climate 200 and Advance were negative, as were nearly half the articles covering the ACL. By contrast, a minority of articles on GetUp! were negative rather than neutral (38 per cent and 62 per cent, respectively). This is similar to the finding in 2016, when a little more than one-third of articles were negative (Vromen 2018).

Table 15.8 Orientation of media articles featuring third-party organisations

Organisation	Orientation of articles (%)	
	Negative	**Neutral**
GetUp!	38	62
Climate 200	66	34
Advance	67	33
ACL	47	53

Sources: Factiva and ProQuest, 9 April 2022 to 4 June 2022 (n = 72).

Conclusions

A lot of money was spent by both third-party organisations and political parties in the 2022 Australian election campaign. There will be ongoing debate about how to best regulate expenditure and make it more transparent, particularly when it comes to social media–based advertising. There will also be a larger debate about truth and social media advertising that will affect the polemics of third parties in particular. With a new Labor Government, conservative third-party organisations now find themselves in an unwelcoming political context and will need to change their tactics to increase their influence over both public opinion and like-minded politicians. The future role of lobbying organisations with a large supporter base, like the ACL, will remain important. Arguably, progressive third parties and interest groups have been more successful when the government is conservative and they can construct themselves as the outsiders and as a moral political opposition.

This election does not spell the end of GetUp! as a generalist campaigning organisation despite its muted showing after a decade of extensive success. It may, however, signal a shift in focus away from episodic elections and towards ongoing radical and locally based progressive political work. This tension has surfaced within the organisation in each election campaign evaluation: elections are good for fundraising, media attention and mobilising the supporter base, but it is harder to see success when it is mainly based on mobilising against conservative incumbents (see Vromen 2017). Its election work was eclipsed in 2022 by Climate 200, but the relative lack of overlap between the two groups in terms of both their campaign issues and their local campaign tactics suggests there could be space for both in coming elections. The same can arguably be said for the two conservative groups analysed in this chapter, with our analysis of social media posting and advertising by Advance and the ACL highlighting the differences between them in tone, content and target audiences.

Yet in the end, having the extensive fundraising revenue to do both local on-the-ground campaigning and mass broadcast and social-media-targeted advertising matters for the success of promoting an issue agenda. There has been extensive analysis of the success of Climate 200 but what is less clear is the impact its emergence has had on Australian politics and on third-party campaigning. What Climate 200 did in fundraising for Independent candidates was a historic shift in Australia. Others have described this as akin to the arrival of political action committees or Super PACs that generate very large funding bases and political expenditure in the United States (Lopez and Douglas-Kinghorn 2022). It is not necessarily the sign of a healthy democratic competition over ideas or a vision for an equitable future in Australian politics when money buys the most influence.

References

Australian Electoral Commission (AEC). 2022a. '2020–21 political campaigner return: Advance Australia'. *AEC Transparency Register*. Canberra: AEC. Available from: transparency.aec.gov.au/AnnualSignificantThirdParty/ReturnDetail?return Id=53302.

Australian Electoral Commission (AEC). 2022b. 'Significant third parties'. *Financial Disclosure*. Canberra: AEC. Available from: www.aec.gov.au/Parties_and_Representatives/financial_disclosure/guides/significant-third-parties.htm.

Barlow, Karen. 2022. 'Who is spending the most political money on Facebook?'. *The Canberra Times*, 20 April. Available from: www.canberratimes.com.au/story/7704083/advance-australia-pours-negative-labor-greens-and-pocock-ads-onto-facebook/.

Calcino, Chris. 2022. 'Row over GetUp!'s bananas'. *Cairns Post*, [Qld], 18 May.

Cameron, Sarah and Thomas Wynter. 2018. 'Campaign finance and perceptions of interest group influence in Australia'. *Political Science* 70(2): 169–88.

Dommett, Kate and Sam Power. 2019. 'The political economy of Facebook advertising: Election spending, regulation and targeting online'. *The Political Quarterly* 90(2): 257–65.

Durkin, Patrick. 2022. 'Simon Holmes à Court's personal battle with Josh Frydenberg'. *Australian Financial Review*, 13 April.

Elias, Michelle. 2022. 'Behind "Advance Australia": The lobby group causing a stir with its ads'. *The Feed*, [SBS News], 27 April. Available from: www.sbs.com.au/news/the-feed/article/behind-advance-australia-the-lobby-group-causing-a-stir-with-its-ads/jtcpkuk9l.

Grattan, Michelle. 2019. 'Politics with Michelle Grattan: Paul Oosting responds to GetUp's critics'. *The Conversation*, 24 July. Available from: theconversation.com/politics-with-michelle-grattan-paul-oosting-responds-to-GetUp!s-critics-120886.

Hall, Nina. 2022. *Transnational Advocacy in the Digital Era: Think Global, Act Local.* Oxford, UK: Oxford University Press.

Harris, Rob. 2022. Tweet, 22 April, 6.20 pm. @serpenteye, *Twitter*. Available from: twitter.com/serpenteye/status/1517418044787949568?s=20.

Karp, Paul, Nick Evershed and Christopher Knaus. 2022. 'Anthony Pratt gave Liberals $1.3m while upstart political groups gain sizeable donations'. *The Guardian*, [Australia], 1 February. Available from: www.theguardian.com/australia-news/2022/feb/01/anthony-pratt-gave-liberals-13m-while-upstart-political-groups-gain-sizeable-donations.

Karpf, David. 2012. *The Move-On Effect: The Unexpected Transformation of American Political Advocacy*. Oxford, UK: Oxford University Press.

Karpf, David. 2016. *Analytic Activism: Digital Listening and the New Political Strategy*. Oxford, UK: Oxford University Press.

Knox, Malcolm. 2022. 'The left may think Australia has seen the light, but don't expect the Christian right to retreat'. *Sydney Morning Herald*, 28 May. Available from: www.smh.com.au/national/the-left-may-think-australia-has-seen-the-light-but-don-t-expect-the-christian-right-to-retreat-20220526-p5aox8.html.

Lopez, Daniel and Zowie Douglas-Kinghorn. 2022. 'With Climate 200, political action committees have arrived to Australia'. *Jacobin*, 14 May. Available from: jacobin.com/2022/05/with-climate-200-political-action-committees-have-arrived-to-australia.

Maddison, Sarah and Andrea Carson. 2017. *Civil Voices: Researching Not-for-Profit Advocacy*. Melbourne: Pro Bono Australia and Human Rights Law Centre. Available from: civilvoices.com.au/wp-content/themes/probono_theme/download/CivilVoices_reportfornonforprofitadvocacy_Web.pdf.

Mills, Stephen. 2020. 'Party campaign communications'. In *Morrison's Miracle: The 2019 Australian Federal Election*, edited by Anika Gauja, Marian Sawer and Marian Simms, 455–72. Canberra: ANU Press. doi.org/10.22459/MM.2020.23.

Napier-Raman, Kishor. 2022. 'Advance Australia targets Steggall, Pocock and Labor one provocative billboard at a time'. *Crikey*, 28 April. Available from: www.crikey.com.au/2022/04/28/advance-australia-targets-steggall-pocock-labor-one-provocative-billboard-at-a-time/.

Seibert, Krystian. 2021. 'Are charities being silenced? Why a new law is alarming activists and could scuttle their election campaigns'. *The Conversation*, 2 December. Available from: theconversation.com/are-charities-being-silenced-why-a-new-law-is-alarming-activists-and-could-scuttle-their-election-campaigns-173056.

Vromen, Ariadne. 2017. *Digital Citizenship and Political Engagement: The Challenge from Online Campaigning and Advocacy Organisations*. Basingstoke, UK: Palgrave Macmillan.

Vromen, Ariadne. 2018. 'GetUp! in election 2016'. In Anika Gauja, Peter Chen, Jennifer Curtin and Juliet Pietsch (eds), *Double Dissolution: The 2016 Australian Federal Election*, 397–419. Canberra: ANU Press. doi.org/10.22459/DD.04. 2018.18.

Watson, Finley. 2021. The organisational success and political impact of the Australian Christian Lobby. MA thesis, La Trobe University, Melbourne.

Zhou, Naaman. 2019. 'Captain GetUp!: Conservative group's satirical superhero debuts to ridicule'. *The Guardian*, [Australia], 9 April. Available from: www.the guardian.com/australia-news/2019/apr/09/captain-GetUp!-conservative-groups-satirical-superhero-debuts-to-ridicule.

Part 3: Results

16

The House of Representatives results

Ben Raue

The House of Representatives contest at the 2022 Australian federal election was a decisive defeat for the Liberal–National Coalition, which won the smallest proportion of seats in the House since World War II. The ALP won a small majority, with half of all seat gains going to members of the crossbench, producing by far the largest postwar crossbench in the House of Representatives. After nine years in power, the ruling Coalition Government was swept out, with its lowest primary vote in the House since 1943.

While the result was a landslide defeat for the Coalition, it was a relatively modest victory for Labor. The new Labor Government won 77 seats, just one more than the minimum needed for a majority. While Labor won a clear majority of the two-party-preferred vote, with a swing of 3.66 per cent compared with 2019, it did not improve its primary vote.

Members of Australia's House of Representatives are elected using the alternative vote, where voters mark numerical preferences for candidates in single-member electorates. This system has traditionally produced results dominated by the ALP and the Liberal–National Coalition (referred to here as the 'major parties'), although this domination declined in 2022.

The 'primary vote' measures how many voters gave their first preference to a party. The 'two-party-preferred vote' measures which of the major parties (Labor or the Coalition) was marked higher on each voter's ballot and has traditionally correlated with a major party winning a majority in the House.

Labor polled its lowest primary vote in the House of Representatives since 1934, and slightly less than it did in 2013, but a shift away from the Coalition and towards minor parties and Independents meant Labor was able to win a majority of the two-party-preferred vote and a slim House majority.

The combined vote for all minor parties and Independents surpassed 30 per cent in the House of Representatives, after narrowly exceeding 25 per cent for the first time in modern Australian elections in 2019.

With a record-low combined primary vote for the major parties, this has increased the pool of preferences available from minor parties and Independents, thus making it possible for a party to win a majority of the two-party-preferred vote off a much lower primary vote than would have been possible in the past, when the major-party vote was higher.

Overall, the election result came in two parts: a relatively modest swing from the Coalition to Labor, changing just enough seats for a slim majority, while the Coalition suffered losses mostly in traditionally safe inner-urban electorates to Independents and Greens, turning a modest defeat into the Coalition's worst result in almost 80 years.

This chapter will analyse the House of Representatives results, with a particular focus on the decline in the vote for the major parties, how that declining vote is changing the operation of the electoral system, the breakthroughs for Independent candidates and minor parties and diverging trends between States and regions.

2019 election

The 2019 election produced a narrow and surprising victory for the incumbent Liberal–National Coalition Government (Table 16.1). The Coalition won 76 of 150 seats at the 2016 election and ended up losing its majority by the time of the 2019 election, with polls suggesting a small but persistent lead for Labor right up to election day, when the Coalition regained its majority, with one more seat than in 2016, in a House consisting of one more seat in total.

The Coalition won 77 seats in the House of Representatives, Labor won 68 seats, there were three Independents and three seats for minor parties. The Greens, Katter's Australian Party and the Centre Alliance each won a single seat.

Table 16.1 Results of the 2019 federal election by party

Party	Votes	Percentage	Swing	Seats	Seat change
Liberal–National Coalition	5,906,875	41.4	–0.6	77	+1
ALP	4,752,160	33.3	–1.4	68	–1
The Greens	1,482,923	10.4	+0.2	1	0
UAP	488,817	3.4	+3.4	0	0
PHON	438,587	3.1	+1.8	0	0
Katter's Australian Party	69,736	0.5	–0.1	1	0
Centre Alliance	46,931	0.3	–1.5	1	0
Independent	479,836	3.4	+2.8	3	1
Other	587,528	4.1	+0.2	0	0

Source: Compiled by author from AEC data (AEC 2022).

Redistribution of electoral boundaries

Redistributions in Australia are conducted independently of political parties and partisan officials, and electoral boundaries are drawn with little regard to their political impact. Australia does not see the partisan decision-making that is present in many States in the United States or the gerrymandered electoral boundaries those decisions produce (see Newton-Farrelly 2015).

Electoral redistributions are required when one of three criteria is met:

- The number of members to which a State or Territory is entitled changes.
- Seven years has elapsed since the last redistribution process.
- The number of electors in more than one-third of electorates deviates from the average divisional enrolment by more than 10 per cent for more than two months.

In the term of parliament before the 2022 federal election, House of Representatives electoral boundaries were redrawn in Victoria and Western Australia. Redistributions in both States were necessitated by a change in the entitlement for the number of members for each State. Victoria's entitlement increased from 38 seats to 39, while Western Australia's entitlement was reduced from 16 seats to 15. The new Victorian seat of Hawke was created in north-western Melbourne, with a notional Labor majority, while the Liberal seat of Stirling in northern Perth was abolished.

These changes resulted in a net gain of one seat for Labor and a net loss of one seat for the Coalition. This left the governing Coalition with just 76 seats, alongside 69 for Labor and six for minor parties and Independents.

By-elections

Two federal by-elections were held during the 2019–22 parliamentary term (Table 16.2). Both were triggered by a voluntary retirement of the sitting member. Unusually, both were contested by Labor and the Coalition and, in both cases, there was a swing away from the incumbent party, but not enough to change the result. Eden-Monaro was a very marginal NSW seat, held by Labor's Mike Kelly by a 0.8 per cent margin, which was cut to less than half at the by-election. Groom was a much safer seat, held by a margin of more than 20 per cent, and the swing, while larger than in Eden-Monaro, left the seat as still very safe for the Liberal National Party of Queensland (LNP).

Table 16.2 By-elections held during the 2019–2022 parliamentary term

Electorate	Date	Outgoing MP	Result
Eden-Monaro	4 July 2020	Mike Kelly (ALP)	+0.5% to Lib. (2PP)
Groom	28 November 2020	John McVeigh (LNP)	+3.3% to ALP (2PP)

2PP = two-party-preferred
Source: Compiled by author from AEC data.

Candidate nominations

A record 1,203 candidates nominated for the House of Representatives in 2022 (see Figure 16.1). This was an increase from the 1,056 candidates who nominated in 2019 and broke the previous record of 1,188 candidates in 2013.

The increase in nominations came despite reforms to party registration rules that made it harder to register a party. There were fewer parties running candidates, but the overall number of candidates increased thanks to a handful of minor parties running significantly more candidates. In total, 38 parties ran candidates in 2019 (including four Liberal–National Coalition parties) and 35 ran in 2022.

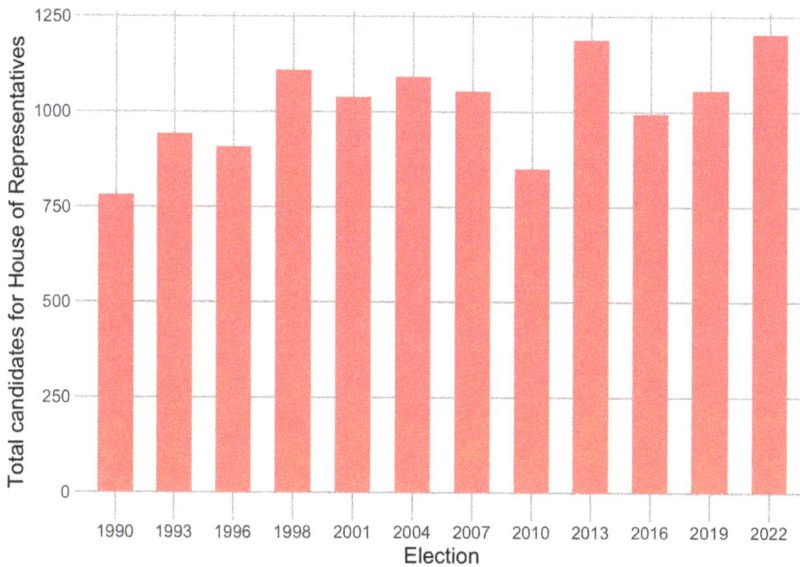

Figure 16.1 Total House of Representatives candidates per election, 1990–2022

Sources: Raue (2019, 2022a).

Table 16.3 Change in nomination numbers per party, 2019–2022

Party	2019 nominations	2022 nominations	Change
Liberal Party of Australia	107	108	1
LNP	30	30	0
The Nationals	23	15	–8
Country Liberal Party of the Northern Territory	2	2	0
Liberal–National Coalition	162	155	–7
ALP	151	151	0
The Greens	151	151	0
UAP	151	151	0
PHON	59	149	90
Liberal Democrats	10	100	90
Animal Justice Party	46	48	2
16 other parties running in 2019 and 2022	103	115	12
Australian Federation Party	0	61	61
7 other parties that did not run in 2019	0	24	24
Conservative National Party	48	0	–48

Party	2019 nominations	2022 nominations	Change
Christian Democratic Party	42	0	–42
10 other parties that did not run in 2022	36	0	–36
Independent/unaffiliated	97	98	1

Source: Compiled by author from AEC data.

Labor, the Greens and the UAP ran a full complement of 151 candidates, which was the same as in 2019. The four parties of the Liberal–National Coalition ran 155 candidates between them—a decline from 162 candidates in 2019, largely thanks to the Nationals running in eight fewer seats. Twelve parties ran in 2019 that did not run in 2022, with 126 candidates between them, including 90 candidates from Fraser Anning's Conservative National Party and Fred Nile's Christian Democratic Party.

Sixteen smaller parties ran in both 2019 and 2022, running fewer than 20 candidates each at both elections, and that group of parties ran just 12 additional candidates in 2022 than in 2019. The Animal Justice Party ran two more candidates than in 2019. Seven small parties that did not run in 2019 ran 24 candidates between them in 2022.

The big increases in candidate numbers are due to a surge in nominations from three minor parties. PHON ran 149 candidates, up from 59 in 2019, while the Liberal Democrats ran 100 candidates, up from 10 in 2019. The Australian Federation Party, which did not run any candidates in 2019, ran 60 candidates. These three parties ran 240 more candidates in 2022 than in 2019, which more than offset the reductions in nominations from other parties.

This follows several legislative changes with the goal of limiting the size of ballot papers. Reforms after the 2019 election made it significantly more difficult to register a political party in the absence of a member already in federal parliament, requiring 1,500 members (instead of just 500). This was preceded by reforms increasing the size of the financial deposit for nomination.

These reforms could have prevented very small parties from running and did reduce the overall number of parties on the ballot paper, but any gains were swamped by the large increase in candidates running for a handful of larger minor parties that were not bothered by the restrictions on party registration and had the budget to pay nomination fees.

Once a party is successfully registered, it is no longer obligated to have local electors sign the candidate's nomination form (as is the case for Independent candidates). An alternative approach could be to require nominators for party candidates, which would reduce the privileges of party registration and shift the burden from a financial to an organisational one, perhaps making it easier for small parties to run a handful of candidates in areas where they have supporters while requiring a greater effort if they want to run a full slate of candidates across the country.

There was very little change in the number of Independent candidates: 97 Independent or unaffiliated candidates ran in 2019, which increased to 98 in 2022. But this consistent number of Independents masked a significant change in the type of candidate running, with many high-profile Independents running much more prominent campaigns than in the past, and a major shift in the gender balance. In 2019, 22.7 per cent of Independent candidates were women, compared with 44.9 per cent in 2022 (Raue 2022a).

National result

The 2022 Australian federal election was a resounding defeat for the governing Liberal–National Coalition. The election produced a majority for the Labor Opposition, but most seat gains were for candidates outside the major parties, specifically Independents and members of the Greens.

Labor polled 52.13 per cent of the two-party-preferred vote—a swing of 3.66 per cent from 2019. On primary votes (Table 16.4), the Coalition suffered a 5.74 per cent swing nationally, while Labor suffered a small swing on primary votes of 0.76 per cent.

All the larger minor parties gained swings, with the Greens gaining a swing of 1.85 per cent, PHON a swing of 1.88 per cent, UAP a swing of 0.69 per cent and the Liberal Democrats a swing of 1.49 per cent. It should be noted that the swings to PHON and the Liberal Democrats are largely artefacts of them running more candidates, and PHON mostly suffered negative swings in seats where it had run in 2019. Independent candidates gained a significant swing of 1.92 per cent nationally.

Table 16.4 Results of the 2022 federal election by party

Party	Votes	Percentage	Swing	Seats	Seat change
Liberal–National Coalition	5,233,334	35.70	–5.74	58	–18
ALP	4,776,030	32.58	–0.76	77	8
The Greens	1,795,985	12.25	1.85	4	3
PHON	727,464	4.96	1.88	0	0
UAP	604,536	4.12	0.69	0	0
Liberal Democratic Party	252,963	1.73	1.49	0	0
Katter's Australian Party	55,863	0.38	–0.11	1	0
Centre Alliance	36,500	0.25	–0.08	1	0
Independents	776,169	5.29	1.92	10	7
Other	400,198	2.73	0.54	0	0

Source: Compiled by author from AEC (2022).

Declining primary vote for the major parties

While levels of support for the two major-party voting blocs (Labor and the Coalition) go up and down, there has been a long-term decline in the total level of support for these groups and an increasing vote for minor parties and Independents (Figure 16.2). The combined primary vote for the major parties dropped below 75 per cent for the first time in 2019 and to just 68.3 per cent in 2022.

Labor managed to form a majority government off a primary vote that was lower than its primary vote in 2013, when the Coalition won a large majority. Meanwhile, the Coalition vote had dropped below 40 per cent only once before—just narrowly, in 1998—but has now dropped to 35.7 per cent.

This increase in the minor-party and Independent vote has changed how the electoral system functions at the electorate level, with more seats where an Independent or minor-party candidate makes it to the final round of the count, fewer seats where a candidate wins a majority of the primary vote and an increasing number of seats with more than two candidates competing for the final round of the distribution of preferences. All these points will be discussed further in this chapter.

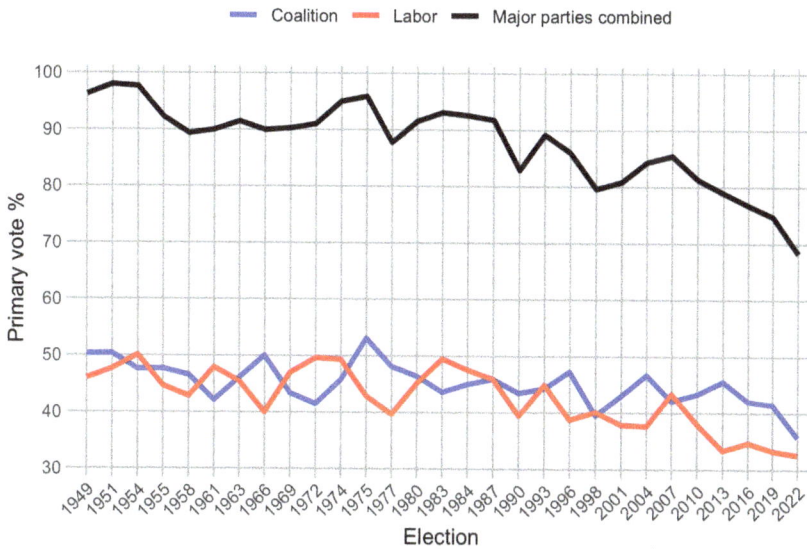

Figure 16.2 Primary vote for Labor and the Liberal–National Coalition, 1949–2022

Sources: Raue (2022b); AEC (2022).

Seats changing hands

Twenty seats changed hands in 2022, with 18 of those lost by the Coalition (all previously held by Liberals or LNP members who belong to the Liberal Party room) and two lost by Labor (Table 16.5). Labor gained 10 seats, Independents gained seven seats and the Greens gained three.

Six of the seven Independent gains were off the Liberal Party in urban electorates, in Sydney, Melbourne and Perth. These seats were won by the Teal Independents. The seventh Independent gain was the former Labor seat of Fowler in south-western Sydney. All three Greens gains were in central Brisbane, two off the LNP and one off the ALP. Labor's 10 gains were mostly in urban electorates, including four in Perth, two in Sydney, two in Melbourne, one in Adelaide and the seat of Robertson on the NSW Central Coast.

Table 16.5 Seats that changed hands at the 2022 election

Seat	State	Incumbent	Winner	Margin (%)
Bennelong	NSW	Liberal	ALP	1.0
Boothby	SA	Liberal	ALP	3.3
Brisbane	Qld	LNP	Greens	3.7
Chisholm	Vic.	Liberal	ALP	6.4
Curtin	WA	Liberal	Independent	1.3
Fowler	NSW	ALP	Independent	1.6
Goldstein	Vic.	Liberal	Independent	2.9
Griffith	Qld	ALP	Greens	10.5
Hasluck	WA	Liberal	ALP	6.0
Higgins	Vic.	Liberal	ALP	2.1
Kooyong	Vic.	Liberal	Independent	2.9
Mackellar	NSW	Liberal	Independent	2.5
North Sydney	NSW	Liberal	Independent	2.9
Pearce	WA	Liberal	ALP	9.0
Reid	NSW	Liberal	ALP	5.2
Robertson	NSW	Liberal	ALP	2.3
Ryan	Qld	LNP	Greens	2.6
Swan	WA	Liberal	ALP	8.8
Tangney	WA	Liberal	ALP	2.4
Wentworth	NSW	Liberal	Independent	4.2

Source: Compiled by author from AEC (2022).

Differences between States

Each State has a long-term historical trend distinct from the remainder of the country, but there were some significant changes in the State balance in 2022 when examining the two-party-preferred vote as a simple statistic that is collected in every electorate.

Every jurisdiction except Tasmania swung to Labor on two-party-preferred terms. Labor gained its largest swing in Western Australia, of 10.55 per cent. Swings in the Australian Capital Territory and Queensland were larger than the national swing, while those in New South Wales and South Australia were slightly smaller than the national swing. There was a smaller swing in Victoria.

Table 16.6 Two-party-preferred vote by State

State	ALP	Coalition	Swing to ALP
NSW	51.42	48.58	3.22
Vic.	54.83	45.17	1.69
Qld	45.95	54.05	4.39
WA	55.00	45.00	10.55
SA	53.97	46.03	3.26
Tas.	54.33	45.67	−1.63
ACT	66.95	33.05	5.34
NT	55.54	44.46	1.34
Australia	52.13	47.87	3.66

Source: AEC (2022).

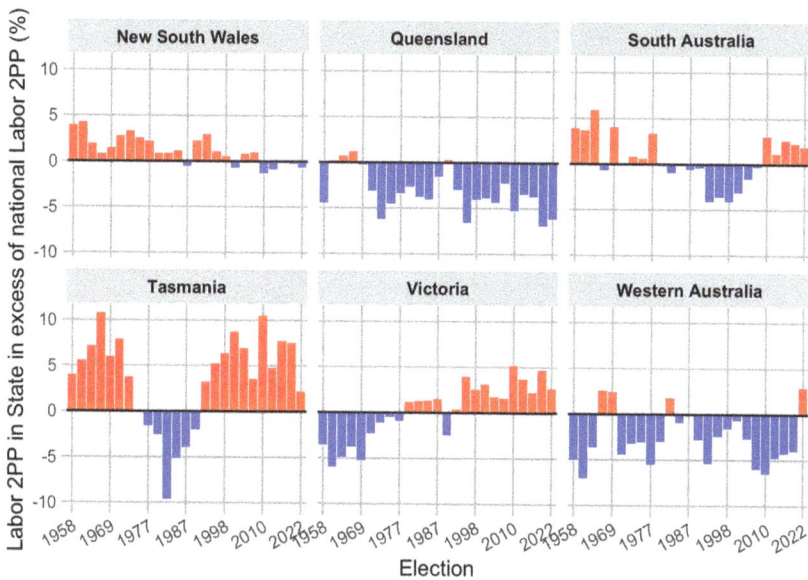

Figure 16.3 Difference between State and national two-party-preferred figures by State, 1958–2022

Sources: Compiled by author from various data sources.

345

There have been long-term trends where some States vote more strongly for one of the major parties relative to other States (Figure 16.3). New South Wales used to lean towards Labor and has shifted to sit at the national average. Victoria leaned strongly to the Coalition in the 1960s, but now leans to Labor. Queensland and Western Australia have traditionally leaned to the right, while South Australia and Tasmania have swung back towards Labor after swinging to the Liberal Party in the 1980s (in Tasmania) and 1990s (in South Australia).

Some of these trends have continued in 2022, but others changed dramatically. Figure 16.3 shows the difference between each State's two-party-preferred figure and the national figure over the past six decades.

Tasmania and Victoria had a smaller lean towards Labor in 2022 than in 2019, while there was little change in South Australia and New South Wales. Queensland had slightly less of a lean towards the LNP than in 2019, but it was still greater than in any election between 1998 and 2016.

The biggest shift was in Western Australia, which leaned strongly towards the Liberal Party at most federal elections in recent decades, but now has a 3.1 per cent lean towards the ALP. This shift accompanied the Liberal Party's loss of five seats in the State—one-third of all West Australian seats. The result in Western Australia was key to Labor gaining a majority in the House of Representatives.

Almost every jurisdiction shifted closer to the national average in 2022. Only New South Wales and the Australian Capital Territory voted more differently than the country overall in 2022 than in 2019, and the difference in New South Wales was very slight.

Differences between regions

The AEC broadly categorises all electorates based on their geography: inner metropolitan, outer metropolitan, provincial and rural. This has been the case for many decades, which allows us to see how the 2022 election differed from recent history according to electorate geography (Table 16.7). Almost all changes in 2022 took place in inner-metropolitan electorates, with the Liberal Party losing three-quarters of its seats in inner-urban Australia. Most of the remaining seat changes occurred in outer-metropolitan seats, with the only other change being in the NSW Central Coast electorate of Robertson, which is classified as provincial. There were no changes in rural electorates, although Labor did come close to losing two seats in rural Australia.

Table 16.7 Seat results by regional classification

	ALP	Coalition	Crossbench
Inner metropolitan	31 (+5)	4 (–12)	10 (+7)
Outer metropolitan	25 (+2)	15 (–5)	3 (+3)
Provincial	14 (+1)	11 (–1)	0
Rural	7	28	3

Source: Compiled by author from AEC (2022).

Looking over a longer time frame, the two-party-preferred results show a growing gap in voting patterns between inner-urban and regional Australia (Figure 16.4). While Labor gained a two-party-preferred swing in inner-metropolitan electorates in 2019 and lost ground in rural electorates in 2019, there was even more of a shift in 2022. Labor gained a 2.3 per cent swing in rural electorates, which was much less than the national swing, while gaining a 5.8 per cent swing in inner-metropolitan seats. Swings in outer-metropolitan and provincial electorates were roughly in line with the national swing.

Difference between election-day and early voting

This was the first election in modern Australian history for which most votes were cast before election day (see Chapter 19, this volume). There is usually a gap between the results for votes cast on election day and those cast early. Labor won the early vote by an extremely narrow margin, outpolling the Coalition by about 35,000 votes (Table 16.8 and Figure 16.5). This is the first time Labor has won the early vote since at least 2001, and this is much more important than it used to be. Labor narrowly lost the early vote in 2007, which made up less than 15 per cent of the total national vote, whereas it now makes up a slight majority.

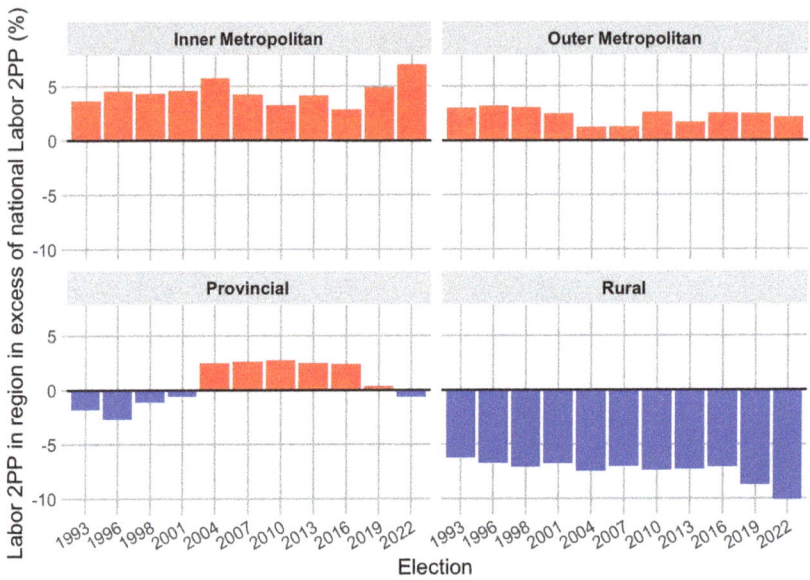

Figure 16.4 Difference between two-party-preferred vote for each regional classification and national two-party-preferred figures, 1993–2022

Source: Compiled by author from AEC data.

Table 16.8 ALP's two-party-preferred vote before and on election day (per cent)

Election	ALP election day	ALP early	Difference	Proportion voting on election day
2001	49.44	45.14	4.30	89.72
2004	47.66	44.05	3.61	87.59
2007	53.23	49.76	3.47	85.32
2010	50.87	46.82	4.05	81.36
2013	47.76	43.22	4.54	72.06
2016	51.15	46.50	4.65	67.21
2019	50.64	45.50	5.14	57.72
2022	53.98	50.24	3.74	47.89

Sources: Compiled by author from AEC (2022).

Informal votes

Despite an increase in ballot sizes due to a record number of House of Representatives candidates, the informal voting rate dropped slightly, to 5.19 per cent from 5.54 per cent in 2019 (Figure 20.6). The informal voting rate went down in New South Wales, Queensland and the Australian Capital Territory (Table 20.9), rose slightly in Victoria, Western Australia and South Australia and went up by more in Tasmania. The effective participation rate (the number of formal votes as a proportion of the eligible population) decreased slightly in every jurisdiction, due to a small reduction in turnout and an increased informal rate.

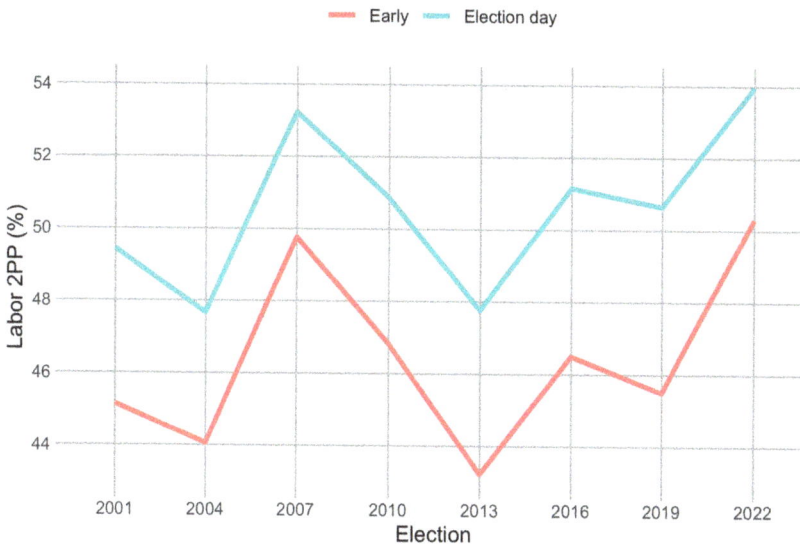

Figure 16.5 ALP two-party-preferred vote before and on election day

Notes: Election-day votes include ordinary and absentee votes. Early votes include remote, pre-poll and postal votes. Telephone, provisional, mobile and special hospital votes are not included as it is not clear whether they are cast on election day or earlier.

Source: Compiled by author from AEC (2022).

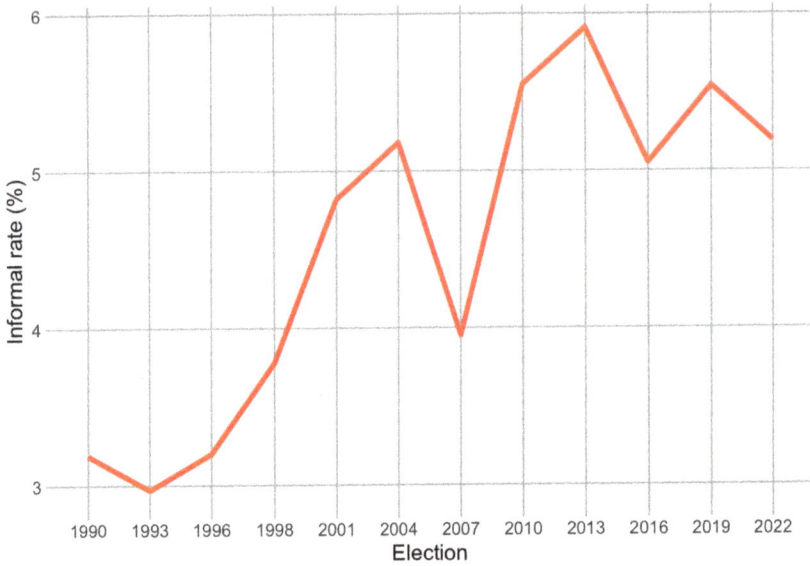

Figure 16.6 Informal voting rate at federal elections, 1990–2022

Sources: Constructed by author from Carr (1990); AEC (1998, 2001, 2022).

Table 16.9 Informal voting rate by State (per cent)

State/Territory	Informal rate	Informal rate change	Effective participation rate
NSW	6.22	−0.78	82.66
Vic.	4.71	0.08	83.20
Qld	4.17	−0.76	81.32
WA	5.52	0.12	80.47
SA	5.12	0.32	84.72
Tas.	5.85	1.48	85.47
ACT	2.46	−1.01	88.11
NT	5.31	0.63	59.24
National	5.19	−0.32	82.39

Source: Compiled by author from AEC (2022).

Increasing impact of preferences

With the increasing vote share for minor parties and Independents, there are very few electorates where one candidate wins a majority of the primary vote, and there is an increasing number of seats that are not simple Labor versus Coalition contests. Until 2016, more than two-thirds of electorates were decided with one candidate winning a majority of the first-preference vote (Figure 16.7). This number dipped just below one-third in 2016 and 2019, with preferences required in 102 and 105 electorates, respectively. In 2022, less than 10 per cent of electorates were decided on the first-preference vote, with preferences required in 136 electorates.

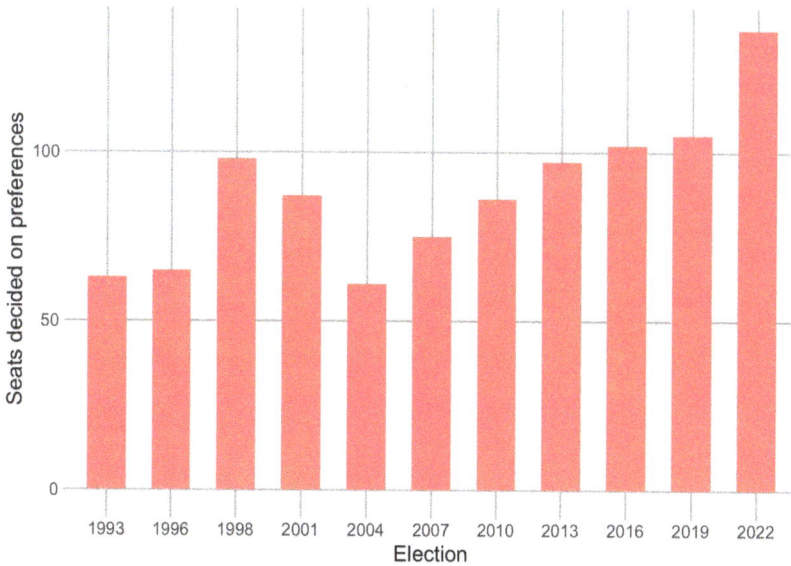

Figure 16.7 Seats decided on preferences, 1993–2022
Sources: Constructed by author from AEC (1998, 2001, 2022).

There has also been a significant increase in the number of electorates where the final two-candidate-preferred count is not between the major parties—a phenomenon the AEC refers to as a 'non-classic' contest (see also Chapter 19, this volume, for examples in opinion polling). The number of non-classic races in 2022 was 27—up from a previous record of 17 in 2016 and 15 in 2019. Sixteen of these races involved Independents, 10 of whom were elected. Another nine involved the Greens, four of whom were elected. Two other minor parties each retained a single seat.

Even beyond these races, the growing minor-party and Independent vote has added another complexity. The gap between the second-placed and third-placed candidates on the first-preference count has been steadily shrinking, which has led to more races where it is not clear who is in the top two.

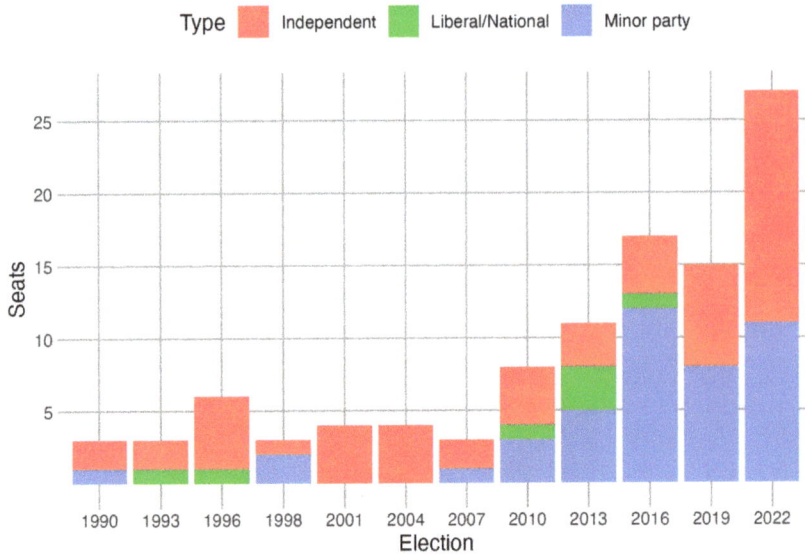

Figure 16.8 Non-classic contests in federal elections, 1990–2019
Sources: Constructed by author from Carr (1990); AEC (1998, 2001, 2022).

There were four races in 2022 where a candidate who did not poll in the top two ended up making it to the two-candidate-preferred count, one of whom was elected. Greens candidate Stephen Bates, who won the seat of Brisbane, polled 27.24 per cent of the primary vote, just 11 fewer votes than the Labor candidate, but overtook his ALP rival on preferences from other candidates and then won a small but comfortable majority over the LNP.

In the ALP-held seats of Macnamara and Richmond, the Coalition candidate came third on primary votes but managed to overtake the Greens to come second at the end of the distribution of preferences, with the preferences of Greens voters flowing strongly to the Labor incumbent. In both seats, the gap between the first-placed and third-placed candidates was less than 3.5 per cent on primary votes, and this produced complex counts in which the three-candidate-preferred rather than the two-candidate-preferred count was critical to knowing the outcome.

There was also another seat where a fourth-placed candidate managed to make it to the top two. In Groom, Independent candidate Suzie Holt polled 8.3 per cent, trailing the ALP and PHON candidates but managed to overtake both on the distribution of preferences and ended up polling 43.1 per cent on the two-candidate-preferred count.

ALP–Coalition contests of interest, by State

New South Wales

The Coalition was defending three seats in New South Wales with margins of less than 6 per cent against Labor, while Labor was defending 11 seats with margins of less than 6 per cent.

Labor gained three NSW seats off the Coalition: Robertson on the Central Coast and Reid and Bennelong in central Sydney. Robertson, covering parts of Sydney's outer commuter belt, was the least-urban seat to change hands at this election. Reid and Bennelong are both very diverse electorates with relatively large Chinese-Australian populations. A significant number of Labor's gains occurred in multicultural seats, with swings highest in suburbs with large Chinese-Australian populations.

Overall, Labor did suffer some negative swings in various regions but in every case, there were other nearby marginals where the ALP did much better. It lost ground in the outer-suburban seat of Lindsay but gained a large swing in Greenway and held its ground in Werriwa. Likewise, it lost votes in Paterson in the Hunter region but gained some in the neighbouring marginal seats of Hunter and Shortland.

Labor lost support in the South Coast seat of Gilmore but gained a large swing in Eden-Monaro, producing the largest margin seen in the former bellwether electorate since at least 1984.

Victoria

Labor gained two seats from the Coalition in Victoria: Chisholm and Higgins, both in the eastern suburbs of Melbourne. Labor also gained strong swings in Deakin and Menzies, both of which border Chisholm.

Michelle Ananda-Rajah won Higgins for the party with a 4.7 per cent swing, leaving her with a 2.1 per cent margin. Higgins is bordered by Goldstein and Kooyong, both of which the Liberal Party lost to Independents; Higgins is demographically similar to its neighbours but had a less prominent Independent campaign.

Labor did not do as well on the outer fringes of Melbourne, gaining small swings or losing ground in many seats. The Liberal Party gained swings in the marginal seats of Flinders and La Trobe, with swings of 1.1 per cent and 3.6 per cent, respectively. Labor gained a 3.1 per cent swing in the outer-suburban seat of Casey, but it was not enough to overturn the 4.6 per cent margin.

Queensland

Queensland is famous as the State with the largest number of marginal seats compared with its population and was crucial to Labor's victory the last time it won a majority government, in 2007. At that election, Labor gained nine seats in Queensland from a net gain of 23 seats nationally. The story was very different in 2022, with Labor gaining no seats off the LNP, and both parties losing seats to the Greens.

The LNP held four seats on margins of less than 6 per cent before the election, with Labor also holding four seats under the same threshold. Those seats on a margin of less than 6 per cent did not include any of the four in central and northern Queensland that were won by Labor in 2007: Capricornia, Dawson, Flynn and Herbert. Of those eight marginal seats, each major party lost one to the Greens—Griffith (Labor) and Brisbane (LNP)—along with Ryan, another LNP seat on a slightly larger margin.

Labor gained two-party-preferred swings in the remaining six seats, but with larger swings in the seats it held. It gained a swing of 9.9 per cent in Lilley and 7.2 per cent in Moreton—both mid-suburban ALP marginals. It also gained a 4 per cent swing in the Ipswich-area seat of Blair. Labor gained a 2.9 per cent swing in the outer-suburban LNP seat of Dickson, but just 0.2 per cent in the neighbouring seat of Longman and 0.7 per cent in the far north Queensland electorate of Leichhardt.

There are nine more LNP seats that were held by margins of between 6 and 13 per cent, including three central and northern Queensland electorates. The swings to Labor were larger in most of these seats. The LNP did gain a 3.4 per cent swing in the Townsville-based seat of Herbert, but Labor gained an average 4.3 per cent swing across the other eight, ranging from 2.9 per cent in McPherson to 5.8 per cent in Capricornia.

Overall, Labor did gain substantial swings in many seats, but they just were not in the right places. The LNP did not have many marginal seats, and it managed to minimise the swing in those seats. In the context of Liberal losses in inner-urban seats across Australia, Labor's best chances were in the inner-city seats of Brisbane and Ryan. Labor won the two-party-preferred count in both, but was overtaken by the Greens, which went on to win those seats, along with the neighbouring Labor seat of Griffith. Thus, the LNP did lose seats to the left in Queensland, but not to Labor.

Western Australia

Western Australia was Labor's best State in 2022, where it won a majority of House seats and three Senate seats for the first time at a half-Senate election.

The Liberal Party lost four seats to Labor (Pearce, Hasluck, Swan and Tangney), plus another to Independent Kate Chaney (Curtin), leaving it with just five of 15 West Australian seats—down from 10 before the election.

Two-party-preferred swings to Labor were smaller in other electorates but were generally among the biggest in the country. The seven biggest two-party-preferred swings to Labor were in Western Australia, and all 15 seats in the west were ranked among the top-24 nationwide. This swing pushed the previously marginal Labor seats of Cowan, Perth and Burt out of that category, while significantly reducing the Liberals' margin in a number of other seats. Of note is the northern Perth suburbs seat of Moore, where a swing of almost 11 per cent reduced Liberal MP Ian Goodenough's margin to just 0.66 per cent.

South Australia

Only one seat in South Australia was held by a margin of less than 6 per cent before the 2022 federal election: Boothby, in the southern suburbs of Adelaide, which was held by the Liberal Party by a 1.4 per cent margin. Labor's most marginal seat was Hindmarsh, held by a 6.5 per cent margin. Sitting Liberal MP Nicolle Flint retired from Boothby and Labor won it with a 4.66 per cent swing, leaving Louise Miller-Frost with a 3.3 per cent margin.

Labor also came close to defeating Liberal MP James Stevens in Sturt, which he had previously held by a 6.9 per cent margin, but this was reduced to just 0.45 per cent.

Tasmania

The Liberal Party performed well in Tasmania on a two-party-preferred basis, gaining swings in three seats and retaining two marginals. Before the election, the Liberal Party held two seats on margins of less than 6 per cent, while Labor held just one seat under that threshold.

Labor MP Brian Mitchell held on to the central Tasmanian seat of Lyons by a slim 0.9 per cent margin after a 4.3 per cent swing to the Liberal Party. The Liberal Party gained swings in both of its northern marginal seats. Bridget Archer gained a 1.0 per cent swing after preferences, which left her with a 1.4 per cent margin. Neighbouring Liberal MP Gavin Pearce gained a 4.9 per cent swing.

Australian Capital Territory

Labor retained all three ACT electorates, gaining similar swings in each: from 5.1 per cent in Fenner to 5.4 per cent in Bean.

Northern Territory

Labor retained both electorates in the Northern Territory—one with significantly more ease than the other. In the vast outback electorate of Lingiari, the ALP won with a 0.95 per cent margin after a 4.5 per cent swing to the Country Liberal Party. In the Darwin-based Solomon, Labor gained a 6.3 per cent swing, retaining the seat with a 9.4 per cent margin.

Non-classic contests

This election produced a record number of non-classic contests, with the final count including an Independent or minor-party candidate in 26 electorates, 16 of whom were elected.

All six incumbent crossbenchers were re-elected—all with relative ease. This included three Independents and one member each from the Greens, Katter's Australian Party and the Centre Alliance. Most candidates in the non-classic contests were Independents, including many who were classified 'Teal' because of to their challenges to Coalition candidates in part over climate change issues, particularly in prosperous inner-urban electorates.

Six candidates who can be loosely categorised as Teal won seats across three large Australian cities (see also Chapters 13 and 14, this volume). Allegra Spender won the eastern Sydney seat of Wentworth, Kylea Tink won North Sydney and Sophie Scamps won the northern Sydney seat of Mackellar. Both North Sydney and Mackellar border Warringah, where fellow Independent Zali Steggall was re-elected to a second term after defeating former prime minister Tony Abbott in 2019. Another Independent, Nicolette Boele, came within 4.3 per cent of winning the neighbouring seat of Bradfield.

Independent candidates Zoe Daniel and Monique Ryan won the inner Melbourne electorates of Goldstein and Kooyong. Former federal treasurer Josh Frydenberg was the biggest scalp for the Independents, losing Kooyong. The sixth like-minded Independent, Kate Chaney, won the western Perth seat of Curtin.

A seventh Independent was elected, in the south-western Sydney seat of Fowler. Dai Le was deputy mayor of Fairfield and defeated former NSW premier and senator Kristina Keneally, who was seeking a House seat to make up for her likely unwinnable Senate seat but did not have any local connections. There were also several Independents who reached the final count in regional electorates, but none came particularly close to winning. These candidates appeared in the seats of Calare, Cowper, Groom, Nicholls and Wannon.

There were no prominent Independent challenges in inner-city Brisbane along the lines of the campaigns in the other major cities, but the Greens did well, gaining three contiguous seats here. Until this election, the Greens had never held more than one seat in the House of Representatives at once, with Adam Bandt sitting alone since 2010.

Greens candidate Max Chandler-Mather topped the primary vote, with the sitting Labor MP Terri Butler dropping into third place, giving Chandler-Mather an easy win on preferences.

Fellow Greens candidates Elizabeth Watson-Brown and Stephen Bates won the LNP seats of Ryan and Brisbane, respectively, with Bates joining a small club of those who have won a seat from third place on the primary vote, falling short of the Labor candidate by just 11 votes (see 'Increasing impact of preferences' section).

There were five other seats in inner-city Sydney, Melbourne and Canberra where the Greens made it to the top two but did not come particularly close to winning. The Greens' two-candidate-preferred vote ranged from 32.95 per cent in Grayndler to 41.43 per cent in Wills. The other seats in this group were Sydney and Canberra. The Greens also came a very close third in Macnamara.

Conclusion

The 2022 Australian federal election was a remarkable election in many ways, in large part due to the results in the House of Representatives.

The election was a landslide defeat for the outgoing Coalition Government, but only a narrow majority win for the ALP. This divergence is explained by a record performance by Independents and minor parties, which won more than twice as many seats as the previous record and reached highs not seen since World War II.

The election saw the worst result for the Coalition, in votes and seats, since the war, but Labor's victory came despite its primary vote dropping to a level not seen since 1934. It was able to convert that primary vote into a two-party-preferred majority and a slim parliamentary majority, but that would not have been possible if the gap between the major parties was narrower.

These changes could prove to be a trend or there could be some reversion at the next election, but it is unlikely we will see a return in the short term to elections dominated by the major parties.

References

Australian Electoral Commission (AEC). 1998. *1998 Federal Election Results*. [Online]. Canberra: AEC. Available from: www.aec.gov.au/About_AEC/Publications/statistics/files/aec-1993-1996-1998-election-statistics.zip.

Australian Electoral Commission (AEC). 2001. *2001 Federal Election Results*. [Online]. Canberra: AEC. Available from: www.aec.gov.au/Elections/federal_elections/Stats_CDRom.htm#cd.

Australian Electoral Commission (AEC). 2022. 'Tally room archive'. *Election Results*. Canberra: AEC. Available from: results.aec.gov.au.

Carr, Adam. 1990. 'The House of Representatives: Australian legislative election of 24 March 1990'. *Psephos: Adam Carr's Election Archive*. [Online]. Available from: psephos.adam-carr.net/countries/a/australia/1990/1990reps1.txt.

Newton-Farrelly, Jenni. 2015. *Fairness and Equality: Drawing Election Districts in Australia*. Melbourne: Australian Scholarly Publishing.

Raue, Ben. 2016. 'Nominations announced: Final update'. *The Tally Room*, 11 June. Available from: www.tallyroom.com.au/29634.

Raue, Ben. 2019. 'Nominations close: Final candidate numbers breakdown'. *The Tally Room*, 25 April. Available from: www.tallyroom.com.au/38508.

Raue, Ben. 2022a. 'Nominations close, 2022 edition'. *The Tally Room*, 23 April. Available from: www.tallyroom.com.au/47463.

Raue, Ben. 2022b. 'Major party vote at all time low'. *The Tally Room*, 23 May. Available from: www.tallyroom.com.au/47834.

17

The Senate results

Antony Green

Australian parliamentary elections are always defined by the battle for government in the House of Representatives. The Senate election held on the same day receives less attention and generally produces similar party vote shares, though both major parties generally record lower shares in the Senate. The combined vote share for major parties has been declining for many elections and reached new lows for both houses in 2022, and the major-party vote share gap between the two chambers was the lowest since 1993.

Where results for the two chambers differed was in the translation of vote shares into party representation and in the pattern of gains and losses by party. These representational differences stem from the different constitutional and electoral arrangements for elections to the two chambers. This chapter will examine how votes were translated into seats in the Senate and the impact on party representation brought about by changes to the Senate's electoral system in 2016.

Vote shares and seats won

The Coalition's loss of seats in the House resulted in gains for both Labor and the parliamentary crossbench. In contrast, Coalition losses in the Senate produced a larger crossbench and no net change in Labor's representation.

While the swing against the Coalition produced a change of government in the House, it produced a changed crossbench in the Senate, though changing it in a way that benefited the incoming Labor Government.

The Coalition lost five seats to five different parties—to Labor in Western Australia, the Jacqui Lambie Network in Tasmania, David Pocock in the Australian Capital Territory, the Greens in Queensland and the UAP in Victoria. The Liberal Party gained a seat in South Australia at the expense of the former Nick Xenophon Team.

The Greens gained three seats to reach 12 senators—a record Senate representation for a minor party. For the second successive election, the Greens elected a senator from each State. The party's three gains were from Labor in New South Wales, the LNP in Queensland and the former Nick Xenophon Team in South Australia.

Labor lost a seat to the Greens in New South Wales but gained one from the Liberal Party in Western Australia. For the first time since six-seat half-Senate elections were introduced in 1990, Labor elected three senators in Western Australia and the Liberal Party only two. Importantly for the new Senate's composition, the Greens also retained their West Australian Senate position, delivering 'left' parties four of the six WA Senate seats for the first time. As in the House, the Senate in the west delivered crucial seats that assisted Labor's control of the new parliament.

The final Senate results left Labor unchanged on 26 senators, which, with 12 Greens senators, gave the two left parties 38 of the 76 seats in the new Senate. When the two parties vote together, the Albanese Government will need one extra vote to pass legislation.

That vote could come from ACT Independent David Pocock, whose election denied the Liberal Party its traditional ACT Senate seat. Labor could also work with the Jacqui Lambie Network's two Tasmanian senators, with that party gaining a second seat in 2022. Less likely to vote with the government would be new Victorian UAP senator Ralph Babet and PHON's two Queensland senators. PHON support declined in Queensland though preference flows ensured Pauline Hanson was re-elected.

Table 17.1 sets out the composition of the Senate before and after the 2022 election, while Table 17.2 provides more detail on the results by party.

Table 17.1 Party composition and changes at the 2022 Senate election

Category (positions)	Coalition	ALP	Greens	Others
Continuing (36) elected 2019	17	11	6	2
Ending term (40) elected 2016	19	15	3	3
Elected 2022 (40)	15	15	6	4
Change	–4	0	+3	+1
2019–22 Senate	36	26	9	5
2022–25 Senate	32	26	12	6

Source: Accumulated by author from tables in AEC (2019a; 2022b).

Table 17.2 Senate result: Votes and seats, 2022

Senate as elected	Percentage of votes	Change	Seats won	Change	New Senate
Coalition	34.2	–3.8	15	–4	32
ALP	30.1	+1.3	15	0	26
Greens	12.7	+2.5	6	+3	12
PHON	4.3	–1.1	1	0	2
UAP	3.5	+1.1	1	+1	1
Legalise Cannabis Australia	3.3	+1.5	0	0	0
Liberal Democrats	2.3	+1.1	0	0	0
Animal Justice Party	1.6	+0.3	0	0	0
Shooters, Fishers and Farmers Party	1.0	–0.7	0	0	0
David Pocock	0.4	+0.4	1	+1	1
Jacqui Lambie Network	0.2	0	1	+1	2
Others	7.0	–2.6	0	–2	0

Notes: The four Coalition parties have been accumulated. Table includes all parties that polled above 1 per cent, elected senators at the 2022 election or had retiring senators.

Source: Summarised by author from AEC (2022a).

At 34.1 per cent, the Liberal–National Coalition's vote share was the lowest since 1943, before the formation of the modern Liberal Party. In Queensland and Western Australia, the Coalition recorded its lowest vote share since Australia's two-party system stabilised in 1910. New South Wales was the only State where Coalition support passed 35.7 per cent or 2.5 quotas. At half-Senate elections between 1990 and 2019, the Coalition always elected between 17 and 21 senators, but it elected only 15 in 2022.

Labor's 30.1 per cent was the party's highest Senate vote since 35.1 per cent in 2010. Around the States, Labor's vote was its highest since 2016 in Queensland, since 2013 in New South Wales and Victoria, since 2010 in South Australia and since 2007 in Western Australia. In contrast, the Tasmanian Labor Party recorded its lowest vote since 1931.

Greens support rose to 12.7 per cent, second only to its high of 13.1 per cent at the 2010 election. The party polled a record vote in New South Wales and Western Australia, its second-highest since 2010 in the other mainland States and the third-highest after 2007 and 2010 in Tasmania.

If you include the Greens in the total for 'Others', the 2022 election was the first time that both major parties were outpolled by others. These one-third splits in Senate support did not translate into one-third representation. The Coalition elected 15 senators, Labor 15 and all other parties ten. Within the vote for others, the Greens elected six senators with 12.7 per cent of the vote while the 23.0 per cent support for all other minor parties and Independents elected only four senators.

This discrepancy is down to the nature of the Senate's electoral system. Support for the Coalition, Labor and the Greens was confined to a single group on each State and Territory ballot paper (there was a second but very low-polling Nationals ticket in South Australia). Support for non-Greens Others could have been at 23 per cent, but it was spread across 126 groups and numerous 'ungrouped' candidates. Support for these parties could have been amalgamated under the group voting ticket system that was abolished in 2016, but running dozens of tickets under the new Senate system allowed preferences to be exhausted or leak to larger parties.

Among the minor parties, a clear hierarchy of results emerged. Nationally and across most States, PHON finished fourth, ahead of the UAP and Legalise Cannabis Australia. PHON finished behind the Jacqui Lambie Network in Tasmania and the UAP in Victoria, while Legalise Cannabis Australia polled 5.4 per cent in Queensland and 3.4 per cent in Western Australia to finish ahead of the UAP.

Changes to party registration rules

The registration of political parties and inclusion of their names on ballot papers were introduced in 1984. In the most significant strengthening of registration rules since 1984, the number of members required for registration was increased from 500 to 1,500 ahead of the 2022 election. Existing parties were given three months to meet the new requirement by December 2021. A second change allowed registered parties to apply for the deregistration of newer parties with the same words in their name. The new rule on party names was supported by both the Coalition and Labor and was clearly aimed at third parties using the words 'Labor' and 'Liberal'.

Between the 2019 election and November 2021, using the 500-member rule, 20 parties were deregistered—11 voluntarily, three for not responding to requests to prove member numbers and five for failing to prove they had 500 members. With the increased-membership rules in place, another 13 parties were deregistered—two voluntarily, five for not responding to requests to prove member numbers and six after failing the new 1,500-member test.[1] The deregistrations included the Democratic Labour Party (DLP), which was first registered in 1984 but had contested elections since the 1950s. The DLP was deregistered for failing to prove it had 1,500 members, though the ALP also lodged a request for the DLP to be deregistered under the new naming rules.

The Liberal Party lodged a name objection to the registration of the Liberal Democratic Party (LDP). The LDP applied to change its name to the Liberty and Democracy Party, causing the AEC to cancel its notice to deregister. Just before the election, the LDP withdrew its application, forcing the AEC to begin the deregistration process again and leaving the LDP free to contest the 2022 election under its old name. The party was finally deregistered in July 2022 (AEC 2022c).

The number of parties contesting the Senate peaked at 52 in 2013—the last election at which parties controlled preferences. The number of parties declined to 45 in 2016, rose to 48 in 2019 and fell to 37 at the 2022 election. The decline began with the abolition of group voting tickets (GVTs) in 2016 and accelerated with the new membership rules in 2022. In the same period, the number of nominated ballot paper groups declined, from 227 in 2013 to 151 in 2022 (not including ungrouped columns), and

---

1   Calculations by the author from 2019–22 registration decisions in AEC (2022d).

there was a drop from 529 to 421 in the number of candidates. All States saw a decline in the number of ballot paper columns—in New South Wales, from 44 in 2013 to 23 in 2022, and from 23 to 14 in Tasmania. With fewer columns on the ballot paper, the AEC has been able to increase the font size, though voters in the mainland States continue to be handed 1-metre-wide ballot papers.[2]

The Senate electoral system

House and Senate elections produce different representational outcomes from similar levels of votes due to the different structure and systems used to elect members. Representation in the House is tied to the population of each State and members are elected from single-member districts, using preferential voting since 1917. In the Senate, States have equal representation with half of each State's senators elected every three years. Senators are elected from Statewide multimember districts, with proportional representation by single transferable vote (PR-STV) used since 1949. The two Territories have two senators elected every three years for single terms.

Senate candidates have been grouped by party on ballot papers since 1922 and parties have determined the order in which their candidates are listed since 1940. Both changes pre-date the introduction of PR-STV. Party names have appeared on ballot papers since 1984 and logos since 2016. Ballot papers have been divided by a thick horizontal line since 1984 (see Plate 17.1), with voters given the choice of voting for parties 'above the line' (ATL) or for candidates 'below the line' (BTL).

The introduction of ATL voting in 1984 included party-controlled preferences using GVTs. Voters could select one ticket above the line and adopt the full list of their chosen party's preferences or were required to preference more than 90 per cent of candidates below the line. From the system's first use, about 90 per cent of votes were cast using the ATL option, turning the race to fill final vacancies in each State into contests controlled by party GVTs. Preferences became tradeable commodities and, over three decades, instances grew of parties with very low vote shares defeating higher-polling competitors (Green 2020; McAllister and Muller 2019). The 2016 Senate reforms abolished GVTs and returned control over interparty preferences to voters.

---

2 Calculations by the author taken from AEC Tally Room sites, 2007–22.

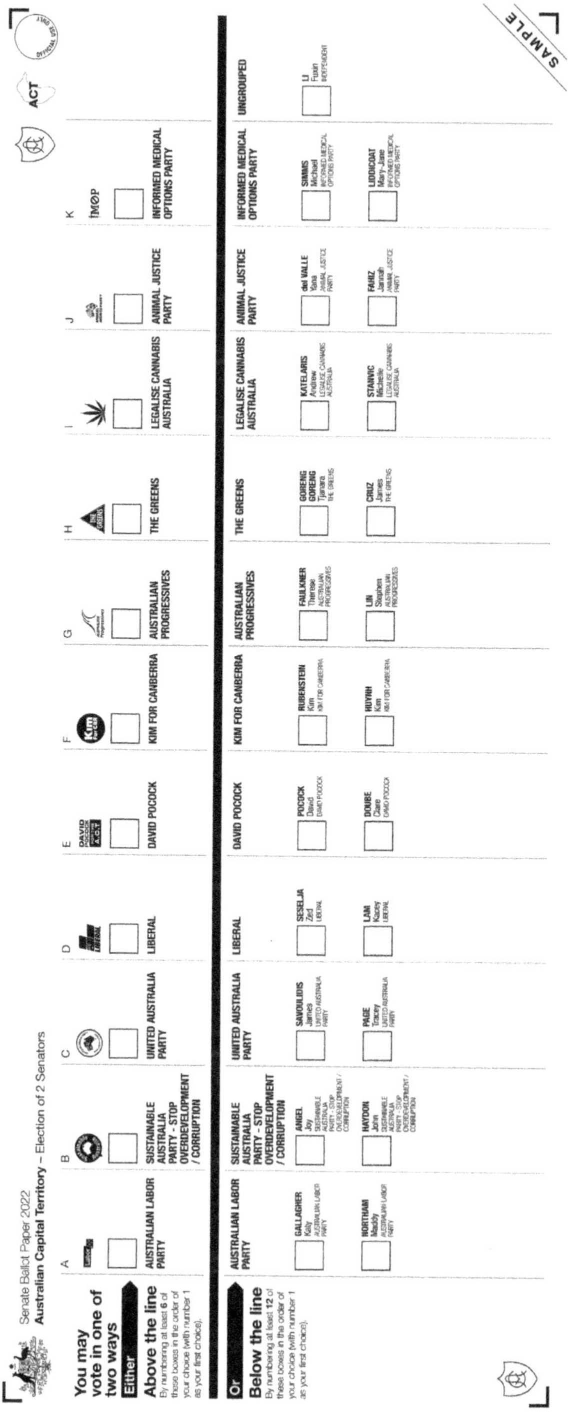

Plate 17.1 2022 Senate ballot paper

Source: Australian Electoral Commission.

The new rules introduced in 2016 were used for the third time at the 2022 Senate election. ATL and BTL voting remained, but GVTs were abolished, ending party control over interparty preferences. A new form of ATL voting permitted voters to indicate preferences for parties, with the instructions stating that a minimum of six preferences should be shown though any vote with a valid ATL first preference was formal. ATL preferences were imputed to be for candidates in each party as listed on the ballot paper. BTL instructions stated a minimum of 12 preferences, though any vote with six preferences was formal.

As discussed by Green (2020), the changes have combined to make the Senate's electoral system behave like list proportional representation (list PR) with a highest remainder method of allocating final seats from partial quotas.

Comparing chamber vote shares

Minor parties received a record vote in both the House and the Senate at the 2022 election, but the difference between minor-party vote shares in the two chambers declined. The share of the vote for minor parties was only 4 percentage points higher in the Senate—the smallest difference since 1993 (see Table 17.3). Two groups accounted for most of the difference: Legalise Cannabis Australia polled 3.3 per cent in the Senate but contested only one House seat; Independents polled 5.3 per cent in the House but non-party candidates under 1 per cent in the Senate.

Support for the Coalition was 1.5 percentage points lower in the Senate than in the House, while support for Labor was 2.5 percentage points lower compared with 5.7 percentage points lower in 2019. The smaller gap for Labor could be explained by strategic voting in seats contested by Teal Independents. In Kooyong, Labor's percentage of the vote was almost four times higher in the Senate (6.9 per cent House, 26.1 per cent Senate), with sizeable differences also in Goldstein (11.0 per cent, 25.3 per cent), Indi (8.6 per cent, 22.5 per cent), Mackellar (8.2 per cent, 20.2 per cent), Warringah (8.4 per cent, 23.9 per cent) and Wentworth (10.9 per cent, 22.7 per cent).

Another reason for the narrowing between the two chambers was parties nominating more House candidates. PHON contested 59 House seats in 2019 and 149 in 2022, and the Liberal Democrats increased their candidates from 10 to 100 in the House. Where PHON's Senate vote was 1.9 percentage points higher than the House in 2019, it was 1.1 per cent lower in 2022 due to the increase in House candidates.

Table 17.3 Candidates/groups contesting elections and minor-party vote share, 1984–2022

Election	Average candidates/groups		Non–major-party vote (%)		
	House	Senate	House	Senate	Difference
1984	4.2	6.9	7.4	18.3	10.9
1987	4.1	8.1	8.1	15.1	7.0
1990	5.3	8.0	17.1	19.7	2.6
1993	6.4	10.3	10.8	13.5	2.7
1996	6.1	10.6	14.0	19.9	5.9
1998	7.5	14.6	20.4	25.0	4.6
2001	6.9	12.6	19.2	23.8	4.6
2004	7.3	15.0	15.7	19.9	4.2
2007	7.0	17.0	14.5	19.8	5.3
2010	5.7	17.0	18.4	26.2	7.8
2013	7.9	28.4	21.1	32.2	11.1
2016	6.6	25.8	23.2	34.7	11.5
2019	7.0	20.4	25.2	33.1	7.9
2022	8.0	18.9	31.7	35.7	4.0

Sources: Calculated by author from Barber and Johnson (2014); AEC (2016, 2019b, 2022e).

Table 17.3 shows changes in the average House candidates and average Senate groups (excluding 'Ungrouped' columns) at elections since party names first appeared on ballot papers in 1984. The table also includes minor-party vote shares in both chambers and differences in vote shares.

The average number of candidates per House contest was unchanged between 2013 and 2022, but the non–major-party vote share rose from 21.1 per cent to 31.7 per cent. Much of the increase was due to the re-emergence of PHON, with 5.0 per cent in 2022, Independents rising from 1.4 per cent to 5.3 per cent and support for the Greens rising from 8.7 per cent to 12.2 per cent.

After the abolition of GVTs in 2013, the average number of groups per Senate contest declined from 28.4 in 2013 to 18.9 in 2022, with only a modest increase in non–major-party support, from 32.2 per cent to 35.7 per cent. Support for the Greens has increased, up from 8.7 per cent to 12.7 per cent, PHON re-emerged with 4.3 per cent and Legalise Cannabis Australia arrived in 2022 with 3.3 per cent. Support for the UAP and Liberal

Democrats has declined and Family First and the Nick Xenophon Team have been disbanded. There has been a consolidation of support for existing minor parties while support for micro-parties has declined in line with the decline in their Senate nomination numbers.

The declining gap in non–major-party support has several causes. The disappearance of the Australian Democrats removed a party that polled significantly in the Senate and there has been a decline in Senate-only parties. As PHON, the UAP and other minor parties have contested more House seats, the difference between their votes shares in the two chambers has narrowed. The emergence of a strong vote for Independents in the House has not seen a similar increase in Independents for the Senate. The rise in non–major-party support that first occurred in the Senate has since been replicated in the House, narrowing the gap in support between the two chambers.

Votes into seats

Since the abolition of GVTs, the Senate's electoral system operates largely as a form of list PR with final seats allocated to groups with the highest partial quotas on first preferences. Preferences can still matter, however, as shown by the come-from-behind victory of Independent David Pocock in the ACT Senate race. As shown in Table 17.4, such wins are less common since the abolition of GVTs.

As explained in Green (2020), it is possible to measure the impact of preferences in the Senate system by comparing the result with what would have been produced using list PR with a highest remainder method of allocating final seats. By treating all votes for candidates in a group as a single total, elected senators can be placed in one of the following categories:

- **Filled quotas:** Seats allocated to groups based on filled first-preference quotas.
- **Highest remainder:** Seats allocated based on having the highest partial quota on first preferences.
- **Trailing wins:** Candidates elected from a trailing partial quota, which is only possible in preferential systems.

Table 17.4 Senators elected classed by list PR category: Half-Senate elections, 2013–2022

Category	2013	2019	2022
Filled quotas	23	25	24
Highest remainder	8	15	15
Trailing wins	9	0	1

Source: Calculations for 2022 by author; see Green (2020).

Table 17.4 shows the number of elected senators in each of the above categories. The 2013 half-Senate election was the last with GVTs, while the new system was used in 2019 and 2022. The lower-quota 2016 double-dissolution election is not included.

At the last election to use GVTs, in 2013, nine of 40 Senate seats were filled by trailing candidates and only eight by candidates who began the count with the highest remainder. No trailing candidates were elected in 2019, with Pocock in the Australian Capital Territory the only candidate in 2022 to win after trailing on first preferences. As was expected when Senate electoral reform was introduced in 2016, the new system tends to reward parties that attract significant first-preference votes over those that rely on preferences.

Results by state

New South Wales

Table 17.5 Senate results: New South Wales

Party	Percentage of vote	Change	Quotas	Elected	Change
Liberal/Nationals	36.7	–1.8	2.57	3	0
ALP	30.4	+0.6	2.13	2	–1
The Greens	11.5	+2.7	0.80	1	+1
PHON	4.1	–0.8	0.29	0	0
UAP	3.4	+1.9	0.24	0	0
Legalise Cannabis Australia	2.6	+0.5	0.18	0	0
Animal Justice Party	2.2	+1.1	0.15	0	0
Liberal Democrats	2.1	+0.2	0.15	0	0
Others	7.0	–4.4	0.00	0	0

Source: Aggregated from AEC (2022a).

Both Labor and the Coalition had been allocated three six-year positions after the 2016 double-dissolution election, which meant New South Wales was the only State without a crossbench senator facing election in 2022. Due to the 2017 citizenship disqualification of Nationals senator Fiona Nash, all three Coalition positions were held by Liberals, with Nash replaced with Liberal Concetta Fierravanti-Wells after a reallocation of terms.

The Coalition polled its highest Senate vote in New South Wales, with 36.7 per cent or 2.57 quotas; the surplus beyond two quotas was enough to ensure the Coalition elected a third senator ahead of PHON. Liberal Marise Payne was re-elected from the head of the ticket and the Nationals' Ross Cadell recovered his party's traditional seat from position two. Fierravanti-Wells was defeated in Liberal preselection and Jim Molan was elected to the third Coalition seat—his first election to the Senate after previously filling casual vacancies or winning recounts.

Labor's Deborah O'Neill and Jenny McAllister were re-elected, but Labor's third seat was won by the Greens' David Shoebridge, with his party recording its highest ever vote in the Senate in New South Wales. With 0.8 of a quota, the Greens easily reached a quota after preferences. The Labor Party's third sitting senator, former NSW premier Kristina Keneally, moved to contest the lower house seat of Fowler, where she was defeated by an Independent.

After the full distribution of preferences, Molan was declared elected with 0.86 of a quota to PHON's 0.69, with 0.44 of a quota of exhausted preferences.

Victoria

Table 17.6 Senate results: Victoria

Party	Percentage of votes	Change	Quotas	Elected	Change
Liberal/Nationals	32.3	−3.6	2.26	2	−1
ALP	31.4	+0.3	2.20	2	0
The Greens	13.9	+3.2	0.97	1	0
UAP	4.0	+1.5	0.28	1	+1
Legalise Cannabis Australia	3.0	+1.5	0.21	0	0
PHON	2.9	+0.1	0.20	0	0
Liberal Democrats	2.4	+1.5	0.17	0	0
Others	10.1	−4.5	0.70	0	0

Source: Aggregated from AEC (2022a).

The turnover of sitting Victorian senators since 2016 meant the Nationals' Bridget McKenzie was the only senator elected in 2016 to seek re-election in 2022. Liberal senators Sarah Henderson and Greg Mirabella, the Greens' Lidia Thorpe and Labor's Jana Stewart had been appointed to fill casual vacancies, while long-serving Labor senator Kim Carr retired at the election.

Labor retained its two seats with Stewart re-elected and Linda White replacing Carr. Thorpe reached a quota after preferences as the Greens recorded its highest Victorian Senate vote since 2010. Henderson and McKenzie were elected on two filled quotas as Coalition support fell to its lowest level in a century.

The filling of the sixth vacancy was a test of the new electoral system, with the UAP on a partial quota of 0.28 and four other parties above 0.20 of a quota. By the time only three candidates remained, the UAP's Ralph Babet led with 0.64 of a quota to Casey Nunn (ALP) on 0.55 and 0.50 for Greg Mirabella (Liberal Party). Liberal preferences then confirmed Babet's election to the sixth seat, the final count being Babet on 0.83 of a quota ahead of Labor on 0.69, with 0.48 of a quota of distributed ballot papers exhausted.

The Coalition's how-to-vote card had recommended preferencing the UAP and, on Mirabella's exclusion, Coalition ATL preferences flowed 55.3 per cent to Babet and 24.5 per cent to Labor, with 20.2 per cent exhausting.

Queensland

Table 17.7 Senate results: Queensland

Party	Percentage of vote	Change	Quotas	Elected	Change
LNP	35.2	−3.7	2.47	2	−1
ALP	24.7	+2.1	1.73	2	0
The Greens	12.4	+2.5	0.87	1	+1
PHON	7.4	−2.9	0.52	1	0
Legalise Cannabis Australia	5.4	+3.6	0.38	0	0
UAP	4.2	+0.7	0.29	0	0
Liberal Democrats	2.5	+1.7	0.17	0	0
Others	8.2	−4.0	0.58	0	0

Source: Aggregated from AEC (2022a).

Up for the 2022 election were the six Senate seats allocated long terms after the 2016 double dissolution. That allocation split the seats four from the right (LNP, three; PHON, one) and two from the left (ALP). The 2019 election had produced a similar 4:2 split, with the LNP electing three senators along with one each from PHON, Labor and the Greens.

Labor had polled only 22.6 per cent in 2019. Any return to a normal level of Labor support was likely to produce a 3:3 right–left split, forcing the third LNP senator into a race for the final seat with Pauline Hanson. The LNP's constitution reserved the first and third positions on the party ticket for Liberal candidates and position two for the Nationals. Victory in Liberal preselection ensured James McGrath was elected from the top of the ticket and the Nationals' Matt Canavan from second place, while third-placed Liberal Amanda Stoker faced the contest with Hanson.

Labor's leading incumbent Murray Watt was elected on first preferences. Second Labor incumbent Anthony Chisholm was re-elected on preferences, with the Greens' Penny Allman-Payne newly elected from the highest Greens vote since 2010. With two LNP and one Labor senator elected on first preferences, the race for the final three seats began with the Greens on 0.87 of a quota, Labor on 0.73, PHON on 0.52 and the LNP on 0.47 of a quota.

Votes of more than 1 quota were distributed from minor parties, with Hanson attracting more than Stoker and Allman-Payne reaching a quota. Labor's Chisholm and Hanson would have reached a quota had Stoker's preferences been distributed.

Western Australia

At the 10 half-Senate WA elections between 1990 and 2019, the Liberal Party had always filled three of the six vacancies. Labor had never elected more than two senators and was reduced to only a single seat at the 2014 WA Senate re-election. The Greens had won the sixth seat at every election since 2004.

Table 17.8 Senate results: Western Australia

Party	Percentage of vote	Change	Quotas	Elected	Change
ALP	34.6	+6.9	2.42	3	+1
Liberal Party of Australia	31.7	−9.2	2.22	2	−1
The Greens	14.3	+2.4	1.00	1	0
PHON	3.5	−2.4	0.24	0	0
Legalise Cannabis Australia	3.4	+1.7	0.24	0	0
Australian Christians	2.2	+0.5	0.15	0	0
UAP	2.1	+0.4	0.15	0	0
Liberal Democrats	1.9	+1.2	0.14	0	0
Others	6.4	−1.5	0.45	0	0

Source: Aggregated from AEC (2022a).

The 2022 Senate election reversed previous results. The WA Liberal Party recorded its lowest vote since its formation in 1946 and the lowest vote in a century for the senior non-Labor party. Labor recorded its highest vote since 2007 and for the first time filled three of the six seats. The Greens easily re-elected their sitting senator, delivering left parties four of the State's six seats. Western Australia was the only State in 2022 where Labor outpolled the Liberal Party and where it elected three senators.

Filled quotas re-elected Sue Lines and Glenn Sterle for Labor and Liberals Michaelia Cash and Dean Smith. The Greens required a few hundred preferences before Indigenous senator Dorinda Cox reached a quota. The sixth vacancy was won by 27-year-old Fatima Payman for Labor. Payman arrived in Australia by boat as a child refugee from Afghanistan. Her victory gave Labor 26 Senate seats, which, when combined with 12 Greens, meant only one more senator would be required to pass legislation.

After the election of filled quotas, Payman led with 0.42 of a quota to PHON on 0.24, Legalise Cannabis Australia on 0.24 and 0.22 for the third Liberal. Preferences generally favoured PHON but at the end of the count Payman was declared elected having reached 0.85 of a quota to PHON's 0.75, with 0.40 of a quota's worth of votes exhausted. The flow of preferences narrowed the gap between Labor and PHON but the exhaustion of preferences prevented the lead narrowing further.

South Australia

Table 17.9 Senate results: South Australia

Party	Percentage of vote	Change	Quotas	Elected	Change
Liberal Party of Australia	33.9	–3.9	2.37	3	+1
ALP	32.3	+1.9	2.26	2	0
The Greens	12.0	+1.0	0.84	1	+1
PHON	4.0	–0.9	0.28	0	0
UAP	3.0	0.0	0.21	0	0
Xenophon/Griff (Ind.)	3.0	+0.4	0.21	0	–1
Legalise Cannabis Australia	2.3	+0.2	0.16	0	0
Liberal Democrats	2.2	+1.5	0.15	0	0
Rex Patrick Team	2.1	+2.1	0.15	0	–1
Others	5.2	–2.4	0.37	0	0

Source: Aggregated from AEC (2022a).

The six-year terms allocated after the 2016 double dissolution were divided between two Liberal, two Labor and two for the Nick Xenophon Team. Xenophon departed for State politics in 2018 and support for the renamed Centre Alliance collapsed to 2.6 per cent in 2019. Both senators holding Xenophon-allocated seats from 2016 failed to win re-election. Stirling Griff was defeated after contesting the election on an Independent ticket headed by Xenophon, while Rex Patrick was defeated at the head of his own party.

Four senators were re-elected on filled quotas: Penny Wong and Don Farrell for Labor and Simon Birmingham and Andrew McLachlan for the Liberal Party. The two former Xenophon seats were won by the Greens' Barbara Pocock and Kerrynne Liddle for the Liberal Party. Liddle became the first Indigenous senator to be elected from South Australia.

After the first five seats were filled, Liddle held a 0.37 partial quota ahead of PHON's 0.28 and 0.26 for Labor's third candidate. When only three candidates remained, Liddle had reached 0.67 of a quota to PHON's 0.61 and 0.56 for Labor. The distribution of Labor's preferences split 33.6 per cent to Liberal and 13.1 per cent to PHON, with more than half of Labor's preferences exhausting. Liddle was elected to the final position with 0.87 of a quota to PHON on 0.67 with 0.46 of a quota of exhausted preferences.

Tasmania

Table 17.10 Senate results: Tasmania

Party	Percentage of vote	Change	Quotas	Elected	Change
Liberal Party of Australia	32.0	+0.6	2.24	2	–1
ALP	27.0	–3.6	1.89	2	0
The Greens	15.5	+2.9	1.08	1	0
Jacqui Lambie Network	8.6	–0.3	0.60	1	+1
PHON	3.9	+0.4	0.27	0	0
Legalise Cannabis Australia	3.0	+1.9	0.21	0	0
Liberal Democrats	1.9	+1.2	0.13	0	0
Others	8.0	–3.2	0.56	0	0

Source: Aggregated from AEC (2022a).

The Tasmanian Senate election saw both the Labor and the Liberal parties poll a record-low vote. In contrast, the Greens recorded its highest vote in more than a decade, and for the third election in a row, the Jacqui Lambie Network polled above 8 per cent.

Five sitting members were re-elected: Liberals Jonathan Duniam and Wendy Askew, Labor's Anne Urquhart and Helen Polley and the Greens' Peter Whish-Wilson. They were joined by Tammy Tyrrell of the Jacqui Lambie Network, who had worked on Senator Lambie's staff for several years.

The Liberals due for re-election in 2019 had been increased from two to three due to a quirk in the recount procedure used to fill two 2017 citizenship vacancies. Long-serving Liberal senator Eric Abetz was demoted to third on the Liberal ticket in preselection. Abetz campaigned for BTL votes but polled only 4.3 per cent of the vote and was unable to win re-election given the total Liberal vote was 2.24 quotas.

Australian Capital Territory

For the first time since Territory Senate representation was introduced in 1975, the Australian Capital Territory's representation did not split one Labor, one Liberal. Both major parties saw record-low votes and the Greens their lowest vote since 2001. Elected in place of Liberal senator Zed Seselja was Independent David Pocock, a former ACT Brumbies and Australian rugby union player but also a well-known environmental activist. Pocock registered a political party called 'David Pocock' to allow his name to appear above the line on the ballot paper.

Table 17.11 Senate results: Australian Capital Territory

Party	Percentage of vote	Change	Quotas	Elected	Change
ALP	33.4	–6.0	1.00	1	0
Liberal Party of Australia	24.8	–7.6	0.74	0	–1
David Pocock	21.2	+21.2	0.64	1	+1
The Greens	10.3	–7.4	0.31	0	0
Kim for Canberra	4.4	+4.4	0.13	0	0
UAP	2.1	–0.1	0.06	0	0
Others	3.8	–4.5	0.11	0	0

Source: Aggregated from AEC (2022a).

Labor's total vote was a fraction over a quota, but Katy Gallagher at the head of the ticket needed the distribution of BTL preferences to achieve a quota. From there, the battle for the second seat was a single-member race for preferences. Seselja led initially with 0.74 of a quota to 0.64 for Pocock.

Of all excluded candidates and groups, 64.6 per cent of preferences flowed to Pocock and 25.8 per cent to Seselja, with only 9.6 per cent exhausting. Pocock finished the count with 1.09 quotas, well ahead the 0.86 for Seselja.

Northern Territory

Table 17.12 Senate results: Northern Territory

Party	Percentage of vote	Change	Quotas	Elected	Change
ALP	33.0	–4.5	0.99	1	0
CLP	31.7	–5.0	0.95	1	0
The Greens	12.3	+2.0	0.37	0	0
Liberal Democrats	9.3	+9.3	0.28	0	0
Legalise Cannabis Australia	6.2	+2.4	0.19	0	0
Great Australian Party	4.4	+4.4	0.13	0	0
Others	3.2	–8.6	0.09	0	0

Source: Aggregated from AEC (2022a).

The Northern Territory produced its traditional Senate result, electing one Labor and one Country Liberal Party (CLP) senator. For the first time, neither party reached a quota on first preferences. The result was also historic in that both elected senators were Indigenous Australians. Labor's Malarndirri McCarthy was re-elected for a third term, joined by new CLP senator Jacinta Nampijinpa Price. The victory of Marion Scrymgour in the lower house seat of Lingiari meant that three of the four Territory members were Indigenous.

Price had defeated Senator Sam McMahon for CLP preselection and McMahon recontested for the Liberal Democrats, who finished fourth with 9.3 per cent.

Conclusion

The election of a new Labor Government and the victories for Teal Independents in traditional Liberal seats were the most notable features of the 2022 election. The enormous swing to Labor in Western Australia also had important consequences, delivering majority government in the House and an extra upper house seat that bequeathed the Albanese Government a more manageable Senate than Labor faced under Kevin Rudd in 2007.

A low first-preference vote did not prevent Labor winning a majority of seats in the House of Representatives, with the swing against the Coalition delivering Labor extra seats. In the Senate, the use of proportional representation translated the swing against the Coalition into an increased Senate crossbench—one that included more members willing to work with a Labor government.

A declining first-preference vote and the rise of the Greens raise questions for Labor's future. At the 24 State half-Senate contests over four elections since 2010, only two have seen Labor elect three senators. In the same period, the Coalition has elected three senators at 14 contests. Labor winning only two seats in each State at the past two elections (Western Australia in 2022 excepted) has allowed the Greens to win the traditional third 'left' seat in each State, lifting its representation to a record 12 seats. The seemingly permanent Greens Senate presence will force Labor to deal with the Greens on a more organised basis into the future.

The 2022 Senate election saw 23 per cent of the non-Greens 'Other' vote cast for a multiplicity of parties. PHON remains the nation's fourth party after Labor, the Coalition and the Greens, but can only be certain of winning seats in Queensland. As in the past, the party could struggle if Hanson retires from politics.

The election of House Independents has a corollary in the Senate with the continued success of eponymous parties. PHON, the Jacqui Lambie Network, the former Nick Xenophon Team, the David Pocock 'party' and even Clive Palmer's association with the UAP point to minor-party Senate success being built on support for individuals rather than more traditional party labels.

References

Australian Electoral Commission (AEC). 2016. *Tally Room: 2016 Federal Election*. Canberra: AEC. Available from: results.aec.gov.au/20499/website/SenateResults Menu-20499.htm.

Australian Electoral Commission (AEC). 2019a. 'Party representation'. *Tally Room: 2019 Federal Election*. [Updated 27 June]. Canberra: AEC. Available from: results.aec.gov.au/24310/Website/SenatePartyRepresentation-24310.htm.

Australian Electoral Commission (AEC). 2019b. *Tally Room: 2019 Federal Election*. Canberra: AEC. Available from: results.aec.gov.au/24310/Website/SenateResults Menu-24310.htm.

Australian Electoral Commission (AEC). 2022a. 'First preferences by Senate group'. *Tally Room: 2022 Federal Election*. Canberra: AEC. Available from: results.aec. gov.au/27966/Website/SenateStateFirstPrefsByGroup-27966-NAT.htm.

Australian Electoral Commission (AEC). 2022b. 'Party representation'. *Tally Room: 2022 Federal Election*. [Updated 1 July.] Canberra: AEC. Available from: results. aec.gov.au/27966/Website/SenatePartyRepresentation-27966.htm.

Australian Electoral Commission (AEC). 2022c. 'Notice of decision on party registration, deregistering a political party and removal from the Register of Political Parties: Liberal Democratic Party'. 19 July. *Party Registration*. Canberra: AEC. Available from: www.aec.gov.au/Parties_and_Representatives/Party_ Registration/Deregistered_parties/files/statement-of-reasons-liberal-democratic-party-s137-deregistration-statement-of-reasons.pdf.

Australian Electoral Commission (AEC). 2022d. *Deregistered Political Parties.* [Updated 26 October]. Canberra: AEC. Available from: www.aec.gov.au/Parties_ and_Representatives/Party_Registration/Deregistered_parties/index.htm.

Australian Electoral Commission (AEC). 2022e. *Tally Room: 2022 Federal Election.* Canberra: AEC. Available from: results.aec.gov.au/27966/Website/SenateResults Menu-27966.htm.

Barber, Stephen and Sue Johnson. 2014. *Federal election results 1901–2014.* Parliamentary Library Research Paper Series 2014–15. Canberra: Parliament of Australia.

Farrell, David M. and Ian McAllister. 2006. *The Australian Electoral System: Origins, Variations and Consequences.* Sydney: UNSW Press.

Green, Antony. 2015. 'Explaining the results'. In *Abbott's Gambit: The 2013 Australian Federal Election*, edited by Carol Johnson, John Wanna and Hsu-Ann Lee, 393–410. Canberra: ANU Press. doi.org/10.22459/AG.01.2015.23.

Green, Antony. 2018. 'The Senate results'. In *Double Disillusion: The 2016 Australian Federal Election*, edited by Anika Gauja, Peter Chen, Jennifer Curtin and Juliet Pietsch, 185–209. Canberra: ANU Press. doi.org/10.22459/DD.04.2018.08.

Green, Antony. 2020. 'The Senate result'. In *Morrison's Miracle: The 2019 Australian Federal Election*, edited by Anika Gauja, Marian Sawer and Marian Simms, 203–21. Canberra: ANU Press. doi.org/10.22459/MM.2020.10.

McAllister, Ian and Damon Muller. 2019. 'Electing the Australian Senate: Evaluating the 2016 reforms'. *Political Science* 70(2): 151–68. doi.org/10.1080/ 00323187.2018.1561153.

18

Seat-by-seat polling versus the pendulum

Murray Goot[1]

Single-seat polls in large numbers, sponsored by the press, have long been a feature of federal election campaigns. Three things were distinctive about the 2022 campaign. First, the almost total collapse of the press as a sponsor of such polls. Second, and largely as a consequence, was the very small number of single-seat polls that were conducted and released—mostly in marginals seats but also in seats, otherwise safe or very safe, under challenge from 'Teal' Independents. Third, was the publication of a poll that sought to predict the outcome not just in some seats but in every seat—a poll whose novel method might have changed election-watching in Australia had it lived up to its promise.

The principal point of conducting polls during the campaign was to track support for the parties and to predict which party (or parties) would form the next government, with every other consideration—even support for the party leaders—being entirely secondary. It is the prospect of a poll successfully predicting the outcome that attracts firms keen to piggy-back their commercial market research off the publicity generated by a successful prediction, that draws the media to commission polls or to report the

1   For their assistance, I thank The Australia Institute, GetUp!, Julian McCrann of Roy Morgan Research, Kos Samaras of RedBridge, James Stewart of uComms, Shaun Ratcliff and Campbell White of YouGov, Chris Williams and Malcolm Mackerras. I am grateful to Rod Tiffen for his comments on an earlier draft and to Ian Watson and the editors.

polls produced by others and that excites readers, listeners and viewers; the 'horserace' element in polls attracts audiences in ways that other elements rarely match.

Polls are usually judged to have worked if they 'pick the winner'. Overwhelmingly, the focus of these assessments is on national polls. In the postwar years, when roughly 90 per cent of the vote was won by parties of government—Labor, Liberal and Country/Nationals—the focus was on the polls' estimates of the government's and Opposition's first-preference votes. In the 1950s and 1960s, the Gallup Poll (the only national poll until the 1970s) adjusted its predictions to consider the preferences of those who voted for the Democratic Labor Party. From 1972, these adjustments were formalised: the two-party-preferred vote was the vote won by Labor and the Coalition after the preferences of other parties and Independents had been distributed, at least notionally, to one side or the other.

To predict the number of seats a party will win, there must be a mechanism to translate the national vote into seats—ideally, a mechanism that also indicates whether one side's share of the vote is sufficient for it to command the majority of seats. Since 1972, that mechanism has been the electoral pendulum. Pioneered in the United Kingdom and adapted by Malcolm Mackerras, the pendulum lists the seats held by the two sides in order of their two-party margins, starting with those held by the smallest margins and finishing with the seats held by the largest margins. Since 1993—the election when all the national polls first estimated a two-party vote—it has been possible to take the polls' figures and derive an estimate of Labor's and the Liberal–National Coalition's share of the seats and to see whether the side with the highest two-party vote is likely to win.

As a guide to the outcome, the national two-party vote has worked well—better, probably, than most reporters, politicians or other students of electoral behaviour realise (Goot 2022). In 2022, it worked well again, even though the Coalition lost no fewer than eight seats—an unprecedented number—not to Labor but to the Greens and Independents. Labor's 52.1 per cent share of the two-party vote—a gain of 3.6 percentage points on its 2019 share—should have netted it an extra seven seats. In the event, Labor increased its seat share by eight—the pendulum underperforming, as it were, by just one.

The pendulum was not designed on the assumption that elections produce *uniform* swings from Labor to the Coalition or from the Coalition to Labor (Mackerras 1972: 5). It was designed with an eye on the *national* swing from one side to the other. Whether the national swing was distributed evenly across electorates was not meant to matter; the swings and roundabouts were assumed to cancel out.

But if the pendulum encourages the belief that the national swing determines the outcome, it also encourages the belief that the outcome can be determined by the success candidates enjoy from more targeted campaigns. This is the paradox of the pendulum (Goot 2018b: 127). Success in certain seats raises the possibility of one side gaining more seats than the pendulum predicts (beating the pendulum, as it were) or losing fewer seats than it predicts (thereby thwarting the pendulum).

Given the predictive power of the pendulum, polls that report the results for seats are not the main game; in the election prediction business, they never have been. The existence of single-seat polls is testimony to the fact that the main game is not the only game; that even if the pendulum works perfectly, it is not designed to predict exactly which seats will change hands and which will not; that the pendulum may not work perfectly—1998 being the outstanding example of this (Goot 2018a); and that some seats may be in play not because they are at risk of falling to Labor or the Coalition but because they could fall to another party or to an Independent—a prospect never more in play, since the war, than in the 2022 election.

The polls in select seats

The six-week campaign, from 11 April to 21 May, saw only 23 single-seat polls flagged on pollsters' websites or published by the press. Most of these polls were commissioned by citizens groups (Climate 200, Get Up! and the Tamar Action Group), think tanks (The Australia Institute) or industry lobbies (Australian Forest Products, South Australian Forest Products). Only five were conducted on behalf of a news organisation (Seven West Media).

Who were the preferred pollsters and how long were they in the field? The interest groups used uComms or RedBridge; Seven West Media used Utting Research. The polls uComm conducted were completed in a single night—'quickies', the British call them. Utting polled over two nights. RedBridge was in the field for much longer. No pollster undertook single-seat polling off their own bat.

Though single-seat polls were conducted for interest groups well ahead of the formal campaign—most notably, by uComms—the campaign itself saw almost no single-seat polls until after the declaration of nominations on 22 April. Pollsters prefer not to run 'generic' polls in individual seats—polls that offer party names or the word 'Independent' in the response options, but not the names of the candidates. They have learnt, usually from work with political parties, that respondents sometimes make different choices when the poll names the candidates. This is especially relevant in seats that attract Independents. Once it was clear who was standing in each seat, single-seat polling gained in terms of validity (what was being measured) even if it did not in terms of reliability (how well it was being measured).

Single-seat polls were conducted, entirely or almost entirely, using interactive voice recognition (IVR) or robopolls; to what was otherwise a robopoll, RedBridge added a relatively small number of computer-assisted telephone interviews. Robopolls are one of the least expensive polling modes. In Australia, their record is comparable with that of other modes (Goot 2014). An alternative in terms of cost would have been to use online panels, but for technical reasons—mostly to do with problems of coverage in certain electorates and demographic skew—single-seat pollsters did not use online panels.

Not all of those who conducted the polls were members of the Australian Polling Council (APC), the industry body established in the wake of the 2019 polling debacle. Both uComms and RedBridge were members; Utting was not. Where members use its 'quality mark', the APC (2022) insists they publish their questionnaires, but where their poll is not to be published, the quality mark need not be used and the questionnaires need not be published. In these circumstances, the only way of uncovering the questions is by feedback from respondents or a leak. Early in the campaign, the APC fielded a complaint from the CT Group (strategists for the Liberal Party) about a poll conducted in Goldstein. The complaint alleged that RedBridge was 'push-polling' (for one discussion of the concept, see Williams 1996–97). RedBridge insisted that the complaint was based on a phone recording that had been edited; it threatened legal action if the complainant persisted (Pers. Comm.). The complaint was dismissed (Koziol 2022).

Where the quality mark is used, the APC requires members to publish details of survey size, mode, target population and the questionnaire. Unlike its UK counterpart, which insists that the computer tables be put on the pollster's website within two working days of the results being published

(BPC 2022), the APC does not insist that the findings from a poll intended for 'the public domain' be published at all. How the questionnaire alone provides an 'adequate basis' on which to judge 'the reliability and validity of results' that are published is not something the APC explains (APC 2022).

Polls commissioned by various interest groups during the campaign were usually not published, even if some version of the results did find their way into the media. Of The Australia Institute's three polls, only one was published. Of the polls Climate 200 commissioned—a number known only to Climate 200—it allowed RedBridge to publish three. (GetUp! published none of its results but made them available to the author.)

The media's—overwhelmingly, the print media's—very limited involvement in commissioning polls contrasts with its much wider involvement in earlier elections. In 2019, the media commissioned 43 single-seat polls (Goot 2020: 151); in 2016, it was 66 (Goot 2018b: 117); in 2013, 83 (Goot 2015: 133). If the reluctance of the press to commission single-seat polls reflects the growing cost pressures facing 'legacy' media, and perhaps an increasing tendency to rely on private polling leaked by the parties, it also reflects a growing view among journalists and media executives that single-seat polling is unreliable. In 2013, roughly 20 per cent of the polls picked the wrong winner (Goot 2015: 134); in 2016, about 40 per cent did so (Goot 2018b: 119); and in 2019, a substantial proportion did so again (Goot 2020: 160–61).

Not until the publication of a YouGov poll nine days out from the election, with its estimates of the two-party vote in each of the 151 seats, could journalists turn to a media-generated poll that purported to measure the vote in even one of the 151 seats.

Classic contests

Traditionally, single-seat polling has focused on marginal seats held by Labor or the Coalition. Marginals are seats defined by the AEC that would fall on a two-party (or two-candidate) swing of less than 6 percentage points; both the category and the cut-off are derived from Mackerras (1969: 29–30; 1972: 5). The AEC (2022a) describes contests where the final two candidates in the ballot are likely to come from Labor and the Coalition as 'classic contests'.

Table 18.1 Labor versus Liberal–Nationals (classic contests), robopolled during the election campaign

Electorate	Fieldwork	State	Pre-2022 ALP	Pre-2022 Lib–Nats	Poll ALP	Poll Lib–Nats	Actual ALP	Actual Lib–Nats	Error ALP	Error Lib–Nats	Sponsor	No.	Pollster
Lyons	12 April	Tas.	5.2		n.a.		0.9		n.a.		Aust. Forest Products	814	uComms
Higgins	2 May	Vic.		3.7	4		2.1		–1.9		The Australia Institute	836	uComms
Boothby	2 May	SA		1.4*		n.a.	3.3		n.a.		SA Forest Products	1,018	uComms
Bass	5 May	Tas.		0.4		n.a.		1.4		n.a.	Tamar Action Group	600	uComms
Eden-Monaro	12 May	NSW	0.8			1	8.2		+9.2		Get Up!	833	uComms
Macquarie	12 May	NSW	0.2		6		7.8		+1.8		Get Up!	818	uComms
Gilmore	12 May	NSW	2.6		7		0.2		–6.8		Get Up!	828	uComms
Page	12 May	NSW		9.4		2		10.7	–8.7		Get Up!	847	uComms
Ryan#	12 May	Qld		6.0	5			–2.6		+2.4	Get Up!	812	uComms
Hasluck	12–13 May	WA		5.9		5	6.0		+11.0		Sunday Times	400	Utting
Pearce	12–13 May	WA		5.2*	2			9.0	+7.0		Sunday Times	400	Utting
Swan	12–13 May	WA		3.2*	3		8.8		+5.8		Sunday Times	400	Utting
Tangney	12–13 May	WA		9.5		4	2.4		+6.4		Sunday Times	400	Utting
Mean/median									6.5/+5.8				
Std dev.									6.63				

* New candidate
# Won by the Greens
n.a. not available
+/–Better/worse than poll predicted
2PP = two-party-preferred
Note: Seats in bold changed hands.
Sources: Green (2021) for the 2PP margins; AEC (2019) for regions; AEC (2022b) for classification; uComms (2021); Scarr and Zimmerman (2022) for Utting.

In 2022, there were classic contests in 124 seats, including 45 marginals. In 13 of these seats, 10 of which were marginals—the sort of seats one would expect to attract most interest—there were polls. The three other seats were 'fairly safe': Page, Ryan and Tangney. Most of these polls were conducted closer to the end of the campaign than to the beginning (Table 18.1).

The accuracy of the polls for which we have results varied considerably; the standard deviation was 6.6 percentage points. Across the nine polls for which we have a two-party vote, the average error was 6.5 percentage points. Six polls underestimated the Labor vote and three overestimated it; the median result underestimated Labor's two-party vote by 5.8 points (Table 18.1).

Least accurate were the polls conducted by Utting in four Liberal Party seats in Western Australia—the State where the swing to Labor was easily the biggest. Each of these polls underestimated how well Labor would do; the average error was 7.6 percentage points. Smaller samples (n = 400) than those used by others could be part of the explanation. Utting's underestimates of Labor's two-party vote were considerable: between 5.8 and 11 percentage points. In two seats (Hasluck and Tangney), Utting had Labor behind in seats that it would go on to win comfortably.

The polling uComms did for GetUp! produced a lower average absolute error but appears to have been more erratic. Across five seats—a mixture of marginals and seats rated 'fairly safe'—four of them in New South Wales, uComms' average error was 5.8 points. Two of its polls underestimated Labor's vote; two overestimated it.

Non-classic contests

Single-seat polls were also used to predict the outcome of 'non-classic' contests—seats where only one of the two candidates in the final count was (or was likely to be) a Labor or Coalition candidate. These seats have always been difficult for a single pendulum to accommodate, though Mackerras insisted they could be. At the end of the count, 27 of the 151 contests were non-classic, including 16 in which one of the final two candidates was an Independent and nine in which one of the final two candidates represented the Greens or the Queensland Greens.

Which candidates—successful or unsuccessful—were Teals is not something that is universally agreed (contrast, for example, Wikipedia [2022b] with Hawley and Smiley [2022]; see also Chapter 14, this volume). Here, they are defined as the Independents who stood against sitting members and who appear to have been funded by Climate 200, a citizens' group-cum-industry lobby. Sitting members, even those funded by Climate 200, are excluded. Along with other MPs who were not Labor, Liberal or Nationals, sitting Independents are treated separately (see below).

Non-classic contests generated fewer polls—or fewer polls that sponsors were prepared to release—and in fewer seats. Three were commissioned by Climate 200 from RedBridge, three were commissioned by The Australia Institute from uComms, two by GetUp! from uComms and one by the Independent Sophie Scamps from Climate 200 from uComms (though attributed by her office to Climate 200). Goldstein attracted polling on behalf of Climate 200, The Australia Institute and Get Up!; North Sydney also stirred Climate 200 and Get Up!. One poll was commissioned by the *West Australian* from Utting (Table 18.2).

Four polls underestimated the Independents' vote, while three overestimated their vote. If the campaign favoured the Independents—if they became better known or if they benefited increasingly from being seen as a real chance—we would have expected their support to have been underestimated more often than overestimated. The least accurate polls—both conducted in Goldstein—overestimated support for the Independent; they pushed the mean error to 3.6 points and the standard deviation to 4.42. The other polls were remarkably good (Table 18.2).

Table 18.2 Liberal versus Independent (non-classic contests), robopolled during the election campaign

Electorate	State	Fieldwork	2CP margin					Sponsor	No.	Pollster
			Pre-2022		**Poll**	**Actual**	**Error**			
			Ind.	**Liberal**	**Ind.**	**Ind.**	**Ind.**			
Indi	Vic.	27 April	1.4		n.a.	8.9	n.a.	The Australia Institute	843	uComms
Warringah	NSW	27 April	7.2		n.a.	11.0	n.a.	The Australia Institute	845	uComms
Goldstein	Vic.	27 April		7.8	12	2.9	+9.1	The Australia Institute	855	uComms
	Vic.	11 May		7.8	9	2.9	+6.1	Get Up!	831	uComms
	Vic.	3–14 May		7.8	0.7#	2.9	−2.2	Climate 200	1,170*	RedBridge
Mackellar	NSW	4 May		13.2	10	12.5	−2.5	Sophie Scamps†	834	uComms
North Sydney	NSW	9 May		9.3	n.a.	2.9	n.a.	Get Up!	834	uComms
	NSW	3–14 May		9.3	0.5#	2.9	−2.4	Climate 200	1,267*	RedBridge
Wentworth	NSW	30 April–14 May		9.8	2.9#	5.2	−2.3	Climate 200	1,267*	RedBridge
Curtin	WA	16 May		13.9	2	1.3	+0.7	*West Australian*	514	Utting
Mean/median							3.6/−2.2			
Std dev.							4.42			

* RedBridge supplemented its IVR (robo) polls, conducted via landline and mobile phone, with about 10 per cent computer-aided telephone interviews.

\# Author's calculation

† Climate 200, according to Chris Williams of Scamps' office (Pers. comm., 3 August 2022).

2CP = two-candidate-preferred

n.a. not available

+/–Better/worse than poll predicted

Note: Seats in bold changed hands to an Independent.

Sources: Green (2021) for the 2CP margins; AEC (2022b) for classification; uComms (2021); RedBridge, 'Goldstein mixed-mode poll', 3–14 May 2022, available from: www.dropbox.com/s/i88aaz1o8ba1ra5/RedBridge%20Goldstein%20Mixed-mode%20Poll.pdf?dl=0; RedBridge, 'North Sydney mixed-mode poll', 3–14 May 2022, available from: www.dropbox.com/s/wg4a306zdhtzg3j/RedBridge%20North%20Sydney%20Mixed-mode%20Poll.pdf?dl=0; RedBridge, 'Wentworth mixed-mode poll', 30 April–14 May 2022, available from: www.dropbox.com/s/06fy6ibqkuw4il8/Wentworth%20Midxed-mode%20Poll.pdf?dl=0from; Chris Williams for Sophie Scamps; Scarr (2022) for Utting.

The MRP poll in every seat

Beyond the single-seat polls conducted in a limited number of seats was the single poll that sought to estimate vote shares in all 151 seats. Using multilevel regression with post-stratification (MRP), YouGov had developed an every-seat poll for the 2017 UK election. It rolled it out, again, for the 2019 UK election, and the main political parties experimented with this approach as well (for the Conservatives and the Liberal Democrats, see Fisher 2020: 203–4; for Labour, see Macqueen 2022: 43, 46, 48).

For Australia, the MRP was a first. Conducted during the first four weeks of the campaign and published 10 days out from the election, the poll was paid for by *The Australian* newspaper and organised for YouGov by Shaun Ratcliff, splitting his time between the University of Sydney and YouGov. (A similar exercise had been undertaken for YouGov in 2019 by Ratcliff, Luke Mansillo and Simon Jackman but not published.) In the United Kingdom in 2017, the MRP poll 'took the campaign by storm', with its figures updated daily in the eight days leading up to the election. By 2019, other pollsters had started to experiment with the technique (Ford et al. 2021: 279–80).

YouGov's Australian version used the weekly Newspoll data collected by YouGov for *The Australian* between 14 April (three days after the election had been called) and 7 May (a fortnight before election day), via online panels (n = 6,109), plus 12,823 additional interviews (how and when were undisclosed). This boosted the sample size to 18,032—a large number, though not the largest on record; in 2010, JWS polled 28,000 voters in the final week of the campaign (Goot 2012: 101). Though very large, a sample of 18,032 represented an average of just 119 respondents per seat. Supplementing the interviews were electorate-level data covering a range of variables: population density, proportion of population with university degrees and previous election results, among others (White and Ratcliff 2022).

Trying to predict the outcome of an election seat by seat was not without precedent. In 2013, the Morgan Research Centre had tried with a poll taken over three days in the final week of the campaign, using a mix of SMS, online and telephone interviewing (Roy Morgan 2013). While it drew on an unusually large national sample (n = 4,937), it relied on a comically small average sample per seat (n = 33) and lots of what might be described as judgement calls (Goot 2015: 135–36). A cheap stunt, it lacked YouGov's sample size, add-ons (the electorate-level variables) and sophisticated modelling.

YouGov boasted a methodology that provided 'a more robust answer' than other polls 'to the question of how the national vote figures translate to number[s] of seats the parties will win than anything commissioned by any media organisation in Australian political history' (White and Ratcliff 2022). Its model generated a national two-party estimate, but this was not what YouGov chose to publicise. The point of the model was to generate a set of predictions, seat by seat. If it worked, projecting an outcome from a national two-party vote would become redundant.

In the United Kingdom, YouGov's MRP had enjoyed mixed success. Using midpoint estimates of the parties' likely seat shares, and very wide confidence intervals, the 2017 poll correctly called 93 per cent of the seats, including seats few others had thought would change hands (Crowley and Kavanagh 2018: 267). In Australia, a similar success rate would have had it incorrectly calling 11 seats—not a performance it would have wanted to write home about. At the 2019 UK general election, the MRP called 18 of the 'Red Wall' seats picked up by the Conservatives from Labour but failed to call seven—a less than impressive success rate of 72 per cent (Ford et al. 2021: 280).

In Australia, YouGov's midpoint estimate (the 'most likely outcome') had Labor winning 80 seats and the Coalition 63. Like all the other national polls, the MRP picked Labor to win. However, like Ipsos, Roy Morgan and Newspoll (another YouGov poll), the MRP anticipated too comfortable a Labor win. The lower bound of its estimate predicted a 76–58 split—almost exactly the number of seats that Labor (77) and the Coalition (58) won; the upper bound was for an 85–68 split.

The MRP's national two-party estimate, says YouGov, was 52.2–47.8 (Pers. Comm.). Since these figures were unpublished at the time of the election, YouGov can make no claim to having the most accurate poll, nor attempt to burnish its image, as Resolve Strategic would seek to do with previously unpublished data (Reed 2022: 16). But, assuming for the sake of the argument that YouGov's figures were what YouGov says they were, the number of seats Labor would have won (76) had YouGov's figures been applied to the pendulum would have been closer to the number of seats Labor won than YouGov's estimate (80) on a seat-by-seat basis. In short, the pendulum—not the seat-by-seat prediction—would have produced the better estimate of the number of seats Labor would win, the clearest estimate of the number of seats the Coalition would win and the better estimate of Labor's majority.

Success, seat by seat

Another way of assessing the MRP's performance is to count the number of seats where it picked the wrong winner. There were nine winners it failed to pick even after allowing for the two seats (Sturt, retained by the Liberals; Ryan, won by the Greens) out of six (including Bennelong and Corangamite, won by Labor; Longman and Lindsay, won by the Coalition) that in print it rated 'too close to call' (seats it reported as 50–50, two-party preferred; The Australian 2022), but online labelled 'likely' to go to the Liberals or to Labor (Benson 2022). Nine misses were better than Roy Morgan managed in 2013, where it failed to pick the winner in 15 seats (Goot 2015: 135–36). It was also two less than the 11 misses one would have expected had the MRP poll been no more accurate than the 2017 UK original.

All YouGov's misses were in seats held by the Liberals or the Queensland LNP: four of them 'marginals', five 'fairly safe' and two 'safe'. In the marginals, the misses included Bass, a seat the Liberals were predicted to lose but held, and Hasluck, a seat the MRP poll expected the Liberals to hold but which they lost (Table 18.3). Among the 'fairly safe' seats, the Liberals held one (Sturt); the Liberals lost one (Ryan); and two that the MRP poll predicted the Liberals would hold (North Sydney and Wentworth) were lost to Teals (Table 18.4). The Liberals also lost two safe seats (Mackellar and Curtin) that the poll expected them to hold. One safe seat (Fowler) that the poll expected Labor to hold, it lost (Table 18.5), in one of the biggest swings against the tide in an Australian national election.

Table 18.3 The MRP poll in 'marginal' seats, by order of marginality, YouGov, 14 April – 7 May 2022

Electorate	State	Liberal–Nationals 2PP			
		Margin	Predicted	Actual	Error
Bass[#]	**Tas.**	0.4	**49**	**51.4**	**+2.1**
Chisholm	**Vic.**	0.5	**47**	**43.6**	**–3.4**
Boothby	**SA**	1.4	**47**	**46.7**	**–0.3**
Braddon	Tas.	3.1	52	58.0	+6.0
Reid	**NSW**	3.2	**44**	**44.8**	**+0.8**
Swan	**WA**	3.2	**43**	**41.2**	**–1.8**
Longman	Qld	3.3	50	53.1	+3.1
Higgins	**Vic.**	3.7	**47**	**47.9**	**+0.9**
Leichhardt	Qld	4.2	51	53.4	+2.4
Robertson	**NSW**	4.2	**49**	**47.7**	**–1.3**
Casey	Vic.	4.6	52	51.5	–0.5
Dickson	Qld	4.6	53	51.7	–1.3
Deakin	Vic.	4.7	53	50.2	–2.8
Brisbane	**Qld**	4.9	**46**	**46.3**	**+0.3**
Lindsay	NSW	5.0	50	56.3	+6.3
Pearce	**WA**	5.2	**48**	**41.0**	**–7.0**
La Trobe	Vic.	5.5	53	58.7	+5.7
Flinders	Vic.	5.6	52	56.7	+4.7
Hasluck	**WA**	5.9	**52**	**44.0**	**–8.0**
Mean/median					3.1/0.3
Std dev.					3.90

Electorate	State	Labor 2PP			
		Margin	Predicted	Actual	Error
Macquarie	NSW	0.2	53	57.8	+4.8
Lilley	Qld	0.6	54	60.5	+6.5
Eden-Monaro	NSW	0.8	57	58.2	+1.2
Cowan	WA	0.9	59	60.8	+1.8
Corangamite	Vic.	1.0	50	57.6	+7.6
Blair	Qld	1.2	54	55.2	+1.2
Dobell	NSW	1.5	54	56.5	+2.5
Moreton	Qld	1.9	56	59.1	+3.1
Gilmore	NSW	2.6	53	50.2	–2.8

Electorate	State	Labor 2PP			
		Margin	Predicted	Actual	Error
Dunkley	Vic.	2.7	54	56.3	+2.3
Greenway	NSW	2.8	53	61.5	+8.5
Griffith	Qld	2.9	60	39.5	−20.5
Hunter	NSW	3.0	60	54.0	−6.0
Solomon	NT	3.1	56	59.4	+3.4
Perth	WA	3.2	63	64.8	+1.8
Parramatta	NSW	3.5	57	54.6	−2.4
Richmond	NSW	4.1	59	58.2	−0.8
Shortland	NSW	4.4	60	55.8	−4.2
Paterson	NSW	5.0	58	53.3	−4.7
Lyons	Tas.	5.2	54	50.9	−3.1
McEwen	Vic.	5.3	55	53.3	−1.7
Lingiari	NT	5.5	57	50.9	−6.1
Werriwa	NSW	5.5	53	55.8	+2.8
Burt	WA	5.5	62	65.2	+3.2
Jagajaga	Vic.	5.9	57	62.3	+5.3
Mean/median					4.3/1.8
Std dev.					5.81

Did not change

2PP = two-party-preferred

Notes: 'Marginal' seats are those requiring a 2PP swing of less than 6 percentage points to change from Liberal to Labor or from Labor to the Coalition; seats in bold predicted to change hands; omitting −20.5 (Griffith), SD = 4.08, absolute mean = 3.66, median = 1.8.

Sources: Green (2021) for the 2PP margins; AEC (2019) for regions, AEC (2022b) for classification; The Australian (2022) for the MRP poll.

Table 18.4 The MRP poll in 'fairly safe' seats, by order of marginality, YouGov, 14 April – 7 May 2022

Electorate	State	Liberal–Nationals 2PP			
		Margin	Predicted	Actual	Error
Ryan*	**Qld**	6.0	**50**	47.4	**−2.6**
Banks	NSW	6.3	52	53.2	+1.2
Kooyong	**Vic.**	6.4	**47**	47.1	**+0.1**
Monash	Vic	6.9	55	52.9	−2.1
Sturt*	SA	6.9	50	50.5	+0.5
Bennelong	**NSW**	6.9	**50**	49.0	**−1.0**

Electorate	State	Liberal–Nationals 2PP			
		Margin	Predicted	Actual	Error
Menzies	Vic.	7.0	56	50.7	–5.3
Bonner	Qld	7.4	54	53.4	–0.6
Goldstein	**Vic.**	**7.8**	**48**	**47.1**	**–0.9**
Herbert	Qld	8.4	56	61.8	+5.8
Petrie	Qld	8.4	56	54.4	–1.6
Forde	Qld	8.6	55	54.2	–0.8
Flynn	Qld	8.7	54	53.8	–0.2
North Sydney	**NSW**	**9.3**	**53**	**47.1**	**–5.9**
Page	NSW	9.4	52	61.7	+9.7
Tangney	**WA**	**9.5**	**55**	**47.6**	**–7.4**
Hughes	NSW	9.8	56	57.0	+1.0
Wentworth	**NSW**	**9.8**	**56**	**45.8**	**–9.2**
Mean/median					3.1/–0.9
Std dev.					4.27

Electorate	State	Labor 2PP			
		Margin	Predicted	Actual	Error
Macnamara	Vic.	6.1	59	57.8	–1.2
Oxley	Qld	6.4	58	61.6	+3.6
Isaacs	Vic.	6.4	54	56.9	+2.9
Rankin	Qld	6.4	58	59.1	+1.1
Hindmarsh	SA	6.5	58	58.9	+0.9
McMahon	NSW	6.6	56	59.5	+3.5
Brand	WA	6.7	60	66.7	+6.7
Fremantle	WA	6.9	59	66.9	+7.9
Bruce	Vic.	7.3	58	56.6	–1.4
Bean	ACT	7.5	63	62.9	–0.1
Adelaide	SA	8.2	60	61.9	+1.9
Wills	Vic.	8.2	58	59.8	+1.8
Macarthur	NSW	8.4	62	58.5	–3.5
Kingsford Smith	NSW	8.8	59	64.5	+5.5
Bendigo	Vic.	8.0	60	62.1	+2.1
Holt	Vic.	8.9	57	57.1	+0.1
Barton	NSW	9.4	59	65.5	+6.5
Makin	SA	9.7	61	60.8	–0.2

Electorate	State	Labor 2PP			
		Margin	Predicted	Actual	Error
Mean/median					2.1/1.9
Std dev.					3.08

* 'too close to call'

2PP = two-party-preferred

Notes: 'Fairly safe' seats are those requiring a 2PP swing of between 6.0 and 9.9 percentage points to change from Liberal to Labor or from Labor to the Coalition; seats in bold predicted to change from Liberal to Independent.

Sources: Green (2021) for the 2PP margins; AEC (2019) AEC (2022b) for classification; The Australian (2022) for the MRP poll.

Table 18.5 The MRP poll in 'safe' seats, by order of marginality, YouGov, 14 April – 7 May 2022

Electorate	State	Liberal–Nationals 2PP			
		Margin	Predicted	Actual	Error
Aston	Vic.	10.1	60	52.8	–7.2
Wannon	Vic.	10.2	58	53.9	–4.1
Bowman	Qld	10.2	55	55.5	+0.5
Canning	WA	1.6	53	53.6	+0.6
Moore	WA	11.6	55	50.7	–4.3
Cowper	NSW	11.9	68	52.3	–15.7
McPherson	Qld	12.2	56	59.3	+3.3
Capricornia	Qld	12.4	59	56.6	–2.4
Fisher	Qld	12.7	55	58.7	+3.7
Hume	NSW	13.0	59	57.7	–1.3
Wide Bay	Qld	13.1	59	61.3	+2.3
Mackellar	**NSW**	13.2	**53**	**47.5**	**–5.5**
Calare	NSW	13.3	60	59.7	–0.3
Grey	SA	13.3	57	60.1	+4.1
Fairfax	Qld	13.4	58	59.0	+1.0
Durack	WA	13.5	61	54.3	–6.7
Curtin	**WA**	13.9	**56**	**48.7**	**–7.7**
Fadden	Qld	14.2	61	60.5	–0.5
Hinkler	Qld	14.5	60	60.1	+0.1
Forrest	WA	14.6	60	54.3	–5.7
Wright	Qld	14.6	56	60.9	+4.9
Dawson	Qld	14.6	56	60.4	+4.4

Electorate	State	Liberal–Nationals 2PP			
		Margin	Predicted	Actual	Error
Lyne	NSW	15.2	56	63.8	+7.8
Moncrief	Qld	15.4	64	61.2	–2.8
O'Connor	WA	15.4	61	57.0	–4.0
Berowra	NSW	15.6	58	59.8	+1.8
Mallee	Vic.	15.7	56	69.0	+13.0
Bradfield	NSW	16.6	58	54.2	–3.8
Gippsland	Vic.	16.7	61	70.6	+9.6
Parkes	NSW	16.9	54	67.8	+13.8
New England	NSW	17.6	68	66.4	–1.6
Mean/median					4.7/-0.3
Std dev.					6.11

Electorate	State	Labor 2PP			
		Margin	Predicted	Actual	Error
Hawke	Vic.	10.2	60	57.6	–2.4
Ballarat	Vic.	10.3	54	63.0	+9.0
Maribyrnong	Vic.	10.3	66	62.4	–3.6
Corio	Vic.	10.3	61	62.9	+1.0
Fenner	ACT	10.6	64	65.7	+1.7
Whitlam	NSW	10.9	64	60.1	–3.9
Hotham	Vic.	11.2	61	64.3	+3.3
Kingston	SA	11.9	64	66.4	+2.4
Franklin	Tas.	12.2	63	63.7	+0.7
Chifley	NSW	12.4	60	63.5	+3.5
Lalor	Vic.	12.4	60	62.8	+2.8
Gellibrand	Vic.	13.0	63	61.5	–1.5
Cunningham	NSW	13.4	63	64.5	+1.5
Watson	NSW	13.5	65	65.1	+0.1
Newcastle	NSW	13.8	67	68.0	+1.0
Fowler	**NSW**	14.0	**62**	**48.4**	**–13.6**
Spence	SA	14.1	62	62.9	+0.9
Gorton	Vic.	14.3	63	60.0	–3.0
Cooper	Vic.	14.6	66	58.7	–7.3
Blaxland	NSW	14.7	64	64.9	+0.9
Grayndler	NSW	16.3	69	67.1	–1.9

Electorate	State	Labor 2PP			
		Margin	Predicted	Actual	Error
Canberra	ACT	17.1	72	62.2	−9.8
Mean/median					3.4/0.9
Std dev.					4.74

2PP = two-party-preferred

Notes: 'Safe' seats are those requiring a 2PP swing of between 10.0 and 17.9 percentage points to change from Liberal to Labor or from Labor to the Coalition; seats in bold predicted to change from Liberal to Independent.

Sources: Green (2021) for the 2PP margins; AEC (2019) AEC (2022b) for classification; The Australian (2022) for the MRP poll.

Of the six seats the Liberals lost that the MRP poll did not see coming, four (Curtin, Mackellar, North Sydney and Wentworth) were lost to Teals, one (Hasluck) was lost to Labor and one (Ryan) went to the Greens. The Curtin result was predicted by a subsequent poll conducted by Utting (Scarr 2022), while the Hasluck result was not (Scarr and Zimmerman 2022). In Mackellar, North Sydney and Wentworth, uComms or RedBridge predicted the winners (Table 18.2). The MRP poll 'predicted only eight crossbenchers when there are now 16' (Reed 2022: 17).

Accuracy, seat by seat

Predicting who will win is one thing; producing figures that reflect the vote in each seat is another. How accurate were YouGov's figures? Not very. Across all four seat categories—'marginal', 'fairly safe', 'safe' and 'very safe'—the average errors were large and the spread of the errors (the standard deviation) broad. While some errors were modest, some were much larger.

Across the Coalition's marginal seats, the (absolute) mean error was 3.1 percentage points, with 3.90 as the standard deviation. In half these seats (nine), the MRP poll overestimated the Coalition's vote, while in half (10) it underestimated it. Across Labor's marginals, the mean error (4.3 points) was even bigger, as was the standard deviation (5.81). In 10 of these seats, the poll overestimated Labor's vote—in the case of Griffith, a three-cornered contest with the Liberals and the Greens, by 20.5 points; in the other 15, it underestimated it (Table 18.3).

In the Coalition's 'fairly safe' seats, the mean error, again, was 3.1 points, with 4.27 as the standard deviation. In more than half these seats (11), the poll overestimated the Coalition's vote and in half (seven) it underestimated it, with some overestimates (Wentworth, 9.2 points) or underestimates (Page, 9.7 points) approaching double figures. In Labor's 'fairly safe' seats, the mean error (2.1 points) was smaller, as was the standard deviation (3.1). In five of these seats, it overestimated Labor's vote; in the other 13, it underestimated it (Table 18.4).

Across the Coalition's 'safe' seats, the mean error blew out to 4.7 points with 6.11 as the standard deviation. In half these seats (16), the poll overestimated the Coalition's vote share and in half (15) it underestimated it, with some of its overestimates (Cowper, 15.7 points) or underestimates (Mallee, 13.0 points) well into double figures. Across Labor's 'safe' seats, the mean error (3.4 points) was again smaller, as was the standard deviation (4.74). In nine of these seats, the poll overestimated Labor's vote, but in the other 13, it underestimated it (Table 18.5). Again, some of the errors— a mix of overestimates and underestimates—nearly reached double figures (Ballarat, 9.0 points; Canberra, 9.8 points) or did reach double figures (Fowler, 13.6 points).

Finally, in the Coalition's 'very safe' seats, the mean error was 4.3 points with 4.89 as the standard deviation. In half these seats (four), the poll overestimated the Coalition's vote and in half (four), it underestimated it. Again, across Labor's safe seats, the mean error (2.7 points) was smaller, as was the standard deviation (2.05). In three seats, the poll overestimated Labor's vote; in the other one, it underestimated it (Table 18.6).

Table 18.6 The MRP poll in 'very safe' seats, by order of marginality, YouGov, 14 April – 7 May 2022

Electorate	State	Liberal–Nationals 2PP			
		Margin	Predicted	Actual	Error
Mitchell	NSW	18.6	59	60.7	+1.7
Barker	SA	18.9	62	66.6	+4.6
Cook	NSW	19.0	62	62.4	+0.4
Riverina	NSW	19.5	59	64.8	+5.8
Farrer	NSW	19.8	73	66.6	−6.4
Nicholls	Vic.	20.0	61	53.8	−7.2
Groom	Qld	20.5	64	56.9	−7.1
Maranoa	Qld	25.4	73	72.1	−0.9
Mean/median					4.3/−0.3
Std dev.					4.89

Electorate	State	Labor 2PP			
		Margin	Predicted	Actual	Error
Fraser	Vic.	18.1	65	66.5	+0.5
Sydney	NSW	18.7	72	66.7	–5.3
Calwell	Vic.	19.6	65	62.4	–2.6
Scullin	Vic.	21.7	68	65.6	–2.4
Mean/median					2.7/–4.0
Std dev.					2.05

2PP = two-party-preferred

Note: 'Very safe' seats are those requiring a 2PP swing of 18 percentage points or more to change from Liberal to Labor or from Labor to the Coalition.

Sources: Green (2021) for the 2PP margins; AEC (2019) AEC (2022b) for classification; The Australian (2022) for the MRP poll.

Altogether, as Table 18.7 shows, there were 82 Labor or Coalition seats in which the Coalition vote was overestimated and 63 seats in which it was underestimated. In Coalition seats, the number of overestimates of the Coalition's vote (40) was slightly greater than the number of underestimates (36). In Labor seats, however, the number of overestimates (42) of the Coalition's vote easily exceeded the number of underestimates (27).

Could the overestimates of the Coalition's vote be explained by the poll being conducted too early, missing a shift to Labor in the final two weeks of the campaign? This seems unlikely. During the campaign, the national polls showed a shift to the Coalition rather than to Labor. Had the poll suffered from being concluded too soon, there should have been more seats in which the Coalition's vote was underestimated, not overestimated—precisely the reverse of the YouGov poll.

But if the two-party vote shifted towards the Coalition during the campaign, the two-candidate-preferred did not necessarily shift against the Teals. In Coalition seats under challenge from Teals, the mean error was large (4.7 points), as was the standard deviation (5.7). In 12 of these seats, the poll overestimated the Coalition vote; in Wentworth (10.2 points), Page (12.7) and Cowper (15.7), the errors were in double digits. Only in four seats was the Coalition vote underestimated and in three of these, Teals were not really in the race (Table 18.7). Ignoring the six seats where the final contest was between Labor and Coalition candidates, there were nine seats in which the poll overestimated the Coalition vote and just one in which it underestimated it.

Table 18.7 Number of seats in which the Coalition's two-party vote was underestimated/overestimated by YouGov's MRP poll, by seat type

Seat type	Coalition seats		Labor seats		Combined	
	Underestimates	Overestimates	Underestimates	Overestimates	Underestimates	Overestimates
Marginal	10	9	10	15	20	24
Fairly safe	7	11	5	13	12	24
Safe	15	16	9	13	24	29
Very safe	4	4	3	1	7	5
Total	36	40	27	42	63	82

Table 18.8 Number of seats in which the Coalition's two-party vote was underestimated/overestimated by YouGov's MRP poll, before and after subtracting seats in which Teal candidates were in contention

Seat type	Coalition seats		Labor seats		Combined	
	Underestimates	Overestimates	Underestimates	Overestimates	Underestimates	Overestimates
Before	36	40	27	42	63	82
After	35	31	27	42	62	73

On this evidence, the campaign worked to the Teals' advantage. The tendency of the poll to overestimate the Coalition's vote, therefore, is partly explained by its overestimate of the Coalition's vote in seats where the threat came not from Labor but from an Independent—the Teals, in particular. Setting aside the 10 seats that came down to a battle between Coalition and Teal candidates, the number of Coalition seats in which the Coalition's vote was underestimated slips from 36 to 35 while the number in which its vote was overestimated drops markedly, from 40 to 31. This, as Table 18.8 shows, narrows the difference between the number of seats in which the Coalition's vote was overestimated and the number of seats which it was underestimated, from 19 to 11 (73–62).

Even less accurate than the poll's estimates in the Coalition's seats where Teals were challenging were the poll's estimates in the six seats held by Independents (Helen Haines, Zali Steggall, Andrew Wilkie), the Greens (Adam Bandt), the Katter Australian Party (Bob Katter) and the Centre Alliance (Rebekha Sharkie), as shown in Table 18.9. Across these seats, the mean error was 5.5 points with a standard deviation of 5.07. Except for Bandt, the vote for each of these members was greater than the poll estimated; in some cases—for example, Wilkie, whose vote was underestimated by 9.8 points, and Sharkie, by 10.3—much greater.

As with the Teals, the campaigns of candidates not endorsed by the parties of government seemed to have worked in their favour. Whether these members were defending seats they had held for one parliamentary term (Haines, Sharkie and Steggall), where the average error was 6.1 percentage points, or three terms (Bandt and Wilkie), where the average error was 6.8 points, seemed not to matter.

Table 18.9 The MRP poll's predictions and the vote in Coalition seats with Teal Independents

Electorate	State	Region	Candidates	2PP margin	Classification	Predicted 2PP/2CP			Actual 2PP/2CP			Error (Lib–Nats)
						Ind.	Lib–Nats	ALP	Ind.	Lib–Nats	ALP	
Bradfield	NSW	Inner metro	Fletcher (Lib.) v Boele	16.6	Safe		58	42	45.8	54.2		–3.8
Calare	NSW	Rural	Gee (Nats) v Hook	13.3	Safe		60	40	40.3	59.7		–0.3
Cowper	NSW	Provincial	Conaghan (Nats) v Heise	11.9	Safe		68	32	47.7	52.3		–15.7
Hughes#	NSW	Outer metro	Ware* (Lib.) v Steele	9.8	Fairly safe		56	44		57.0	43.0	+1.0
Mackellar	NSW	Outer metro	Falinski (Lib.) v Scamps	13.2	Safe		53	47	**52.5**	47.5		–5.5
North Sydney	NSW	Inner metro	Zimmerman (Lib.) v Tink	9.3	Fairly safe		53	47	**52.9**	47.1		–5.9
Page	NSW	Rural	Hogan (Nats) v Lake	9.4	Fairly safe		52	48		60.7	39.3	–12.7
Wentworth	NSW	Inner metro	Sharma (Lib.) v Spender	9.8	Fairly safe	44	56		**54.2**	45.8		–10.2
Casey	Vic.	Rural	Violi* (Lib.) v Miles	4.6	Marginal		52	48		51.5	48.5	–0.5
Flinders	Vic.	Rural	McKenzie* (Lib.) v O'Connor	5.6	Marginal		52	48		56.7	43.3	+4.7
Goldstein	Vic.	Inner metro	Wilson (Lib.) v Daniel	7.8	Fairly safe	**52**	48		**52.9**	47.1		–0.9
Kooyong	Vic.	Inner metro	Frydenberg (Lib.) v Ryan	6.4	Fairly safe	**53**	47		**52.9**	47.1		+0.1
Wannon	Vic.	Rural	Tehan (Lib.) v Dyson	10.2	Safe		58	42	46.1	53.9		–4.1

Electorate	State	Region	Candidates	2PP margin	Classification	Predicted 2PP/2CP			Actual 2PP/2CP			Error (Lib–Nats)
						Ind.	Lib–Nats	ALP	Ind.	Lib–Nats	ALP	
Boothby	SA	Outer metro	Swift* (Lib.) v Dyer	1.4	Marginal		47	**53**		46.7	**53.3**	**–0.3**
Grey	SA	Rural	Ramsey (Lib.) v Habermann	13.3	Safe		57	43		60.1	39.9	+3.1
Curtin	WA	Inner metro	Hammond (Lib.) v Chaney	13.9	Safe		56	44	**51.3**	48.7		–7.3
Mean/median												4.7/ –2.4
Std dev.												5.67

Held by Craig Kelly (UAP), elected in 2019 as a Liberal; so, treated as Liberal.

* New candidate

2CP = two-candidate-preferred

2PP = two-party-preferred

Note: Seats in bold changed hands or were predicted to change hands.

Sources: Wikipedia (2022b) for the candidates; Green (2021) for the 2PP/2CP margins; AEC (2022a)AEC (2022b) for classification; The Australian (2022) for the MRP poll; AEC (2022c) for the election results.

Table 18.10 The MRP poll in seats not held by Labor or the Coalition, YouGov, 14 April – 7 May 2022

Electorate	State	Region	Candidates	2CP margin	Classification	Predicted 2CP			Actual 2CP			Error (Other)
						Other	Lib–Nats	ALP	Other	Lib–Nats	ALP	
Warringah	NSW	Inner metro	Steggall (Ind.) v Deves	7.2	Fairly safe	59	41		61	39		2
Indi	Vic.	Rural	Haines (Ind.) v Lyman	1.4	Marginal	53	47		58.9	40.9		5.9
Melbourne	Vic.	Inner metro	Bandt (Greens) v Paterson	21.8	Very safe	64		36	60.3		40.1	–3.7
Kennedy	Qld	Rural	Katter (KAP) v McDonald	13.3	Safe	62	38		63.1	36.9		1.1
Mayo	SA	Rural	Sharkie (CA) v Buck	5.1	Marginal	52	48		62.3	37.7		10.3
Clark	Tas.	Inner metro	Wilkie (Ind.) v Davis	22.1	Very safe	61		39	70.8		29.2	9.8
Mean/median												5.5/4.0
Std dev.												5.07

CA = Centre Alliance

2CP = two-candidate-preferred

Sources: Green (2021) for the 2PP/2CP margins; AEC (2019) for regions; AEC (2022b) for classification; The Australian (2022) for the MRP poll.

Conclusion

Because it reported a result for each of the 151 seats, the only single-seat poll that could have trumped the pendulum's estimate was YouGov's MRP poll. It did not. If Labor was going to win 53 per cent of the two-party vote—as the final polls from Ipsos, Roy Morgan and Newspoll suggested—according to the pendulum, it was likely to finish with 79 seats. For Labor to govern in its own right, this would have been three more seats than it needed. If Labor was going to win 51 per cent of the two-party vote—as the final polls from Essential and Resolve suggested—it was likely to finish with 72 seats. To form majority government, this would have been four fewer than Labor needed. Labor won 52.1 per cent of the two-party vote—roughly the midpoint of these two estimates. This should have given it an extra seven seats, taking its tally to 76—one less than it achieved. The MRP poll's estimate of 80—the midpoint in its range—overestimated Labor's majority by three seats.

What of its estimate of the votes? Promoting the merits of the MRP poll, YouGov emphasised the poll's large sample, its incorporation of other metrics and its use of an online panel rather than IVR (White and Ratcliff 2022). But the poll was hardly a poster child for MRP. Its mean errors were large—larger than those registered by RedBridge and not very different from those recorded by single-seat robopolls in 2013, 2016 or 2019 (Goot 2015: 133–35; 2018b: 120; 2020: 158). The standard deviations were also substantial, with large overestimates figuring alongside large underestimates. Whether the sample size was adequate, the electorate-level measures appropriate or online polling any better than robopolling (Goot 2014: 24 ff.; Mansillo and Jackman 2020: 145) is something YouGov needs to review.

In its call of the seats—something it might have done with more caution—YouGov overestimated Labor's position and underestimated the Coalition's. On this score, it could have been the victim of a late swing. But its overestimate—not underestimate—of the Coalition's vote, seat by seat, when the national polls during the campaign pointed to the Coalition's narrowing of the gap, makes 'late swing' a difficult line to run.

What might the single-seat polls tell us about the dynamics of the campaign that the national polling cannot? In Liberal seats under challenge from the Teals—notably, in New South Wales and Victoria—the MRP poll's overestimate of the Coalition vote suggests that the vote for the Independents grew in the campaign's closing stages. In Liberal seats under challenge from Labor in Western Australia, the Utting polls' overestimate of the Coalition vote suggests that the vote for Labor also grew in the campaign's closing stages.

Polls in select seats, though becoming less common, are likely to stay; if the media does not stump up to fund them, others will. Seat-by-seat polling, nationwide, is also likely to stay—provided there are newspapers prepared to pay for it. The emergence of the Teals, the success of the Greens and a sense that the old party system is morphing into something more complex should help see to that.

A growing sense that a single pendulum is an anachronism is a likely corollary of these developments. In the United Kingdom, in 2005, the BBC replaced its 'swingometer' with three swingometers—an acknowledgement that in some seats the Liberal Democrats were more important than Labour while in other seats the Liberal Democrats were more important than the Conservatives (Wikipedia 2022a). With 27 of the 151 contests in 2022 classified by the AEC as non-classic—no fewer than 14 involving Coalition candidates against Independents, six involving Labor candidates against Greens and three involving Coalition candidates against Greens—a similar development in Australia seems inevitable. Whether that makes the old Mackerras pendulum that treats all contests as essentially classic contests a less reliable guide to which side will form government, and with how many seats, remains to be seen.

References

Australian Electoral Commission (AEC). 2019. '2019 federal election results maps'. *Maps and Spatial Data*. Canberra: AEC. Available from: www.aec.gov.au/electorates/maps.htm.

Australian Electoral Commission (AEC). 2022a. 'Electorate profiles, 2022 federal election'. *Federal Elections*. Canberra: AEC. Available from: www.aec.gov.au/Elections/federal_elections/2022/profiles/index.htm.

Australian Electoral Commission (AEC). 2022b. *Glossary*. Canberra: AEC. Available from: www.aec.gov.au/footer/glossary.htm.

Australian Electoral Commission (AEC). 2022c. 'House of Representatives: Divisional results'. *Tally Room*. Canberra: AEC. Available from: results.aec.gov.au/27966/Website/HouseDivisionalResults-27966.htm.

Australian Electoral Commission (AEC). 2022d. 'House of Representatives: Non-classic divisions'. *Tally Room*. Canberra: AEC. Available from: results.aec.gov.au/27966/Website/HouseNonClassicDivisions-27966.htm.

Australian Polling Council (APC). 2022. *Code of Conduct*. [Online.] APC. Available from: www.australianpollingcouncil.com/code-of-conduct .

The Australian. 2022. 'National seat-by-seat poll'. *The Australian*, 12 May. Available from: www.theaustralian.com.au/federal-election-2022/results.

Benson, Simon. 2022. 'Labor to win modest majority with 80 seats, YouGov poll predicts'. *The Australian*, 11 May. Available from: www.theaustralian.com.au/nation/federal-election-2022-labor-to-win-modest-majority-with-80-seats-yougov-poll-predicts/news-story/84c4634d4fd3671e5194a2c5739b3e2c.

British Polling Council (BPC). 2022. *Objects and Rules*. [Online.] BPC. Available from: www.britishpollingcouncil.org/objects-and-rules/.

Crowley, Philip and Dennis Kavanagh. 2018. *The British General Election of 2017*. Cham, Switzerland: Palgrave Macmillan.

Fisher, Justin. 2020. 'Party finance in 2019'. In *Britain Votes: The 2019 General Election*, edited by Jonathan Tonge, Stuart Wilks-Heeg and Louise Thompson, 189–207. Oxford, UK: Oxford University Press.

Ford, Robert, Tim Bale, Will Jennings and Paula Surridge. 2021. *The British General Election of 2019*. Cham, Switzerland: Palgrave Macmillan. doi.org/10.1007/978-3-030-74254-6.

Goot, Murray. 2012. 'To the second decimal point: How the polls vied to predict the national vote, monitor the marginals and second-guess the Senate'. In *Julia 2010: The Caretaker Election*, edited by Marian Simms and John Wanna, 85–110. Canberra: ANU Press. doi.org/10.22459/J2010.02.2012.06.

Goot, Murray. 2014. 'The rise of the robo: Media polls in a digital age'. In *Australian Scholarly Publishing's Essays 2014: Politics*, 18–32. Melbourne: Australian Scholarly Publishing.

Goot, Murray. 2015. 'How the pollsters called the horse-race: Changing polling technologies, cost pressures, and the concentration on the two-party preferred'. In *Abbott's Gambit: The 2013 Election*, edited by Carol Johnson and John Wanna, 123–41. Canberra: ANU Press. doi.org/10.22459/AG.01.2015.08.

Goot, Murray. 2018a. 'An extraordinary victory: Winning the election while losing the vote'. In *Back from the Brink: The Howard Government. Volume II: 1997–2001*, edited by Tom Frame, 1–26. Sydney: UNSW Press.

Goot, Murray. 2018b. 'National polls, marginal seats, and campaign effects'. In *Double Disillusion: The 2016 Federal Election*, edited by Anika Gauja, Peter Chen, Jennifer Curtin and Juliet Pietsch, 107–32. Canberra: ANU Press. doi.org/10.22459/DD.04.2018.05.

Goot, Murray. 2020. 'The perilous polling of single seats'. In *Morrison's Miracle: The 2019 Australian Federal Election*, edited by Marian Sawer, Marian Simms and Anika Gauja, 149–76. Canberra: ANU Press. doi.org/10.22459/MM.2020.08.

Goot, Murray. 2022. 'It's time to switch to the national vote'. *The Australian*, 21 April.

Green, Antony. 2021. '2022 federal electoral pendulum'. *Antony Green's Election Blog*, 2 August. Available from: antonygreen.com.au/2022-federal-electoral-pendulum/.

Hawley, Sam and Stephen Smiley. 2022. 'Who are the "teal" independents? Your questions answered about the candidates fighting for some of Australia's wealthiest electorates'. *ABC News Daily*, 20 April, [Updated 21 May]. Available from: www.abc.net.au/news/2022-04-20/teal-independents-who-are-candidates-what-electorates/101000412.

Koziol, Michael. 2022. 'Polling Council rejects Liberal complaint against Climate 200 polls'. *Sydney Morning Herald*, 21 April. Available from: www.smh.com.au/politics/federal/polling-council-rejects-liberal-complaint-against-climate-200-polls-20220413-p5ad82.html.

Mackerras, Malcolm. 1969. *The 1968 Federal Redistribution*. Canberra: Australian National University Press.

Mackerras, Malcolm. 1972. *Australian General Elections*. Sydney: Angus & Robertson.

Macqueen, Rory. 2022. 'No time for real change: Labour'. In *Political Communication in Britain: Campaigning, Media and Polling in the 2019 General Election*, edited by Dominic Wring, Roger Mortimore and Simon Atkinson, 41–52. Cham, Switzerland: Palgrave Macmillan. doi.org/10.1007/978-3-030-00822-2.

Mansillo, Luke and Simon Jackman. 2020. 'National polling and other disasters'. In *Morrison's Miracle: The 2019 Australian Federal Election*, edited by Anika Gauja, Marian Sawer and Marian Simms, 125–48. Canberra: ANU Press. doi.org/10.22459/MM.2020.07.

Reed, Jim. 2022. 'Are we asking the right questions?'. *Research News* 39(2)(August–October): 14–17.

Roy Morgan. 2013. 'L-NP set to win federal election and over 90 seats. High vote for Palmer Party (6.5% – 10.5% in Queensland), helps the L-NP vote'. Morgan Poll Article No. 5169. Melbourne: Roy Morgan.

Scarr, Lanai. 2022. 'It'll be a game Chaney'. *West Australian*, [Perth], 18 May.

Scarr, Lanai and Josh Zimmerman. 2022. 'Photo finish for key seats'. *Sunday Times*, [Perth], 15 May.

uComms. 2021. *uComms Australian Polling Council Info*. [Online.] Brisbane: uComms. Available from: ucommsapc.info/.

White, Campbell and Shaun Ratcliff. 2022. 'New way of polling offers answer to question of seats'. *The Australian*, 11 May.

Wikipedia. 2022a. 'Swingometer'. *Wikipedia*. Available from: en.wikipedia.org/wiki/Swingometer.

Wikipedia. 2022b. 'Teal independents'. *Wikipedia*. Available from: en.wikipedia.org/wiki/Teal_independents.

Williams, George. 1996–97. *Push Polling in Australia: Options for Regulation*. Parliamentary Library Research Note No. 36. Canberra: Parliament of Australia.

19

The rise and rise of early voting

Ferran Martinez i Coma and Rodney Smith

The 2022 federal election made history in several ways. Among them was the fact that for the first time a minority—just less than one-half—of Australian voters cast their ballots at a polling place on polling day. Record numbers and proportions of citizens voted before polling day—almost all either voting in person at early voting centres (5,541,757 voters, or 35.82 per cent) or voting by post (2,210,408 voters, or 14.30 per cent).[1]

As Figure 19.1 shows, the 2022 figures continued a trend since 2010 of declining polling-day voting and growing early voting. During this period, pre-poll voting rates registered an extraordinary fivefold rise. Increased postal voting contributed strongly to the growth in overall early voting from 2019 to 2022, ending a run of three elections (2013–19) in which rates of postal voting had been stable. While rates of postal voting in federal elections more than doubled after 2010, most of this increase took place between 2019 and 2022.

---

1 Most but not all postal votes would have been cast before polling day (see Note 2). Mobile voting and telephone voting services were also provided to small numbers of voters who were not able to vote on polling day, such as people living in remote communities, military personnel deployed overseas and people working in Antarctica (AEC 2021). These forms of voting will not be a focus in this chapter.

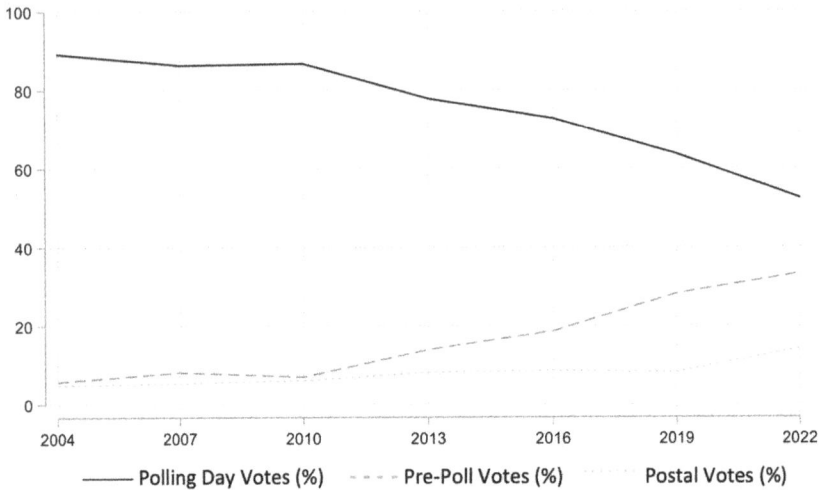

Figure 19.1 The evolution of polling-day and early voting (postal and pre-poll) in Australian federal elections, 2004–2022

PPVC = Pre-poll voting centre

Source: Developed by the authors from Australian Electoral Commission data.

These figures raise questions about how much of the rise in early voting to its 2022 record high was simply part of an ongoing trend and how much was the result of politicians, the AEC and voters themselves adapting voter behaviour to cope with the Covid-19 pandemic. They also raise questions about whether the record early vote affected the campaign and the outcome of the election. The rest of this chapter explores these questions. It traces the shift in early voting from minority necessity to widespread convenience; discusses the ways in which early voting in the 2022 federal election was primed by recent voter experiences at State and local elections; explores the spatial and temporal patterns of early voting in 2022; suggests that early voting was not a disadvantage for competitive minor parties and Independents; and concludes with some reflections on the extent to which early voting is erasing old 'rituals and rhythms' (Orr 2015) in federal elections and creating new ones.

From necessity to convenience: Early voting in federal elections

Australian federal elections allow two main types of early voting that can be initiated by electors: postal voting and in-person early voting, called 'pre-poll' voting. Postal and pre-poll voting were both originally legislated as contingency measures for what were expected to be relatively small numbers of voters who could not reasonably access the default option of voting at a polling place on election day. Schedule 2 of the *Commonwealth Electoral Act 1918* specifies the same eligibility criteria for pre-poll and postal voting, including distance from a polling place, travel, health issues, caring responsibilities, safety, imprisonment, religious restrictions and occupational obligations.

Postal voting in federal elections began in 1902 for eligible voters. Its provision was initially a source of conflict between the non-Labor parties (supportive) and Labor (opposed) but has been available at every federal election since 1918 (Aitkin and Morgan 1971). Voters typically have had a four–five-week period to apply for and return postal ballots.[2] Voters unable to attend polling places on an ongoing basis, due to circumstances such as their age or ill health, can apply to be placed on a 'general postal voter' list and automatically receive a postal ballot at every federal election (*Commonwealth Electoral Act 1918*, ss 184A–186).

Pre-poll voting was introduced for federal elections only in 1990. As early as the 1998 federal election, suspicions emerged that voters were increasingly casting pre-poll votes 'as a matter of convenience rather than for the grounds specified' in the Act (Newman 2004: 9). Until 2010, voters who attended an early voting centre to cast a pre-poll vote had to complete the same declarations as postal voters and place their votes within envelopes for later verification and processing. From 2010, this requirement ceased for voters who cast a pre-poll vote within their electoral districts, making early voting much simpler.[3] This simplification coincided with the start of marked increases in pre-poll voting at each federal election, while the proportion of postal votes remained steady (see Figure 19.1).

2　Part XV of the *Commonwealth Electoral Act 1918* specifies that voters can apply for postal votes from the AEC between the issuing of writs for an election and up to three days before polling day. The AEC then provides eligible voters with ballot papers, along with declaration documentation and envelopes for returning their ballots. Voters have until the close of polling day to post their ballots in the mail or return them directly to electoral officials (see Orr 2019: 193–95).
3　Since 2010, only pre-poll voters voting outside their electoral district have been required to use declaration envelopes (*Commonwealth Electoral Act 1918*, Part XVA).

While pre-poll and postal voting remained measures necessary for some Australians to access the ballot, for increasing numbers of other Australians, voting early was seen as a convenient way of fitting a democratic obligation into a twenty-first-century lifestyle (Rojas and Muller 2014: 6; Maley 2018: 19; Sheppard and Beauregard 2018; Smith et al. 2018; Orr 2019: 195).

The context of early voting at the 2022 federal election

Without Covid-19, it is highly likely that early voting at the 2022 federal election would have been less widespread than it turned out to be. This is not just because without Covid-19 fewer electors would have had a reason to seek an early vote, but also because Covid-19 forced parliamentarians to reassess what they saw as the risks of early voting against the dangers of a business-as-usual election in a pandemic.

In its December 2020 review of the 2019 federal election, the Joint Standing Committee on Electoral Matters (JSCEM 2020: 2) highlighted the 'risk' that the take-up of early in-person voting 'was creating a "voting period" rather than a polling day'. The JSCEM expressed disquiet about the cost and safety of early voting centres, as well as the difficulties parties encountered finding volunteers to give out how-to-vote cards to voters over the three-week early voting period (JSCEM 2020: 3–4, 35). The committee also had more general normative concerns about early voting. The AEC's practice of allowing citizens to 'self-assess' their eligibility for an early vote drew suspicion that some voters were making 'disingenuous' eligibility claims (JSCEM 2020: 2–3). Committee chair Senator James McGrath asserted that 'voters who choose to vote early should be required to explain why they are unable to attend on [polling] day rather than it being a matter of convenience' (JSCEM 2020: iv). Echoing the critique of early voting found in some academic literature (for example, Thompson 2004; Orr 2015: 60), the JSCEM suggested that citizens who voted in person before polling day were doing so with 'incomplete information' about rival candidates and policies (JSCEM 2020: 3, 34). Interestingly, the committee raised no similar concerns about postal voting, perhaps because of its far longer history in Australia and more limited use in recent elections compared with pre-poll voting.

The committee proposed to address these concerns by reducing the early voting period from three to two weeks, repeating a recommendation it had made after the 2016 federal election (JSCEM 2020: 37; Mills 2019). To prevent citizens from deliberately subverting the eligibility requirements, the JSCEM (2020: 3, 37) recommended that the AEC ensure voters meet the legislative criteria and advertise these criteria.[4] In addition, to address the possibility that the increasingly large numbers of pre-poll and postal ballots would delay vote counts and therefore election results being known, the committee recommended allowing the AEC to check and count pre-poll and postal votes before the end of polling day (JSCEM 2020: 47).

By mid 2021, Covid-19 had considerably modified the JSCEM's view of early in-person voting. Reporting on 'the future conduct of elections operating during times of emergency situations', the committee surveyed the successful voting arrangements used in local, State and Territory elections throughout 2020 in response to the pandemic (JSCEM 2021: 5–21). It acknowledged 'the benefit of in person and postal pre-poll voting … during emergency situations' (JSCEM 2021: 27). Rather than demanding that the AEC enforce existing early voting eligibility criteria more rigorously, the JSCEM now proposed allowing the electoral commissioner to 'extend the reasons electors can vote by post or pre-poll' and to 'streamline application and/or declaration requirements for postal and pre-poll voting' during emergencies (JSCEM 2021: 35).

The government took up key elements from both JSCEM reports. In August 2021, it introduced the Electoral Legislation Amendment (Counting, Scrutiny and Operational Efficiencies) Bill 2021, the provisions of which included shortening the maximum pre-poll period to 12 days before polling day and allowing preliminary sorting but not counting of pre-poll ballot papers before voting had concluded on polling day. In October, the government introduced the Electoral Legislation Amendment (Contingency Measures) Bill 2021, which gave the electoral commissioner powers to, among other things, expand the early voting eligibility criteria in response to an emergency declaration. Both bills also made the procedures for completing a postal vote less onerous. The bills were passed with support from Labor and the Greens.

---

4   Neither Senator McGrath nor the committee specified the measures that would ensure such voter compliance. One measure would have been to return to the pre-2010 process of pre-poll voters having to complete a declaration. Given the growing demand for early voting and the range of eligibility criteria, it is difficult to imagine measures the AEC could have adopted that would have proven effective and efficient.

As indicated above, significant subnational elections were held between the 2019 and 2022 federal elections. Six of the eight States and Territories held general elections, while New South Wales and Victoria ran Statewide local council elections. Seven of these eight elections included pre-poll voting, with New South Wales also allowing voters to use remote electronic voting in local council elections for the first time. In Victoria, voting at all local council elections was by post (see Table 19.1).

Table 19.1 Rates of early voting between the 2019 and 2022 federal elections

Election	Pre-poll votes	Postal votes	Remote electronic voting	Total early votes	Total votes
NT, 22 August 2020	53.34% (56,460)	6.41% (6,790)	n.a.	60.04% (63,550)	105,853
ACT, 17 October 2020	69.91% (190,964)	6.28% (17,172)	n.a.	76.20% (208,136)	273,143
Vic. local councils,[a] 24 October 2020	n.a.	100.00% (3,473,718)	n.a.	100.00% (3,473,718)	3,473,718
Qld, 31 October 2020	43.13% (1,280,679)	23.82% (707,298)	n.a.	66.95% (1,987,977)	2,969,347
WA, 13 March 2021	39.87% (585,234)	14.75% (216,457)	n.a.	54.62% (801,691)	1,467,732
Tas., 1 May 2021	19.36% (69,644)	7.49% (26,942)	n.a.	26.84% (96,586)	359,805
NSW local councils,[b] 4 December 2021	25.5% (1,053,224)	5.15% (213,012)	16.87% (697,598)	47.48% (1,963,834)	4,136,254
SA, 19 March 2022	18.46% (208,136)	11.72%[c] (132,187)	n.a.	30.18% (340,323)	1,127,642
Total	**24.76% (3,444,341)**	**34.45% (4,793,576)**	**5.01% (697,598)**	**64.22% (8,935,515)**	**13,913,494**

[a] 76 local councils

[b] 119 fully or partly contested local council elections

[c] Estimated from postal vote applications, using the ratio of applications to postal votes at the 2018 election (ECSA 2019: 50).

Sources: NTEC (2021: 98); Elections ACT (2021: 7); VEC (2021: 48); ECQ (2021: 11); WAEC (2021: 8); TEC (2022: 26); NSW Electoral Commission (n.d.); Green (2022).

One result of these elections was that by the 2022 federal election, 8.9 million Australian voters had recent experience of casting an early vote in person, by mail or online. This represented almost two-thirds (64.22 per cent) of those who voted. Setting aside the all-postal Victorian local council elections still leaves a total of roughly 5.5 million of 10.4 million citizens (52.37 per cent) opting to vote early. Overall, postal voting was the most common form of early voting in these elections (34.45 per cent); however, once the Victorian results are removed, pre-poll voting was clearly the preferred early voting channel (24.76 per cent to postal voting's 12.64 per cent), with remote online voting also popular relative to postal voting in New South Wales (16.87 to 5.15 per cent).

These experiences undoubtedly primed many Australians to vote early at the 2022 federal election; however, different jurisdictions appear to have primed voters to varying extents. Among the jurisdictions offering voters a choice of voting channels, early voting rates ranged widely, from highs of 76.20 per cent (Australian Capital Territory), 66.95 per cent (Queensland) and 60.04 per cent (Northern Territory) to lows of 30.18 per cent (South Australia) and 26.84 per cent (Tasmania). These differences align with government signals regarding the availability and ease of early voting. Electoral commissioners and key ministers in the Australian Capital Territory and Queensland publicly repeated terms such as a 'mixed model' election, a 'voting period' and an 'election period rather than an election day', encouraging citizens to vote early (Brown 2020; Lynch 2020; McCutcheon 2020; Elections ACT 2021). The Northern Territory Electoral Commission (NTEC 2020: 4) recommended 'as many voters as possible opt to use early and postal voting services'.

By contrast, Tasmanian electoral commissioner Andrew Hawkey stressed measures for Covid-safe voting on polling day and presented early voting as a less-preferable fallback option: 'We want to find a way for everyone to be able to vote for this election, preferably on polling day' (Baker 2021). He later expressed surprise at the number of Tasmanians voting early (Inglis 2021). In South Australia, a preference for polling-day voting was less explicit; however, South Australia retained the requirement for voters to make a written declaration to cast a pre-poll vote, making it a more time-consuming and complex process than in other jurisdictions (Stewart-Rattray 2022). As will be shown, these contrasting approaches appear to have spilled over into different levels of early voting in different jurisdictions at the 2022 federal election.

Spatial variations in the 2022 early vote

The trend away from in-person polling-day voting to early voting has occurred across all House of Representatives electoral divisions. As Figure 19.2 shows, the maximum polling-day vote in any division in 2019 (82.3 per cent) sat just above the minimum polling-day vote in any division in 2004 (81.0 per cent). By 2022, the maximum polling-day vote was 66.2 per cent—below the minimum percentage recorded in any division for all federal elections before 2013.

Figure 19.2 also indicates that the ranges of pre-poll and postal voting across all electorates were very similar to one another in 2004 (ranging from 2.5 per cent to 12.2 per cent in the case of postal voting and 2.4 per cent to 15.4 per cent for pre-poll voting). Postal voting ranges remained close to their 2004 levels until the 2022 federal election, when the minimum postal vote in any division increased to 4.5 per cent and the maximum jumped more dramatically to 22.9 per cent. Both these increases were minor compared with those in pre-poll voting over the same period. The minimum pre-poll vote in any division more than doubled from 2016 to 2019 (3.9 to 9.9 per cent) and almost doubled again in 2022 (to 18.4 per cent). The maximum pre-poll vote in any division increased more steadily from 2010, reaching 49.9 per cent in 2019 and 49.2 per cent in 2022.

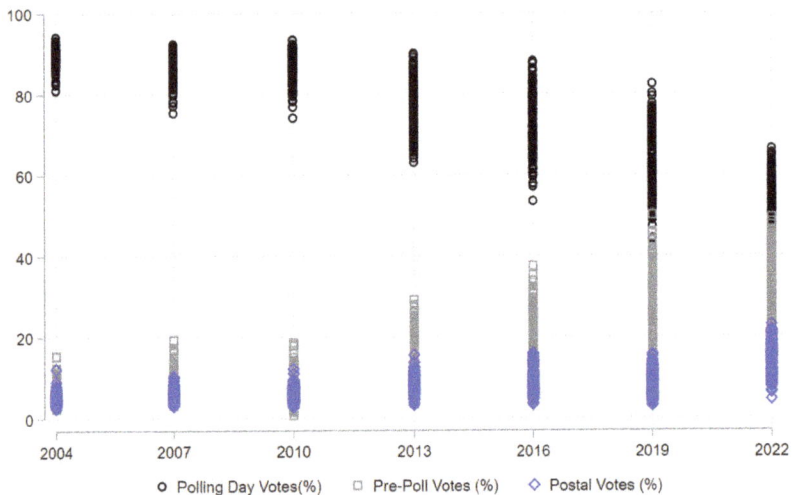

Figure 19.2 Evolution of polling-day, pre-poll and postal voting by division, 2004–2022

PPVC = Pre-poll voting centre

Source: Developed by the authors from Australian Electoral Commission data.

Looking at individual divisions within this pattern, it is striking that all five Tasmanian electorates are among the top eight overall for rates of polling-day voting (62.6 to 66.3 per cent). South Australian divisions are also overrepresented among the highest polling-day voting, with Adelaide, Spence and Grey all in the top eleven. The bottom six divisions for polling-day voting (ranging from 37.1 to 40.8 per cent) are all in Queensland (as are 11 of the bottom-22 divisions).

Perhaps not surprisingly, the Tasmanian divisions of Lyons, Franklin, Clark and Bass, along with South Australia's Adelaide and Spence, recorded the lowest levels of in-person early voting. Solomon registered the highest pre-poll vote (49.3 per cent), with the electorates of Hinkler, Fairfax and Fisher (all in Queensland), Gippsland (Victoria) and Gilmore (NSW) all registering more than 45 per cent. In 15 divisions (six in Queensland, five in Victoria, three in New South Wales and one in the Northern Territory), pre-poll voting surpassed polling-day voting—most strikingly, in the Queensland electorate of Hinkler, where the margin was 11.1 per cent.

Regarding postal voting, two of the electoral divisions that relied on it the least in 2022 were the Northern Territory's electorates of Lingiari (4.4 per cent) and Solomon (6.4 per cent). Calare and Riverina, both in New South Wales, were the other two electorates to register postal voting rates under 7 per cent. NSW divisions were overrepresented among those least reliant on postal voting, with 22 of the lowest-30 divisions in that State. By contrast, 17 of the 30 divisions in which postal voting was highest were in Queensland, with the remaining 13 in Victoria. No divisions recorded a higher postal than pre-poll vote; the two divisions that came closest were both in Queensland (Moreton, 23.39 per cent pre-poll versus 22.9 per cent postal; and Brisbane, 22.7 per cent pre-poll versus 20.5 per cent postal).

The fact that some electoral districts record relatively high levels of some modes of voting and relatively low levels of others leads to the question of whether these modes are simply substitutes or whether they have their own dynamics. On the one hand, logically, they are substitutes, as Australia has compulsory voting; since citizens must vote, they must use one or another method to cast a vote. On the other hand, there are three options and it is logical to expect that different dynamics are at play in leading voters to choose one type over the other two. How the two early voting alternatives relate to the dominant and more traditional ordinary polling-day vote ought to be explored. We present such an exploration in Figure 19.3.

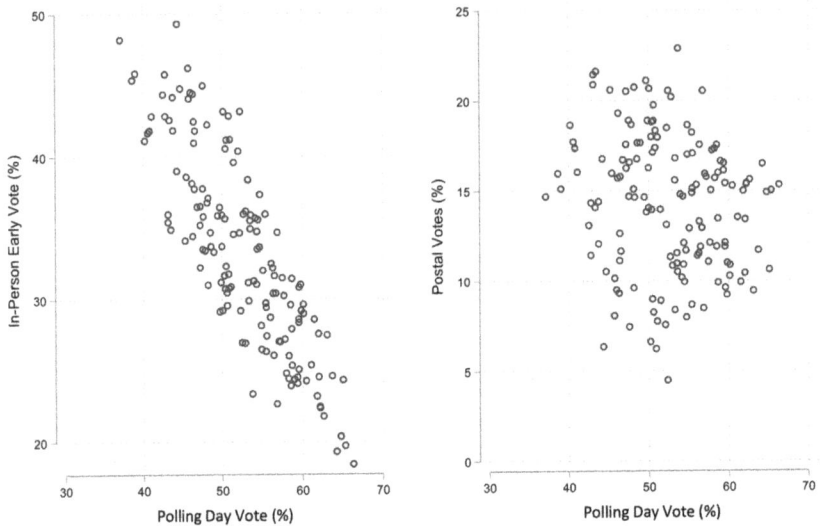

Figure 19.3 Relationships between polling-day voting and the two types of early voting

Source: Developed by the authors from Australian Electoral Commission data.

Figure 19.3 displays two very interesting and clear patterns. The first is that early voting does indeed serve as a substitute for polling-day voting: there is a clear negative relationship between the two and as one increases the other declines and vice versa (r –0.835). The second is that there seems to be no clear relation between polling-day voting and postal voting (r –0.180). In short, while early in-person voting is a substitute for polling-day voting, it is not the case for postal voting. One plausible explanation for the difference is that postal voting still serves as the main backup voting option for Australians whose circumstances—illness, old age, etcetera—prevent them from voting in person, whether on polling day or before. These Australians are spread relatively evenly throughout electorates, meaning they have little effect on variations in polling-day voting.

Our previous research on early voting in federal elections between 2004 and 2019 indicates that older voters are more likely than younger voters to cast a postal ballot. It also shows that two electoral-district-level variables have an impact on the rates of early voting, net of other individual and district-level variables. The first has to do with convenience. Early voting tends to be higher in districts where the polling places available on polling day are few and far between. Anticipating long travel and waiting times on polling day leads voters to cast their ballots early. Voters who face shorter travel times and less waiting to vote on polling day are more likely to delay voting until then. The second factor has to do with the competitiveness of an electoral district. Voters in safe districts are more likely to cast an early ballot than voters in marginal districts. The more intense campaigning in marginal electorates signals the importance of the electoral choice and seems to cause more voters to delay their decisions until the final day (Martinez i Coma and Smith 2023). The same variables are likely to have been in play in 2022, although we do not yet have the data to test this.

Table 19.2 Pre-poll and postal voting at the 2022 federal election by State and Territory (per cent)

State/Territory	Pre-poll	Postal	Total early
NT	47.72	6.51	53.23
Qld	38.91	17.65	56.56
ACT	38.11	9.45	47.56
Vic.	37.24	15.96	53.20
NSW	36.33	10.82	47.15
WA	32.80	15.20	48.00
SA	26.99	15.40	42.39
Tas.	22.59	14.25	36.84
Total	**35.81**	**14.30**	**50.21**

Source: AEC data.

The patterns of early voting at the 2022 federal election are consistent with the idea that voters took cues about how to vote from their recent experiences in State and Territory elections. As Table 19.2 indicates, the highest rates of early voting were in Queensland and the Northern Territory, where voters had been encouraged to vote early, and in Victoria, which had conducted all-postal local council ballots, while the lowest rates were in South Australia and Tasmania.

Temporal variations in the 2022 early vote

The next question we address is the distribution of early votes across the early voting period. Here, we focus by necessity on pre-poll votes since we do not know when postal voters received their voting packs or returned their ballots. As indicated earlier, the pre-poll period in 2022 was 12 days from 9 May—a week shorter than pre-polling in 2019. The fact that, as Figure 19.4 shows, most early in-person votes in 2019 were cast in the two weeks leading up to polling day meant this change was likely to deter relatively few early voters in 2022. Indeed, comparing the final two weeks of pre-poll voting in 2019 (Monday, 6 May to Friday, 17 May) with the two weeks of pre-poll in 2022 reveals very similar patterns. In each case, daily rates of pre-poll voting were relatively steady throughout the first week but then jumped on the last Monday of pre-poll voting and increased throughout the final week, culminating in a final-day rush of voting. The main difference between 2019 and 2022 is one of scale. The final-Friday turnout in 2022, for example, exceeded that of 2019 by an average 1,229 voters per electorate—an increase of 185,630 voters across Australia.

The result of this pattern is that some of the early voting at recent federal elections has not been very early at all. In 2022, almost two-thirds of the pre-poll votes (63.9 per cent) were cast in the final five days before polling day, while almost three-tenths (29.68 per cent) were cast on the final two days. If, as the JSCEM feared, early voters were missing out on key information about candidates, leaders and policies, for many, it would have to be information that came to light late in a six-week campaign. Voters casting their ballots in the last week of pre-polling had already had the opportunity to absorb all three leaders' debates, both the major parties' campaign launches and five weeks of campaign advertising.

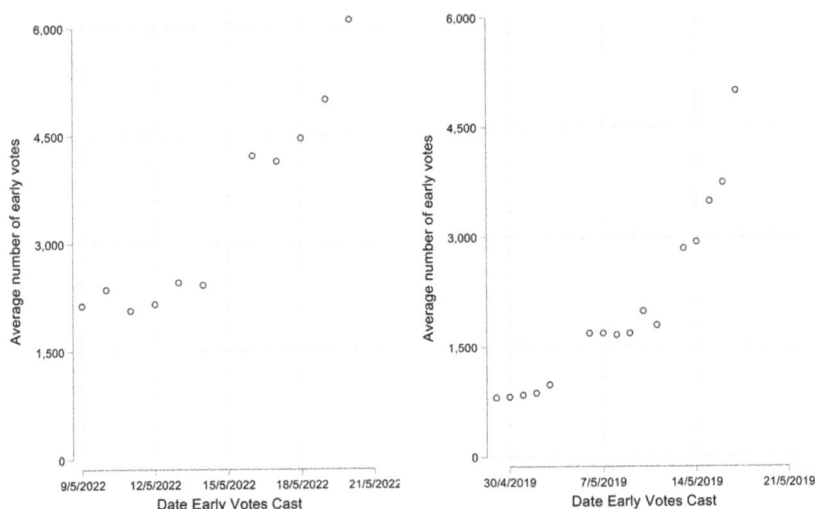

Figure 19.4 Average pre-poll vote per electoral division per day, 2022 and 2019

Source: Developed by the authors from Australian Electoral Commission data.

Time and space: Variations in pre-poll voting by day and division

The previous section of this chapter explores the evolution of early voting per day across the whole country. Here, we take this a step further, disaggregating the daily evolution of early votes by electoral divisions. Overall, as Figure 19.5 shows, there is considerable variation within the general pattern of record take-up of early in-person votes. More than 8,000 pre-poll votes were cast in some electorates on the final Friday before polling day, while in other electorates, the number was less than half that. Figure 19.5 also shows that the dispersion in the numbers of early in-person votes between electorates was higher in the second week than in the first week of the pre-poll voting period.

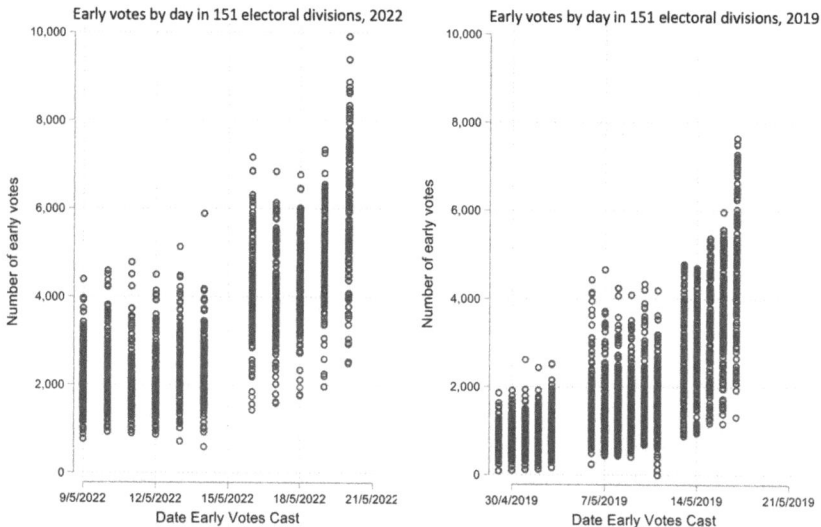

Figure 19.5 Evolution of early voting by electoral division
Source: Developed by the authors from Australian Electoral Commission data.

Focusing on a few selected cases illustrates these patterns. On the first day of in-person early voting on 9 May, 771 votes were taken in the Tasmanian division of Lyons, while 4,395 were taken in the Queensland division of Hinkler. By the end of the first week, on Saturday, 14 May, Franklin and Hobart (both in Tasmania) received 595 and 928 votes, respectively, while in Cowper and Riverina (both in New South Wales), the totals for the day were 4,179 and 5,883, respectively. The next Monday, the divisions that received the lowest number of in-person early votes were Clark and Lyons in Tasmania, with 1,429 and 1,564 votes, respectively, while Fairfax and Maranoa both received more than four times as many votes. Friday, 20 May—the day before polling day—saw the divisions of Bass and Lyons register the fewest early votes (about 2,500 each), compared with Fisher (Queensland) and Riverina (New South Wales), which took 9,387 and 9,914 votes, respectively. Considering the smaller enrolments in Tasmanian electoral divisions, the differences are still large, with final-Friday pre-poll votes of 3.2 and 3.4 per cent in the Tasmanian electorates, compared with 8.4 in Fisher and 9.3 per cent in Riverina.

Parties and campaigning

The rise in early voting offers opportunities as well as risks for candidates and parties contesting federal elections. On the one hand, parties can use early voting channels to target electors effectively. Parties have long done this through their ability to solicit postal vote applications and follow up with targeted campaign material around the time they know those voters will be receiving their postal ballots from the AEC (Orr 2019: 194). Increased pre-poll voting gives parties the opportunity to get their supporters' votes 'in the bank' early, so they can concentrate on undecided voters later in the campaign. Early votes also eliminate the risk that citizens leaning to a particular party or candidate will switch sides later in the campaign (Mills 2019).

On the other hand, early voting can mean that parties do not get important campaign messages to citizens before they have voted. Early voting disrupts party strategies about the timing of key policy announcements, campaign launches and party leaders' travel. As noted earlier in this chapter, early voting also requires parties and candidates to find volunteers to attend early voting centres for 11 days in addition to the larger number of polling places on election day. In short, early voting adds complications to the already very imperfect art of election campaigning (Kefford 2021).[5]

---

5   Interestingly, Kefford's fine analysis of contemporary election campaigning in Australia does not discuss the challenges of increasing pre-poll voting, perhaps suggesting that campaign operatives have not yet really come to grips with those challenges.

Some submissions to the JSCEM's review of the 2019 federal election suggested that minor-party and Independent candidates were disadvantaged by higher levels of early voting due to their more limited volunteer base and resources compared with major parties. The results of the 2022 federal election suggest this was not the case. Table 19.3 shows that in the 27 electorates where a minor-party or Independent candidate either won the seat or came second after preferences, the average pre-poll votes (32.5 per cent) and postal votes (14.1 per cent) were almost identical to the averages for all 151 electorates. Independent candidates won Indi and Fowler, which had high overall early voting, as well as seats with relatively low early voting, such as Clark and Mackellar. The Greens won Brisbane, Ryan and Griffith—three electorates with high postal voting. An Independent won Fowler and Independents came close to beating Nationals candidates in Cowper and Nicholls—all seats that had low postal voting and high pre-poll voting. Pre-poll voting in the seven seats won by Teal Independents varied from 26.1 to 37.8 per cent, with postal voting ranging from 12.1 to 18.6 per cent. If there is a lesson in this variation, it is that well-resourced and well-run minor-party and Independent campaigns can succeed regardless of the mix of polling-day, postal and pre-poll voting in an electorate.

Table 19.3 Significant non–major-party candidates and early voting

	2PP vote for non-major candidate (%)	Total pre-poll vote in electorate (%)	Total postal vote in electorate (%)	Total early vote in electorate (%)
Greens in 'Labor' electorates				
Griffith[a] (Qld)	60.46	29.20	18.95	48.15
Melbourne* (Vic.)	60.15	27.05	15.75	42.80
Wills (Vic.)	41.43	24.55	16.10	40.65
Cooper (Vic.)	41.33	29.45	15.11	44.56
Canberra (ACT)	37.80	36.19	10.85	47.04
Sydney (NSW)	33.31	32.03	12.91	44.94
Grayndler (NSW)	32.95	32.22	11.52	43.74
Greens in 'Liberal' electorates				
Brisbane (Qld)	53.73	22.69	20.53	43.22
Ryan (Qld)	52.65	26.97	20.55	47.53
Independents in 'Labor' electorates				
Clark* (Tas.)	70.82	20.37	14.88	35.25
Fowler (NSW)	51.63	44.52	9.50	54.02

	2PP vote for non-major candidate (%)	Total pre-poll vote in electorate (%)	Total postal vote in electorate (%)	Total early vote in electorate (%)
Independents in 'Liberal' electorates				
Warringah* (NSW)	60.96	33.54	12.09	45.63
Indi* (Vic.)	58.94	44.37	13.08	57.45
Wentworth (NSW)	54.19	37.78	14.28	52.06
Kooyong (Vic.)	52.94	26.50	18.63	45.13
North Sydney (NSW)	52.92	27.06	15.91	42.97
Goldstein (Vic.)	52.87	31.76	17.38	49.14
Mackellar (NSW)	52.50	30.25	12.10	42.35
Curtin (WA)	51.26	26.09	17.55	43.64
Wannon (Vic.)	46.08	35.98	11.33	47.31
Bradfield (NSW)	45.77	27.21	15.02	42.23
Centre Alliance in 'Liberal' electorates				
Mayo* (SA)	62.26	30.43	12.93	43.36
Independents in 'Nationals' electorates				
Cowper (NSW)	47.68	41.19	7.74	48.93
Nicholls (Vic.)	46.19	42.26	9.61	51.87
Groom (Qld)	43.11	31.01	20.74	51.75
Calare NSW)	40.32	42.86	6.23	51.09
Katter's Australian Party in 'Nationals' electorates				
Kennedy* (Qld)	63.10	44.41	9.31	53.72
Means for all challengers	50.64	32.52	14.10	46.69

* Incumbent

a Two-party-preferred vote measured against the Liberal candidate

Source: AEC data.

Conclusions

The rise of early voting has challenged long-established electoral rhythms and rituals based on most Australians casting their ballot at a local polling place on election day. Most voting was still local in 2022; however, much of it occurred over two weeks rather than one day. More postal voting in 2022 meant less involvement in the public rituals of gathering to vote with other citizens (see Orr 2015).

Whether 2022 marked an irreversible stage in a movement away from the old polling-day rituals or represented a high point in early voting caused partly by Covid-19 precautions cannot be said at this stage. Many Australian voters have clearly embraced early voting over the past decade. In some cases, they have been encouraged to do so by politicians and electoral commissions. In 2022, recent experiences of early voting in subnational polls appeared to influence levels of early voting at the federal election. The effects of Covid-19 almost certainly contributed to the growth of early voting, and particularly the increase in postal voting, between 2019 and 2022.

The increase in early voting has implications for other electoral stakeholders. Federal legislators must decide whether to try to wind back the 2022 levels of early voting and, if so, how that might be done. These decisions will affect the AEC's approach to future elections. As the Electoral Commission of Queensland (ECQ 2021: 1) has noted: 'It is possible the pandemic may have long-term impacts on the normal model of election delivery, for example, many electors may continue to vote early, and the ECQ will need to plan and prepare accordingly for future elections.' The same considerations apply to the AEC.

Finally, legislators will have an eye on the impact of early voting on their own fortunes and those of their parties. On the one hand, most pre-poll voters cast their ballots in the five days before polling day and pre-poll voting is more common in safe seats than in the marginal contests that usually matter much more to who wins government. This suggests that the major parties may not have to do much to adjust their campaigns in response to the rise of early voting. On the other hand, the 2022 successes of well-organised and well-resourced minor parties and Independents in House of Representatives seats in which there were average to high levels of postal and/or pre-poll voting indicate that early voting will not protect major-party candidates from defeat, even in previously safe seats.

References

ACT Electoral Commission (Elections ACT). 2021. *Report on the ACT Legislative Assembly Election 2020*. Canberra: Elections ACT. Available from: www.elections. act.gov.au/__data/assets/pdf_file/0007/1746097/2020-Election-report.pdf.

Aitkin, Don and Kim Morgan. 1971. 'Postal and absent voting: A democratic dilemma'. *The Australian Quarterly* 43(3): 53–70. doi.org/10.2307/20634455.

Australian Electoral Commission (AEC). 2021. *Planning Voting Services*. Canberra: AEC. Available from: www.aec.gov.au/elections/planning-voter-services.htm.

Baker, Emily. 2021. 'Who is responsible for Tasmania's coronavirus response during the State election?'. *ABC News*, 31 March. Available from: www.abc.net.au/news/2021-03-31/who-manages-tasmanias-coronavirus-response-during-an-election/100039448.

Brown, Natalie. 2020. 'Your guide to the 2020 Qld election'. *news.com.au*, 8 September.

Electoral Commission of Queensland (ECQ). 2021. *2020–2021 Annual Report*. Brisbane: ECQ. Available from: www.ecq.qld.gov.au/__data/assets/pdf_file/0030/28776/2020-21-ECQ-Annual-Report_v2.1Interactive.pdf.

Electoral Commission of South Australia (ECSA). 2019. *Election Report: 2018 South Australian State Election*. Adelaide: ECSA. Available from: ecsa.sa.gov.au/html/publications/2018-election-report/ECSA_2018-Election-Report_Web.pdf.

Green, Antony. 2022. '2022 SA election: Pre-poll and postal voting rates'. *Antony Green's Election Blog*, 13 March. Available from: antonygreen.com.au/2022-sa-election-pre-poll-and-postal-voting-rates/#comments.

Inglis, Rob. 2021. 'Surge in pre-poll voting shocks Electoral Commission'. *The Advocate*, [Burnie, Tas.], 30 April. Available from: www.theadvocate.com.au/story/7232904/huge-surge-in-pre-poll-voting-shocks-electoral-commission/.

Joint Standing Committee on Electoral Matters (JSCEM). 2020. *Report on the Conduct of the 2019 Federal Election and Matters Related Thereto*. December. Canberra: Parliament of the Commonwealth of Australia. Available from: parlinfo.aph.gov.au/parlInfo/download/committees/reportjnt/024439/toc_pdf/Reportontheconductofthe2019federalelectionandmattersrelatedthereto.pdf;fileType=application%2Fpdf.

Joint Standing Committee on Electoral Matters (JSCEM). 2021. *Report of the Inquiry on the Future Conduct of Elections Operating during Times of Emergency Situations*. June. Canberra: Parliament of the Commonwealth of Australia. Available from: parlinfo.aph.gov.au/parlInfo/download/committees/reportjnt/024638/toc_pdf/Reportoftheinquiryonthefutureconductofelectionsoperatingduringtimesofemergencysituations.pdf;fileType=application%2Fpdf.

Kefford, Glenn. 2021. *Political Parties and Campaigning in Australia: Data, Digital and Field*. Cham, Switzerland: Palgrave Macmillan. doi.org/10.1007/978-3-030-68234-7.

Lynch, Lydia. 2020. 'Queensland postal vote applications open weeks before election starts'. *Brisbane Times*, 9 September. Available from: www.brisbanetimes.com.au/politics/queensland/queensland-postal-vote-applications-open-weeks-before-election-starts-20200909-p55tuf.html.

Maley, Michael. 2018. 'The secret ballot in Australia: What does it mean and how secret is it really?'. Paper presented to the International Political Science Association World Congress, Brisbane, 21–25 July.

Martinez i Coma, Ferran and Rodney Smith. 2023. 'Correlates of early voting'. *Government and Opposition*, 1–18.

McCutcheon, Peter. 2020. 'Record surge in postal vote applications for the Queensland election means it could be days before the result is clear'. *ABC News*, 20 September. Available from: www.abc.net.au/news/2020-09-20/record-surge-postal-vote-queensland-election-result-delay/12678818.

Mills, Stephen. 2019. 'Three weeks of early voting has a significant effect on democracy. Here's why'. *The Conversation*, 29 April. Available from: theconversation.com/three-weeks-of-early-voting-has-a-significant-effect-on-democracy-heres-why-115909.

Newman, Gerry. 2004. *Analysis of declaration voting*. Research Paper Number 3. Canberra: Australian Electoral Commission. Available from: www.aec.gov.au/About_AEC/research/files/research_report_3.pdf.

Northern Territory Electoral Commission (NTEC). 2020. *2020 Territory Election COVID-19 Management Plan*. Darwin: NTEC. Available from: ntec.nt.gov.au/__data/assets/pdf_file/0004/887206/NTEC-COVID-19-Management-Plan.pdf.

Northern Territory Electoral Commission (NTEC). 2021. *2020 Territory Election Report*. Darwin: NTEC. Available from: ntec.nt.gov.au/__data/assets/pdf_file/0015/1010814/2020-Territory-Election-Report.pdf.

NSW Electoral Commission. n.d. '2021 NSW local government elections'. *Elections*. [Online.] Sydney: NSW Electoral Commission. Available from: www.elections.nsw.gov.au/Elections/Past-elections-folder/Local-government-elections/Local-Government-Elections-2021.

Orr, Graeme. 2015. *Ritual and Rhythm in Electoral Systems: A Comparative Legal Account*. Farnham, UK: Ashgate. doi.org/10.4324/9781315606620.

Orr, Graeme. 2019. *The Law of Politics: Elections, Parties and Money in Australia*. 2nd edn. Sydney: The Federation Press.

Rojas Lopez, Angelo and Damon A. Muller. 2014. 'Early voting in Australian federal elections: Causes and consequences'. Paper presented to the Australian Political Studies Association Annual Conference, University of Sydney, 28 September – 1 October. Available from: www.aec.gov.au/About_AEC/research/files/apsa-2014-early-voting-in-australian-federal-elections-causes-and-consequences.pdf. doi.org/10.2139/ssrn.2440075.

Sheppard, Jill and Katrine Beauregard. 2018. 'Early voting in Australia: The costs and benefits of convenience'. *Political Science* 70(2): 117–34. doi.org/10.1080/00323187.2018.1561155.

Smith, Rodney, Ian Brightwell, Richard Buckland, Martin Drum, Justin Harbord, Annabelle McIver, Stephen Mills, Carroll Morgan, Mark Radcliffe and Roland Wen. 2018. *Implications of Changes to Voting Channels in Australia*. A Research Report Commissioned by the Electoral Regulation Research Network. December. Melbourne: ERRN, University of Melbourne. Available from: law.unimelb.edu.au/__data/assets/pdf_file/0008/2943386/Changes-to-Voting-Report-December-2018-FINAL.pdf.

Stewart-Rattray, Justin. 2022. 'Tick for online voting'. *The Advertiser*, [Adelaide], 28 February.

Tasmanian Electoral Commission (TEC). 2022. *2019 to 2021: Report on Parliamentary Elections*. June. Moonah, Tas.: TEC. Available from: www.tec.tas.gov.au/Info/Publications/ElectionReports/Report_on_Parliamentary_Elections_2019-2021_w.pdf.

Thompson, Dennis F. 2004. 'Election time: Normative implications of temporal properties of the electoral process in the United States'. *American Political Science Review* 98(1): 51–63. doi.org/10.1017/S0003055404000991.

Victorian Electoral Commission (VEC). 2021. *Annual Report 2020–21: Delivering Elections in Lockdown*. Melbourne: VEC. Available from: www.vec.vic.gov.au/-/media/7d1ac60d3fd24ea181936ea5adbc607f.ashx.

Western Australian Electoral Commission (WAEC). 2021. *Annual Report 2020–2021: Take Your Seat at the Table*. September. Perth: WAEC. Available from: www.elections.wa.gov.au/sites/default/files/2020_2021%20WAEC%20Annual%20Report%20online%20vf.pdf.